To Come to the Land

JUDAIC STUDIES SERIES

Leon J. Weinberger

GENERAL EDITOR

To Come to the Land

Immigration and Settlement in Sixteenth-Century Eretz-Israel

Abraham David
Translated by Dena Ordan

THE UNIVERSITY OF ALABAMA PRESS
Tuscaloosa and London

The University of Alabama Press
Tuscaloosa, Alabama 35487-0380

Manufactured in the United States of America

1 2 3 4 5 6 7 8 9 10 / 07 06 05 04 03 02 01 00 99

Parts of chapters 6 and 10 appeared in somewhat different form in Abraham David, "The Spanish Exiles in the Holy Land," in *The Sephardi Legacy,* ed. H. Beinart (Jerusalem, 1992), 2: 77–108.

The Jewish Publication Society gave permission for quotation of selected passages from the following publications: Cecil Roth, *The House of Nasi: The Duke of Naxos* (1948); and Norman Stillman, *The Jews of Arab Lands* (1979).

∞

The paper on which this book is printed meets the minimum requirements of American National Standard for Information Science–Permanence of Paper for Printed Library Materials, ANSI Z39.48-1984.

Library of Congress Cataloging-in-Publication Data

David, Avraham.
['Aliyah ve-hityashvut be-Erets-Yisra'el ba-me'ah ha-16. Hebrew]
To come to the land : immigration and settlement in sixteenth-century Eretz-Israel / Abraham David ; translated by Dena Ordan.
p. cm. — (Judaic studies series)
Includes bibliographical references and index.
"Parts of chapters 6 and 10 appeared in somewhat different form in Abraham David, "The Spanish Exiles in the Holy Land," in *The Sephardi Legacy,* ed. H. Beinart (Jerusalem, 1992)"—T.p. verso.
ISBN 0-8173-0935-7 (cloth : perm paper)
1. Jews—Palestine—History—16th century. 2. Jerusalem—Ethnic relations. 3. Tsefat (Israel)—Ethnic relations. 4. Jews—Jerusalem—History—16th century. 5. Jews—Israel—Tsefat—History—16th century. 6. Rabbis—Palestine—Biography. I. Title. II. Series.
DS124 .D3813 1999
305.892'4056944'0931—ddc21 98-2524

British Library Cataloguing-in-Publication Data available

Dedicated to the memory of my father, Eliezer David

Contents

Maps and Tables

MAPS

TABLES

Preface

More than forty years have elapsed since Israel's second president, Itzhak Ben-Zvi, published his pioneering study *Ereẓ Yisrael ve-Yishuvah taḥat ha-Shilton Ha-Ottmani* (The Land of Israel and Its Jewish Community under Ottoman Rule; Jerusalem, 1957), a survey of the entire four-hundred-year period of Ottoman hegemony. The chapter specifically devoted to the sixteenth century is only some sixty pages in length. In the intervening period Eretz-Israel studies have made tremendous strides, both in the discovery of new texts and in the renewed analysis of previously known ones. The fruits of these discoveries and this analysis have appeared in hundreds of scholarly articles and dozens of monographs. Especially noteworthy are the examination and publication of Muslim sources from Turkey and Jerusalem that greatly elucidate aspects of Jewish life in Eretz-Israel, of the Jerusalem community in particular, in conjunction with known and newly discovered Hebrew sources, specifically dozens of Geniza documents. This monograph represents the fruits of years of study and source analysis. Basing my effort on the work of my worthy predecessors for the background—primarily on the studies of the late Professor Uriel Heyd and of Professors Amnon Cohen and Bernard Lewis, who together and separately laid the foundations for the study of the Jewish and non-Jewish populations of Eretz-Israel during the period under consideration—I set before me as my goal the critical assessment of all the known sources, including many from the Cairo Geniza, which I myself have published, in order to draw a new portrait of Jewish society in Eretz-Israel during this period of radically significant changes in the history of Eretz-Israel and its Jewish society.

This comprehensive investigation of the history of Jewish settlement in sixteenth-century Eretz-Israel is a slightly revised and updated version of the Hebrew original, *Aliyah ve-Hityashvut be-Ereẓ Yisrael ba-Meah ha-16* (Jerusalem, 1993). The sixteenth century bears witness to the strong influence of the Iberian exiles and their descendants, as significant numbers of these individuals made their way to Eretz-Israel in the century's early part, leaving their mark on the social, economic, and intellectual spheres. The beginning of the period is demarcated by the Ottoman conquest, which temporarily brought improved conditions for the Jews in Eretz-Israel, and its end by the severe economic crisis that affected the Ottoman Empire in the century's last quarter, intensifying at the century's end. The effects of this crisis are clearly reflected in the local Jewish society in Eretz-Israel in its search for solutions to contemporary problems.

This study focuses on sixteenth-century patterns of communal institutional structure and leadership in Eretz-Israel against the background of patterns of immigration and settlement and the prevailing economic and legal conditions. Emphasis is placed on the two main settlements of Jerusalem and Safed: the composition of their *kehillot,* their administrative structure, institutions of learning, and leadership. Consequently, the significant intellectual-spiritual trends in both the exoteric and esoteric realms that characterized this century remain excluded from the purview of this book. Let me comment here specifically on the exclusion of the sphere of kabbalah from this book, its indisputable status as one of the outstanding achievements of this century notwithstanding. This is surely a realm better left in the hands of specialists in Jewish mysticism. Along with the century's other intellectual trends and accomplishments, this topic certainly merits monographs in its own right. The book's final chapter is a collection of brief biographies (listed in alphabetical order by first names) of the important rabbinic personalities of that period; rather than provide detailed biographical and bibliographical references in the body of the book, I have elected to concentrate this material in a separate chapter.

As a result of the restricted scope of this book, some of the more interesting issues and phenomena of the period are treated only in passing. Nor did I view this work as the appropriate context for an intensive examination of topics already investigated in detail: for example, the ordination controversy, taxation in the Safed kehillah, Safed's wool industry, the rebuilding of Tiberias, and the Jerusalem academies.

The seeds of this study lie in a series of articles devoted to textual study—both newly discovered texts and corrected versions of known texts—as well as to examination of various aspects of the Jewish society in sixteenth-century Eretz-Israel. Parts of this study were carried out under the aegis of Haifa University's "Yishuv Project" in cooperation with the *Tübinger Atlas des Vorderen Orients—TAVO.* A condensed version of this project's results appeared as "The Jewish Settlement in Palestine at the Beginning of the Ottoman Empire (1517–1599)," in *Settlement in Palestine, 634–1881,* ed. A. Carmel, P. Schäfer, and Y. Ben-Artzi (Wiesbaden, 1990), 86–141.

The initial draft of the Hebrew original was written while I was a research fellow at the Harvard Center for Jewish Studies in winter 1990. The late Professor Isadore Twersky, then chairman of the center, provided willing and able assistance. I would also like to thank my colleagues who shared their knowledge and offered guidance, especially Professor Jacob Barnai of Haifa University, who read the Hebrew manuscript and made pertinent comments, as well as my teacher, Professor Haim Beinart, and Professor Haim Zalman Dimitrovsky, both of Hebrew University.

It is my pleasant duty as well to express my appreciation to the Maurice Amado Foundation, whose grant made this translation possible, and to Dr. Tamar Frank, former program officer of the Foundation's Sephardic Education Program, for her significant efforts to promote this project. I would also like to thank the translator, Dena Ordan, for her painstaking efforts to create an accurate translation of the original, as well as for her practical editorial suggestions.

To my wife, Hava, and our five children—Yossi, Yair, Akiva, Hemda, and Hagit—my sincere appreciation for their long-suffering patience and support.

Abraham David
Hebrew University

Abbreviations

AAS—Asian and African Studies

BJPES—Bulletin of the Jewish Palestine Exploration Society

BSOAS—Bulletin of the School of African Studies

HUCA—Hebrew Union College Annual

IEJ—Israel Exploration Journal

IJMES—International Journal of Middle Eastern Studies

IMHM—Institute of Hebrew Microfilmed Manuscripts, Hebrew University, Jerusalem

JQR—Jewish Quarterly Review

JRAS—Journal of the Royal Asiatic Society

MGWJ—Monatsschrift für Geschichte und Wissenschaft des Judenthums

PAAJR—Proceedings of the American Academy for Jewish Research

REJ—Revue des Etudes Juives

To Come to the Land

Introduction

The Ottoman Turks made their initial entrance on the Mediterranean scene in the early fourteenth century as Seljuk vassals in western Anatolia. Within a two-hundred-year period their empire spanned the borders of India to the African shores of the Atlantic Ocean, extending to the gates of Vienna in central Europe. The appearance of the Turks on the Mediterranean scene constituted a severe threat to several existing major powers: to the Istanbul-based Byzantine kingdom; to the Egyptian-based Mamluk kingdom; and to the integrity of the Persian kingdom in the East. The Turkish armies swiftly demonstrated their superior military prowess, securing impressive victories on the battlefield, emerging victorious in the region of the Near East as well.[1]

In the Middle Eastern region, the decisive confrontation between the Mamluks and the Ottoman Turks took place at the battle of Marj Dābiq (near Aleppo, Syria) on 24 August 1516. Led by Sultan Selim the First, the Ottomans inflicted a crushing blow on the troops of Mamluk Sultan Ḳānṣūh al-Ghūrī, who was killed in battle. Not only was the Ottoman victory secured by virtue of their numerical superiority, their greater military proficiency certainly contributed to their success. The battle of Marj Dābiq marked the inception of the Ottoman campaign to conquer Syria, Eretz-Israel, and Egypt. From that point on, the Ottoman path of conquest proceeded uninterruptedly, albeit leaving the local populace generally unharmed. The Ottoman campaign against the Mamluks culminated in their victory at the decisive battle of Ridaniyya (north of Cairo) on 29 December 1516.[2]

Eretz-Israel remained under Ottoman rule for the next four centuries (1516–1917); however, it is the initial period of Ottoman rule that concerns us here. During the early period of Ottoman administration, Eretz-Israel was under the jurisdiction of the governor of the Damascus district (*Iyalet as-Sam*). Officially titled pasha, this governor's authority extended over southern Syria and Eretz-Israel.[3] Eretz-Israel itself was divided into four large administrative districts (Turkish—*sanjak;* Arabic—*liwā*)—Jerusalem, Gaza, Nablus, and Safed. A fifth district, *Sanjak Lagun,* was incorporated later. The *sanjaks* were further subdivided into smaller administrative units, subdistricts (Turkish—*nāḥiya*), each ruled by its own special governor. The four major cities mentioned above functioned as the regional seats of government whose Turkish rulers bore the title of *sanjak bey*, or *Mir al-Liwā* in Arabic.[4]

Momentous changes followed in the wake of the Ottoman conquest, which opened a new era of prosperity in Eretz-Israel. With the defeat of the oppressive Mamluk regime, Eretz-Israel now found itself part of a large, stable, well-organized kingdom. Not only did internal security improve but also new economic opportunities arose. *Taḥrir* registers from the first decades of Ottoman rule extant in Turkish archives clearly indicate a sharp increase in Eretz-Israel's population, both urban and rural. At the same time, industry, commerce, and agriculture experienced rapid growth.[5] Bernard Lewis has suggested an estimated figure of 300,000, including some 10,000 Jews, for the population of Eretz-Israel in the sixteenth century's latter half.[6] It is by no means definite, however, that this estimate accurately reflects the contemporary reality.[7]

It appears that approximately 20 to 25 percent of Eretz-Israel's population were city dwellers, whereas the majority resided in villages.[8] With an eye to advancing its policy aimed at encouraging economic development, for which practical implementation was in the hands of the local rulers, the Ottoman regime took steps to attract residents to Eretz-Israel from both nearby and distant regions. Jewish settlement was no exception.[9]

The reign of Sultan Suleiman the Magnificent, which spanned two generations (1520–1566), is justifiably considered the "Golden Age" of the Ottoman Empire. Not only did Suleiman expand and fortify the borders of his kingdom, which extended to Persia in the east and to the gates of Vienna in central Europe, but he also left his mark on Eretz-Israel by means of construction projects, economic rehabilitation, and augmented trade and industry.[10] Moreover, Suleiman and his agents took steps to block Beduin incursions into Eretz-Israel and to bring the Beduins under government control. Additionally, Suleiman directed substantial resources to the fortification of the empire's large cities, constructing strong defensive walls on their perimeters.

The present walls of Jerusalem's Old City, constructed by Suleiman between 1537 and 1540, belong to this defensive project.[11] A seventeenth-century Jewish source attributes the actual overseeing of the construction to Abraham Castro, an eminent Jew from Egypt who immigrated to Jerusalem.[12] In 1549, a perimeter wall was built around Safed as well, and in 1557, the *Ḥan al Basha* (The Khan of the District Ruler) fort, where Jews resided, was erected.[13] Moreover, during the 1550s and 1560s, Suleiman promoted the planned restoration of the city of Tiberias from its ruins, calling upon two of his senior advisers in Istanbul, Don Joseph Nasi and his aunt (and mother-in-law) Dona Gracia Nasi, for assistance.[14]

In Jerusalem, Suleiman devoted particular attention to engineering projects with an eye to repairing and improving the city's water supply system. As part of this plan, he repaired Solomon's Pools near Bethlehem, which supplied water to Jerusalem, and the large reservoir known as the Sultan's Pool, constructing a public fountain (*sabīl*) for passersby. On the outskirts of the city, additional aqueducts were constructed to convey water to the fountains strategically located within.[15] Concurrently, local Jerusalem industries underwent rapid development and expansion. New olive presses, flour mills, and storehouses for flax were built. Soap manufacture expanded and even an arms manufacturing plant was founded.[16] Commercial ventures, also encouraged by the regime, took an upswing as well; the local markets, which dated from the Mamluk period, were now renovated and enlarged.

The positive effects of the sultan's growth-oriented economic initiatives were even more pronounced in Safed, the second focal city of this study. Because of its superior geopolitical status, Suleiman gave priority to the development of Safed's industrial infrastructure. Its status as the gubernatorial seat of a district that controlled a major highway was by no means Safed's sole advantage. Factors such as Safed's plentiful water supply and rich agricultural hinterland enhanced its position as the preferred site for the establishment of a broad-based textile industry largely devoted to the manufacture and processing of wool and silk dry goods. A significant portion of this industry's world-renowned wares were exported to foreign markets.[17] As we shall have occasion to see, Jews played a crucial role in this industrial enterprise.

But the Ottoman golden age of territorial expansion and economic growth was short-lived, essentially lasting only a few years beyond Suleiman's reign. Starting in the 1570s, and during the reign of Murad III (1574–1595) especially, the Ottoman Empire experienced a severe economic and political crisis that plunged the empire into a prolonged decline, bringing material and social instability in its wake.[18] Naturally, its negative effects were also experienced in Eretz-Israel, where population declined. This process will later be examined at length.

As noted, the Ottoman conquest brought an influx of population to Eretz-Israel. Jewish immigration was no exception, and Jews from the far-flung corners of the Diaspora began to converge on Eretz-Israel.[19] The partial demographic data extracted from Ottoman censuses of taxpayers (conducted at several-year intervals) reflect this upward trend in Jewish population, which evidently lasted more or less until the 1550s.[20] The 1560s saw the beginning of a persistent decline that was only exacerbated by the deepening empire-wide economic crisis.

Who were these Jews who now swelled the ranks of the existing Jewish community? The overwhelming majority of Jewish immigrants to Eretz-Israel during the Ottoman period were Jews exiled from Spain in 1492. Following the expulsion, they had turned eastward, finding temporary homes in the Mediterranean basin in hopes of ultimately reaching Eretz-Israel. In the preceding Mamluk period, the significantly more difficult conditions prevailing in Eretz-Israel had acted as a deterrent to Jewish immigration, reducing it to a mere trickle. The improved circumstances that followed the Ottoman conquest now led to an influx of Spanish exiles, who rapidly constituted an influential majority in the Safed and Jerusalem Jewish communities. Their rapid domination of the Jewish community in Eretz-Israel within a short period after the Ottoman conquest is reflected in both Muslim and Hebrew sources.[21] On the whole, the new immigrants of Spanish extraction settled in the cities, whereas the majority of the village Jews belonged to the *Musta'rab* (Morisco) community.[22] The explanation for this phenomenon lies in socioeconomic factors related to the immigrants' background. Primarily city dwellers, not farmers, the European and Mediterranean-based immigrants naturally settled in Eretz-Israel's urban centers, with conditions being ripe for their absorption there.

As a rule, Safed, not Jerusalem, was the immigrants' chosen destination. Only a minority settled in Jerusalem, which offered fewer economic opportunities by comparison. Under Muslim rule, Jerusalem's status was no more than that of a provincial city in a large empire. It could in no way compare with the imperial centers of Damascus, Baghdad, Cairo, or Istanbul. Indeed, Jerusalem's status within the empire declined for generations. Not only was it far removed from the kingdom's economic and political centers, but also it lacked strategic or commercial importance, for it lay in close proximity to no major highway. Safed, on the other hand, as a regional capital and seat of government during both the Mamluk and Ottoman periods, possessed distinct political, strategic, and economic advantages.[23] By virtue of its geographical position controlling the Damascus-Acre highway, its productive agricultural hinterland, and its preferential status as a site for industrial development from the early Ottoman period,[24] in the textile branch especially, Safed attracted immigrants. Nor can we discount Safed's mystical pull. Contemporary belief held that the Messiah would appear in the Galilee region, whose inhabitants would thereby be saved from the agony preceding the Messiah's advent.[25] Taken as a whole, these reasons were compelling enough to direct the steps of most immigrants north to Safed, rather than south to Jerusalem.

Basing this work on diversified primary sources, I propose first to survey briefly aspects of sixteenth-century Eretz-Israel—origins of immigration, patterns of settlement, economic life, and the regime's attitude toward the Jews. The heart of this monograph focuses on the two major Jewish settlements of Jerusalem and Safed, placing emphasis on their communal and institutional infrastructure. Brief biographies of major rabbinic personalities conclude this work. Three types of sources have been utilized in the main:

1. Hebrew sources: travel books, correspondence to and from Eretz-Israel, historical notes, rabbinic literature (responsa, judicial rulings, and sermons).[26] In addition, documents from the Cairo Geniza, many discovered or analyzed by the present author, have been utilized for their considerable contribution toward clarifying our picture of Jewish society in sixteenth-century Eretz-Israel.[27]

2. Christian sources: travelers' itineraries and diaries kept by Christian pilgrims en route to Eretz-Israel; chronicles kept by the Franciscan order in Jerusalem.[28] Although these sources undoubtedly contribute significantly to our knowledge of Jewish life in Eretz-Israel during the period under consideration, we must note the subjective and prejudicial nature of much of this material.

3. Muslim sources: documentary material from the Ottoman archives in Istanbul and in Ankara concerning Eretz-Israel, and the *sijill* documents of the Jerusalem *sharia* court, whose eighty sixteenth-century volumes unveil many details of contemporary Jewish life in Eretz-Israel. These documents constitute an important supplement to the existing data, as they illuminate many aspects of Jewish life as viewed through the eyes of the Ottoman regime.[29]

These sources provide insight into Jewish settlement in Eretz-Israel to varying degrees. Taken in conjunction, they inform my attempt to develop a portrait of the sixteenth-century Jewish community in Eretz-Israel.

1 Immigration to Eretz-Israel

The Jewish population of Eretz-Israel has ever been subject to cycles of contraction and expansion. During the medieval and modern periods especially, because of the harsh living conditions in Eretz-Israel, more than one population low was reached—the outgrowth of constant warfare, natural disasters, and the effects of despotic rule.

From the Arab conquest to the end of Mamluk rule, the Muslim potentates evinced no interest in developing the land. For them, Eretz-Israel's significance was mainly religious in nature and centered on Jerusalem and Hebron; they therefore felt no compulsion either to develop the country or to advance its population.[1] The prevailing harsh conditions during the Mamluk period, coupled with the regime's oppressive policies and ineptness, made *aliyah* a matter for individuals only, keeping the Jewish population of Eretz-Israel numerically small for centuries. As noted, a marked change occurred with the Ottoman conquest.[2] The pronounced hardships of life in Eretz-Israel notwithstanding, throughout the medieval period its Jewish settlement was periodically reinforced by waves of immigration from western and eastern Europe, Mediterranean countries, and the Orient.

Even the darkest periods saw a trickle of immigrants. Their story is told in the fascinating accounts and letters written by those who reached their goal, singly and in groups. Their letters unfold for family or intimate friends spellbinding descriptions of experiences en route, by land or by sea, giving full weight, of course, to the initial encounter with Eretz-Israel. Not only do these descriptions form a significant primary source of historical data concerning Eretz-Israel and its inhabitants at different times, they also sketch the alternative travel routes to the Land (to be discussed below), adding local color in the form of comments on the Jewish communities encountered on the way.

Immigration to Eretz-Israel was stimulated by a variety of factors, including religious, national, and messianic impulses.[3] On occasion, harsh persecution, restrictive measures, or even expulsion from their homelands expedited individual or group plans for aliyah. Upon being forced to relocate, certain individuals chose to settle in Eretz-Israel. Nonetheless, it appears that only a minority of immigrants actually achieved a successful foothold in Eretz-Israel; others, some thirteenth-century Provençal and Ashkenazi rabbis for example, left after only a brief sojourn, returning either to their countries of origin[4] or putting down roots in nearby Levantine communities—Damascus, Cairo, and Alexandria, among others. Many Jews left Jerusalem in the aftermath of the "Jerusalem elders affair," a late-fifteenth-century crisis that affected the leadership of the Jerusalem kehillah.[5] According to the testimony of Israel Ashkenazi, in the early sixteenth century economic difficulties forced Jacob Berab, an exile from Spain who headed a Jerusalem yeshivah in the 1520s, to relocate to Egypt with his students.[6]

Physical hardships alone by no means constituted the sole obstacle the immigrants faced. Frequently, they found themselves engaged in sharp conflict with the local Jewish population, which evidently lacked both the desire and the means to provide a warm welcome. The natives viewed the newcomers with suspicion, assessing them as potential rivals for jobs and status, as bearers of a different culture and mentality. Thus, in addition to unfamiliar physical conditions, settlers in Eretz-Israel from medieval to modern times also confronted social hostility, both internal and external, as an integral part of their adjustment to their new milieu.[7]

Further differences divided newcomers and natives. The immigrants generally represented the cream of Jewish society, having held eminent posts in their homelands as communal leaders, officials (*parnassim*), or rabbis. Others were men of substantial wealth and social stature. Friction arose within and between the various congregations (*kehalim*) that composed the larger Jewish community when the newcomers attempted to impose their lifestyles on the existing structure. Against the background of such conflicts, we find individuals and groups relocating within Eretz-Israel, or even leaving its boundaries for varying lengths of time.[8]

This intercongregational friction notwithstanding, more than one immigrant rose to prominence in the local Jewish community. Following their rapid social integration, Naḥmanides, Obadiah of Bertinoro, David ben Solomon ibn Abi Zimra (Radbaz), Isaiah ben Abraham ha-Levi Horowitz (Ha-Shelah Ha-Kadosh), among others, assumed preeminent positions in the communal leadership.[9]

Going back in time to the fourteenth century, sparse documentation is available for immigration from Spain and Ashkenaz.[10] But for the fifteenth century, additional information is extant regarding aliyah from various parts of the Diaspora—western Europe, Spain, Italy, and North Africa.[11] These more extensive data are by no means indicative of a radical change in immigration patterns to Eretz-Israel. Not only did physical conditions remain difficult in that period, but also after 1354 the attitude of the Mamluk regime toward its non-Muslim minorities (*dhimmi*) took a turn for the worse. Harsh restrictive measures were enacted, affecting various spheres of daily life.[12] Although contemporary appeals for aliyah to Eretz-Israel are extant,[13] the response to these calls in the fifteenth century can be gauged only with difficulty, and the number of groups that actually implemented their plans for aliyah remains unknown. Individual Jews did continue to reach Eretz-Israel from the far-flung corners of the Diaspora nonetheless, and there is clear evidence for a moderate increase in Eretz-Israel's Jewish population during the fifteenth century.

Certainly the harsh conditions that characterized life in Eretz-Israel under the Mamluk regime impeded aliyah.[14] The significant improvement wrought by the Ottoman rulers, which included the active endorsement of large-scale settlement by the new regime, encouraged many Diaspora Jews to seize this propitious moment to settle in Eretz-Israel,[15] both north and south, and not in the large concentrations of Jerusalem and Safed alone. In the south, apart from Jerusalem, Jews resided in Hebron and Gaza. But, as we shall see, the main area of settlement was in the north—in Safed, the destination of choice, in the villages of the Upper, Western and Lower Galilee, and possibly in Nablus as well.[16] We must note, however, that even in the late Mamluk period, that is, in the early sixteenth and perhaps the late fifteenth century as well, Spanish expellees did make their way to Eretz-Israel.[17] Among them we can identify individuals representing that generation's leading figures in the fields of halakhah—Jacob Berab and Levi ibn Ḥabib; science—Abraham Zacuto; and kabbalah—Abraham ha-Levi. With their arrival, these Spanish exiles rapidly captured key positions in the spiritual and public domains, in both Jerusalem and Safed.[18]

But, as Jews were not magically transported to the Land of Israel, the more mundane processes of travel warrant exploration.

TRAVEL ROUTES

Potential immigrants to Eretz-Israel had a choice of several routes—by sea, from Italian shores, especially Venice, via the ports of the Peloponnesian Peninsula or the Aegean Islands to Alexandria, Tyre, Beirut, Tripoli, Acre, or Jaffa;[19] by land from western or eastern Europe via Turkey and Syria.[20] Alternately, they could journey over the Atlas Mountains to Egypt[21] and continue by sea or join an overland caravan through the Sinai Peninsula. These routes will be examined in greater detail below.

Sea Routes

Extant contemporary descriptions of the sea and land routes from Europe to Eretz-Israel, composed by the travelers themselves, indicate that, of the available routes, the most popular was by sea from Italian ports—Ancona, Naples, and Venice in particular. After landing in the ports of the Peloponnesian Peninsula the traveler proceeded to Alexandria, Tyre, Beirut, Acre, or Jaffa, continuing overland to destinations in Eretz-Israel. Other travelers took the long land route through Alexandria, Abu Qir, or Rosetta to Cairo, proceeding from there via the Sinai Peninsula.[22] This route will be discussed in greater detail below.

Two late-fifteenth-century Jewish travelers, a wealthy Florentine merchant and a rabbi, embarked from Naples and journeyed to Eretz-Israel by the almost identical combined sea and land route. The merchant, Meshullam of Volterra, completed his pilgrimage to Eretz-Israel in 1481. The rabbi, Obadiah of Bertinoro, the well-known commentator on the Mishnah, arrived in Jerusalem in spring 1488, following a nine-month-long journey protracted by visits of varying lengths with the Jewish communities he encountered en route.[23]

Briefly, we can trace the essential points of the route followed by both travelers. After embarking from Naples, both Meshullam of Volterra and Obadiah of Bertinoro sailed across the Mediterranean to Rhodes.[24] (The extant portion of Meshullam's account, which is only partially preserved, describes his route from Rhodes alone.) Both men then sailed south. Meshullam made landfall on the Alexandrian coast,[25] while Obadiah landed nearby, at Abu Qir.[26] Their next port of call was Rosetta, reached by an overland journey and followed by a river trip up the Nile to Cairo. At this point, each joined a caravan whose route wound from the eastern Delta to the northern Sinai Peninsula, then along the Mediterranean coast to Eretz-Israel's southern gateway—Gaza. From Gaza, both Meshullam and Obadiah journeyed first to Hebron, then to Jerusalem.[27] The accounts of these journeys follow the accepted norms of the day for measuring distances, alternately referring either to miles or number of days.

Although no essential differences set them apart from known medieval travel books, Meshullam's account and Obadiah's letter to his father have the capacity to enrich our knowledge of Mediterranean seamanship and of the overland route from Cairo to Eretz-Israel. Through them, the hardships encountered en route, the many dangers facing the traveler, especially on the personal level, come alive for the reader. Also, although superficial, their eyewitness accounts provide a sense of local color, noting exotic natural and social regional phenomena and commenting on the practices of local and Jewish populations in their ports of call. Unfamiliar local Jewish customs also attracted their notice, particularly the customs of the Samaritan and Karaite communities they encountered in Cairo.[28]

Other travelers embarked on their sea journey from Venice, which was, from the early fifteenth century, the port of choice for travelers to the East from western or central Europe. The major European seapower at that point in time, the Venetian republic, controlled oriental trade via its merchants and consuls.[29]

Christian and Jewish pilgrims alike, whether originating from Italy or western and central Europe, viewed Venice as a popular way station.[30] In effect, the Venetian route was regarded not only as more reliable but also as more regularly available because of the republic's massive trade with the Orient. During the thirteenth and fourteenth centuries, the significant numbers of pilgrims traveling to Eretz-Israel made the use of special passenger ships economically feasible. From the fifteenth century, however, these passenger ships were put out of service, as a result of both the drastic decline in pilgrimages (a process with roots in the fourteenth century) and the greatly enhanced Venetian mercantile trade to the East. Cargo and merchant vessels allotted berths to traders traveling with their wares, to travelers, and to pilgrims,[31] including Jews. The extant travel accounts apprise us that even under the most favorable conditions the sea voyage from Venice was, at the very least, of several weeks' duration. One informant, Obadiah of Bertinoro, who arrived in Jerusalem in 1488, noted that the voyage from Venice to Eretz-Israel lasted "forty days."[32] A second, anonymous traveler provides a similar figure of an estimated five-week sailing time from Venice to Beirut in a letter written in late 1495. He observed: "In general, it takes thirty-four days to go from Venice to Beirut."[33]

Venice's popularity as an embarkation point is attested by other travelers. In his travel book from 1522, Moses Basola opened the section offering advice to would-be travelers, as follows: "He who wishes to go to the land of life [Eretz-Israel] in a seagoing vessel should travel in a Venetian galley only."[34] Similarly, in a letter sent to relatives in Italy, dated October 1563, Elijah of Pesaro described his trip from Venice to the Orient.[35] The opening salutation reads: "To you, my friend and companion, who desires to know all the details necessary for a person whose heart moves him to travel to these regions via a Venetian vessel."[36]

Also extant are accounts written by Christian pilgrims and travelers, preserving their impressions of their journeys and their encounters with the Holy Land, with the occasional addition of advice and instructions for potential voyagers. A wealth of information on the *realia* of the times and the contemporary techniques of sailing can be extracted from the concentrated and/or scattered references contained in these firsthand accounts, including references to the ship's route after embarkation from Venice, computations of distances between ports of call, estimated lengths of stay in various ports, descriptions of the ship's layout coupled with advice on where to find the best berths, information about provisions and their quality, along with informative details concerning the captain and crew.[37]

Evidently, separate "guidebooks" unattached to a particular travel account were also in circulation, intended for use by Jews planning to visit or settle in Eretz-Israel. Over a century ago A. Neubauer published a fifteenth-century itinerary that described the sea route from "Venice to Eretz-Israel" alongside additional geographical itineraries tracing routes from Venice to other destinations.[38] Titled "How to Go from Venice to Eretz-Israel and to Egypt," this itinerary delineated the sea route from Venice to the East, noting the following ports of call: Venice, Pola (south of Venice on the eastern shore of the Adriatic); the islands of Corfu, Crete, Rhodes, and Famagusta. From this point the route diverged depending upon whether the final destination was Beirut, Tyre, Jaffa, Alexandria, or Damietta (Egypt). Contemporary Christian pilgrim literature cites a nearly identical sea route. For example, in 1494 the Italian pilgrim Canon Pietro Casola sailed from Venice to Jaffa via a similar route.[39] Recently, two additional guidebooks for immigrants sailing to Eretz-Israel, from the late-fifteenth and mid-sixteenth centuries, have been published.[40] Other sixteenth-century sources shed light on travel routes as well as on aspects of related issues.

A similar picture emerges from letters and travel books written by Italian Jews; for example, the letter of the previously mentioned anonymous traveler; he sailed from Venice to Beirut in thirty-four days and then journeyed overland to Safed via Damascus.[41] Nearly a quarter of a century later, in 1522, the Italian-Jewish traveler and tourist Moses Basola followed a similar route.[42] He landed at the port of Tripoli (not mentioned in the earlier itinerary) after a month; from there he proceeded by caravan via the land route that hugged the Mediterranean shore. He then journeyed through Beirut, Sidon, Tyre, and the Upper Galilee en route to Safed. Another Italian Jewish traveler, Elijah of Pesaro, sailed East using a similar route, but his account ends in Famagusta, Cyprus, in 1563. From his port of call in Famagusta he described the sea journey at length, providing detailed factual information on ship design, provisioning, and sailing routes, among other points.[43] We have no means of ascertaining whether he continued on to Eretz-Israel; what we do know is that news of an epidemic in Syria and Eretz-Israel detained him in Famagusta. In 1611 or 1616 another traveler, Shemaiah Min ha-Nearim, described his journey from Venice to Tripoli in a brief letter posted from the latter port to the dignitaries of the Casale Monferrato community (Italy).[44]

Generally speaking, the plotting of sea routes was affected by a number of factors: economic and political conditions that fostered ties with specific commercial centers, climatic factors, and considerations of safety. As we shall see, from the 1530s until the late eighteenth cen-

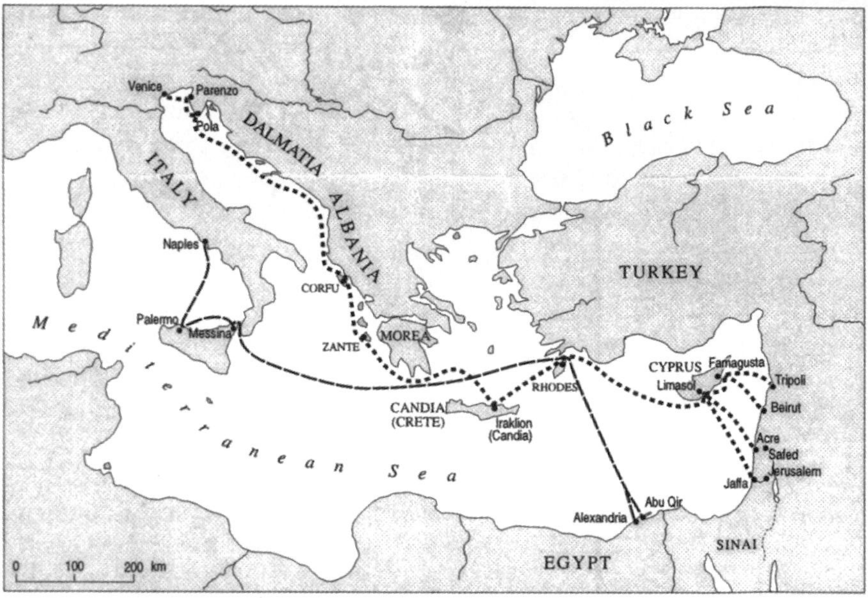

Map 1. Maritime Travel Routes (Tamar Soffer)

tury, piracy, especially by the Knights of the Order of St. John of Jerusalem (the Knights Hospitalers on Malta), posed a major threat to maritime ventures.[45]

Although Venetian ships were certainly a most popular means of transportation, the option of traveling on Venetian vessels was not always open to Jews. For an interval of at least several years in the fifteenth century (and perhaps for two intervals), Jews were barred from booking passage on Venetian ships bound for Eretz-Israel, a punitive measure dictated against the background of extreme Christian-Jewish tension in Jerusalem sparked by an Ashkenazic Jew's attempt to purchase the putative site of David's tomb on Mt. Zion in the 1420s. The tomb, directly below the Cenaculum, the church that marks the site of the Last Supper in Christian tradition, was then in Franciscan hands. The Jewish overtures to the Muslim regime requesting that the site be turned over to them in exchange for monetary recompense elicited sharp Franciscan countermeasures. The Muslim authorities ordered the destruction of the church located above the tomb in 1428 and designated the site as a mosque. Not surprisingly, the Franciscans, led by Pope Martin V, called for a crusade against the Jews. This Franciscan anti-Jewish campaign influenced the Venetian authorities as well, prompting them to issue in response an edict forbidding ships' captains to transport Jews to Eretz-Israel. The existing evidence suggests, however, that this edict was in force only until the 1440s at the latest, as the Christians were granted permission to rebuild the Cenaculum in 1448.[46]

The Land Route from Eastern Europe

This two-decade-long restriction on sea travel by no means caused the cessation of Jewish traffic to Eretz-Israel. Two sources, one Jewish and the other Christian, clearly indicate the existence of an alternate overland route that wound from western to eastern Europe, then south through central Europe via Bessarabia to Turkey and Syria.[47] Some ten years after the implementation of the so-called Sea Decree, Isaac Ṣarfati corresponded with his coreligionists in Germany about the feasibility of reaching Eretz-Israel.[48] In his letter sent from Turkey, he addressed: "the Ashkenazic communities in Schwaben and the Rhine Valley, Steiermark, Moravia, and Hungary, to tell them of the goodness of this land [Turkey]. As they intend to reach the far corners of the earth, and are perhaps unaware of the true reason why the route to Zion is barred to them, I have been asked to write the reason for the ban and its remedy. For the Lord has taken note of his people, and has made available another route through Turkey, a safe nearby overland route to escape by" [Yellinek, *Quntres Gezeyrot Tatnu,* 15].

Ṣarfati briefly described the edict and its background, as follows: "When I heard how for more than ten years our diaspora brethren in Ashkenaz and Italy [have been affected] by the dispute with priests and monks who despise God's name over Mt. Zion. . . . In hopes of reversing the situation . . . [the monks and priests] said 'we will persecute them severely.' . . . Therefore they passed an edict . . . that any captain . . . who finds a Jew bound for Jerusalem on board his ship shall throw him overboard" [Yellinek, *Quntres Gezeyrot Tatnu,* 17–19].

In recognition of the restrictions imposed by this edict, he recommended using a land route through Turkey. He wrote: "For through Turkey is the lifesaving way, a land route to Jerusalem, with only a six-day journey by sea. Every day large caravans with Muslim traders and many Jews travel from city to city, from community to community" [Yellinek, *Quntres Gezeyrot Tatnu,* 20–21].

But Ṣarfati did not furnish a specific outline of the land route, for which details we turn to a Christian source. In his 1479 travel book, Christian pilgrim Sebald Rieter described this route,[49] which was one of many existing trade routes from western Europe to Turkey:

> The following is the description of the overland route from Nuremberg and its neighboring districts to Jerusalem, as described to me by a Jew in Jerusalem, who recently took this road. The route can be traveled in great safety. Most of the Jews who come from the lands of Germany to Jerusalem make their way overland. First they

> travel from Nuremberg to Posen, in Poland . . . from Posen to Lublin, also in Poland . . . from Lublin to Lemberg, from Lemberg through Walachia [present-day Bessarabia, Rumania], to Khotin, from Khotin to Akjerman on the shore [of the Black Sea]; then a five-six day journey to Samsun, a Turkish city, and from Samsun, a six-seven day trip to Tokat . . . from Tokat a fifteen-day journey through Turkey to Aleppo . . . a week-long trip from Aleppo to Damascus . . . from Damascus, a six-day journey to Jerusalem.[50]

Ṣarfati also noted the dangers connected with the Walachian leg of the journey, where astute travelers hired armed guards. But this was not the case in Turkey. Presumably, Jews continued to utilize the overland route from Turkey even after the edict banning sea passage from Venice was revoked. Extant evidence from the mid-sixteenth century, an unpublished Hebrew source, indicates that German Jews crossed Poland en route to Eretz-Israel at this later date as well.[51]

North African Land Route

An additional overland route, used mainly by Jews from the Maghreb and Spanish exiles, wound through the Atlas Mountains to Egypt. Upon their arrival in Egypt, some travelers then sailed to Eretz-Israel from Alexandria or other port cities, while others proceeded by land from Cairo through the Sinai Peninsula via a route identical to the one used by Meshullam of Volterra and Obadiah of Bertinoro. It was not unusual, however, for travelers to make temporary stops in the Jewish communities en route. We learn from an anonymous letter, almost certainly written between 1520 and 1566,[52] that the overland journey to Eretz-Israel—via Algiers, Tunis, Jerba, Alexandria, Cairo, and Jerusalem—lasted "a month and seven days." Because of the activity of pirates on the Barbary coast, sea passage from North African ports presented greater hazards than land travel. The Corsairs—Algerian pirates—ambushed every Christian vessel that neared their shores.[53]

Difficulties of Travel

Although it is now evident that Jews were willing to brave the dangers of the by no means easy journey to Eretz-Israel, what we have not noted are the pitfalls unique to the Jewish traveler, whether on the high seas or in the desert. First, Jewish dietary restrictions made acquiring provisions problematic; their special requirements could not always be met. Second, the Jewish traveler was vulnerable to outbursts of hatred, both physical and verbal, against the background of the global Jewish-Christian conflict. In his letter (1488), Obadiah of Bertinoro relates one such incident involving the Jewish merchant Meshullam of Volterra referred to earlier. In 1488 the two men sailed together on the Palermo-

Alexandria leg of their journey. Obadiah recounts that as the ship rounded the shore of Rhodes, "one of the sailors used insolent language to the worthy Meshullam." Although the ship's captain punished the culprit, Obadiah observed that as a result of this incident, the ship's crew "began to hate us and no longer treated us as they had done before." Upon reaching Rhodes, Meshullam elected to change his destination to Istanbul.[54]

As a result of religious requirements and because of the fear of physical outbreaks of anti-Jewish hostility, Jews generally chose to travel in groups. More than one traveler noted this phenomenon, including Obadiah of Bertinoro, who remarked on the presence of fourteen Jews aboard ship on the Messina–Rhodes leg of the journey,[55] and Elijah of Pesaro, who commented in a letter (1563) that "every ship contains large numbers of Jews."[56] At least ten adult Jewish males, the minimum for a quorum, were on board when the early-seventeenth-century traveler Shemaiah Min ha-Nearim made his journey from Venice to Tripoli en route to Eretz-Israel: "On Rosh Ha-Shanah [New Year's] we prayed in a quorum of ten and blew the *shofar* [ram's horn] on board ship."[57] It appears then that where feasible Jews traveled in groups.

ORIGINS OF IMMIGRATION

The sixteenth century witnessed a significant change in the magnitude of immigration to Eretz-Israel. The interrelated factors underlying this shift included, on the one hand, the atmosphere of deep despair among the Jews expelled from the Iberian peninsula in the late fifteenth century,[58] which was accompanied by a concomitant intensification in messianic expectations (as we shall see below). On the other hand, the improved standard of living fostered by the political, economic, and social changes that ensued following the Ottoman conquest of Eretz-Israel enhanced recognition of the importance of immigration to and settlement in Eretz-Israel in the eyes of Diaspora Jews. This was especially true for Iberian Jews, who, following their expulsion from the peninsula, had taken up temporary residence elsewhere, in North Africa and other lands under Ottoman control in particular. This group, particularly the first and second generation expellees among them, enthusiastically hailed the emerging new order in Eretz-Israel. The moment was now ripe, they felt, to settle in the Land.[59]

Immigrants to Eretz-Israel, both potential and actual, originated from a broad spectrum of Jewish settlements in the Diaspora: the Balkan lands, Turkey, Italy, western and central Europe, North Africa, Yemen, and Egypt. Each of these areas will be broadly treated below. (For personal data on the outstanding individuals mentioned in the course of discussion—family origin, place of birth, date of aliyah—see the concluding chapter on rabbinic personalities.)

A. The Balkan Lands

The influx of expellees from the Iberian peninsula swelled the population of the Jewish communities in the Greek cities, Salonika in particular. For some, Salonika served as a brief port of call on the way to Eretz-Israel; for others, it served as a temporary home prior to embarking for Eretz-Israel at a later date.[60]

More than one source mentions Salonika as a point of origin for aliyah. In the context of a letter written several years after the Ottoman conquest (1523) concerning messianic pretender David ha-Reuveni, Safed resident Abraham Raphael Trabot mentioned an impending plan by Salonikan householders to settle in Safed. In his words: "A letter that arrived from Damascus this week tells of a missive sent from Salonika to a *ḥakham* in Damascus, bearing news of the king's emissary, a member of the tribe of Reuben, who arrived in Salonika bearing a letter. . . . As a result of the letter's contents, and its bearer, three hundred Salonikan households are preparing to come here immediately after Passover, which we have just celebrated" [Neubauer, "Qibuṣim," 33].[61]

Trabot indicated, however, that a severe local housing shortage made the absorption of such a large number of immigrants virtually impossible. In his estimation, "due to the multitude of immigrants from the far corners of the earth, not a cubit of space is available for purchase or rent." Notwithstanding the apparently hyperbolic assertions of this letter, its mixture of reality and imagination, it does constitute a guide both to contemporary reality and to the atmosphere of messianic expectations in Eretz-Israel.

Other sixteenth-century sources paint a revealing picture of the vicissitudes of contemporary sea travel. The threat of piracy on the high seas truly imperiled the traveler. To their misfortune, on more than one occasion Jews bound for Eretz-Israel from Salonika fell captive to the Knights of St. John (Knights of Malta), notorious for their acts of piracy.[62] Witness the following account by the Italian-Jewish historian Gedaliah ibn Yaḥya describing the misadventure that befell eighty Jews on board a Salonikan vessel bound for Safed.

> The following year [1554], the Knights of Rhodes who live on Malta captured a ship from Salonika on the high seas whose destination was Safed in the Upper Galilee. Eighty Jews were on board, plus Christians. After putting up a fight, the [ship] was captured, and the Jews plundered, along with the goods on board. They were then taken to Malta. Ransom was set at ten thousand *zecchinos* [Venetian gold currency]. Within a few days only they were redeemed, for

> among their numbers were many donors from Italy, Turkey, and Eretz-Israel. Other captives from the ship were ransomed as well. [*Shalshelet ha-Qabbalah,* MS. Günzburg 652, fol. 214r–v][63]

It is not known whether this group ultimately succeeded in reaching its destination.

A similar incident is recounted in an undated anonymous letter. Its writer urged Jewish communal leaders to take the initiative in meeting the pressing need to ransom captives intercepted en route to Eretz-Israel. "For the assailants on Maltese ships came upon them as they left Rhodes for Eretz-Israel. They were stripped to the skin and paraded naked. They were taken into captivity before their enemies. Eight Jews, including two women, a mother and daughter, were exiled to Malta . . . and with them the venerable wise old man, Rabbi Jacob Marcus of Salonika" [MS. Oxford, Bodleian Library Opp. Add. 8° 26 (2417) (IMHM, no. 21697), fols. 2v–3r].[64]

Against the background of the late-sixteenth-century empire-wide economic crisis, we find reference to a large group of Safed-bound Jews from Salonika in an official Turkish document.[65] As a means of stimulating the Cypriot economy, its governor had sought to import Jews to the island. Following the cancellation of a firman issued in 1575 that had authorized such a transfer of Jews from Safed to Cyprus, the Cypriot governor then turned to the sultan with a request to now appropriate a group of one hundred Salonikan Jews in transit to Safed who had made port at Famagusta.[66] A firman issued in 1579 approved this request.

But Salonika did not harbor Jews alone. There is a strong likelihood that a group of former *conversos* from Portugal, known to have arrived in Eretz-Israel in the late 1530s, passed through this city. With the institution of the Portuguese Royal Inquisition in the 1530s, these conversos, whose numbers included Spanish Jews exiled to Portugal where they had been forcibly baptized, elected to leave Portugal. Although we cannot entirely discount the possibility that these former Spaniards traveled directly to Eretz-Israel, because of the large numbers of conversos absorbed by Turkish and Greek Jewish communities it appears likely that this group made brief stops en route.[67] Solomon Alkabetz's prayer for redemption, composed upon his arrival in Safed from Salonika (1536), insightfully portrays the trials of these temporary converts to Christianity, the spirit that now moved them to come to the Land.

> If there be among them those who abandoned their honor [converted] on a bitter day and prayed to a strange god, You alone know the heart of man, You know his hurt and the pain of his heart. . . . In distress they called upon You and some sanctified Your name in

> *auto-da-fés*. . . . Nonetheless they kept Your Torah, neither leaving nor abandoning it. . . . Now their spirit moves them to go up to Mt. Zion, the Lord's mountain, to delight in its stones and to rebuild the dust of its ruins. All assemble to come to You; they take their lives in their hands and set forth by sea . . . for the Land. [Werblowsky, "Solomon Alkabets," 152–53][68]

B. Italy

The scant evidence available for organized group aliyah from Italy in the sixteenth century is primarily from Hebrew sources. As the major Mediterranean port at that time, Venice naturally served as the starting point for Italian Jews journeying to Eretz-Israel.[69]

Conditions for Jews in Italy during this period were unsettled, with anti-Jewish edicts and even expulsions making aliyah an attractive option. A Christian source indicates that, following their expulsion from Naples in 1541,[70] some Jews chose to immigrate to Eretz-Israel. Interestingly, the evidence for this turn of events comes from none other than a papal bull. On 24 February 1543 Pope Paul III ordered Italian Jews to assist their coreligionists from southern Italy and elsewhere as they advanced through their communities en route to Eretz-Israel.[71] Perhaps Isaac de Lattes was alluding to these circumstances when he stated, "God has remembered His people, and His land, and there the Israelites go from strength to strength in wealth and honor," in a responsum written in that year.[72]

In the mid-1560s rumors of the impending reconstruction of Tiberias by Dona Gracia and her son-in-law Don Joseph Nasi struck a responsive chord throughout Italy. Publicized and supported by Don Joseph Nasi, the Tiberian experiment made waves. The Jews of the Italian town of Cori, caught up in the excitement, composed a letter requesting assistance from their fellow Jews in organizing their aliyah to, and settlement in, Tiberias. An excerpt follows:

> Now, when the groaning of the holy congregation of Cori and their tribulation became great and their weeping became extremely heavy, behold, there came unto us the voice of the coming of the announcer and foreteller of peace. . . . Yea, there came to these poor and miserable Jews, who are eager to go out from this exile, one who announced good tidings and grace and mercy . . . our lord Don Joseph, to whom the Lord God caused to be given the land of Tiberias, wherein God chose to be the sign and symbol for our redemption and the salvation of our souls. . . . According to tradition, Jews will initially return to Tiberias, and be transported from there to the Temple.
>
> We have heard from the corner of the land the songs of glory ad-

> dressed to the righteous one, the Nasi, the aforementioned lord, that he has lavished money from his purse and arranged many places, such as Venice and Ancona, ships and help, in order to put an end to the groaning of the captive . . . to bring out the prisoner from duress and from the dungeon those who dwell in this dark and dreary exile: above all, those who have been brought low and who cannot by themselves go thither with their households. . . .
>
> We have, indeed, learned that many have already set out and crossed the seas, with the assistance of the communities and the aforementioned Prince. It has been told us, moreover, that he seeks especially Jews who are craftsmen, so that he may settle and establish the land on a proper basis. . . .
>
> On hearing all this, we became stirred with a single heart and went as one man . . . to the synagogue. There at our head was Rabbi Malachi Gallico . . . who is employed in our community. . . . There we made agreement among ourselves . . . about our proposed journey hence, to go to dwell under the pinions of the Almighty, at the bidding of the honored lord, the Prince, in Tiberias . . . so as to give proper order to this journey. . . . [English translation cited from C. Roth, *The House of Nasi: The Duke of Naxos* (Philadelphia, 1948), 126–27, slightly revised][73]

This undated epistle almost certainly belongs to the context of Pope Pius V's (1566–69) anti-Jewish edicts. Not content with reinstating all of his predecessor Paul IV's anti-Jewish measures, in 1569 Pius took the more extreme step of expelling the Jews from Papal States. Even before the expulsion, many Jews in the Papal States had begun a peripatetic existence, a situation to which the letter quite clearly alludes.[74] We are unable to ascertain how many, if any, Jews from Cori eventually reached Tiberias.

Italian Jews expelled from the Papal States also fell prey to the Knights of St. John en route to Eretz-Israel. An appeal for help in redeeming the prisoners, addressed by members of the "holy communities of Pesaro and its environs to his excellency the duke, Don Joseph Nasi," described their plight: "For the terrible news has reached us of the capture by the Knights of Malta of some 102 of our brethren, may God protect and preserve them, our coreligionists who were on board ship bound to settle permanently in Eretz-Israel. Like a gazelle or a deer they rush about, fleeing the great evils that have befallen them and us" [Kaufmann, "A Letter from Pesaro," 512].

Further evidence for the immigration of Italian Jews to Safed is found in another Hebrew source. In marginal notations made by the anonymous owner of a manuscript, he noted that his brother, "Moses Beth-el," had joined a group of Jews who left Italy in 1568: "On Thursday, the 15th of Tishri, 18 September [5]328 [1568], on the first day of Sukkot, my esteemed brother, Rabbi Moses, may he have a long life . . . and his two sons and daughter, may God protect and preserve them . . . boarded a ship bound for Safed with another group of Jews. . . . My brother, may God protect and preserve him, wrote . . . how he wrote from their port of call in Arta on the 15th of Elul [5]328 . . . and [that the letters] were lost when he sent them from Venice" [MS. Parma, Biblioteca Palatina, 2095 (1377) (IMHM, no. 13171), fol 34r].

Finally, a halakhic decision by Moses Leone, dating from the late sixteenth or the early seventeenth century, mentions the arrival of a group of Italian Jews in Eretz-Israel.[75] The question at hand, which was where children were to be raised—with their mother or father—also touched on sending a son to study in Jerusalem. In his words: "We see daily in our time eminent families and scholars, wise and worthy men whose hearts have been roused by God to leave [Italy] for Eretz-Israel, may it be speedily rebuilt and reestablished in our day. There are no impediments, for praise God, there is peace between the kings of Venice and Turkey" [MS. Oxford, Bodleian Library, Mich. Add. 67(2317) (IMHM, no. 21009), fol. 15r].

C. Western and Central Europe

Unlike the fourteenth and fifteenth centuries, for which some information on aliyot is extant, virtually no sixteenth-century data have survived for this region.[76] Recall that in the fifteenth century two main routes served immigrants bound for Eretz-Israel from western and central Europe: (1) an overland route via eastern Europe, Turkey, and Syria;[77] (2) a combined land and sea route—overland to Italy, then by ship from Venice. The few extant sixteenth-century references suggest that they continued to function as the primary routes to Eretz-Israel in that century as well, as seen from two responsa by Moses ben Joseph Trani. In one, Trani briefly outlined the land route: "Throughout the years there have been times when one can come from afar. There are people bound for Eretz-Israel from Christian lands, from Italy, from Ashkenaz, from France, via the Turkish kingdom."[78] In a second responsum, written in 1562, Trani commented on the high estimation in which the sea route from Italy was held, noting that it is "generally recognized as readily accessible by the Ashkenazim who dwell in Italy prior to immigrating to Eretz-Israel."[79] These two descriptions evidently reflect a dual reality. While most western and central European Jews traveled to Eretz-Israel via the "readily accessible" Italian route, others must have utilized the alternate overland route.

Abraham ha-Levi's letter "On the Falashas and Martin Luther" (1522) provides additional evidence for the arrival of Jews from Germany and Bohemia in Eretz-Israel in the 1520s. These newcomers served as the writer Abraham ha-Levi's informants on current Euopean religious trends, the Lutheran reformation in particular, as he noted: "Recently, loyal Jews have come to Jerusalem from the lands of Germany and Bohemia, with letters from different places, bearing witness and recounting wondrous things about the exalted man who arose in those lands, named Martin Luther" [Scholem, "Chapters from Cabbalistical Literature," 444].[80]

D. North Africa

In the second half of the fifteenth century, a group of Moroccan Jews from the Dr'aa district banded together for the purpose of aliyah to Eretz-Israel under the leadership of Ḥalafta ben Levi. It appears, however, that their departure was delayed,[81] that the group achieved its goal only near the century's end, as attested by the presence of Ḥalafta family members in Jerusalem from that time henceforth.[82] The lack of substantive evidence for Jewish group immigration from North Africa to Eretz-Israel in the sixteenth century notwithstanding, the presence of North African kabbalists in Eretz-Israel has been documented for the century's last quarter, for Safed in particular. This almost certainly suggests the arrival of a group of North African kabbalists in Safed about this time, or perhaps earlier, drawn in response to the magnetic allure of Isaac Luria (the ARI) and his coterie.[83]

An anonymous propagandizing letter, sent from Jerusalem to Morocco in the early to the mid-sixteenth century, outlined the route from North Africa to Eretz-Israel via Egypt.[84] The journey, which according to the writer lasted "a month and seven days," commenced in Algiers, and continued to Tunis, Jerba, Alexandria, and Egypt (=Cairo), before reaching its final destination, Jerusalem.

E. Egypt

Naturally, by virtue of its close geographical proximity, as well as its role as a major junction on the occidental-oriental travel route, mutual population exchange between Egypt and Eretz-Israel was not infrequent. On the one hand, it was a relatively convenient matter for local Jews to make pilgrimages to Eretz-Israel.[85] On the other, Diaspora Jews bound for Eretz Israel ultimately landed in Egypt, whether traveling by sea from Italy to Alexandria, or by land from North Africa over the Atlas Mountains, a route utilized in particular by Iberian exiles who had settled in the Maghreb following the expulsion, some as permanent settlers, others with the aim of finding a temporary haven.[86] From Egypt such travelers as Meshullam of Volterra and Obadiah of Bertinoro as well as settlers set out with the caravans that traversed the highway across the Sinai peninsula to Gaza.

Many Jewish arrivals in Egypt viewed themselves as potential immigrants to Eretz-Israel. It was not uncommon, however, for their aliyah to be delayed due to the adverse conditions in Eretz-Israel under the despotic Mamluk regime. They bided their time in Egypt, awaiting more auspicious circumstances. As David ibn Abi Zimra (Radbaz), an Egyptian scholar of the post-expulsion generation, succinctly noted: "The majority of scholars and prominent men come to Egypt on their way to Eretz-Israel."[87] Not surprisingly, the improved conditions in Eretz-Israel under the Ottoman regime led to increased immigration from Egypt to Eretz-Israel, as reflected in a letter sent to Italy by Safed scholar Abraham Raphael Trabot (1523): "We await a large caravan from Egypt [with Jews] to settle in this land."[88] Among the sages who later rose to prominence in Eretz-Israel, some made temporary homes in Egypt, remaining for varying lengths of time. Obadiah of Bertinoro, Joseph Saragossi, Jacob Berab, Abraham ben Eliezer ha-Levi (who arrived in Jerusalem from Egypt several years prior to the Ottoman conquest), David ibn Abi Zimra, and Moses Alashkar must be counted among these figures.

It was not unheard of for immigrants who had settled in Eretz-Israel, including prominent rabbinical figures, to return to Egypt following a brief sojourn there. Among these notable figures we find, for example, Jacob Berab, David ibn Abi Zimra, and Joseph Corcos, head of a Jerusalem yeshivah. Various motives prompted Jews to leave Eretz-Israel for Egypt: marital ties, inability to adjust to the harsh conditions in Eretz-Israel, and/or the desire to acquire riches. Others were drawn to Egypt by the presence of spiritual giants. One such outstanding rabbinical authority, who had briefly resided in Jerusalem, David ibn Abi Zimra, himself stated: "It is a commonplace that [Jews] from Eretz-Israel come to Egypt all the time."[89]

Sixteenth-century sources also indicate that the traffic between Egypt and Eretz-Israel was not confined solely to the living. During that period it was an accepted practice to transport the bones of deceased Jews from Egypt to Jerusalem for reinterment.[90]

Immigration to Eretz-Israel in the late medieval age was an ongoing process with dimensions fixed by the contingencies of reality. The all too real vicissitudes of travel to the East and Eretz-Israel emerge from letters and travel accounts written by Jewish immigrants and pilgrims from the second half of the fifteenth century on, as do their itineraries. As a rule, European immigrants sailed from Italian ports, Venice in particular, to eastern ports in Egypt and Syria where they joined caravans traveling overland to Eretz-Israel. Immigrants originating from the Maghreb and the Near East traveled by land.

The expulsion from Spain sparked an increase in immigration; the Ottoman conquest in 1516 provided further impetus, reinforced by the new regime's positive attitude toward the Jewish population of Eretz-Israel. The extant sources shed light on the peripatetic existence of many immigrants, particularly the Spanish expellees and their descendants who made such a vital contribution to the social, economic, and intellectual development of Jewish society in Eretz-Israel, their travel routes, and the religious, national, or messianic factors that fostered their aliyah. Nor can we ignore the inherent instability of Diaspora Jewish life as a prime incentive for aliyah.

Following this brief excursus concerned with incentives for immigration, means of travel, and points of origin, we now turn to the distribution of Jewish settlement in sixteenth-century Eretz-Israel.

2 Distribution of Settlement

The extant Hebrew sources, Turkish documents, and Christian pilgrim accounts provide but a partial picture of Jewish settlement in sixteenth-century Eretz-Israel. Demographic data on the size of various sixteenth-century Jewish communities, both urban and rural, derive in the main from partial lists of taxpayers in the taḥrir registers housed in the Turkish archives in Istanbul and Ankara. In addition, Moses Basola's travel book (1522) will be mentioned time and again in this chapter as a source of data for the Jewish settlements he visited during his travels. I have chosen to exclude the largest Jewish concentrations, in Jerusalem and Safed, from the present discussion; they will be treated separately below. Sixteenth-century Jewish settlement, however, was by no means restricted to these two cities. Jews lived both in other urban centers and in numerous villages, particularly in the northern regions. This survey, whose disparities in length and detail reflect the uneven nature of our data, opens with the southern and central regions.

SOUTHERN AND CENTRAL REGIONS

Sanjak Jerusalem

Hebron belonged to the *sanjak* of Jerusalem. Its Jewish population was tiny; in the 1480s, Hebron's entire Jewish presence reportedly totaled twenty families.[1] Evidently, with the Ottoman incursion to Eretz-Israel, Hebron's Jewish community was decimated in the course of rioting by the local populace, as a document of uncertain origin indicates.[2] Generally speaking, for Hebron's Jewish community, the postconquest period may be summed up as one of growth and subsequent decline. The extant data, not necessarily an accurate reflection of reality, attest that Hebron's sixteenth-century Jewish population fluctuated between eight and twenty families. In 1522 Moses Basola reported that "eight or ten householders reside there,"[3] while the relevant taḥrir registers reflect a total of twenty households in 1538/39, eight in 1553/54, eleven in 1562 and 1596/97.[4] From Basola's account it appears likely that Hebron's Jews resided in the courtyard that adjoined the synagogue. The location of the town's Jewish quarter has been identified—in close proximity to the northern end of the Kazzazin quarter.[5]

No substantive information is available for the century's first half regarding individual members of the Hebron kehillah. From its second half, however, scattered data on several community members[6] and a yeshivah that functioned despite severe financial straits have survived. The following mid- to late-sixteenth-century responsum refers to this yeshivah: "The Spanish congregation in Sidhirokastron [Bulgaria], may it be well founded, has collected a sum of money for the Talmud Torah society in Hebron, may it be speedily rebuilt and reestablished. It seems that this society may now be defunct; what then will happen if it turns out that the yeshivah in Hebron is no longer functioning?" [Samuel de Medina, *Responsa, Yoreh Deah,* no. 167].

The doors of this yeshivah were still open in 1589 when the noted scholar Joseph Trani made a visit to Hebron. His diary entry for that year reads as follows: "5349 [1589]. I arrived in and traversed Jerusalem with difficulty. I came to Hebron in time for the festival of Shavuot. We studied tractate *Ḥullin* at the yeshivah."[7]

As I have already hinted, the statistical data extant for the Hebron kehillah in Ottoman archives may understate the demographic reality. Indeed, the constant flow of important rabbinic figures from Jerusalem and Safed to Hebron, which, as we have seen, boasted its own yeshivah, suggests that Hebron experienced a period of growth from midcentury on. In the mid-sixteenth century, Hebron's communal leaders included the renowned kabbalist Malkiel Ashkenazi. At a later date, the town's noted scholars included Elijah de Vidas, a former student of Isaac Luria in Safed, who came to Hebron in the 1570s; Solomon Adeni the Yemenite, the author of the Mishnaic commentary *Melekhet Shelomo,* known to have lived in Safed and Jerusalem as well in the century's latter half; Menaḥem ha-Bavli; and Ḥiyya Rofe.[8]

Sanjak Gaza

Gaza, the capital of Eretz-Israel's southernmost sanjak, was an important city in its own right. By virtue of its geographical position as the southern entrance to the land, mercantile and passenger caravans from Egypt passed through its gates, making Gaza the major commercial inland center for both Egypt and Eretz-Israel. It therefore comes as no surprise that many of Gaza's Jews engaged in commerce, a reality reflected by late-fifteenth- to early-seventeenth-century Genizah documents.[9] Other Gazan Jews worked precious metals in the *saga* (jewelers' market) or engaged in agriculture.[10]

Gaza's Jewish population rose until midcentury; the late sixteenth century saw a decline. Taḥrir registers reflect both trends, reporting the number of Jewish households as 95 in 1525/26, 98 in 1538/39, and 115 in 1548/49. But, in 1556/57 we find a total of only 81 Jewish households and in 1596/97 only 73.[11]

A responsum written in 1600 reflects this late-sixteenth-century downward trend. It touches on steps taken by the communal leaders to encourage Jewish settlement, including the incentive of reduced taxes:

> Reuben, who resided in Jerusalem, may it be speedily rebuilt and reestablished in our day, had commercial dealings in Egypt. On the return trip he passed through Gaza. The local residents who sought to encourage settlement [approached him], saying: "Would you like to become a resident of our city? Bring your wife here and become as one of the city elders. We will charge you only four *grossos*[12] yearly for taxes, etc." Reuben replied, "If you take an oath to this effect, I will agree." When the town's residents saw that he had consented to bring his wife to Gaza and to pay the agreed-upon amount annually, they gave Reuben a signed and sealed document [to that effect]. [Jacob Castro, *Shu"t Ohaley Yaaqov,* no. 119]

The Gaza taḥrir register for 1525/26 provides a partial breakdown, which allows us to identify some of its component congregations (kehalim).[13] The register notes the presence of thirty-one Maghrebi families (North African Jews), seven French (actually, Provençal) families,[14] and two Shami (Syrian) families. The total Jewish population figures make it obvious that members of other kehalim also resided in Gaza: Musta'rabs (or Moriscos—arabized Oriental Jews) and Sefardim, for example. Sefardim constituted the dominant component of the Jerusalem and Safed Jewish communities at that point in time,[15] and there is no evidence to suggest that this was not the case in Gaza as well. An Ashkenazi presence may also be inferred, based on a late-fifteenth-century reference to a scholar, one "Moses of Prague," as a Gaza resident.[16] A Hebrew document from the early 1480s indicates that Gaza's sixty Jewish households occupied a separate quarter.[17]

Although we have no specific knowledge of scholars based in sixteenth-century Gaza, with the exception of R. Isaac Shalom ibn Arḥa, who signed a legal writ there in 1605,[18] the Jewish community's size alone suggests that Gaza's infrastructure certainly encompassed educational institutions and a rabbinic court of law.

Ramla, also situated in the sanjak of Gaza, was probably the site of a tiny Jewish community. A single Hebrew source alludes to Jews living in "a Christian village near Ramla,"[19] whereas the German-Christian pilgrim Solomon Schweiger made a more explicit reference to a Jewish presence in Ramla.[20]

Sanjak Nablus

Nablus was the capital of the sanjak bearing this name. Some five years after the Ottoman conquest, Moses Basola found "twelve Morisco (Musta'rab) householders" there.[21] The taḥrir registers indicate that its Jews resided in three separate, noncontiguous neighborhoods: Dabbura, Kalyun, and Ḥabala,[22] with the Musta'rabs to whom Moses Basola referred concentrated mainly in the latter. In addition, several families resided in the Akaba quarter.

According to taḥrir registers from 1538/39, the Jewish population in the three main neighborhoods totaled seventy-one heads of family. The Ḥabala quarter, although populated mainly by Musta'rabs, also housed several families of different origin: a family from Kurdistan, three from North Africa, and five French (Provençal) families. By 1548/49 Nablus' Jewish population had been reduced by half—we find only thirty-six heads of families residing in the three neighborhoods. By 1596/97 the number of Jewish families residing in Nablus had declined to fifteen.[23] A Portuguese-Christian pilgrim, one Pantaleao de Aveiro, commented in 1564 on the prevailing enmity between the city's Jewish and Samaritan residents.[24]

NORTHERN REGION

Sanjak Safed

Eretz-Israel's largest Jewish concentration was in the sanjak of Safed, with its subdistricts of Safed, Tibnin, Tyre, Shaqif, Acre, and Tiberias. Jewish settlement in Acre was evidently renewed after the Ottoman conquest. Although this premise receives no substantiation in the taḥrir registers, mid-sixteenth-century rabbinic sources do indicate that local Jews were involved in commercial ventures in this port city, which served Aleppo, Sidon, and Egypt.[25] The port served undoubtedly Safed as well, the absence of explicit testimony to this effect notwithstanding. Eretz-Israel's rural Jewish population was concentrated mainly in the northern part of the country, in the sanjak of Safed: in the upper, lower, and western Galilee and in the valleys.

Acre subdistrict

The following rural settlements were located in the Acre subdistrict:

Peqiin (Buqaia): The late tradition regarding continuous Jewish settlement in Peqiin from Second Temple times notwithstanding, no authentic evidence exists for a Jewish presence here prior to the initial years of Ottoman rule.[26] According to the taḥrir registers, thirty-three Jewish families resided here in 1525/26, fifty-four in 1533/34, and forty-five in 1556/57 and 1572/73.[27] The noted Safed scholar Joseph Trani stayed in Peqiin on a number of occasions.[28]

Ein Tiriah: There is evidence for a Jewish settlement here in the sixteenth century.[29]

Gulis: Taḥrir registers from 1555/56 and 1572/73 indicate the presence of nine Jewish families.[30]

Kefar Yasif: The earliest evidence for Jewish settlement is found in a Geniza document dating from the sixteenth century's first decade.[31] Taḥrir registers indicate the presence of ten Jewish families in 1533/34, twenty-nine in 1555/56, and eighteen in 1572/73.[32]

Kabul: Taḥrir registers provide the sole evidence for a tiny Jewish settlement. Kabul's Jewish population was five families in 1533/34 and fifteen in 1572/73.[33]

Shefaram (Shafa Amr): Taḥrir registers reflect a total Jewish presence of three families in 1525/26 and ten in 1533.[34]

Safed subdistrict

Jews resided in villages in the Safed subdistrict as well, particularly in the environs of the city of Safed itself. These villages often served as a refuge for the Jews of Safed in times of persecution, natural disaster, and pestilence.

Ein Zeitim (Ein Zitun): This village apparently had a continuous Jewish presence from an earlier period. Jews are known to have resided in Ein Zeitim as early as the first decade of the sixteenth century; there is even a report of a death, that of Abraham Besodo, in 1509.[35] In 1522 Moses Basola reported that Ein Zeitim's synagogue housed twenty-six Torah scrolls and that "some forty Jewish householders, all Moriscos [Musta'rabs]" lived there.[36] Taḥrir registers indicate a Jewish population high of forty-two families in 1525/26 and a subsequent low of five families in 1555/56.[37]

From the century's second half, Ein Zeitim boasted its own yeshivah, headed by Moses ben Makhir in the last quarter of the century until its doors closed in 1599.[38] In that year, against the background of Druze emir Faḥr ed-Din II's early-seventeenth-century attempt to bring all of southern Lebanon and large parts of Eretz-Israel under his control,[39] there were outbreaks of anti-Jewish violence by Muslim brigands. These resulted in the yeshivah's relocation to Safed, thus ending Jewish settlement in Ein Zeitim. A letter written by Solomon Shlomil Meinstral of Safed in 1607 reflects this state of affairs: "In the village of Ein Zeitim, and in Meron, there are abandoned synagogues, and no [Jewish] inhabitants."[40]

Birya's Jewish settlement dates from an earlier period. A Geniza document contains a laconic reference to a Jewish presence here in the first decade of the sixteenth century.[41] Taḥrir registers indicate that the

Jewish population was nineteen families in 1525/26 and sixteen in 1555/56.[42] Like Ein Zeitim and other nearby settlements, this village was evidently abandoned in the early seventeenth century because of the outbreaks of violence.[43]

Kefar Anan (Inan), or Kefar Ḥananiah, located near Safed, also had a Jewish population in an earlier period.[44] In his travel report, Moses Basola noted the presence of a "Musta'rab community of some thirty householders, mostly *kohanim* [individuals of priestly descent]."[45] Taḥrir registers cite a Jewish population of fourteen families in 1525/26 and seventeen in 1555/56.[46]

Alma had a Jewish presence even prior to the sixteenth century.[47] According to Moses Basola, "there was a Jewish community of some fifteen households" in Alma.[48] Taḥrir registers show a population of eight Jewish families in 1555/56 and only three in 1572/73.[49]

Meron (Mirum) was the site of an ancient Jewish settlement.[50] According to an early Jewish tradition, it was also the reputed burial site of the renowned tanna Simeon bar Yoḥai, whose holy gravesite was a popular destination for pilgrims.[51] A later tradition ascribes the erection of a building and a courtyard at the gravesite to one of Safed's notable late-sixteenth-century scholars, Abraham Galante.[52] Jewish sources provide no indication as to whether or not there was a permanent Jewish settlement in Meron. In 1522 Moses Basola reported that "no Jews live here."[53] As we saw above, the same was true in 1607.

Kadesh Naftali: There is evidence for a sixteenth-century Jewish settlement here.[54]

Kefar Firim, located near present-day Rosh Pinah, was the home of the Safed scholar Yom Tov Ṣahalon in the late sixteenth century.[55]

Shaqif subdistrict

Jews also resided in northern Eretz-Israel in the sanjak of Shaqif—present-day southern Lebanon.

Ḥaṣbayah: A Jewish settlement existed here prior to and during the sixteenth century.[56] Several sources, including a responsum written by Yom Tov Ṣahalon, suggest the presence of a sizable Jewish community in Ḥaṣbayah.[57]

Tiberias subdistrict

Another Jewish population concentration was to be found in the Tiberias district, but its dimensions never reached those of the Safed region.

Tiberias: Until nearly midcentury, there is simply no information extant for Jewish settlement in Tiberias. Tiberias was not a popular destination for immigrants arriving in Ottoman Eretz-Israel, who preferred to wend their way to Jerusalem, Safed, and elsewhere. Moses Basola's travel report (1522) sheds light on the reason for its lack of popularity, largely attributable to its desolation. In his words: "Tiberias was formerly a great city . . . but now, it is desolate and waste. . . . No man can go there for fear of the Arabs, except at the time of the caravan."[58]

Christian sources from the 1540s indicate the existence of tiny Jewish communities in Tiberias and the nearby villages—Capernaum, Bethsaida, and Korazin—to the north of Lake Kinneret.[59] In the 1560s, however, Tiberias itself experienced a brief flowering as word (and rumors) spread of its impending reconstruction and repopulation by the Mendes-Nasi family with the backing of Suleiman the Magnificent.[60] Two extant reports, that of the Italian-Jewish historian Joseph ha-Kohen and that of the French consul in Istanbul, note Don Joseph Nasi's crucial role in the rebuilding of Tiberias and its perimeter wall, some fifteen hundred cubits long, accomplished in 1563/64.[61] According to Joseph ha-Kohen's account, the rehabilitation was orchestrated by Nasi's representative, Joseph ben Adret. Ha-Kohen summarized Don Joseph Nasi's Tiberian project as follows:

> Then Don Joseph Nasi came to Ferrara, among those who escaped from the iron cauldron, Portugal, and lived there for some time. Thence he went to Turkey, where he found grace in the eyes of the King Sulayman, who loved him greatly. And the king gave him the ruins of Tiberias and of seven country villages around it, and made him lord and prince over them at that time.
>
> Don Joseph sent there R. Joseph Adret (Ibn Ardut), his attendant, to rebuild the walls of the city, and he went and he too found favor in the king's eyes, and he gave him sixty aspers each day. The king sent with him eight men born in his house, and gave him the order written and sealed with the imperial seal, and recommended him to the pasha of Damascus and the pasha of Safed, saying: "All that this man desires of you, you shall do."
>
> The law was given in the king's name, saying: "All builders and porters who are in those cities shall go to build Tiberias; and he who does not go shall bear his sin." There was there much stone, for Tiberias had been a great city before the Lord, before the hewer [Arabs] went up against them, and there were twelve synagogues there in the days of R. Ammi and R. Asi. He commanded the inhabitants of those seven country villages to make mortar to do the work, and more also; and there was there moreover much sand, for the Lake of Tiberias was near to them. But Arabs were jealous of them; and a certain *sharīf* who was advanced in years arose and called in the ears of the inhabitants of that land, saying: "Do not permit this city to be built, for it will be bitter for you in the end; for I have assuredly found it written in an ancient book, that when the city that is called Tiberias is built, our faith will be lost, and

> we will be found wanting." They harkened to his voice, and they were unwilling to go to rebuild the walls. At that time, an end was made to the building of the walls of Tiberias, and R. Joseph b. Adret was very sad. He went to the pasha of Damascus and called before him: "O my Lord, for the inhabitants of the villages refuse to do the king's bidding." Then the pasha was afraid, and he hastened to send thither, and they took two of the heads of those people, and brought them down in blood to Sheol, so that those who remained might see and not act presumptuously any more. . . .
>
> Now the city of Tiberias which they built was one thousand and five hundred cubits in compass. The work ended in the month of Kislev 5325 (November–December 1564). Don Joseph greatly rejoiced and gave thanks unto God. [Joseph ha-Kohen, *Emeq ha-Bakha,* 93; English translation cited from Stillman, *Jews of Arab Lands,* 293–94][62]

Contemporary and later Christian pilgrim accounts as well as those by Ottoman firmans indicate that the moving force behind the plans to build, develop, and fortify Tiberias was none other than Dona Gracia, Don Joseph Nasi's aunt and mother-in-law, an influential personage in Suleiman's court in her own right.[63] In exchange for an annual payment, in 1560 the sultan granted her the concession to Tiberias and its environs, including permission to colonize the city with Jews. The income from the area was allocated to the Damascus soup kitchen. At the time and again in 1566 the sultan sent firmans confirming the leasing of Tiberias and its environs to Dona Gracia and granting her permission to erect a perimeter wall around the city both to the head of the Damascus *waqf* and to the *defterdar* of the Aleppo region.[64] The Sublime Porte set forth the conditions of the lease as follows: "A Jewess named Gracia has undertaken to pay the fixed annual sum of 1,000 gold pieces [for the concession for Tiberias] together with the villages in the vicinity, on condition that all income from the area belongs to them [her]" [Heyd, "Turkish Documents on Tiberias," 204].

It appears then that both Don Joseph Nasi and Dona Gracia were actively involved in the rebuilding and recolonizing of Tiberias with Jews. Our informants, Joseph ha-Kohen and the French consul in Istanbul, suggest that while Don Joseph served as go-between and coordinator of construction, Dona Gracia's role primarily consisted of furthering the town's development, which included the responsibility for leasing the site from the Ottoman authorities.

Don Joseph's and Dona Gracia's comprehensive plans to turn Tiberias into a Jewish center by means of encouraging massive immigration apparently roused broad interest in Italy. Let us recall in this context the letter written sometime between 1566 and 1569 by members of the Cori Jewish community requesting aid from their coreligionists in implementing their planned aliyah to Eretz-Israel and their projected settlement in Tiberias.[65] Although primarily motivated by political reasons, we cannot discount the influence of the contemporary messianic atmosphere on this colonization effort.[66] It is not clear what number, if any, of Cori's Jews eventually succeeded in reaching Tiberias.

Jews in the Tiberias area—Capernaum, Beth Saida, and possibly in other villages near Lake Kinneret[67]—as did the region's other residents, engaged in the following occupations: commerce, agriculture (including the cultivation of oranges), and fishing. Some Tiberian Jews were also involved in beekeeping.[68] Don Joseph Nasi's plans for Tiberias envisioned this city as a second center of the textile industry, similar to Safed. With this in mind, he ordered the planting of mulberry trees in Tiberias to lay the ground for the cultivation of silkworms, and he also made arrangements for the importation of wool from Spain.[69] It is not within our power to determine the success of these projects, as the Jewish community experienced a debilitating crisis only a decade later. Even during Don Joseph's lifetime (d. 1579), Jews continually fled Tiberias, leaving only the community's most impoverished members.[70]

The most plausible explanation for the failure of Nasi's plan to rebuild and recolonize Jewish Tiberias appears to be lobbying by local Franciscan monks.[71] Of particular relevance in this context are the words of Bonifacio di Ragusa, custodian of the Franciscan order in the Holy Land:

> Due to its multitude of snakes, Tiberias is an uninhabitable city. . . . The infidel Jew Zaminex [Don Joseph Nasi—apparently the name used here is a distortion of his Portuguese name, João Miques—A.D.] hoped to expel the snakes [Muslims] and settle his brethren the poisonous vipers [Jews] there, to turn our church into a synagogue. In order to stand in the breach, I consulted in utmost secrecy with Rustem Pasha and Ali Pasha [governor of Damascus] and they promised me that no such thing would come to pass during Sultan Suleiman's lifetime. Their deeds matched their words.[72]

We have some further knowledge of the existence of one or two institutions of learning and a synagogue in Tiberias. A yeshivah headed by Eleazar ben Yoḥai functioned in Tiberias, although we have no inkling as to when it was founded. Its upkeep was subsidized by Dona Gracia for many years. Following her death in 1569, the yeshivah enjoyed the support of Diaspora Jewry, and its doors remained open at least until the early seventeenth century.[73] Tiberias' synagogue was located in the city's eastern sector, adjoining the city wall on the Kinneret shore.[74] This supports the conjecture that the city's Jewish quarter also was situtated in the eastern part of Tiberias. A later tradition suggests that Tiberian Jews also resided outside the city wall and that another yeshivah functioned outside its perimeter.[75]

Don Joseph's death in 1579 did not spell the immediate death of the Tiberian dream. Several years later, the concession for Tiberias was granted to another influential Jewish political figure in the sultan's court—the former Portuguese converso Alvaro Mendes (d. 1603), known also by his Hebrew name, Solomon ibn Yaish. Mendes returned to Judaism in Turkey in 1585. The sultan conferred upon him the duchy of the island of Mytilene (ancient Lesbos) in the Aegean Sea, as well as the lease on Tiberias and its vicinity. Ibn Yaish appointed his son Jacob overseer of Tiberias in turn. Of Jacob it was said that he combined "many buildings into a handsome palace, and was much beloved by the Arabs."[76]

Jews lived elsewhere in the Tiberias subdistrict, at a distance from the city itself. Among the locations to be cited we must note the following:

Kefar Kanna, at the foot of Mt. Tabor, boasted a large Jewish community in the late Mamluk period.[77] Scant attention is paid to this settlement in sixteenth-century Hebrew sources. In 1522 Moses Basola reported the presence of "some forty householders,"[78] while taḥrir registers show a Jewish population of fifty families in 1525/26, fifty-two in 1533/34, sixty-five in 1555/56, and seventy-seven in 1572/73.[79] From the testimony of a Christian pilgrim dating from the 1560s we can infer that there was a large Sefardi presence here.[80] One of Safed's foremost scholars, Joseph Trani, stayed in Kefar Kanna in 1602.[81]

Not far from Kefar Kanna (near Kefar Tabor) was the Ḥan al-Tugar. Located on the border between the Safed and Nablus districts, it boasted an important commercial center. According to a source dating from the first half of the seventeenth century, Jews involved in trade resided there.[82]

Sanjak Lagun

Jinin, on the southern border of the Safed district, in Sanjak Lagun, also had a tiny Jewish community. Only a few sketchy references to this Jewish community, cited by the Christian pilgrim Nicolai Christopher Radzivill, who traveled in Eretz-Israel in 1583/84, are extant. Nonetheless, clear evidence for a Jewish presence in Jinin emerges from Joseph Trani's temporary residence there in early 1594 and again in 1602 for instructional purposes.[83]

Sanjak Ajlun

According to fourteenth- and sixteenth-century sources, Ajlun, the capital of the sanjak by that name, located on the eastern bank of the

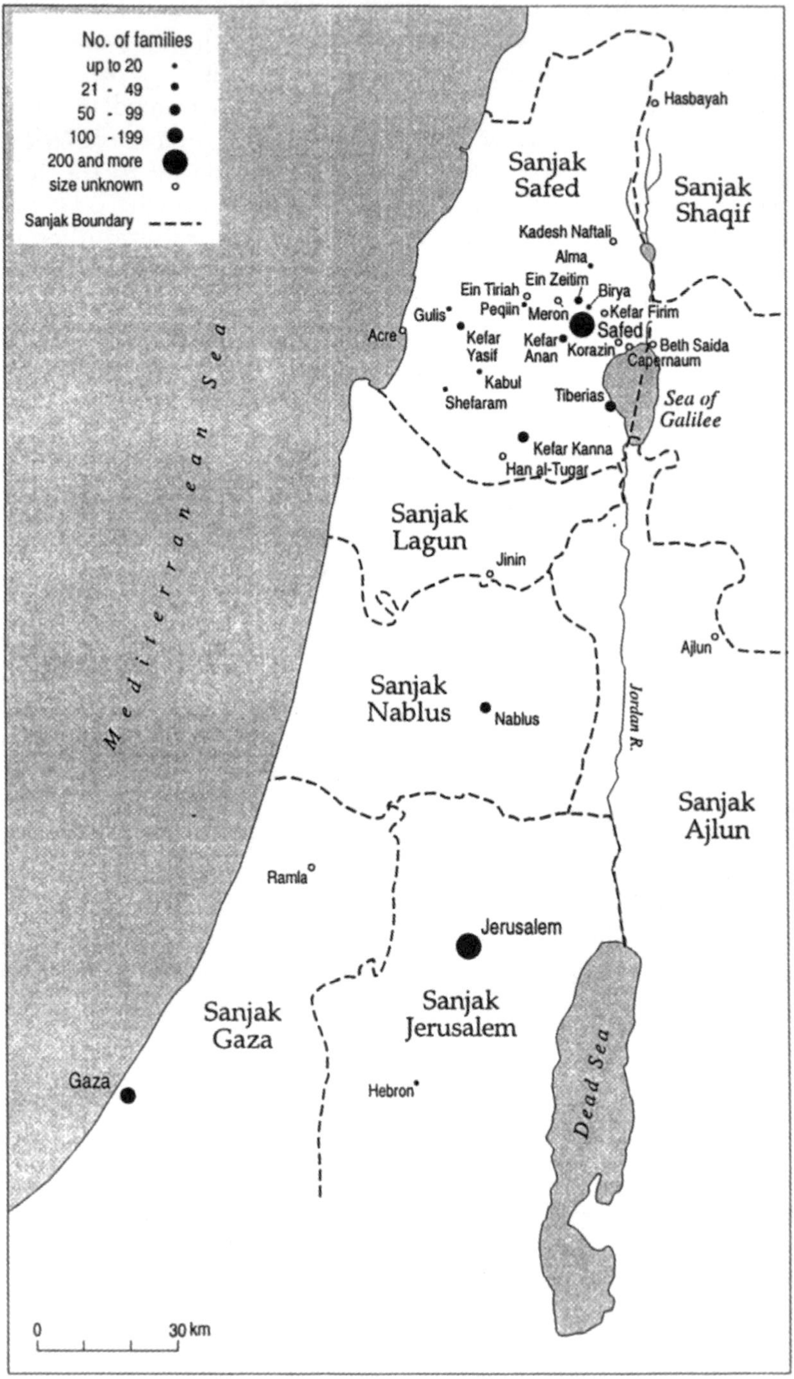

Map 2. Jewish Population in Sixteenth-Century Eretz-Israel (Tamar Soffer)

Jordan, also had a Jewish settlement. It seems likely that the sixteenth-century community was new and that there was no continuous Jewish settlement from the fourteenth century.[84]

In summation, apart from the two main cities of Jerusalem and Safed, we have seen that Jews resided in the central and southern regions—Hebron, Ramla, and Gaza—but were primarily concentrated in the north. Naturally, the economic opportunities to be discussed in the following chapter played a significant role in determining the patterns of Jewish settlement in sixteenth-century Eretz-Israel.

3 Economic Life

The inception of the Ottoman regime brought with it significant economic growth. In the absence of restrictions on their choice of economic endeavor, Jews engaged freely in a broad spectrum of occupations. In effect, any branch of sixteenth-century economic endeavor may justifiably be considered a potential Jewish occupation.[1] This chapter first surveys the main areas of Jewish economic enterprise—agriculture, industry, trade, and finance—and then proceeds to discuss the dramatic change in cost of living under the newly instated Ottoman regime. It concludes by documenting the continuing need for Diaspora support of the community in Eretz-Israel despite the new era of relative prosperity ushered in by the Ottoman conquest.

A. AGRICULTURE

Eretz-Israel's agricultural centers were located in the rural areas, where 75 percent of the population resided.[2] Wheat, barley, legumes, fruits, and vegetables formed the backbone of rural agriculture; nonetheless, vineyards, fruit orchards, and vegetable gardens were also located in and near urban centers. Other major crops, cultivated primarily for industrial purposes, were sesame seed and olives for oil and soap production; cotton for thread manufacture; mulberry trees for silkworm culture (Safed and Tiberias); and grapevines for wine production (pursued only by the non-Muslim minorities). Another specialized sector, restricted to specific villages, was apiculture. Nor can we neglect to mention that important fisheries operated from Lake Kinneret and the Ḥuleh valley region and in the coastal cities of Tyre, Acre, and Jaffa.[3]

The formal Muslim legal ban on Jewish ownership of land notwithstanding, Jews by no means forsook agricultural pursuits. Nevertheless, this discriminatory legislation regulating the status of "unbelievers," *ahl al-dhimma,* did give rise to a strange misconception among the Muslim population, as David ibn Abi Zimra noted: "In this kingdom Jews generally refrain from purchasing fields or vineyards, and in general, make no attempt to move in this direction. This is politic for many reasons. This [tendency] has gained recognition among the non-

Jews, to the extent that some foolish ones say [in consequence] that if the Jews sowed, nothing would grow" [David ibn Abi Zimra, *Responsa,* no. 1208].

In actual practice, the ban against landowning by dhimmi was not universally enforced. The picture that emerges from Hebrew (mainly halakhic) and Muslim sources is one of Jewish involvement in agrarian pursuits both as landowners and as tenant farmers, particularly in the rural north. Jews were represented in nearly all the contemporary agricultural sectors, in addition to beekeeping and fishing.[4]

B. INDUSTRY AND CRAFTS

Textiles

The importance of textiles as sixteenth-century Eretz-Israel's leading industry cannot be overstated. Whereas the Safed area's unquestioned primacy, attributable to its terrain and plentiful sources of flowing water, went unchallenged, nevertheless, it by no means constituted sole center of the local textile industry. Under the patronage of Don Joseph Nasi this industry flowered briefly in Tiberias during the 1560s and 1570s; another textile center was located in Nablus.[5] Raw material for manufacture of fabrics was derived in part from locally produced cotton and silk. (Silkworms were cultivated in and around Safed and Tiberias, on mulberry trees specifically planted for this purpose.[6]) But the industry's backbone was imported woolen goods, which were shipped to the ports of Sidon and Acre from cities in Turkey, the Balkans, and Spain[7] via the wool depot in Adrianople. Dyeing, an important adjunct of the textile industry, was also primarily Safed-based; however, dyeing centers were situated in other cities—Nablus, Gaza, and Jerusalem, for example.[8]

Jews, Spanish exiles in particular, were the leaders of the local textile industry. The Spanish Jewish concentration in Safed was naturally attracted to the wool and weaving industries because of prior familiarity with these processes. Fully a third of the Castilian population earned its living from wool manufacture, and weaving ranked first among Spanish-Jewish crafts.[9] This state of affairs was aptly summed up in a letter sent from Safed in 1535 by David min ha-Adummim (de Rossi): "He who saw Safed ten years ago, and observes it now, has the impression of a miracle. For more Jews are arriving here continually, and the tailoring trade grows daily. I have been told that more than 15,000 suits of kersey[10] have been manufactured in Safed during this year, besides fancy suits.[11] Every man and every woman who works woolen fabric earns an abundant living" [Yaari, *Letters,* 184. Translation cited from Stillman, *Jews of Arab Lands,* 290, slightly revised].

Safed and its textile industry experienced a sharp decline in the last quarter of the sixteenth century, partly attributable to economic bankruptcy. Mediterranean wool centers as a whole were adversely affected when world markets were flooded with competitively priced quality goods imported from western countries, England in particular. Safed's rich merchants relocated, leaving the craftsmen unemployed.[12]

Soap Manufacture

Soap manufacture was another major industry on Eretz-Israel's economic scene. Olive trees cultivated in the Safed, Nablus, and Jerusalem regions supplied the oil that was the basic ingredient for soap. Evidence is extant for two operational soap factories, one in Jerusalem and the other in Hebron.[13] Muslim sources clearly reflect the role played by Jerusalem's Jewish residents in this industry, whose final product was generally exported to Egypt in the main; a Hebrew letter notes its ready availability in the city.[14]

Sundry Occupations

Because of the dietary restrictions imposed by Jewish law, Jews were naturally drawn to food processing, in order to meet the requirements for the proper preparation of meat, cheese, grape and bee honey, bread, and wine.[15] In addition to the branches of industry and crafts already noted, Jews engaged in a variety of additional occupations: precious metals, carpentry, smithing, saddle- and harness-making, shoemaking, hide-tanning, medicine, and construction.[16] This diversity reflects their untrammeled freedom of choice.

C. TRADE

Trade and commerce on both the local and the international levels provided another notable outlet for Jewish economic activity.[17] The role played by Jews in local trade, as shopkeepers in the markets and elsewhere, for example, has been well documented.[18] Of Jerusalem's four quarters one was the "Jewish quarter" where "*merceria* [notions] and perfumes" were sold.[19] According to Muslim sources, fully one-quarter or approximately thirty-five of the shops in Jerusalem were in Jewish hands.[20] It appears that Safed had a substantial number of Jewish shopkeepers as well and that Jews sold fruits and vegetables and other culinary products in its local market.[21] Not unexpectedly, given the intense Jewish involvement in the manufacture of textiles, the sale of dry goods and clothing was another notable branch of Jewish commercial endeavor.[22] In Gaza, southern Eretz-Israel's principal trade center with Egypt, Jews maintained shops in the jewelers' market (*saga*).[23] These scattered references are certainly suggestive of active Jewish involvement in local trade in additional urban centers and perhaps also in some of the villages where they resided.

Shopkeeping by no means represents the full range of Jewish commercial venture. Enterprising Jewish peddlers hawked their wares in the cities where they resided and in the outlying villages.[24] The Jewish shopkeepers in Jerusalem and Hebron viewed these peddlers as a thorn in the flesh, and in the early sixteenth century they voiced their objections to this practice to the communal authorities. The following *takkanah* promulgated in the sixteenth century's first quarter was specifically aimed at solving this problem:

> On Friday . . . the clothing and pepper merchants in the holy community of Jerusalem gathered in the synagogue and protested . . . before the congregational officials about individuals who peddled their wares from house to house and on the street, making a profit, preventing the shopkeepers from making a profit or negotiating. It was unanimously agreed that no merchant shall . . . peddle his wares in the city. . . . The congregational officials realized that this *haskamah* [agreement], far from causing damage, would rather bring the opposite, preserving them from grievous dangers and evils, heaven forbid. They observed that in larger communities the royal authorities had restricted the Jews, mandating that no Jew could peddle wares from house to house. It was then [seen as] preferable for us to regulate this matter on our own, rather than wait for the non-Jewish authorities to impose their oppressive yoke. We heard that [a similar takkanah] was adopted by the holy community of Hebron, may God protect and preserve it. . . . The entire congregation agreed. . . . This ends the quotation. [Elijah Mizraḥi, *Responsa,* no. 45][25]

Consumer goods—food, notions, clothing, and various luxury items such as spices, perfumes, jewelry, and medicinal plants—formed the backbone of local trade in the cities and their surrounding areas. David de Rossi's letter to Italy (1535) reflects the active Jewish role in import and export to and from Safed, as follows: "All articles of commerce are available in these regions. Fibers, spun and unspun,[26] are exported from Safed in great quantities, also gallnuts, scammony,[27] oil, honey, and silk in smaller quantities. From the adjoining regions come crimson silk, Cordovan carpets, and all kinds of spices, including pepper, cloves, ginger, and cane-spices. Many people including Jews buy these goods as merchandise" [Yaari, *Letters,* 187. English translation, Stillman, *Jews of Arab Lands,* 292].[28]

During this period, international trade flourished in Eretz-Israel, not only with neighboring Syria and Egypt,[29] but with more distant overseas destinations as well. Jews acted as importers and exporters, mainly in the context of Safed's thriving textile industry. Various sources, primarily halakhic in nature, touch upon Jewish involvement in the importation of wool to Safed from Turkey (Istanbul and Adrianople) in the main, but even from Rhodes. In Eretz-Israel, as we saw earlier, the wool was shipped to the ports of Tripoli, Sidon, and, in all likelihood, Acre.[30] Safed's Jews were heavily represented in the exportation of finished textiles, as well as of spun and unspun fibers.

During the sixteenth century Safed's merchants played an active role in exporting clothing to Damascus and to Egypt, and cotton and silk to Venice.[31] The Hebrew sources also indicate that Safed-based merchants exported oil and grain to Damascus and elsewhere, importing in turn fruits and vegetables not available in Eretz-Israel.[32] As we have seen, Jews were also involved in the exportation of luxury items—scammony, perfumes, and spices[33]—but their destination remains obscure. In the second half of the sixteenth century, however, Jewish traders are known to have been involved in shipping some or all of these items to Venice via Egypt.[34]

Jerusalem's Jews also had a hand in international trade. Soap manufacture was the city's best-developed industry, and Jewish merchants exported its products to Syria and Egypt.[35] In turn, Jews imported spices and dry goods from Syria and rice from Egypt.[36] In Gaza and Acre, too, Jewish merchants played a role in import-export trade across the borders of Eretz-Israel.[37]

Like their counterparts in Europe and the Orient, Jewish traders in Eretz-Israel employed the *fattoria* method; that is, wealthy merchants employed agents (*fattore*) in the various commercial centers whom they empowered to transact business in their names.[38]

D. FINANCIAL ACTIVITY

The regime's evenhanded treatment in the early Ottoman period, coupled with the absence of restrictions on their choice of economic endeavor, enabled Jews to engage actively in financial matters on behalf of both the central and the provincial governments.[39] Nor was Eretz-Israel an exception in this regard. Generally speaking, there were three major areas of Jewish financial activity: tax-farming, moneychanging, and moneylending.

1. Tax-farming

The large extent of Jewish involvement in the different facets of tax-farming in Jerusalem and elsewhere is well documented in the records of the Jerusalem sharia court. These sources reflect intense Jewish involvement in the tax-collection apparatus (*amil* or *multazim*) between 1538 and 1557, even specifying individual tax commissioners by name.[40] Following this date, no Jewish tax commissioners are known to have served in Jerusalem. Jews played a prominent role in the leasing of revenues in Safed as well. In the words of a Safed resident (1535): "The exile here is not like in our homeland [Italy]. The Turks hold respectable Jews in esteem. Here and in Alexandria, Egypt, Jews are the chief officers and administrators of the customs, and of the king's revenues" [Yaari, *Letters,* 186–87. English translation, Stillman, *Jews of Arab Lands,* 291–92].[41]

The individuals who engaged in tax-farming, often wealthy merchants who thereby sought to increase their income, belonged to the affluent upper echelon of Jewish society. On the most prominent the noble title *al-muallim* was conferred.[42]

2. Moneychanging

Jewish moneychangers, officially known as *ṣarrāf* or *ṣayrafī,* received official appointments from the kadi both to monitor the money currently in circulation and to detect counterfeit coins. Others functioned as treasurers for financial institutions, waqfs, for example. Jerusalem sharia court documents list ten Jewish moneychangers, including two Karaites.[43]

3. Moneylending

Extremely affluent Jews, in both Jerusalem and Safed, evidently turned a profit by extending credit at interest to Muslim or Christian public institutions in financial straits. Hebrew and Muslim sources alike indicate that district governors employed the services of Jewish moneylenders to raise funds,[44] as did Church institutions that experienced delays in receiving stipends from abroad.

The permissibility of Jewish financial support for church institutions was a stormy, much-debated issue among late-sixteenth-century Jerusalem sages. The question at stake was whether a Jew living in Eretz-Israel could enhance Christian strength in Eretz-Israel in general, and in Jerusalem in particular, by means of advancing them financial aid. A takkanah prohibiting moneylending to Christians was enacted. As certain Jews depended on moneylending at interest as their sole means of livelihood, this regulation was untenable. If this regulation was enforced, these individuals would be compelled to leave Jerusalem. In a responsum addressing this issue, the leading late-sixteenth/early-seventeenth-century scholar in Egypt, Meir Gavison, ruled in favor of allowing Jews to lend money to Christians:

> The holy flock of Israel, the first fruits of His harvest, who are dispersed among the lands of the nations, their souls long for the courts of the house of the Lord, to frequent His Temple on Jerusa-

> lem's holy mountain. [Jerusalem's] residents feel the yoke of the nations more strongly, and must constantly propitiate them with pieces of silver in addition to what they require for their own households. They honor its judges and officials with regular and additional sacrifices at the appointed and special times. . . . And they took the initiative, seeing that the Christians and priests who lived there used to borrow money at interest from the town notables and merchants to cover their expenses pending the arrival of their stipends from their native lands. Therefore, it was decided that a few recently arrived designated persons would fulfill the positive commandment "you may deduct interest from loans to foreigners" [Deut. 23:20], "but [within the limits of] while a tenth part yet remains in it" [Isa. 6:13][45] so that they would be able to support themselves. [Meir Gavison, *Responsa,* no. 43, pp. 163–64]

Thus the validity of the ban on Jewish moneylending to the Church was questioned, and it was eventually nullified. Moneylending by Jews to Church institutions became a recognized and legitimate means of earning income then and for generations thereafter.[46]

E. COST OF LIVING (AFTER THE OTTOMAN CONQUEST)

The fiscal changes ushered in by the Ottoman conquest found their expression in a drastic rise in the prices of basic commodities in Jerusalem. The lack of direct evidence notwithstanding, it is more than likely that a similar situation prevailed elsewhere. Prices jumped four- or fivefold in the course of a single year, as documented in Abraham ha-Levi's letter (1520): "Prior to the change in regime, everything in Eretz-Israel was very cheap, everything, that is wheat, meat, wine, and fruit, for the land is exceedingly good. But at present, everything is very expensive. What cost ten . . . cannot [now] be found for forty or even fifty" [David, "A Letter from Jerusalem," 56].

This letter not only pertains to this specific point but also is indicative of a general trend. It faithfully mirrors the difference between the economic policies practiced by the two regimes, or at the very least, the changes engendered by the shift. Under Mamluk rule, due to its precarious economic status, basic commodities were imported to Jerusalem from Gaza and elsewhere.[47] Contemporary Hebrew sources relating to Jerusalem indicate that, far from rising, basic consumer goods remained low in price, commensurate with the population's restricted purchasing power and limited demand.[48] The significant improvement in the economy that followed the Ottoman takeover, its expanded sources of income and concomitantly greater fiscal ability, led to a correspondingly drastic hike in the cost of living.[49]

F. DIASPORA SUPPORT FOR COMMUNITIES IN ERETZ-ISRAEL

The picture of intensive economic activity that emerges from the sources notwithstanding, it appears that in the early decades of Ottoman rule, Jews in Eretz-Israel in general and Jerusalemites in particular experienced substantial difficulty in meeting their daily economic needs. The sources clearly depict economic hardship, noting in particular the burdensome taxes that crushed a significant segment of the Jerusalem Jewish community. Destitution was not uncommon, as seen from the following letter written by Abraham ha-Levi (1520): "The burden of financial payments is unbearable for a poor and destitute community, for poverty is prevalent. Everyone borrows at interest from the rich Muslims and the interest accumulates daily" [David, "A Letter from Jerusalem," 56].

Moses Basola painted a similar picture in his travel account (1522): "There are some three hundred householders among them aside from more than [. . .][50] widows who earn a good living, who pay no taxes. . . . Those who receive charity number more than two hundred individuals" [Basola, *Masot,* 61–62].

A similar description, written in the same year, is found in a letter sent from Jerusalem by Israel Ashkenazi: "As far as food is concerned, everyone is in trouble, because meat is not available daily in Jerusalem as it is in our land [Italy], nor are fish and fruits, with the exception of figs and grapes. Other fruits, apples and pears, are imported from Damascus and are very expensive" [David, "Letter of Israel Ashkenazi," 115].

Levi ibn Ḥabib (Ralbaḥ), a leading Jerusalem rabbi, provided a more dramatic description of Jerusalem in the 1530s: "The residents of Jerusalem eat no delicacies; their food is bitter. He who succeeds in acquiring sufficient funds to purchase the head of a small animal with its innards, even of a goat, for the Sabbath or holidays, regards himself as having been freed from servitude to sit in the place of honor" [Levi ibn Ḥabib, *Semikha Pamphlet*].[51]

Although the acutely felt problems of daily life during the early days of the Ottoman regime have been documented for sectors of Jerusalem's Jewish population, it seems likely that these problems were not restricted to Jerusalem alone. In this respect Safed constituted an exception—there, as we shall see, poverty became acute only in the sixteenth century's last quarter. Hebrew sources, including the following responsum by Moses Trani, indicate that Jerusalem's Jews owed their survival to monetary support from Diaspora Jews: "All the *kehillot* that send contributions to Jerusalem know that apart from what is disbursed to scholars and the poor, [the money] is used to pay debts incurred by the community. For the residents of Jerusalem are able to pay the annual poll tax alone. Other indebtedness is covered from funds sent from abroad, for if this were not the case, no one would desire to settle in this city" [Moses Trani, *Responsa,* pt. 3, no. 228].[52]

Individual donors to the Jewish communities in Eretz-Israel were motivated by a variety of factors—by generous impulses or by the desire to show gratitude to God for having been rescued from danger or disaster. Others willed money and property to the poor of Eretz-Israel as a means of gaining penance for their souls, of ensuring their elevation after death.[53] Often moved by individual entreaties, donors also responded to appeals made by rabbinic emissaries (*shadarim*) dispatched by Jewish communities in Eretz-Israel who traveled far and wide in search of contributions. From the sixteenth century on, information is available regarding such rabbinic emissaries from Jerusalem, Safed, Hebron, and Tiberias. Safed's precarious economic situation during the sixteenth century's last quarter has been relatively well documented. Because of the general recession in Eretz-Israel and its severe effect on Safed in particular, its Jews now found themselves addressing more frequent requests for material assistance to the Diaspora. Although it seems reasonable to assume that the depressing conditions described in the letters borne by the emissaries were almost certainly overstated, nonetheless, we must note that emissaries were nearly always dispatched in times of real crisis—severe economic depression or newly enacted decrees requiring the immediate payment of large sums.[54]

The impression conveyed by the sources is that Italian Jewry bore the brunt of material support for Jerusalem and Safed's Jews.[55] From the fifteenth century, Italian cities were an important destination for emissaries dispatched from Eretz-Israel. As early as the 1520s, Venice served as an important junction for funds bound for Eretz-Israel from kehillot in Italy and western Europe. In the sixteenth century, many emissaries initiated their fund-raising campaigns in this port city, using it as a base for their activities. Some of the larger Italian Jewish communities even appointed special officials to collect funds for Eretz-Israel, who assisted the emissaries in the solicitation and collection of funds, providing them with letters of recommendation as well. On occasion, these officials for Eretz-Israel saved the emissaries time and trouble by appealing to nearby and distant communities in their name and even collecting a portion of the donations. These brief comments by no means indicate the full extent of the active interest in Eretz-Israel demonstrated by the Italian communities.[56]

But communities in the Near East—Egypt, Syria, and Turkey—also contributed to the upkeep of kehillot in Eretz-Israel.[57] Contemporary Jewish sources, including Geniza documents, partially acquaint us with the philanthropic activity of kehillot and affluent individuals in Egypt on behalf of Eretz-Israel's Jews. Institutions of learning as well as individuals were its beneficiaries.[58] During his tenure as Egypt's last *nagid* (1502–17), Isaac Sholal nurtured Jerusalem's spiritual life by means of continuous massive support for the two yeshivot there, one of which he founded whereas the other reopened at his initiative.[59] In the sixteenth century's first decade, Sholal also contributed to the upkeep of a Sefardi yeshivah in Safed.[60] But his assistance to the communities in Eretz-Israel extended beyond the material sphere. In Jerusalem, for example, not only did the nagid provide aid in the form of economic relief; he also sought to legislate order in the Jewish community's public affairs.[61]

With the Ottoman conquest, the office of nagid was terminated.[62] Isaac Sholal's personal circumstances underwent a dramatic change. He now found himself unable to support the yeshivot in Jerusalem,[63] as seen from the following remarks by Abraham ha-Levi (1520): "Prior to the change in regime, an eminent man resided in Egypt, the perfect sage, the great rabbi named Isaac Sholal, may he be exalted. He supported Torah scholars throughout Eretz-Israel, teachers and students as well . . . and his largesse was great. Now that a new face has come to the land, and the sons of Japheth, the Turks, rule, the aforesaid exalted nagid . . . had to leave Egypt. He suffered great losses, to the extent that he subsists on bread and water" [David, "A Letter from Jerusalem," 59]. Nonetheless, the Egyptian Jewish community as a whole and its individual members continued to make philanthropic contributions and to set up charitable trusts for the Jewish population in Eretz-Israel, as attested by various sources, including halakhic sources and Geniza documents.[64]

In addition to their regular ongoing support, Egyptian Jewry responded swiftly with massive aid in times of emergency. Two examples, from Safed and Jerusalem respectively, illustrate this point.

Shortly after the Ottoman conquest of Egypt, due to attacks by Muslims still loyal to the Mamluk regime, Safed's Jews found themselves in need of substantial financial assistance. Elijah Capsali, the well-known historian from Candia (Crete), recounted how the Jews of Egypt rallied to the aid of their coreligionists in Safed:

> Men and women came, all who were moved to make a contribution. More than thirty thousand florins were collected. And the aforesaid Rabbi Nissim was saved by his arm and his righteousness supported him. He asked himself: "Who will provide clothing for so many and when will we have time to sew clothes for them?" The spirit of the

> Lord enveloped him, and he took off his vestments, and put on others, stating: "This clothing shall be for charity, it must go into the treasury of the Lord." And those that saw him, said: "We shall do the same." Everyone whose spirit moved him came bringing his offering of vestments—a checkered tunic, a headdress, and a sash [Exod. 28:4]—the rich in accord with his wealth and the poor in accord with his poverty. [Capsali, *Eliyahu Zuta,* chap. 127, p. 350][65]

In 1520 the renowned Jerusalem kabbalist Abraham ha-Levi noted in a letter that Jerusalem's Jews had experienced persecution of an unspecified nature. He stressed the help provided by Egyptian Jewry in those circumstances: "For we were falsely accused this year, and feared expulsion, had it not been for God's mercy. In any event, this holy congregation had to disburse three thousand florins in three days, in order to abate the anger of the land's rulers . . . and the interest mounted daily until our brethren in Egypt provided help in the amount of six hundred florins" [David, "A Letter from Jerusalem," 56ff.].[66]

Egyptian Jews taxed traders with whom they did business in the amount of a half-*muayyadi* (an Egyptian coin in circulation in the fifteenth and sixteenth centuries).[67] This fee, which was allocated to Jerusalem's poor, is referred to in a responsum: "In Egypt they did the following—the merchants who came from overseas agreed to take upon themselves to contribute one half-muayyadi per bale for Jerusalem's poor" [David ibn Abi Zimra, *Responsa,* no. 2248].

Geniza documents attest to appeals addressed by individuals in Eretz-Israel to their counterparts in Egypt requesting material aid both for communal needs and for specific cases.[68] Aside from the nagid, Isaac Sholal, we know of three outstanding Egyptian Jewish philanthropists who provided material assistance to the Jews of Eretz-Israel from the late Mamluk period to the end of the sixteenth century—Abraham Castro, Abraham ibn Sanji, and Solomon Alashkar.

Abraham Castro, one of Egyptian Jewry's outstanding figures in the early Ottoman period, has recently captured scholarly interest since the discovery of documents that shed light on his life and personality. He was of Spanish origin and perhaps himself an expellee from Spain. Contemporary Hebrew and Muslim sources indicate that he moved in government circles, especially in the financial realm, leasing duties on customs and trade and serving as the master of the mint (*muallim dar al ḍarb*) from 1520 at least (and perhaps earlier). Castro was renowned for his broad philanthropic activity on behalf of individuals and institutions both in Egypt and in Eretz-Israel.[69] Hebrew sources as well as documents from Jerusalem's sharia court indicate that Castro was a Jerusalem resident from the late 1530s and that he assumed a central role in local society there, primarily as an economic force, dealing in real estate and tax-farming.[70]

Concerning the second personality, Abraham ibn Sanji (d. prior to 1547[71]), we have some knowledge of his involvement in various branches of commerce[72] and his close philanthropic ties with Jerusalemites beginning in the sixteenth century's second decade. Two Geniza documents, letters sent from Jerusalem, shed light on Ibn Sanji's philanthropic activity on behalf of Jerusalem's Jews.[73]

Solomon Alashkar, the third philanthropist, was a wealthy merchant known for his dynamic activity on behalf of the yeshivot in Jerusalem and Safed and for additional cultural undertakings as well.[74] In his *Shalshelet ha-Qabbalah,* the Italian-Jewish historian Gedaliah ibn Yaḥya mentions him as "a great prince who supported the yeshivot in Eretz-Israel from his own pocket, for he was an extremely affluent man and the customs collector for the king of Egypt."[75]

In sum, the brief fifty-year period of economic prosperity ushered in by the Ottoman regime saw Eretz-Israel's Jewish population engaged in all branches of economic endeavor, ranging from agriculture, industry, trade, and finance, with textiles playing a lion's share in Jewish occupations. The new prosperity and economic opportunities in Eretz-Israel notwithstanding, Jews still bore the burden of heavy taxation and owed their survival, in Jerusalem especially, to massive support by Diaspora Jews.

4 Governmental Policy Toward the Jews

The evenhanded policy pursued by the Ottoman regime did not carry over to all aspects of its treatment of non-Muslim minorities. In certain areas the Ottoman rulers, like their Mamluk predecessors, continued to be guided by the discriminatory laws grounded in Islamic doctrine.[1] In addition to its insistence on the strict enforcement of discriminatory legislation, not only did the Ottoman regime require that its non-Muslim subjects (*ahl-al-dhimma*) take cognizance of their inferior status, but also it anticipated that they would adjust their behavior accordingly.[2] It seems, however, that in Eretz-Israel the early Ottoman regime was by no means either as harsh or as despotic as its Mamluk predecessors.[3] This more lenient attitude toward "non-believers" is reflected, along with the prescribed conventions for dhimmi behavior, in a letter written in 1522 by Israel Ashkenazi—a leading Jerusalemite sage in the 1520s:

> Those who accept the yoke of exile and subservience, shall lift neither hand nor foot against the Ishmaelites, even if they cheat you. One should not speak arrogantly even to the very lowly. [Rather] one should act deaf and dumb, speak placatorily and offer a small bribe. Then all is well, for when the Ishmaelite sees humility and subservience, he is placated. Even if he seeks food, he is satisfied with a small amount . . . and after humbling oneself, then one can trade everywhere, and have a store in the market like an Ishmaelite without anyone raising objections. One can go everywhere with a green turban, even travel if he likes, and be honored by all. The only thing is—he is obliged to pay a high customs tax. [David, "Letter of Israel Ashkenazi," 117–18]

These remarks clearly prescribe acquiescence to the discriminatory reality. In Ashkenazi's view, dhimmi compliance with the discriminatory rules governing the social and economic spheres was potentially rewarding in terms of unrestricted mobility and choice of profession. A similar, more laconic description cited earlier noted the esteem in which "respectable Jews" were held and mentioned their high positions as administrators of customs and revenues, explicitly stating, "no injuries are perpetrated against them in all the empire."[4]

This optimistic statement notwithstanding, Jews and other non-Muslim minorities were subject to discrimination in two main areas: taxation and the social sphere, in addition to the already mentioned restrictions on landowning.

A. TAXATION

Jews, like other dhimmi, bore the burden of special taxes: the poll tax—*jizya*—and the toll or protection tax—*khafar.*[5] In Safed and elsewhere, the tax collection apparatus was unable to cope efficiently with the dramatic rise in population engendered by the new prosperity, necessitating the enactment of special firmans by the Sublime Porte.[6] There is some evidence to suggest that in its early years the Ottoman regime may have canceled additional taxes the Mamluk regime collected from the dhimmi, including the ubiquitous tax on wine;[7] however, the documentation for such a step dates from the late sixteenth century.[8] It is not unlikely that the Ottomans also canceled the ancient tax normally paid upon a new ruler's accession to the throne.[9]

The picture that emerges from the Jerusalem sharia court documents suggests that the Jewish community did not find the special taxes especially burdensome.[10] Various Hebrew sources, dating mainly from the latter half of the sixteenth century, convey a very different impression of a community suffering from a heavy tax burden. In the late sixteenth century especially, regular tax collection was supplemented by additional legal and illegal levies. The exigencies of life in Jerusalem are reflected in a responsum penned by Meir Gavison at the turn of the sixteenth to seventeenth centuries:

> The holy flock . . . their souls long for the courts of the house of the Lord . . . on the Lord's holy mount in Jerusalem. As the residents there feel the yoke of the nations more strongly, and must constantly propitiate them with pieces of silver, in addition to what they need for their own households. (They must unfailingly pay the judges their daily reckoning.) They honor its judges and officials with regular and special sacrifices. It is well known publicly that is how it is in Jerusalem (living in Jerusalem, may it be speedily rebuilt and reestablished, entails suffering). [Meir Gavison, *Responsa,* no. 43, p. 164][11]

Gavison's contemporary, Samuel de Uceda of Safed, confirmed the particularly heavy burden of taxation the Jews of Eretz-Israel bore: "We see in our time, that of all the lands where the king's sway extends, may he be exalted, no other country collects as many taxes and fees from Jews as Eretz-Israel, Jerusalem in particular. If money were not sent from all the regions where Jews live toward payment of their taxes and fees, they would be unable to reside there [Jerusalem] due to the multitude of taxes" [Samuel de Uceda, *Leḥem Dimah* (Commentary on Lamentations), fol. 3r, lemma: *hayyetah la-mas*].

B. DISCRIMINATORY LEGISLATION

The restrictions imposed on Jews included dress regulations. Local potentates insisted on compliance with the Mamluk ordinance requiring Jews to wear a yellow turban,[12] well documented in Hebrew, Muslim, and Christian sources.[13] On one occasion, Jews were accused of masquerading as Muslims when they covered their heads with prayer shawls that were white and therefore forbidden to them.[14] Jerusalem's Jews were required in addition to forewarn the Muslims before entering the public bath by wearing a small bell around their necks in order to allow the Muslims time to cover themselves.[15]

Synagogue construction was also subject to legal restrictions. In the case of Jerusalem, the renovation of its main synagogue, the so-called Ramban Synagogue, whose traditional attribution to Naḥmanides is unfounded, gave rise to Muslim-Jewish tension, partly attributable to its close proximity to the al-Umari mosque. In late 1474 Muslim fanatics destroyed the synagogue, claiming that it had been built illegally, in defiance of the standing order forbidding the construction of new synagogues adjoining old ones. The synagogue was rebuilt several years later at the order of Sultan Qaitbay when the Jews supplied documentary proof of its legality.[16] Under the Ottoman regime in the 1530s, further Muslim attempts to encroach upon the area under Jewish control were made, even going so far as to seek total revocation of their rights. Rumors were spread of illegal renovations; the claim that the synagogue had been rebuilt was also advanced. Attempts to prove that the synagogue had been illegally constructed continued down to the late 1580s.[17] In late 1587 the synagogue was confiscated by order of Abu Seifin; however, a temporary restraining order was obtained from the sultan. This brief period of grace ended in April 1588, when the kadi of Jerusalem issued an order expressly forbidding Jews to utilize the structure.[18] As the ban on the construction of new synagogues did not apply to informal or semiformal worship, the local authorities permitted the Jews to worship in private homes.[19] Several decades were to pass before the Jews were again allowed to pray openly in an officially designated public setting, the Yoḥanan ben Zakkai synagogue.

In 1534 the kadi's representative renewed another discriminatory measure issued in the late Mamluk period, during the reign of Qaitbay (1468–96). This order forbidding Jews ingress to Mount Zion, sparked by incessant Jewish-Franciscan tension, was reinstated at the insistence of the Franciscan order.[20]

The existing pattern of anti-Jewish discrimination notwithstanding, the Ottoman central government adamantly protected Jewish rights; new restrictions, in addition to those already found in the *kānūn* or the sharia, were not to be enacted. Dozens of firmans dispatched by the Sublime Porte to the governors and kadis of Jerusalem, Safed, and Damascus reinforced this stance,[21] firmly reiterating the obligation not to diverge from the parameters of Jewish privileges as defined by Islamic doctrine and banning detraction from established Jewish rights. These documents clearly illustrate that when their rights were infringed in Jerusalem, Safed, and Damascus, Jews had recourse to the Sublime Porte. When investigation proved Jewish allegations correct, the sultan, for his part, had no compunctions about reprimanding the kadis or governors involved, demanding on more than one occasion that the injustice be rectified. If taxes were collected in excess of the legal ceiling, for example, local officials could be and were ordered to make restitution. Government officials who overstepped the established bounds and tried to encroach on Jewish status and rights were punished. Sometimes appeals to the sultan did not elicit an immediate decision on his part; rather, the Sublime Porte directed the kadi or local ruler to investigate Jewish allegations.

An interesting picture emerges from these documents, one of give-and-take between Jews and the central regime. When local authorities infringed on their rights, Jews had no qualms about seeking recourse from the central government. On the one hand, this attests to a high level of tolerance on the central government's part; on the other, the number of these appeals clearly demonstrates that serious violations of Jewish rights by the local authorities were far from infrequent.[22]

C. RELIGIOUS AUTONOMY AND DEPENDENCE ON THE MUSLIM COURTS

Under the Ottoman regime, Jews enjoyed religious autonomy as well as legal independence. This independence was by no means absolute. In Jerusalem and Safed, as was the case elsewhere in the Ottoman empire, the appointment of Jewish officials was subject to the local kadi's approval;[23] in reality, then, the ostensibly independent Jewish judicial system was actually at the mercy of the local kadi who alone was empowered to instate the *dayyan,* the Jewish community's chief judicial authority.[24] As a rule, Jewish communities made intensive efforts to prevent the Ottoman authorities from intervening in their judicial process. Jews determinedly refrained from appealing to the Muslim courts, which, in their view, undermined Jewish communal autonomy. It is not without cause that we find repeated warnings issued from Jerusalem against appealing to the Muslim courts during this period. For example, "We do not litigate in the [Muslim] courts at all . . . and if an occasional poison weed elects to go to the [Muslim] court, all of Israel immediately unites as one against the destroyer, and they pay a bribe to the local ruler to flog him with sticks for his disobedience, as is the custom of the land. He is then ostracized until he repents and makes monetary restitution to the community" [David, "Letter of Israel Ashkenazi," 111–12].[25]

Sharia court documents clearly indicate that Jews did seek legal rulings from the kadi. In essence, they sought authorization for verdicts handed down by the Jewish courts, which had limited punitive powers. The kadi was approached when the Jews sought to mete out more drastic punishment than the ostracization and excommunication at their disposal;[26] for example, Jews turned to the Muslim judicial system in the case of habitual offenders who refused to submit to internal Jewish authority.[27] According to the takkanot of the Jerusalem community, in such a case it was permissible to turn to the Muslim courts; however, they also stipulated that "no Jew can summon a coreligionist to a non-Jewish court unless he has warned him of his failure to comply three times."[28] Jews involved in litigation against Muslims or Christians had recourse to the Muslim courts as well. Sharia court documents provide evidence of verdicts that favored Jews over Muslims,[29] despite the natural tendency to suspect a pro-Muslim bias on the part of the judges, regardless of the question of guilt or innocence. Jews were also occasionally summoned to the sharia court to give evidence or to serve as witnesses, generally in cases involving dhimmi vs. dhimmi, or Muslim vs. Christian.

Evidence presented by Jews was admissible in the Muslim courts in cases where other Jews or Christians were involved and as auxiliary evidence backing Muslim testimony. In the Muslim judicial system, however, it was inadmissible as sole evidence in Jewish-Muslim litigation.[30]

We have characterized the Ottoman regime as more tolerant toward the Jewish population in Eretz-Israel than were its Mamluk predecessors. Nonetheless, the discriminatory laws anchored in early Muslim law governing dhimmi behavior were enforced—Jews carried the burden of extra taxes, dress regulations, and restrictions on public worship. Whereas the Ottoman regime upheld the existing measures, it was also careful not to encroach upon existing Jewish rights, including the Jewish community's religious and judicial autonomy. Although Jews assiduously avoided litigation in the Muslim courts when possible in the interests of maintaining this autonomy, we do find Jewish dependence on the Muslim authorities for appointment of its leaders and for the administration of punishments that exceeded the powers of the Jewish court. Although the regulations governing dhimmi behavior were certainly burdensome, at the same time the central regime preserved the Jewish right to redress when basic rights were infringed, going so far as to order investigation and restitution. The "yoke of subservience," while certainly not ideal, was tolerable, with the exception of the burden of taxes for which payment the Jewish community of Eretz-Israel continued to rely on Diaspora assistance.

JERUSALEM

5 The Jewish Quarter

The section on Jewish Jerusalem, one of the two major centers of Jewish life in sixteenth-century Eretz-Israel, sets out first to establish the Jewish quarter's physical location and salient demographic features. It then explores the variegated human mosaic of its social composition, bearing witness to the Sefardi element's rapid rise to dominance. The internal communal structure and patterns of leadership form the next topic, which is followed by an examination of the city's educational settings and their curricula. By no means have I tried to present a picture of daily life; the focus here is on the institutional and educational settings and on the roles played by leading personalities within the communal structure.

A. LOCATION

Jerusalem's Jews resided in the area contiguous with the present-day "Jewish Quarter" during the period under consideration. In an earlier period, they lived on Mt. Zion; their relocation dates from the turn of the fourteenth to the fifteenth centuries.[1] Hebrew sources refer to the Jewish neighborhood as "Ẓion," while Arabic ones use "Ṣahyun."[2] Two possible conjectures for this choice of name are the neighborhood's proximity to Mt. Zion or a retrospective reference to the former Jewish quarter on Mt. Zion. The Arabic term *ḥarat al-yahud*, that is, the Jewish neighborhood, was also in use.

Hebrew sources provide but a sketchy picture of the Jewish quarter's location.[3] Moses Basola, for example, reported its location in general terms only: "The nagid, may God protect and preserve him, told me that in Jerusalem the Jewish neighborhood extends from Mt. Zion to near the Temple."[4] Arabic and Turkish sources from the late Mamluk/early Ottoman periods enable us to fix its boundaries more precisely.[5] According to these sources, the Jewish presence in Jerusalem was distributed over three contiguous Muslim neighborhoods—the al-Sharaf, the al-Risha, and the al-Maslakh quarters. The al-Sharaf neighborhood, where the *Tarik al-Maslakh* or Jews' Street was located, lay west of Mt. Zion in close proximity to the *ḥaram* and was bounded by David Street in the north. The al-Risha quarter lay to the west of Jews'

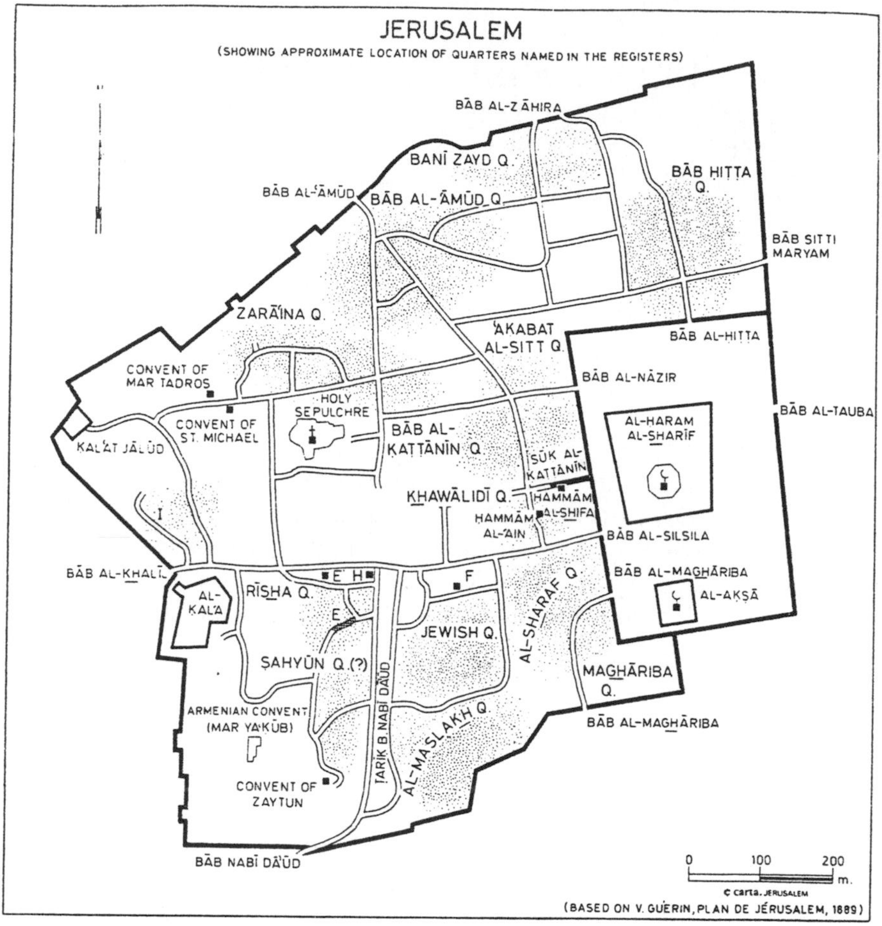

Map 3. Jerusalem's Quarters in the Early Ottoman Period (Princeton University Press)

Street and was situated between this street and the Jacobite (Armenian) quarter, while the al-Maslakh quarter lay between the Zion Gate's southern corner and the Armenian Quarter, toward Dung Gate.[6]

Jews resided outside the city limits as well, in Nabi Samuil, situated north of Jerusalem. As its name indicates, this was believed to be the burial site of the prophet Samuel, a tradition embraced in both Muslim and Jewish lore.[7] Jews exercised control over this site, albeit not continuously, from the late twelfth until the early eighteenth century, and Nabi Samuil was a popular destination for Jewish pilgrims. Mass gatherings were held here, on the 28th of Iyyar in particular, the traditional date of Samuel's death. These gatherings were the venue for a variety of rituals: special prayers in the prophet's memory and bequests of charity in his honor, among others.[8] Various sources dating from the late fifteenth century on indicate that a synagogue and a *bet midrash* (yeshivah) operated here.[9] In the early Ottoman period, ownership of this site was a contested issue, with claims set forth by both Rabbanite and Karaite Jews. Through the intervention of the Sublime Porte, hegemony over Nabi Samuil was awarded to the Rabbanites.[10]

Over the years, Muslims made unceasing efforts to obstruct Jewish activity at the site, which was also holy in their eyes, and even to wrest control of it from the Jews.[11] Sixteenth-century sources indicate that the Jews succeeded in maintaining their hold and that both a yeshivah and a synagogue continued to function there.[12] Between 1565 and 1573, however, it appears that the Muslims did succeed in temporarily evicting the Jews, as documented in a responsum by David ibn Abi Zimra: "He who made a vow to cut his child's hair at Samuel's tomb and came and found that it was in the hands of the idol-worshippers; due to our sins Jews cannot gain entry."[13] Nonetheless, some thirty years later, in 1600, the Jews regained permission to return to this site.[14]

B. DEMOGRAPHIC CHANGES

Jerusalem's Jewish population, like the Jewish population of Eretz-Israel in general, showed a steady increase following the inception of Ottoman rule. Partial demographic data for selected years dating from the 1520s to the 1560s are found in taḥrir registers housed in the Ottoman archives.[15] Although these registers presumably provide an accurate reflection of Jerusalem's population, including the number of its Jews, this is not necessarily the case. We must note the discrepancy between the data they report and the evidence from Hebrew sources. According to the 1525/26 census, the Jewish population figure numbered 199 households. This contrasts with the far larger number attested by Moses Basola approximately three years earlier, "some three hundred [Jewish] households."[16] I believe that, in this instance, Basola's testimony is the more accurate reflection of reality. Earlier, in 1495, an anonymous traveler had reported that Jerusalem's Jewish population then comprised "some 200 households."[17] It is by no means a fanciful assumption that in the intervening twenty-seven-year period until Basola's visit, and after the Ottoman conquest especially, Jerusalem's Jewish population underwent a substantial increase, by as much as 50 percent, well beyond what we would expect based on the birthrate alone. This figure of 300 households must therefore reflect a moderate increase in the number of immigrants who settled in Jerusalem as conditions there improved.

It appears, then, as noted, that the taḥrir registers by no means provide a totally accurate picture of the contemporary reality.[18] An im-

Table 1. Jewish Households According to Taḥrir Registers

Year of Census	1525/26	1538/39	1553/54	1562/63
Number of Households	199	224	324	237

portant factor that must be taken into account is the complete unavailability of data regarding the number of tax-evaders, making it impossible to correct the taḥrir's low estimate by factoring in this figure.[19] Thus the importance of these registers lies primarily in their ability to indicate upward or downward population trends.

The data for Jewish households in Jerusalem can be summarized as shown in Table 1. The second and third censuses show a moderate increase in Jerusalem's Jewish population, while the fourth is indicative of a downward trend. The registers for the Muslim and Christian populations reflect similar trends;[20] for the non-Jewish population, however, the rise reflected in the second and third censuses is sharper, whereas the decline shown by the fourth is more moderate. From a fifth census (1596/97), information only for the Muslim and Christian populations has survived. We can assume that the continued general decline in population reflected there applied also to Jerusalem's Jewish sector.

Sharia court documents indicate that three local censuses were conducted as well: in 1567/68, 1584, and 1587. These censuses similarly reflect a significant decrease in Jerusalem's Jewish population.[21] This decline, already clearly evident in the 1560s, may have begun slightly earlier. Evidently, the incipient signs of the severe economic depression that affected the Ottoman Empire in the last quarter of the sixteenth century, including Eretz-Israel, were felt somewhat sooner in Jerusalem and Safed, as early as the 1550s and 1560s.[22]

For the century's third quarter, there is evidence from a Hebrew source (1575) that Jews left Jerusalem for Safed because of the difficult conditions in the city, which to every indication were rooted in an earlier period. The source also reflects the growing involvement of Safed's communal leaders in Jerusalem affairs.[23] It appears that the leading rabbi of the day, David ibn Abi Zimra, should be included among the Jews who relocated to Safed; he evidently left Jerusalem sometime after 1563.[24] But this exodus to Safed came to a halt in the century's final quarter, when Safed experienced a severe economic crisis in the context of the empire-wide depression. At that point in time, Safed was even more severely affected than Jerusalem, as a letter sent from Jerusalem in 1584 by Samson Back (Bacchi) attests: "How many goodly favors has the Almighty bestowed on me! He took me out of Safed and led me to Jerusalem the holy where nothing is lacking. . . . Since I left

Table 2. Jewish Households According to Neighborhood

Census Year	1525/26	1538/39	1553/54	1562/63
total	199	224	324	237
al-Sharaf	—	85	107	146
al-Maslakh	—	43	79	40
al-Risha	—	96	138	51

Safed, they are in great distress, due to our iniquities . . . and here, praise God, everything except wheat is cheap" [Yaari, *Letters,* 188–89].[25]

The taḥrir registers also provide a breakdown of the number of Jewish households in each of the three Muslim neighborhoods where Jews resided, as shown in Table 2. The 1538/39 and 1553/54 censuses show the greatest concentration of Jews in the al-Risha quarter. The last census reflects a shift to the al-Sharaf neighborhood, with a concurrent decrease in the Jewish population of the other two neighborhoods. This relocation evidently took place during the 1550s or early 1560s.[26]

It is perhaps difficult for us to imagine a major Jewish center whose population totaled only a few hundred families. Moreover, as we shall see in the following chapter, the Jewish population in sixteenth-century Jerusalem, though small, was by no means homogeneous. Over the course of the century, however, the balance of power passed into the hands of the Sefardim who absorbed most of the existing groups. Having briefly placed the Jewish quarter in its geographical and demographic setting, I now turn to a consideration of its social composition.

6 The Communities

Small by modern standards, but diverse nonetheless, the divisions in Jerusalem's Jewish community were broadly outlined by Moses Basola in his eyewitness account, recorded in 1522: "The Jewish community includes all kinds of Jews . . . Ashkenazim, and many Sefardim, and there are Musta'rabs, the ancient inhabitants of the land, and Maghrebis who came from Barbary [North Africa]."[1] Each of these kehalim, with the addition of the Ethiopian and Karaite communities, will be examined separately below. The discussion focuses on the shifting balance of power between the kehalim, tracing the evidence for the rise of the Sefardi *kahal,* the community's dominant element for a substantial portion of the century.

A. ASHKENAZIM

As early as the latter half of the fourteenth century, an Ashkenazi congregation is known to have existed in Jerusalem.[2] By 1475 to 1500, this congregation ranked foremost within the Jewish community at large in Jerusalem. Ashkenazim, among them Italian Jews of Ashkenazi origin,[3] were at the forefront of the Jewish *yishuv*'s spiritual and social leadership.

With the increased influx of Iberian exiles in the late fifteenth/early sixteenth centuries, the Ashkenazim experienced a loss of hegemony, gradually surrendering their dominance to the newcomers. Whereas the Sefardim swiftly overpowered and absorbed the other communities unopposed,[4] the Ashkenazim constituted an exception. Their numerical inferiority notwithstanding, they continued to hold fast to their separate communal identity and to maintain the traditions unique to the Ashkenazi way of life.[5] An important facet of this separatism hinged on economic independence. The Ashkenazim dispatched their own emissaries to the Diaspora,[6] and funds collected in this manner were disbursed at the sole discretion of the Ashkenazi congregation, which felt no obligation to share with the other kehalim. Witness the following statement by Moses Basola: "More than two hundred individuals receive charity, much of which is sent from Egypt, Turkey, and elsewhere. But the Askenazi poor are not included—their support comes from Venice"[7] [Basola, *Masot,* 62].

Basola's remarks imply that Jerusalem's Ashkenazi congregation received massive aid from its fellow communities in Italy, which were clustered in the peninsula's northern urban centers. A different source (to be discussed in greater detail in the following section) illustrates the intercommunal tensions created by the superior Ashkenazi prowess at fund-raising; these peaked in the late sixteenth century when economic exigencies forced the Sefardim to demand that the Ashkenazim hand over half their funds to the Sefardi communal treasury.[8]

Close interpersonal relationships between members of the different kehalim were rare, as were "intermarriages." But such "mixed marriages" were not unheard of. For example, Joseph Caro, famed resident of Safed from 1536 to 1575, who was of Iberian extraction, made his second marriage with the daughter of a Jerusalemite Ashkenazi sage, Zechariah Zaksel Ashkenazi.[9] In some instances, such unions gave rise to disputes. A case in point is that of a Sefardi woman who married an Ashkenazi man, which formed the basis for a query to Yom Tov Ṣahalon regarding the question of the ownership of a pair of Torah finials. Were they the property of the Sefardi synagogue to which they were originally entrusted, or were they now to belong to her new spouse's Ashkenazi congregation? The writer bluntly declared his opinion regarding the undesirability of such a match: "From the day of her arrival in Zion, Miss Esther placed the Torah finials [*rimmonim*] in the Sefardi synagogue. . . . Now it has come to pass that she was seized by a capricious whim and has married an Ashkenazi" [Yom Tov Ṣahalon, *Responsa,* no. 276].[10]

Explicit opposition to marriage between an Ashkenazi man and a non-Ashkenazi woman is documented in another source. In 1567, "Rachel, daughter of R. Abraham of Prague of blessed memory, widow of R. [Eliezer] Sussmann of Jerusalem of blessed memory," wrote in Yiddish to her son Moses who resided in Egypt, as follows: "If Zwillen were here, R. David would give him his daughter in marriage. She's a fine young woman . . . he [only] wants an Ashkenazi."[11]

Although several Ashkenazi sages were active in sixteenth-century Jerusalem—in a nutshell we know no more of their intellectual activity than that, beginning in the 1520s, some of these scholars taught in the yeshivot they had founded.[12] In the first half of the century, the following Ashkenazi scholars resided in the city: Israel ben Yeḥiel Ashkenazi and Peretz Feyvush ha-Zaqen; while in the middle and late century we find records of David Frank, Yeḥiel ben Moses Ashkenazi Castellazzo, Kalonymos (to be identified as Rabbi Kalman), Abraham Pollack, Ephraim Fish ben Moses Judah, Simeon ben Isaac ha-Levi Eshenberg,

Bezalel Ashkenazi, who arrived in Jerusalem in 1587, Meir ben Samuel Back Ashkenazi, and Samson Back, who left Safed for Jerusalem before 1584.[13]

Extant among the Geniza documents are letters sent by members of the Jerusalem Ashkenazi congregation to relatives in Egypt,[14] including an exchange of letters in Yiddish between a mother (Rachel bat Abraham of Prague, the wife of Eliezer [called Sussmann] ben Abraham Ẓarit) and her son Moses, who resided in Cairo (1564–67),[15] one of which has been cited above. These letters shed light on various personalities in the Ashkenazi congregation, its lifestyle, and communal institutions.[16]

Within the rubric of the Ashkenazi congregation we must include not only individuals who originated in Ashkenaz (Germany),[17] but other Diaspora communities in western and central Europe as well: France,[18] Bohemia,[19] Hungary,[20] Italy,[21] and Poland.[22]

B. SEFARDIM

Following the expulsion from Spain and the episode of forced conversion in Portugal in 1497, Iberian exiles flooded the lands of the Mediterranean basin, founding new Jewish settlements and reinforcing existing ones. In this context it suffices to mention the following centers in passing: Istanbul, Salonika, Fez, Naples, Ferrara, and Cairo.[23] Nor was Eretz-Israel neglected, as seen from Don Isaac Abrabanel's remarks: "And in the year two hundred and fifty-two [1492] the Lord inspired the kings of Spain to expel all the Jews from their land, some three hundred thousand souls, so that they entirely left the western parts and all set out toward the Holy Land; not only the Jews, but the Conversos who had left Judaism also made their way there, and thus they gathered on the soil of the Holy Land" [Abrabanel, commentary to Isa. 43:6. Translation based on David, "Spanish Exiles," 80].[24]

Additional contemporary testimony for this phenomenon is found in an apocalyptic missive written by the Italian-Jewish sage Bonet de Lattes: "The expulsions from Spain and Naples and other places . . . are a good sign. . . . blessed be the Lord who inspired the hearts of the monarchs to expel all the Jews from their lands so that they would go to Eretz-Israel or somewhere near it as they are doing each and every day" [David, "Spanish Exiles," 80].[25]

But in late-fifteenth-century Jerusalem, the Sefardi presence was of little weight. The available evidence—an anonymous letter sent from Jerusalem (late 1495) by a disciple of Obadiah of Bertinoro that alludes both to the shipboard presence of an unspecified number of Sefardim on the Venice to Eretz-Israel leg of his journey[26] and to the presence of a Sefardi sage in Jerusalem, one "Zechariah Sefardi, may he live long and see many descendants," who expounded Torah every day[27]—provides no clues, however, as to the contemporary Sefardi kahal's importance. This changed with the ever-increasing waves of immigration to Eretz-Israel following the expulsion from Spain, when the Sefardim began to reinforce their position in the local communities there. Nonetheless, it appears that their proportional representation in the early-sixteenth-century Jerusalem community remained small, as only four or five identifiably Sefardi names[28] are to be found among the twenty signatories on Isaac Sholal's well-known regulation (1509) exempting religious students from taxes.[29] The other signatories included Ashkenazim, Musta'rabs, and Maghrebis (Jews of North African origin).

Sixteenth-century Safed, by way of contrast, bears witness to a different balance of power. As early as 1504, the Sefardim held a preferential position in the Jewish community there; unlike the previously cited example from Jerusalem, most signatories on a letter dispatched by the Safed sages to their Jerusalem counterparts concerning the fixing of the sabbatical year were of Spanish origin.[30] The names appended to this misssive, as well as to one sent to the nagid, Isaac Sholal, in 1510,[31] suggest the presence of two main kehalim in Safed at this time—Musta'rab and Sefardi, of which only the latter benefited from the nagid's support.[32] The extant sources provide no evidence for the presence of Spanish exiles in Hebron or other Jewish communities in Eretz-Israel.

For Jerusalem, as we have seen, the sparse evidence extant suggests that for the century's initial decades the Sefardi influence was counterbalanced by that of the other kehalim. From the 1520s to the mid-to-late 1570s, however, the Sefardim rose to dominance within the communal structure, even absorbing some of the other kehalim. In late century their influence was on the wane. We shall now trace this process in greater detail.

Starting from 1510, additional information is available on the presence of Spanish exiles in Jerusalem, alongside their counterparts from the other kehalim. Various sources, including recently discovered ones, reveal that outstanding Spanish exiles were active in Jerusalem as early as the sixteenth century's second decade. These noteworthy individuals, renowned for their public and intellectual activity in Jerusalem, Safed, and elsewhere both earlier than and at the beginning of the Ottoman period, included: Levi ibn Ḥabib (Ralbaḥ); the kabbalist Abraham ben Eliezer ha-Levi; his brother-in-law, the renowned astronomer and historian, Abraham Zacuto, who reached Jerusalem in 1513; and Jacob Berab, who definitely headed a Jerusalem yeshivah shortly after the Ottoman conquest and perhaps before that date. Less known figures in Jerusalem include: scholar and physician David ibn Shoshan; Moses Castro, who held a central position in the community's administration in the early part of the century's second decade; Judah Albotini, a scholar and kabbalist of Portuguese origin; Moses ben Shem Tov Alfaranji; and Abraham Abzardiel.

I have already noted, the general though not dramatic improvement in Eretz-Israel's material and administrative status following the Ottoman conquest that brought a moderate increase in Jewish population in its wake. Within a short period of only a few years, its Sefardi constituent showed a steady increase, rapidly becoming the dominant element. Hebrew sources dating to the early 1520s, some of which will be cited below, indicate that the Sefardi kahal constituted the prime force in both Jerusalem and Safed's Jewish communities at that time. Witness, for example, the remarks of Israel Askenazi of Perugia, made in 1522: "But now that the Sephardim, may the Lord preserve them, have arrived, almost all the other communities have become insignificant, and they do as the Sephardim wish. Of the cantors, three are Spanish and one a Musta'rab" [David, "Letter of Israel Ashkenazi," 110–11. Translation cited from David, "Spanish Exiles," 83].

It is interesting that the writer omits any mention of the Ashkenazi congregation, although he himself was one of its leading members.[33] Moses Basola's account of his journey to Eretz-Israel (1522) reinforces this impression of Sefardi ascendancy: "The community includes all kinds of Jews. There are 15 Ashkenazi householders and many Sephardim, and there are Musta'rabs, the ancient inhabitants of the land, and Maghrebis who came from Barbary, all in all some three hundred householders" [Basola, *Masot,* 61. Translation cited from David, "Spanish Exiles," 83].

Moses Basola goes on to recount that the customs in Jerusalem's only or at least main synagogue followed the Sefardi rite. In his words: "The liturgy closely resembles the Sefardi tradition."[34] It appears that this uniformity of synagogue ritual and liturgy was imposed on the disparate kehalim by force of *ḥerem* (excommunication). The relevant passage, found in the takkanot issued by Jerusalem's sages in the first half of the sixteenth century, reads: "That no one may change anything whatsoever in the liturgy and hymns, this [at the risk] of the ḥerem" (par. 15).[35] From the 1520s, then, Jerusalem's Sefardi Jews must be considered that city's elite, setting the tone for the lifestyle and culture of the other kehalim, with the exception of the Ashkenazim, who maintained their autonomy (see preceding section).

The outstanding Spanish scholars mentioned earlier, the best minds among the Spanish expellees, rapidly displaced the scholars from the other kehalim, of whom we hear but little from this time forth. Even the exceptional Ashkenazi figures left little permanent mark on Jerusalem's Jewish community.[36] Nonetheless, unlike the Musta'rab, Maghrebi, Italian, and other elements that made up the Jewish community, who were now absorbed by the large and dominant Sefardi kahal, the Ashkenazim succeeded in maintaining their individuality, conducting their lives as a minority kahal according to Ashkenazi tradition and culture. The dominant Sefardi element was forced to accept this state of affairs, much to its leaders' distaste. The Ashkenazi congregation's special status was even granted recognition in the communal takkanot; the Askenazim were explicitly exempted from two of its regulations governing social issues.[37] Its numerical inferiority notwithstanding, apparently the Ashkenazi congregation owed its survival to its independent and exclusive sources of financial assistance, mentioned in the previous section. Ashkenazi independence extended to the intellectual sphere as well. Two Hebrew sources dating from the early 1520s indicate the existence of two yeshivot in Jerusalem, one under Sefardi administration and the other under Ashkenazi.[38] In 1522 Moses Basola made the following observations:

> Our honorable teacher, R. David ibn Shoshan, physician and head of the Sephardi yeshivah, and with him the distinguished, modest and honorable teacher Abraham ha-Levi who is the author of *Meshareh Kitrin,* around whom gather eight or nine Sephardim . . . Our honorable teacher R. Israel [Ashkenazi], head of the Ashkenazi yeshiva, and with him our honorable teacher R. Pereẓ who has just arrived from Germany[39] . . . and four or five Musta'rabs gather there, and R. Judah of Corbeil who is a Sephardi and R. Solomon from Camerino, twelve or thirteen in all. [Basola, *Masot,* 62–63. Translation cited from David, "Spanish Exiles," 85]

A similar, more succinct description was provided by Israel Ashkenazi: "You should know that there are two yeshivot here, one headed by the honorable R. David Shoshan, may the Lord preserve him, with whom a group of five or six students study, and some ten people who gather [to study] with me."[40]

Basola's account suggests that attendance at the "Sefardi yeshivah" was restricted to Sefardim only, whereas the "Ashkenazi yeshivah" encompassed a broader mix of students that included some from other kehalim: Musta'rabs, a Sephardi, and an Italian (Solomon of Camerino). In all probability, the method and course of study in the two yeshivot differed in accord with the respective traditions represented by their heads.[41] The existence of two yeshivot divided along communal lines reflects the delicate balance between the kehalim that now came into play. It appears that shortly before this time, the Jerusalem yeshivot were not yet divided along communal lines. A letter sent from Jerusalem in 1521 by yeshivah heads and their students bears the signatures of Musta'rab and Sefardi sages and a French one as well.[42]

Nor did the Sefardim dominate the court at that time. An act issued in 1525 by the Jerusalem *bet din* was signed by three judges, each of whom represented a different kahal.[43] First was Israel ben Yeḥiel, an Ashkenazi already mentioned above; second was the renowned kabbalist Abraham ha-Levi, a Sefardi; third was Joseph Colon ben Peretz, a scion of a French family who had migrated to Italy several generations earlier.

Generally speaking, however, for a sixty-year period from the early 1520s until Bezalel Ashkenazi's time, that is, until the late 1580s, Sefardi sages were at the forefront of Jerusalem's Jewish community. As early as 1520, Abraham ha-Levi remarked on their level of learning in a letter sent from Jerusalem: "As for the sages, there are certainly great Sephardi sages there who study Torah day and night."[44] This writer also noted the recent arrival of two Ashkenazi scholars: Rabbi Joḥanan and Rabbi Israel (none other than the Israel ben Yeḥiel Ashkenazi mentioned earlier), neither of whom left a lasting impression on his contemporaries or on subsequent generations.

Until the 1560s and 1570s, the leading Sefardi sages, including the majority of sages who lived and taught in Jerusalem in the late Mamluk period, belonged to the first- and second-generation Spanish expellees. From the century's last quarter, however, Sefardi dominance was on the wane in both Jerusalem and Safed as these spiritual giants and their descendants, heirs to the pure Spanish tradition, died out. Moreover, the century's second half brought new waves of immigration to Eretz-Israel from Diaspora communities with local traditions that matched the Spanish heritage. Finally, the empire-wide economic depression that started in the 1560s had an especially adverse effect on the status of the Sefardim in both centers.

Nonetheless, the decades-old division into kehalim was still operative in late-sixteenth-century Jerusalem. The Sefardi kahal acted as the umbrella organization for members of the other congregations, while the Ashkenazim continued to preserve their specificity. The severe economic crisis dried up the Sefardi kahal's external sources of income, derived mainly from contributions by individuals and communities throughout the Ottoman empire (who likewise suffered from the recession), to the extent that the kahal found itself hard-pressed to meet its daily needs. The Ashkenazim, whose economic support derived from a variety of communities in Italy and in western and central Europe, were far less affected, and their funding apparently continued to flow uninterruptedly. This disparity forced the Sefardi kahal to turn to the Ashkenazi one for financial assistance. A responsum composed by Yom Tov Ṣahalon, a scholar active in Safed and Damascus in the late-sixteenth/early-seventeenth century, attests to this ongoing Ashkenazi success in fund-raising and to their autonomous disbursement of monies.[45] In their appeal to Ṣahalon, the Sefardim referred to an earlier rabbinic decision issued by Bezalel Ashkenazi, which had awarded them a sixth of the Ashkenazi income. That agreement having lapsed with Ashkenazi's demise in the 1590s, they now demanded that the Ashkenazim hand over half of their funds to help meet the Sefardi kahal's needs, presenting their argument as follows:

> For at the time of the *haskamah* [Bezalel Ashkenazi's ruling] the alien peoples did not cast their eyes on the Jews' wealth and the Sephardim were also wealthy and disposed of ample funds, and they used to send [emissaries] to Egypt and Istanbul and they were sent large sums of money. But now their means are limited, fortunes have dwindled to nothing and the alien peoples do not levy according to the assessment, but raise taxes upon those to whom funds are sent, and the major part of those funds are sent today to the Ashkenazim. [Yom Tov Ṣahalon, *Responsa,* no. 160. English translation cited from David, "Spanish Exiles," 103–4]

In his reply, Ṣahalon upheld Ashkenazi's prior ruling. As for any sum in excess of a sixth of the Ashkenazi income, he suggested binding arbitration by two representatives, one from each kahal. Nonetheless, he also underscored the Ashkenazi kahal's autonomy by noting: "It is certainly inconceivable that a Sephardi sage should issue an order to Ashkenazi sages, however prominent the scholar who issues it may be."

Further evidence for the decline in Sefardi preeminence emerges from the fact that an Ashkenazi—Bezalel Ashkenazi[46]—was Jerusalem's leading intellectual figure in the late 1580s and early 1590s. It appears that this division between the Sefardi and Ashkenazi kehalim remained in effect in the seventeenth century as well. Although the contemporary sources reflect ongoing conflict between the Ashkenazim and Sefardim over economic issues, there was a marked degree of cooperation on the organizational level.[47] In 1625 the general administration of the Jerusalem community was still in Sefardi hands, as attested to by an anonymous resident: "And the two community officers (parnassim) are Sephardim, and the Ashkenazim are drawn along after them."[48] Nonetheless, the seventeenth century saw a decline in the status of the scholarly Sefardi elite—as compared to their counterparts from the other kehalim, no Sefardi scholars of outstanding caliber are known.[49]

C. MUSTA'RABS

In the Mamluk period, Musta'rabs, local Jews of Oriental origin, constituted the leading component of the Jerusalem community.[50]

Over time, with the influx of waves of immigration from various Diasporas, the Musta'rabs gradually surrendered their preeminence. Dominance passed from one kahal to another, first to the Sefardim, who were preeminent from midcentury to 1475,[51] and then to the Ashkenazim, who displaced them by that century's last quarter.[52]

Little is known of Jerusalem's Musta'rab kahal in the early Ottoman period. As noted in the introductory section of this chapter, Moses Basola remarked on the presence of a Musta'rab kahal in Jerusalem, noting elsewhere that "four or five Musta'rabs" were to be counted among the students in the Ashkenazi yeshivah. He mentioned a single Musta'rab figure by name: "One of the *dayyanim* [judges] is a Musta'rab named Isaac."[53]

Basola's contemporary Israel Ashkenazi provides a glimpse of the state of affairs prior to the arrival of the Sefardim, when the prayer ritual in Jerusalem followed "the Musta'rab rite." In Ashkenazi's day, of the three cantors in the Jerusalem synagogue only one was a Musta'rab. Ashkenazi commented on the harmonious intercommunal relations as well, noting that "there is excellent rapport between all, Sefardim and Musta'rabs."[54]

Contemporary sources, letters in particular, mention various Jerusalemites whose names disclose their Musta'rab identity. Two were the heads of the Jerusalem yeshivot in 1521: Samuel Masud and Jacob ben Mani. At least two other Musta'rabs—Ezra Kohen Shabi and Moses Tader—can be positively identified as such among the signatories on a letter.[55] Yet another source, a responsum, provides additional information concerning the Jerusalem Musta'rab kahal and its members Nissim Ankari and Maatuk Yerushalmi.[56] The leading Musta'rab sage in the early Ottoman period was Joseph ibn Ṣayyaḥ (Ṣiyyaḥ).

D. MAGHREBIS (MAARAVIM)

Jews from North Africa, including members of the Ḥalafta and the Sholal families,[57] are known to have resided in Jerusalem as early as the mid-fifteenth century. However, scant knowledge has survived regarding Jerusalem's Maghrebi kahal in the sixteenth century. As we have seen, Moses Basola reported their presence. Some data are extant regarding individuals belonging to this kahal, for example, Issachar ibn Susan, originally of Fez. A student of Levi ibn Ḥabib, who was the dominant intellectual figure of his day, Ibn Susan resided in Jerusalem in the 1530s or perhaps even earlier. In 1545 or 1548, he reminisced: "I remember [that] when I dwelled in Jerusalem, which is surrounded by a wall from the time of Joshua bin Nun . . . my teacher the perfect scholar R. Levi ibn Ḥabib of blessed memory was then residing in Jerusalem. About 12 years have passed since that time" [Issachar ibn Susan, *Ibbur Shanim,* fol. 27].[58] At a later date, Ibn Susan moved to Safed.

Additional Maghrebi sages known to have been active in Jerusalem at that time included "the exalted elderly sage, R. Saadiah ha-Maaravi,"[59] and Meir ben Joseph Fassi, who sat on Levi ibn Ḥabib's court in Jerusalem in 1537.[60] Apparently, Isaac ibn Ḥayyim, who resided in Jerusalem in the first half of the sixteenth century, also belonged to the Maghrebi kahal, as did kabbalist Judah Ḥallewa, originally of Fez, who resided in Safed during the first half of the sixteenth century, but spent his final years in Jerusalem, after 1545. Jerusalem sharia court documents mention Maghrebi Jews, as well as Maghrebi pilgrims who arrived in Jerusalem in 1538.[61] A Geniza document conjures up echoes of Maghrebi/Sefardi friction in Jerusalem at the turn of the fifteenth to sixteenth centuries by posing the following question: "Why do you claim that we preferred the Maghrebi to the Sefardi?"[62]

E. ETHIOPIANS

According to Israel Ashkenazi's testimony from the early 1520s, and perhaps before that date, Ethiopian Jews (Falashas) resided in Jerusalem. In 1522, Ashkenazi penned the following description of a Jew who had reached that city:

> [He] had been taken prisoner at sea and changed hands repeatedly until he was sold in Alexandria, Egypt. The Jews paid a large bribe to ransom him, and he is almost like a Cushite [in appearance]. . . . He told us that in his land there are thousands, even tens of thousands of Jews who have a great king who engages in constant battle with the nearby Christians. He lives near the Nile, the Nile river of Egypt . . . and this is certain, for I have spoken to many others from his city, and all the Jerusalemites attest that forty families reside there. [David, "Letter of Israel Ashkenazi," 119]

It is nearly certain that Askenazi's description refers to Ethiopian Jews captured in battle and later ransomed after reaching Egypt, as additional sources attest.[63] Ashkenazi's testimony implies that dozens of Ethiopian Jews made their way to Eretz-Israel and settled in Jerusalem.[64] One of these Jews may have been David ha-Reuveni, who resided briefly in Jerusalem from 1522 to 1523. Although it lies beyond our ken to determine the exact origins of this enigmatic figure, there is a distinct possibility that he too belonged to the Ethiopian kahal.[65]

F. KARAITES

Sparse data survive regarding Jerusalem's tiny Karaite community in the late-fifteenth, sixteenth, and seventeenth centuries.[66] Shortly after the Ottoman conquest, the Karaites advanced claims to the ownership of the synagogue in Nabi Samuil, in an attempt to dispossess the Rabbanite Jews who had controlled the site for generations.[67] Although the Karaites in Jerusalem maintained separate communal institutions, they were subject to Rabbanite hegemony in certain spheres, collection of the jizya tax, for example. For that reason, Karaites were not listed separately in the taḥrir registers.[68]

Sixteenth-century Jerusalem had a half-dozen constituent kehalim, of which the Ashkenazi, Sefardi, Musta'rab, and North African components were its most visible elements. From the century's second decade, we can trace the enhanced status enjoyed by its Sefardi kahal, whose influence waxed in the 1520s, making it the dominant element in the Jerusalem community at large. The other kehalim, with the exception of the Ashkenazi one, fell under the sway of the dominant Sefardi leadership and were absorbed into its ranks. Despite its numerical inferiority, the Ashkenazi kahal successfully maintained its autonomous communal structure and institutions. Our picture of Jerusalem's sixteenth-century community has focused mainly on the balance of power between Sefardim and Ashkenazim, as its two main divisions, but we must note the scanty evidence for the existence of two additional small constituents—Ethiopians and Karaites—who undoubtedly maintained independent communal structures as well. The broad configuration of the collective reins of leadership in the sixteenth-century Jewish community will be examined in the following chapter.

7 Communal Organization

In the last quarter of the fifteenth century, the collective reins of leadership in Jerusalem's Jewish community were in the hands of some eighteen officeholders: the *parnas*, the *dayyanim*, the *maskilim* (the scholars), the rabbis, the *shofetim* (elders), and the nagid's representative, known as the vice-nagid.[1] It appears, however, that this pattern of collective leadership was no longer in effect in the early sixteenth century. Sometime in the 1480s, the Jerusalem community evidently experienced a severe social crisis precipitated by the high-handed behavior of the community's "elders," a crisis with repercussions that are mirrored in Obadiah of Bertinoro's first letter from Jerusalem (1488).[2] Several years later, we find the last nagid in Egypt, Isaac Sholal (nagid from 1502 to 1517), taking far greater interest than his predecessors in directly overseeing the affairs of the communities in Eretz-Israel.[3] In effect, he unilaterally empowered himself to assume jurisdiction over the organization of communal life in Jerusalem and Safed, almost certainly introducing far-reaching changes in the organizational structure of their leadership, making it directly accountable to him.[4] It seems plausible to ascribe Isaac Sholal's strong intervention in the affairs of the Jerusalem community directly to the intolerable situation there, the result of the elders' brazen behavior prior to his appointment as nagid.

Isaac Sholal made a major contribution to the material and intellectual advancement of Jerusalem by means of a steady infusion of support for the two yeshivot in the city: one reopened at his initiative, and the other he founded.[5] But material support for the community and its institutions by no means encompasses the full extent of his involvement. Isaac Sholal issued regulations aimed at prescribing the conduct of public communal affairs in Jerusalem, even going so far as to attempt to arbitrate in the community's internal disputes.[6] One example is found in a letter sent by the nagid to "the scholars in the holy yeshivah in Jerusalem" sometime between Tammuz (June) 1509 and Nisan (April) 1511; he tried to arbitrate in a dispute that had broken out in the Jerusalem community regarding the yeshivah administration. He wrote: "Since you yourselves have not taken care in this matter, from this day on I will issue instructions to each as he deserves. . . . To my way of thinking, when the reason for these disagreements and arguments amongst yourselves is removed, then love and brotherhood will prevail" [David, "The Yeshivah in Jerusalem," 47]. But the main thrust of his activity is subsumed in the enactment of several basic regulations for Jerusalem's Jews by his court in Egypt. Of these, perhaps the best-known is the takkanah exempting scholars from payment of taxes issued in 1509.[7] It, like the other regulations, was aimed at encouraging scholars to settle in Jerusalem. A related takkanah required that cases involving a scholar or a dayyan be brought before the "duly registered sages," the members of the nagid's court, who possessed sole jurisdiction in matters concerning litigation between members of the Jerusalem community and scholars or dayyanim. In 1514 Isaac Sholal issued a takkanah mandating the equitable distribution of synagogal honors in Jerusalem, which, as we shall see in this chapter's concluding section, had significant implications for other aspects of communal life.[8]

With the termination of the nagidate in the early Ottoman period (1516),[9] radical changes took place in the organizational structure of Jerusalem's Jewish community. No longer dependent on outside leadership, several years after the Ottoman conquest the Jerusalem Jewish community was formulating autonomous principles of communal organization. These were, however, largely based on the solid administrative structure set in place during the tenure of the last nagid, Isaac Sholal. These arrangements, which are reflected in various sixteenth-century sources, found expression in a substantial corpus of takkanot regulating social and religious affairs.[10] In addition, two sets of takkanot from the early Ottoman period, or perhaps earlier, are extant: (1) the ten "takkanot and haskamot [agreements] of the holy congregation of Jerusalem, the holy city, inscribed on a tablet in the synagogue," as attested to by Moses Basola, who recorded selected excerpts in his travel book in 1522;[11] (2) a collection of mid-sixteenth-century takkanot, with regulations that parallel the synagogue tablet to a limited extent.[12]

To be more specific, in essence, two authoritative figures jointly and concurrently held the reins of power in the Jerusalem community: the *shaykh al-yahud,* who may rightly be considered the community's "secular arm," and the dayyan, best defined as its "religious arm."

The shaykh al-yahud[13]—"elder of Jews"—bore direct responsibility for communal affairs in the social and fiscal realm: tax collection, waqfs, and the like. Moreover, he was the Jewish community's official representative to the governmental authorities, both local and central. Sharia court documents indicate that although the appointment of the shaykh al-yahud required the kadi's endorsement, he approved the Jewish community's choice.[14] The sharia court documents also indicate that the Ashkenazi congregation approached the kadi with a request, to which he acceded, to appoint its own leaders, who would not be answerable to the shaykh al-yahud on any matter.[15] This step is consistent with Ashkenazi separatist tendencies, its desire for autonomy from the other congregations who essentially submitted to the authority of the leadership of the Sefardi kahal.[16] Other influential figures served alongside the shaykh. Known as "Jewish elders" or just plain "elders," they are referred to in Arabic sources as *shaykh al-maḥalla, shaykh maḥallat al-yahud* (shaykh of the Jewish neighborhood), or *shaykh al-ḥara* (neighborhood shaykh).[17] Presumably, the bearers of these titles fulfilled a leadership function similar to those of the "elders" in the 1480s,[18] who were also referred to as shofetim, or shaykh, in the singular case. Unfortunately, we have no further details as to their exact area of responsibility.

Sharia court documents mention some eighteen elders, including a Sholal family member, Salamun ibn Musa Shullal,[19] who was almost certainly related to the nagid Isaac Sholal, a Jerusalem resident from 1517 until his death in late 1524. Nevertheless, we have no evidence as to whether or not the former nagid played a role in the Jerusalem Jewish community's leadership during that period.

The second officeholder was the dayyan—the religious judge. The bearer of this title was directly responsible for overseeing the framework of the community's spiritual and religious life. Supervision of the internal Jewish legal apparatus was his main function, as was the making of halakhic decisions with the aid of a three-man court, subject to his authority as its head (av bet din). Like the shaykh al-yahud, the dayyan was chosen by the Jewish communal leaders, but his appointment required the kadi's endorsement. It was official Ottoman policy at that time to make the judicial authority of its non-Muslim subjects dependent on the local kadi, who alone was empowered to delegate judicial powers and grant extremely limited powers of punishment.[20] The dayyan's powers did not even comprehend the authority to order an arrest or to collect a fine. The stiffest punishment at his disposal was excommunication (ḥerem), but its efficacy was plainly limited.[21]

A clearer picture of the dayyan's dependence on the kadi emerges from a responsum by Moses Trani, cited at length below. Essentially, it reveals the degree to which the dayyan's authority was vested in the kadi's approval, bringing to life the story of the appointment of an unnamed dayyan.[22] This figure has been identified as David ibn Abi Zimra, who settled in Jerusalem in 1553. Having assumed the position of dayyan at the Jerusalem kehillah's behest, an agreement defining the dayyan's authority and privileges was drawn up. The document opens as follows:

> We the undersigned and the entire holy congregation, may it be preserved, its officials, and the seven elders have taken upon ourselves with solemn oaths to the Almighty, praised be He, that Reuben [an

> anonymous reference—TRANS.] shall be our head, our chief, our dayyan, and leader, to adjudicate and arbitrate every matter, whether for individuals or for the public-at-large, concerning marriage or divorce, or in every matter where he sees fit to issue a decree, or to erect safeguards, or to issue a haskamah [agreement], or to enforce a prior agreement. We have unanimously taken upon ourselves to accept whatever the abovementioned ḥakham says, and to reimburse him in full from our property for any loss or damages or expenses incurred by the said ḥakham, heaven forbid, by dint of any of the above, [or] by any individual.

Events took a different turn when this dayyan handed down a decision involving a punishment that other members of the kehillah found unacceptable. They appealed to the kadi, whose authorization was necessary both for the dayyan's appointment and for execution of the punishment. Finding a harsh reprimand far from being a sufficient disciplinary action for the offense, not only did the kadi remove the dayyan from his post, but he also stipulated a beating. This last punishment was averted only by the delivery of eighty florins to the kadi and his men.[23] The responsum unfolds the circumstances in vivid detail:

> Sometime later, he [the dayyan] wanted to chastise scoundrels and put them on the straight path. They informed on him [to the kadi] that he issues legal rulings and acts as a judge in the city, performing marriage, divorce, and the like, in his home. In the kadi's court there was much anger at this ḥakham. They said to him, "Beware, for if you perform [these acts] we will chastise you." To which he replied, "I have not done so, nor will I do so. Those who present this claim, lie."
>
> A week or two later, in the evening, the *kehaya* [representative] of the city's governor called for the aforementioned ḥakham in the presence of two Jews. He asked him, "Tell me, from whence do you come?" The ḥakham replied, "From such and such a place." The kehaya asked, "Do you have a writ from the king or a *berat* [an official appointment], like the ones given to the Christians, authorizing you to be a ruling official? If so, show it to me; if not, who appointed you to rule? Is there no governor in this city?" To which the aforementioned ḥakham replied: "Heaven forbid! I did not seek to rule, nor have I done anything [wrong]. I am like one of the king's servants, who if it does not please the king that he resides in City A, he moves to City B. Yet he remains the king's servant." When he concluded these remarks, they dismissed him, and the Jew returned home.

> In the morning, the governor sent for him, and had him brought to his residence in shackles. He asked him, "Who are you?" To which he replied, "I am one of your servants." The governor then inquired: "Who appointed you to rule over the Jews? You are no ḥakham; you are unworthy. A year-and-a-half ago, I fell ill in this city, and all the leaders of the idol-worshippers and the heads of the Christian churches visited me, while you did not respect me enough to come, as if you have no fear of me?!" The ḥakham replied, "We Jews have a shaykh whose duty this is, and this was formerly the custom among all the city's governors. You have no case against the ḥakham, for this was not our practice." He replied, "If indeed this was not the custom, I will teach you the custom." He commanded that they grab him by his beard and remove him from his presence. They prepared sticks to beat him to death. He wanted to [make him] shave his beard and put a hook in his head and parade him thus throughout the city. When the Jews there learned of this, they offered a compromise, paying 60 florins to the governor, and approximately 20 to his men. [Moses Trani, *Responsa,* pt. 3, no. 188]

This authentic account reveals the delicate nature of the relationship betweeen the kadi (and/or the Muslim potentate) and the leadership of the Jerusalem Jewish community, which certainly pertained to other locales as well. The responsum clearly delineates the dayyan's absolute dependence on the local kadi, as well as the necessity to preserve unquestioningly the kadi's honor at all times.

In his role as head of the internal Jewish judicial system, one of the dayyan's functions was to serve as kehillah spokesman before the kadi.[24] It seems logical to assume that he fulfilled an educational function as well, most likely within the framework of one of the city's yeshivot.

In the early Ottoman period, the office of dayyan was governed by a rotation system, with each ḥakham holding office for a year. In the words of a sage of that generation: "The accepted practice among the ḥakhamim in Jerusalem is that each one judges for a year in rotation."[25] Similarly, in 1522 Moses Basola reported: "Every ḥakham in Jerusalem serves as dayyan for a year."[26] The underlying motivation for this rotation system was apparently the desire to prevent any one individual from attaining a permanent hold on this key position in the kehillah administration. Social equality, to be achieved by blocking the creation of class divisions within the kehillah, was viewed as a means of encouraging large-scale settlement in Jerusalem. Within this framework, Isaac Sholal's court issued a takkanah in 1514 that emphatically called for eliminating permanent possession or rights to synagogal or other communal functions. Its authors articulated the underlying rationale of this regulation as follows: "The Holy One, Blessed Be He, wanted to grant all Israel a Jerusalem undivided into tribes [classes]; rather, all Israel is to be on an equal footing there."[27]

This trend toward equality found further expression in another communal position that was rotated on a monthly basis—that of instructor in the Jerusalem synagogue.[28] Nonetheless, it appears that the rotation system for the office of dayyan was not always fully realized; at a later date this system was no longer operative. Sharia court documents specifically mention several dayyanim who held this post for longer periods. Among the better known individuals who held this post, we must note Levi ibn Ḥabib, who acted as dayyan from 1533 to 1536, and David ibn Abi Zimra, who served from 1560 to 1564.[29] Not surprisingly, these men were the foremost halakhic authorities in Jerusalem of their day.

The unique structure of the Jerusalem kehillah led to the creation of a model of dual leadership by the shaykh al-yahud and the dayyan, one that also reflects its division into two main groups, Sefardim and Ashkenazim. As we shall see, this pattern of communal leadership differed significantly from that of Safed, where the kehillah was governed by an umbrella organization that included representatives of all the congregations. Several factors contributed to this model: the elders' crisis that precipitated the intervention of Isaac Sholal; the dream of social equality in Jerusalem that led to the institution of a system of rotation for the important communal posts; the smaller size of the Jerusalem community. Having briefly glimpsed the structure of communal organization, we now turn to an examination of the communal institutions that played an active role in the intellectual life of sixteenth-century Jerusalem.

8 Intellectual Life

Throughout the ages, Jerusalem has ranked as Eretz-Israel's foremost spiritual-intellectual center. At varying times under Muslim hegemony, Jerusalem served as the inspirational center for both local and Diaspora Jewry.[1] Its spiritual ascendancy was, however, by no means unbroken. From the early to the late twelfth century, which spanned the first Crusader period, there was no Jewish community in Jerusalem. Even after its renewal in the late twelfth century, the Jewish settlement in Jerusalem was materially and spiritually impoverished.[2] It was only in the latter half of the fourteenth century, with the arrival of aliyot from Ashkenaz, spurred by the Black Plague to leave Europe, that a marked improvement in the status of Jerusalem's Jewish community took place and that a yeshivah began to function in Jerusalem.[3] As we shall see, Jerusalem's intellectual and spiritual life flowered once again both immediately prior to and following the Ottoman conquest, when it was home to some of the leading sages of the day.

A. RABBINICAL ACADEMIES (YESHIVOT)

The status of Jerusalem's yeshivot cannot be divorced from the general circumstances that governed the fortunes of the community as a whole. In times of relative prosperity, yeshivot opened their doors to students; in times of hardship, their doors closed. A yeshivah, almost certainly founded by immigrants from Ashkenaz in the latter half of the fourteenth century, as mentioned above, functioned in Jerusalem until the 1460s or early 1470s, when the difficult contemporary conditions led to its closing.[4] Evidently, this yeshivah was reopened in the early sixteenth century at the initiative of Nagid Isaac Sholal, who, as we have seen, made a concerted effort to develop Jerusalem's intellectual sphere. Contemporary sources reflect the breadth of his intervention; his initiatives found expression not only in the reopening or founding of two yeshivot in Jerusalem but also in the provision of support for their upkeep. Evidently, he even took a hand in the appointment of ḥakhamim; this impression is confirmed by the contemporary report of the well-known astronomer and historian Abraham Zacuto, who arrived in Jerusalem in 1513. In the introduction to his treatise on astronomical tables composed that year, he wrote: "Thus said Abraham b. R. Samuel Zacuto of blessed memory, '. . . I have been privileged to dwell in Jerusalem the holy city, may it be speedily rebuilt in our day, in the company of scholars appointed by our master the nagid . . . the wise and perfect *kohen,* R. Isaac Sholal, may God preserve him'" [Sassoon, *Ohel Dawid* 1:510].[5]

A letter sent in 1521 by *lomdey ha-torah* (yeshivah students) in Jerusalem to Italy, in all likelihood addressed to the notable Abraham of Perugia,[6] also noted Isaac Sholal's activities on behalf of yeshivot and their students:

> R. Isaac Sholal ha-Kohen, may he be exalted . . . when he served as nagid while the king ruled, inquired after those who studied Torah and the scholars in this kingdom . . . and he founded yeshivot in Jerusalem, in the Upper Galilee, and in Egypt. . . . He assigned us to study in the two yeshivot in Jerusalem, may it be speedily rebuilt in our day. . . . He helps us and the students with contributions from his wealth, and what he spends out of his own pocket yearly for the scholars in Jerusalem comes from his funds alone, for there is no other source of aid. [Yaari, *Letters,* 163, revised][7]

Other contemporary sources substantiate Isaac Sholal's role in funding the upkeep of the Jerusalem yeshivot. In the words of Israel Ashkenazi: "Know then that the most superior [person] possessing all good qualities and attributes is our master the nagid . . . whose name is the esteemed Rabbi Isaac, may God preserve him, the righteous priest [*kohen*]. . . . While in Egypt, he distributed [funds] to the scholars of Eretz-Israel by the hundreds and thousands" [David, "Letter of Israel Ashkenazi," 114].[8]

As noted earlier, the yeshivah that had closed its doors in the third quarter of the fifteenth century apparently reopened shortly after Isaac Sholal's appointment to the nagidate in 1502. This yeshivah was mentioned as early as 1504 in a "letter concerning the sabbatical year sent by the sages of Safed to the rabbis of the holy yeshivah in Jerusalem,"[9] which was headed by Peretz Colon, son of the noted Italian scholar Joseph Colon. The second yeshivah was founded by the nagid at a later date but in all likelihood prior to the Ottoman conquest.[10] The founding and promotion of these two yeshivot are consistent with the nagid's plans to enhance the study of Torah in Jerusalem, which he implemented through a series of practical steps aimed at inducing scholars to settle there. Sholal's ultimate aim seems to have been the establishment of a spiritual center in Jerusalem, which would then act as a magnet, drawing scholars and students to Jerusalem from the Diaspora worldwide. With this end in mind, the nagid's court in Egypt issued a takkanah in 1509 exempting scholars from the payment of taxes.[11] The takkanah's intent was to provide scholars who had no other sources of livelihood—that is, those engaged in teaching and studying in the yeshivot—with a real incentive to settle in Jerusalem. Public furor ensued upon this takkanah's promulgation as the householders were expected to assume payment for the scholars' debt. Significant social tensions emerged in Jerusalem, Safed, and elsewhere when the householders refused to remit the scholars' portion of the communal tax.[12] Among the householders themselves were some unable to meet the tax payments; these individuals were granted an exemption as well.

From the period immediately preceding the Ottoman conquest we know the names of three heads of yeshivot: Peretz Colon (first decade of the sixteenth century[13]); Samuel Masud (1512 and later); and Jacob Berab, who headed the yeshivah prior to the Ottoman conquest but continued in office for another two years afterward, perhaps until mid-1519, as seen from these remarks by Israel Ashkenazi: "There was a great scholar here, an uprooter of mountains, named R. Jacob Berab, may God preserve him, who went to Egypt. And all the prominent students left this place to save themselves from starvation" [David, "Letter of Israel Ashkenazi," 113–14].

Hebrew sources from 1522 indicate that the two Jerusalem yeshivot founded during Isaac Sholal's tenure as nagid were divided along communal lines—a Sefardi yeshivah headed by a Sefardi, David ibn Shoshan, and an Ashkenazi yeshivah, headed by Israel Ashkenazi.[14] We have already seen that the dominant Sefardi kahal absorbed the other kehalim, with the exception of the Ashkenazim, who maintained their status as a minority congregation.[15] Naturally, the heads of the Ashkenazi yeshivah, Israel Ashkenazi and Rabbi Peretz from the "land of Ashkenaz" (Germany), brought with them instructional styles and thought patterns that differed from those of the Spanish scholars or the Musta'rabs. A somewhat conflicting picture of the yeshivah administration emerges from the extant sources: Israel Ashkenazi's testimony conveys the impression that each yeshivah had one head; whereas Moses Basola's implies that each yeshivah's administration was composed of two scholars. Nonetheless, the two reports are not necessarily contradictory. It is quite possible that Basola simply supplied additional information in this case, i.e., the names of lecturers and preachers, while the first-named individuals, David ibn Shoshan and Israel Ashkenazi, actually headed the respective yeshivot.[16]

From the 1530s scant information has survived regarding Jerusalem's institutions of Jewish instruction. However, we can safely assume that with the rise in the city's population, swelled by waves of immigration from among the Spanish expellees and other Diaspora communities, the number of yeshivot and their student bodies also increased proportionally.[17] A responsum written by Levi ibn Ḥabib, who settled in Jerusalem for a second time in 1525,[18] cites his involvement in instruction in the yeshivah: "The reason was indeed attributable to lack of spare time due to involvement in public affairs and instructing the students [in the yeshivah], may God preserve them."[19]

A mid-sixteenth-century letter from the Geniza provides further confirmation for the continued increase in the number of rabbinical students and yeshivot in Jerusalem. Sent from Jerusalem by Johanan ben Solomon to his cousin "Simeon [A]shke[na]zi b. R. Yeḥiel, may God preserve him," who resided in Egypt, the letter alludes to the existence of two rival Ashkenazi yeshivot: "And I wish to inform his excellency . . . that we study together in the yeshivah of my esteemed uncle R. Yeḥiel[20] and R. Abraham Pollack, and God knows that we study for altruistic reasons alone, whereas in the yeshivah of R. Kalman and R. David,[21] they do not study for the sake of Heaven" [David, "Ashkenazic Community in Jerusalem," *Vatiqin,* 31].

The writer of this letter cast these two yeshivot in a very different light: whereas in "his" yeshivah altruistic motives for study prevailed, in the rival yeshivah he adduced that this was definitely not the case. From the known existence of two yeshivot serving the Ashkenazi congregation, its numerical and social inferiority notwithstanding, we can postulate that the dominant Sefardi community certainly maintained several institutions of learning. An additional reference to one of the Ashkenazi yeshivot in Jerusalem is found in a Geniza document, a letter sent from Jerusalem by Abraham Sagis to Joseph Corcos in Egypt reporting the arrival of supplies sent to the Ashkenazi yeshivah in Jerusalem.[22]

We know of two eminent scholars who resided in Jerusalem, albeit not continuously, from the late 1580s to the early 1590s: Ḥayyim Vital (foremost disciple of the kabbalist Isaac Luria) and Bezalel Ashkenazi (who studied under David ibn Abi Zimra in Egypt prior to arriving in Jerusalem sometime after October 1587). Both men expounded Torah in Jerusalem's yeshivot, perhaps in the same one, as may be inferred from the testimony of their student, Solomon Adeni: "And in Jerusalem the holy city, may it be speedily rebuilt, . . . I sat in the dust at the feet of the scholars there; are they not the pillars of the Diaspora and Jerusalem, including the perfect scholar, the divine kabbalist, R. Ḥayyim Vital, may he rest in paradise, and our teacher, the Ashkenazi rabbi, R. Bezalel, may he rest in paradise, among other teachers" [Solomon Adeni, *Melekhet Shelomo,* introduction].[23]

Shortly prior to his aliyah to Jerusalem in the course of 1587, Bezalel Ashkenazi sent a letter from Egypt to Italy, describing the study of Torah in Jerusalem, as well as the distressed condition of the

Jewish community there.[24] He also touched upon the appropriation of the community's main synagogue by the Muslims in 1586:[25]

> For the synagogue is still locked with a binding seal—unhappy, storm-tossed one, uncomforted [Isa. 54:11]—and . . . shut up tight. But, praise God, unlike earlier times the land is filled with [the study of] Torah. There is a Talmud Torah for over a hundred children, and Torah is expounded publicly, without censure. There is a yeshivah[26] there where they are never silent by day or by night, and with God's help, when I go there may His teaching be magnified and glorified. [Marx, "Zwei Briefe," 169; Dimitrovsky, "Notes to the History of the Jews in Italy," 178]

According to Bezalel Ashkenazi's testimony, Jerusalem was "filled with the study of Torah." Over a hundred children studied in a special setting for young boys (to be discussed below), while in the yeshivah study proceeded by day and by night. Ashkenazi hoped to make his own contribution to the enhancement of Torah study in the city, and as we have seen, his student, Solomon Adeni, attested to the realization of Ashkenazi's wish to expound Torah at Ḥayyim Vital's side.

A late-sixteenth-century reference to the Jerusalem yeshivah is also found in the agreement (haskamah) of the "*baaley Torah* [scholars] in Jerusalem" to the nagid's takkanah exempting them from taxes. In 1596 Rabbi Ephraim, son of Rabbi Judah of blessed memory, known as Fish Ashkenazi, led the list of signatories.[27] Ephraim certainly held the post of head of the yeshivah at that time. Hyperbolic praise for him is found in Yom Tov Ṣahalon's writings: "And I have heard that there were more than two hundred great scholars in his yeshivah."[28]

The Ottoman conquest saw a decline in philanthropic activity on behalf of the Jerusalem yeshivot. As we have seen, Isaac Sholal, who earlier had been the mainstay of the city's two yeshivot, was unable to continue his support following the conquest. He himself settled in Jerusalem, an impoverished man.[29] Others stepped in as promoters of the welfare of the Jews in Eretz-Israel, including Solomon Alashkar, an Egyptian-Jewish notable in the latter half of the sixteenth century. His financial assistance to the yeshivot in Eretz-Israel in general and to Jerusalem in particular is reflected in more than one source. By way of example, I shall cite Joseph Sambari's testimony: "The noble R. Solomon Alashkar built a Talmud Torah and donated several buildings for the Talmud Torah's children, and supported scholars in Egypt, and the yeshivot in Eretz-Israel. His contribution was approximately 1,000 rials or 1,000 groszy for Jerusalem, may it be speedily rebuilt, or 1,000 muayyadi for charity" [Sambari, *Divrei Yosef,* 417].[30]

B. THE STUDENT BODY

The picture that emerges from the extant sources is one of a student body composed of mature men. Included among their number were halakhic authorities—famed scholars and posekim of great stature—who gathered from the far corners of the Diaspora to engage in study. Various terms are used in the Hebrew sources to refer to the scholars who studied at the yeshivah: *baaley Torah, beney ha-yeshivah,* or *ḥaverim maqshivim* (auditors).[31] The latter appellation, and its abbreviated form—*ḥaverim*—then current in the yeshivot in Safed, Istanbul, Salonika, and elsewhere, denoted pairs of scholars who studied under the supervision of the head of the yeshivah or ḥakham.[32] Evidently, we cannot limit our conception of the Sefardi and Ashkenazi yeshivot in Jerusalem simply to their role as academic institutions; rather we must recognize that they also functioned as a forum for the practical examination of halakhic issues, for the formulation of legal decisions and responsa, as practiced in Jacob Berab's yeshivah in Safed.[33] Some of the discussions held by Jerusalem's sages in the sixteenth century's first quarter have been preserved in *Quntres Ḥiddushey Dinim mi-Rabbaney Ir Qodshenu Yerushalayim . . . bi-Zeman ha-Nagid Rabbenu Yiṣḥak ha-Kohen Sholal* (Novellae by the Rabbis of Jerusalem our holy city . . . from the time of the nagid Rabbi Isaac Sholal).

Based on a single extant reference, a letter written by the Jerusalem dayyanim in 1456, it seems that the ḥaverim were accompanied by their students, who studied separately. It states: "Recently, great scholars have arrived with their students . . . and they joined the yeshivah and the study of Torah has increased substantially."[34] Although this information reflects the state of affairs in the fifteenth century's latter half, it appears that in the sixteenth century a similar arrangement existed in Jacob Berab's yeshivah in Safed, and in yeshivot in Turkey and Salonika as well.[35]

References to the educational framework for youths and young children in Jerusalem are virtually nonexistent. Youths evidently studied in the Jerusalem yeshivah, as seen from Joseph Colon's letter to Rabbi Nissim the dayyan, who resided in Egypt (1512): "The bearer of this letter, the youthful student Yom Tov, studies in the yeshivah of the perfect scholar, R. Samuel Masud." Regarding the writer's son Peretz, also mentioned in the letter as "now studying tractate *Taaniyot* and as having studied tractate *Berakhot,*" it is not clear whether he acquired his knowledge of these tractates at the yeshivah. From computation of the child's age in 1512, then seven or eight, we can infer that his studies were most likely under the aegis of a *melammed* (teacher of young children).[36]

In his travel book, Moses Basola also provided a scrap of information on the education of young children in early-sixteenth-century Jerusalem: "There is an honored man who teaches halakhah to youths in his home and he is blind." He mentioned "another notable, who teaches children, by the name of Joseph Midrash."[37] Also extant are two late-fifteenth- or early-sixteenth-century letters by a Jerusalem melammed, Moses ben Isaac ibn Latif, which shed light on the teacher's lot. In these letters, he cited his indigence and the impossibility of earning an adequate wage because of the unbearable economic situation in Jerusalem: "At present, I have insufficient funds, for I have become greatly impoverished. Nor am I able to teach the sons of others as I was used to doing formerly. For at present, payment is non-existent, and if I receive anything it is far too little to support my family and myself" [MS. New York, Jewish Theological Seminary of America Library, ENA 2050 (IMHM, no. 33577)].[38] Moreover, we learn from these letters that melamdim were hired by the parents on an individual basis and were not kehillah employees.

C. THE CURRICULUM

Despite the paucity of sources from this period regarding Jewish educational institutions, which provide little in the way of information on the nature of study, close examination of the available material enables us to outline broadly some of its guiding principles. As early as the fifteenth century, two distinct educational frameworks operated in the Jerusalem kehillah—the synagogue and the bet midrash (or yeshivah). The synagogue at that time was more than a house of worship; it served a variety of social functions; for example, it also was used as a study hall for householders who did not devote their time exclusively to Torah. Short periods devoted primarily to the study of practical halakhah were set aside daily either before or after the public recitation of the prayers. In contrast, the yeshivah setting was reserved for the scholars and their students, who devoted their energies to Torah study exclusively. Their curriculum of study, which consisted mainly of the examination of academic issues based on advanced study of the Talmud with the classic commentaries of Rashi and the Tosafists, was a daylong pursuit.[39]

This functional division, with the synagogue serving as the venue for classes in practical halakhah based on Maimonides' *Mishneh Torah* (Code), continued into the sixteenth century, as seen from Israel Ashkenazi's letter (1522): "They honored me greatly in my teaching, for I read to them from Maimonides in the synagogue during my appointed month. Each one instructs for a month in rotation."[40] In his travel book, Moses Basola gave a similar report: "Each scholar reads Maimonides for a month in the synagogue following the morning prayer service."

He continued: "All the ḥaverim [scholars] listen to him and then proceed to the yeshivah."[41] We can infer on this basis that the daily study sessions in the synagogue were attended by scholars and householders alike. In the interval between prayer times, the yeshivah students attended their own study sessions in the yeshivah, which was probably located in a different building.

Both sources note the monthly rotation system among the instructors in the synagogue. As we have seen, this arrangement was apparently instituted as a means of preventing any one individual from acquiring a permanent hold on key positions in the kehillah or its institutions.[42]

A letter sent by yeshivah students in 1521, most likely to the notable Abraham of Perugia, provides some details of the course of study in the yeshivah: "We study the entire Talmud in consecutive order with Rashi of blessed memory and the *tosafot* (glosses) of our French rabbis. In the morning we also learn *halakhot* in the long [Babylonian] Talmud [as opposed to the abbreviated compendium of Isaac Alfasi, popular among Spanish Jews—A. D.], two, or one-and-a-half pages daily, however it works out. And in the evening one chapter of the Mishnah with the commentary of Maimonides of blessed memory" [Yaari, *Letters,* 163].[43]

It appears that at the time when this missive was written, both Jerusalem yeshivot followed a similar course of study. Mornings were devoted to intensive study of the complete version of the Talmud, covering one and a half to two folios daily, and evenings were devoted to the study of a chapter of the Mishnah with Maimonides' commentary.

This inclusion of Mishnah as an integral part of the curriculum represents an innovation, a singular phenomenon in the medieval age. Until the late fifteenth century, no known program of study in the yeshivot of Germany, Spain, or Italy included this subject. I have no adequate explanation for this new interest in Mishnah; I can only suggest that it may have been related to the development and increased influence of kabbalistic trends on the early-sixteenth-century Jerusalem kehillah, as the link between kabbalah and Mishnah has been clearly demonstrated.[44] Alternately, the emphasis on Mishnah may be attributable to other factors. A late-fifteenth-century letter by an anonymous traveler who reached Jerusalem in late 1495 provides evidence that the study sessions in the synagogue incorporated both Mishnah and Talmud: "Every day after the prayer service and the *derashah* (sermon) people remain in the synagogue for about three hours to study Mishnah and Talmud."[45] It is possible that this refers to study by householders rather than scholars and that the emphasis on Mishnah may be attributable to the influence of Obadiah of Bertinoro, then engaged in writing his commentary on the Mishnah. Although not singled out in the yeshivah students' letter to Abraham of Perugia cited above, it seems logical to assume that Obadiah of Bertinoro's commentary had its place in the curriculum of the Jerusalem yeshivot, based on his prestige among the most eminent scholars of his day in Eretz-Israel and Egypt.[46] Nor can we discount the possibility that the study of Mishnah received practical impetus following its publication with Maimonides' commentary in Naples in 1492.

How did the heads of the yeshivot assess their academic level? Israel Ashkenazi, himself the head of one of the two Jerusalem yeshivot, by no means held the level of study in high estimation; indeed, he regarded it as superficial as compared to his yeshivah in Perugia, Italy. He wrote, "There is no in-depth study of the halakhic material in the Talmud by the students, especially not of the Tosafists in particular." Worse still, in his opinion, was the sparse amount of material covered: "For what we studied in Perugia in one day exceeded what is studied here in a month."[47] Although undoubtedly exaggerated, this observation must be seen as an indication that the level of study in Jerusalem fell far short of that in the best Italian yeshivot.[48]

Israel Ashkenazi's complaints notwithstanding, Jerusalem was home not only to yeshivah heads and their students but also to the greatest scholars of the day, who served as dayyanim and posekim (decisors). Most were Spanish scholars of the first and second generation after the expulsion. Listed below are sages whose works of rabbinic scholarship have survived in the form of responsa and legal decisions, novellae or commentaries on the Talmud and halakhah: Abraham ben Samuel Zacuto, Bezalel ben Abraham Ashkenazi, David ben Solomon ibn Abi Zimra, Ephraim Fish ben Moses Judah, Ḥayyim ben Joseph Vital, Israel ben Yeḥiel Ashkenazi, Issachar ben Mordecai ibn Susan, Jacob Berab, Joseph Corcos, Joseph ben Abraham ibn Ṣayyaḥ (Ṣiyyaḥ), Judah Albotini, Levi ben Jacob ibn Ḥabib, Moses ben Isaac Alashkar, Simeon ben Isaac Eshenberg ha-Levi, Solomon ben Joseph Sirillo, Solomon ben Yeshua Adeni.

D. KABBALAH

Halahkhic studies by no means comprehended the sole sphere of scholarly interest. In the first half of the sixteenth century a circle of kabbalists resided in Jerusalem, and whereas some of its members delved into kabbalah in addition to their halakhic studies, others concentrated on kabbalah alone. Its members were almost exclusively Spanish and Portuguese expellees.[49] A letter sent prior to the Ottoman conquest by the well-known kabbalist Abraham ha-Levi of Jerusalem to the nagid, Isaac Sholal, in Egypt, regarding "instruction on the question of angels," stresses that "some new kabbalists have recently arrived" in Jerusalem.[50] Their numbers included: (1) Isaac Mar-Ḥayyim, who left Spain for Italy prior to the expulsion. Known to have been in Naples in 1491, he made his way from Italy first to Salonika and then to Jerusalem, where he resided by 1503; (2) Judah Albotini, of Portuguese origin, the grandson of Joseph Ḥayyun, a leading rabbi and notable in pre-expulsion Lisbon;[51] Albotini arrived in Jerusalem prior to 1509; (3) Joseph ibn Ṣayyaḥ, who resided in Jerusalem in the first half of the sixteenth century; (4) Judah Ḥallewa, a Safed kabbalist who originated from Fez, Morocco. In 1545, while residing in Safed, he composed his kabbalistic work *Ṣafenat Paaneaḥ*. Two Geniza documents indicate that he later settled in Jerusalem. But the group's most celebrated member was certainly (5) Abraham ben Eliezer ha-Levi, who resided in Jerusalem from several years prior to the Ottoman conquest until his death sometime in the early 1530s.

Allow me to comment here that the precise relationship between kabbalah as it developed in Safed in the sixteenth century's latter half and its predecessor in Jerusalem in the century's early part has yet to be fully elucidated. Yet, it seems self-evident that such a link existed.[52] In any event, kabbalists are known to have resided both in Jerusalem and in Safed for varying lengths of time during the latter half of the sixteenth century. Among the figures who roamed from Safed to Jerusalem and back we must note: David ibn Abi Zimra, Ḥayyim Vital, Menaḥem de Lonzano, and Samson Back.

E. APOCALYPSE

The historic upheavals that marked the late fifteenth and early sixteenth centuries gave rise to strong messianic expectations. In Jerusalem and the Diaspora, these expectations were intricately intertwined with the figure of Abraham ha-Levi, whose intriguing personality and kabbalistic and apocalyptic works have merited much scholarly interest.[53] During his time in Jerusalem, he concentrated on apocalyptic revelations and the determination of the "end of days," completing his commentary on *Nevuot ha-Yeled Naḥman,* a thirteenth-century apocalyptic work, in 1517.[54] The foundations of his apocalyptic views were undoubtedly laid in Italy, where messianic hopes and the longing for redemption underwent a multidimensional flowering in the sixteenth century;[55] but even earlier, in Spain, ha-Levi had found fertile ground for his apocalyptic ideas.[56] In late-fifteenth-century Italy as well, a wide-branched development of apocalyptic literature had taken place against the background of messianic ferment, giving rise to various figures who predicted the "end of days" and the future redemption. Concurrently, rumors of the discovery of the Ten Tribes spread; their discovery and hoped-for redemption, as we shall see below, have ever been a prescient sign of the advent of the messianic age. The sixteenth-century messianic awakening was further advanced by a major historical event—the Ottoman conquest of Eretz-Israel in late 1516—an event that only enhanced that generation's messianic fervor.[57]

Against this background we can perhaps better comprehend Abraham ha-Levi's self-perception as the herald announcing the approaching footsteps of the Redeemer. In this guise, Abraham ha-Levi dispatched numerous missives to the Diaspora regarding the imminent redemption, to Italy mainly, where they found a receptive audience that responded enthusiastically to his calls for repentance.[58] Ha-Levi believed that redemption was imminent and would proceed by stages—in 1520, in 1524, and in 1529, or alternately, 1530–31, when the Messiah would be revealed in Safed, in the Upper Galilee.[59]

Abraham ha-Levi's apocalyptic visions were undoubtedly influenced by the astrological calculations and calendrical charts of his brother-in-law, Abraham Zacuto.[60] We must note, however, that with regard to messianic preaching in Jerusalem Abraham ha-Levi can by no means be considered a trailblazer; rather, he was preceded by others of an apocalyptic bent. At most, we can observe that he functioned within an already existing atmosphere of messianic ferment,[61] which also formed the backdrop for the messianic claims advanced by Solomon Molcho and David ha-Reuveni.[62] Ha-Reuveni, who made Jerusalem the center of his messianic activity at the outset of his career (1522/23), spread his ideas of redemption among Muslims and Jews alike. The account of his visit to Jerusalem on 25 Adar [13 March] 1523 is, however, a combination of fact and fanciful flights of imagination.[63]

Another Jerusalem resident known for his intense involvement in the contemporary messianic atmosphere was Isaac Sholal. After settling in Jerusalem (1517), he was instrumental in prescribing the performance of acts aimed at hastening the hour of redemption, proclaiming vigils "to pray and undergo privation for the sake of all our brethren in the Diaspora" to this end. In 1521 the Jerusalem yeshivah students testified to his concern:

> Our master the nagid, may he be exalted, whose heart is uplifted to the utmost in the ways of God, and all his deeds and thoughts are directed towards doing what is good and right in the eyes of God, said to his people, to his sages, and his court of justice: "Till when will we procrastinate before returning to our God? When will we awake from our deep sleep to call upon Him with all our heart to bring back our captivity and hasten our redemption? Let Him speed, let Him hasten His purpose on Mt. Zion and in Jerusalem to establish His kingdom in the world; as for idols, they shall vanish completely. Did not our sages say that the Israelites despised three

> things in the days of Rehoboam: the kingdom of heaven, the kingdom of David, and the Temple? And that no sign of redemption is shown to Israel until they ask for all three?"[64] He then commanded the organization of prayer vigils to pray and undergo privation for the sake of all our brethren in the Diaspora, may God preserve them, protect them, and turn a merciful forgiving eye upon them. May their captors be merciful to them, and may He return their sons to their country and have mercy on those who make this request before the heavenly King for the three items previously mentioned, to pray and make confession for them. [Yaari, *Letters,* 164–65][65]

The messianically charged atmosphere in the late fifteenth and early sixteenth centuries, both in Eretz-Israel and the Diaspora, with its harbingers of redemption and visions of the "end of days," also saw the circulation of stories and rumors of the existence of the Ten Lost Tribes. The purported discovery of these tribes as an incipient sign of redemption has always heralded the apprehension of the Messiah's approach.[66] Several sources from the early 1520s indicate that in Egypt, and most likely in Jerusalem as well, Isaac Sholal hosted refugees (apparently from war) who spoke the "language of Cush." These individuals claimed descent from several of the Ten Tribes for themselves and their compatriots in their native lands. Witness the following remarks in Israel Ashkenazi's letter from Jerusalem (1522):

> Today I spoke with our master the nagid, may God protect and preserve him, about the Ten Tribes. He told me that a Jew who spoke the language of Cush, the language of the Bible, and the Hebrew language, stayed at his home, and informed him that in his land there are no written books of the Oral Law, and that regarding all their statutes they say: "Joshua said this on the authority of Moses and on divine authority." [He also said] that in his land there are four tribes: the tribe of Simeon, the tribe of Issachar, and two others, that he is unable to remember. [David, "Letter of Israel Ashkenazi," 119–20]

In his travel book (1522), Moses Basola provided the following account:

> When I was in the holy city, Jerusalem, a Jew from the land of Cush came who had been held captive among the nations for ten years until purchased by Muslims and sold to Jews in Egypt. And he came to see Jerusalem. The nagid spoke to him, and he clearly stated that there are many Jews in the south, kings and nobles. . . . The nagid,

> may God preserve and protect him, said that thirty years earlier, a Jew from the tribe of Simeon had stayed at his home, and related that in his land there were four tribes, one of them the tribe of Issachar which studied Torah. [Basola, *Masot,* 88–89]

Abraham Rafael Trabot also had something to relate on this matter:

> Then a young man from one of the Ten Tribes arrived, whose father was from the tribe of Reuben and whose mother was from the tribe of Dan, and divulged great things and wonders concerning the redemption, that the tribes will come soon, and that Reuben will be the first to arrive. . . . He said that he was sent to Jerusalem by the king of Reuben, to remove a stone from the Western Wall of our house of glory built by Yeroboam ben Nebat . . . and this young man boasted that he removed it in the presence of our brilliant master the nagid, the great kohen, R. Isaac Sholal, may God protect and preserve him. . . . From here this young man proceeded to Damascus. After his departure, [that is] our master, the nagid, may God protect and preserve him, wrote to me from Jerusalem . . . that the things he said in his name, like the removal of the stone in his presence, and the like, are all lies and falsehood, for he is an instigator and provocateur. [Neubauer, "Qibuṣim," 32–33]

These sources have sparked much scholarly debate as to the identity of the nagid's informant. Some identify him as David ha-Reuveni;[67] others do not find the evidence for this identification conclusive, postulating that two personalities were involved instead.[68] In any event, the sources clearly demonstrate that Isaac Sholal was already receptive to the incipient signs of messianic redemption in Egypt and that this continued to be the case in Jerusalem at a later date. Consequently, he desired not only to scrutinize these men and their strange customs closely but also to examine their claim to descent from the Ten Tribes. As we have seen, he was by no means alone in this interest.

In conclusion, this section has attempted to define characteristic features of the Jerusalem kehillah's social and intellectual life during the post-expulsion era. It touched upon the location of the Jewish quarter and the social fabric of its inhabitants, members of communities who hailed from both East and West. With the increased influx of immigrants following the Ottoman conquest, we are witness to an attempt to create a homogeneous society, from which the Sefardim emerged as the leading element in all spheres.

From the Ottoman conquest the community's organizational structure, its institutions and legislation, was vested in two officeholders:

the dayyan and the shaykh al-yahud, whose authority was vested mainly in the backing of the local rulers. The community's intellectual and spiritual life found expression in various branches of Jewish creativity, particularly in the realm of halakhah, Mishnaic and talmudic commentaries, and to a large extent, in Jewish mysticism as well. (The fruits of this activity are briefly surveyed in the concluding chapter on rabbinical authorities in Eretz-Israel.) This section also explored the educational settings and course of study in Jerusalem as they developed in the early sixteenth century—yeshivah, bet midrash, and synagogue—where once again the strong Sefardi influence is readily apparent.

Finally, I took a brief look at the strong messianic expectations that found expression in the early decades of the sixteenth century in apocalyptic visions that proved attractive to the Jews of Italy, at actions taken to hasten the advent of the messiah, and at the spread of rumors about the existence of the Ten Tribes, whose purported discovery has ever been linked to messianic expectations.

SAFED

9 The Jewish Quarter

The section on Safed essentially follows the same structure as the one on Jerusalem, opening with a brief excursus on the location of Safed's Jewish quarter and the century's demographic trends. It then proceeds to examine the fabric of its social composition, the multiplicity of congregations that formed its constituent parts. This is followed by an attempt to delineate the structure of the Safed Jewish communal leadership, which differed significantly from that of Jerusalem. A detailed examination of Safed's educational settings and the sages who functioned as their heads is the topic of the next chapter, which parallels the examination of Jerusalem's intellectual life. The section concludes with a brief consideration of the rivalry for hegemony between Jerusalem and Safed, the main centers of Jewish life in sixteenth-century Eretz-Israel.

A. LOCATION

In the early Ottoman period, various sources place Safed's Jewish quarter to the northwest of al-Kala (the present-day citadel), on one of the slopes of what was known as the "summit" or the "mountain."[1] Following his visit to Safed in 1522, Moses Basola described the city and its Jewish quarter: "Safed is the northernmost district of the land of Naftali, [with] a strong walled enclosure at the mountain-top. The walled enclosure on the peak is surrounded by four mountains, two [inhabited] entirely by Muslims, and the slopes of [the other] two are entirely covered with Jewish homes" [Basola, *Masot,* 43].

The English Christian pilgrim William Biddulph penned a similar description following his visit to Safed three-quarters of a century later, in 1600. "When we came to the top of the mountains, we saw Saphetta on the right hand a universitie of the Jewes, where they speake Hebrew and have their Synagogues there. The citie Saphetta is situated on a very high hill with three tops and so the citie hath three parts. One part is inhabited by Jewes, the other two by Turkes" [Biddulph, *Travel into Africa, Asia and to the Blacke Sea,* 105].

Safed's sixteenth-century Jewish population found the city wall constructed in 1549 insufficient for their protection; indeed, Hebrew sources indicate that it had been seriously breached by the late sixteenth/early seventeenth century.[2] Consequently, they sought the erection of a fortified sector for their homes whose gates could be locked at nightfall. Evidently, about midcentury this requirement was fulfilled when the pasha (district ruler) erected a special fortress near the Jewish quarter. Named for its builder, the fortified *Ḥan al Basha* housed Jews, providing them with maximum protection against robbers and brigands. Its ground floor contained warehouses, and its upper stories (apparently three in number[3]) served as living quarters.[4] The number of Jews who actually resided in this edifice is unascertainable, and we do not even know whether it housed all or only part of the Jewish population. The Jews paid a yearly rental fee of four hundred florins for its use.[5]

In a responsum, Joseph Caro described the evolution of the Jewish initiative to build a khan in Safed:

> Beforetimes it occurred to several notables to send to our master the king, may he be exalted, a request that he build a khan for them near the summit. They drew up a detailed reckoning of each one's participation in the construction, wrote letters and had them witnessed. They then forwarded this request to the court of the Sublime Porte, to a certain individual there who could promote this project, who requested a thousand florins as his fee. Upon receiving this reply the notables withdrew from the project and canceled their intentions; it was as if it had never been, and each went his own way. Several years later a pasha (district ruler) arrived from Damascus who wished to build a khan here in Safed, may it be speedily rebuilt, in order to collect its rent. The kehalim banded together and appointed R. Moses Bibas, may God preserve him, to buy up the fields near the summit, regardless of whether or not they contained olive trees. All were purchased and presented to the said pasha as a gift, so that he would build a khan on the aforementioned fields. The matter was settled and it came to pass that he built the khan. [Joseph Caro, *Shu"t Avqat Rokhel,* no. 125]

This khan was still standing in the mid-seventeenth century, as attested by Turkish tourist Evliya Tshelebi, who visited Eretz-Israel in 1649. He described the building as "a large caravanserai, with an iron gate like that of castle, and square in plan. Right round it measures six hundred paces. It stands four stories high. Previously twelve thousand Jews lived in it. But at present they number only two thousand" [*Evliya Tshelebi's Travels in Palestine,* 23].[6]

No further references to the khan are known following the renewal of the Safed Jewish community in 1672. The khan's exact location is unknown, for all the buildings from that period were destroyed by earthquake in 1837.

B. DEMOGRAPHIC CHANGES

For the late Mamluk era, scant information has survived regarding Safed's Jewish community. According to an anonymous traveler from that period (1495), Safed's Jewish population then numbered "about three hundred households."[7] But as the sixteenth century unfolds, our knowledge of this community is augmented. It appears that shortly after the Ottoman conquest in 1517, Safed's Jewish population suffered a severe blow following the dissemination of unfounded reports that the Ottoman sultan had met defeat at the gates of Cairo. A contemporary Hebrew source described the results of the bloody clash between Mamluk supporters and representatives of the Ottoman authorities; the rioters killed many of Safed's Jews and robbed others and left them destitute. Those Jews who escaped physical harm sought refuge in the nearby villages, "for due to sins it happened that our brethren were evicted from their homes, robbed, and plundered, and they fled naked to the villages, without any provisions."[8] Despite this setback, five years later Moses Basola reported that the Safed community had again reached its former level of "more than three hundred households."[9] Many of the Jews who had fled to the surrounding villages evidently returned to the city; moreover, we must remember that after the Ottoman conquest Safed was the leading destination for immigrants to Eretz-Israel.

Following this initial setback, Safed's Jewish population continued to grow for several decades, until the 1570s, as did the city's non-Jewish component. Nonetheless, the attempt to determine more precisely the size of Eretz-Israel's Jewish population in general and that of Safed in particular from the available statistical data has failed to reach definitive conclusions. As for Jerusalem, the periodic censuses found in the Ottoman taḥrir registers by no means reflect the true demographic picture of Safed's Jewish population. A renewed evaluation of the Jewish population data from censuses and other sources gives rise to a somewhat altered demographic picture than the previously accepted one. It does not, however, affect relative size or demographic trends; thus it is possible to compare the size of the city's Jewish and Muslim components. In the 1525/26 census, the Jewish population numbered half the Muslim one. In the subsequent census, taken thirty years later in 1555/56, the gap had closed, and by 1567/68, the census reflects equality between Safed's Jewish and Muslim populations. These data clearly indicate a massive increase in the city's Jewish population, even in comparison to its Muslim one. But thirty years later, in 1596/97, the census reflected a decline in Jewish population as compared to the Muslim one.[10]

The mid-1570s marked a downward turning point in the fortunes of Safed's Jewish community. The empire-wide economic recession had disastrous results for Safed's Jewish community, which depended largely on textile production and marketing for its livelihood. A concurrent deterioration in the central government's attitude toward the Jews of Safed further exacerbated this decline.[11] Ottoman documents reveal that a group of affluent Safed Jews was targeted for transfer to Cyprus as a means of assisting the Cypriot ruler to stabilize that island's economy, a step consistent with the Ottoman policy of sürgün. In 1576 Sultan Murad III issued an order for the deportation of a thousand of the Safed area's wealthiest Jews and their families to Cyprus. Less than a year later this firman was superseded by another one, later rescinded, authorizing the transfer of five hundred affluent Jews from Safed.[12]

In actual fact, incipient signs of decline were already apparent in the mid-sixties, which saw a drastic decrease in Safed's Jewish population.[13] Concurrently, in order to maintain a semblance of a decent standard of living, Safed's Jewish community made more frequent appeals for assistance via emissaries dispatched to the Diaspora.

In 1591 Moses Alshekh, one of late-sixteenth-century Safed's leading scholars and kabbalists, described Jewish Safed's economic and demographic setbacks in a letter: "For from the beginning of the exodus until we left, the majority of the city's population had relocated. It declined to the extent that of the five thousand people who formerly resided in the city, some four hundred alone remained" [Pachter, "'Ḥazut Kasha,'" 184].

Although some suggest that these statistics refer to families, logic dictates that the figures cited above refer to individuals.[14] (Nonetheless, the figures are far removed from the reality reflected in the final census below.) As Alshekh's letter covers the three-year period from 1588 to 1591, this suggests that Safed's Jewish population reached its nadir in the late eighties/early nineties, as the result of a coalescence of factors that led to the harsh conditions he described. In actuality, Safed's Jewish population was already in decline from the mid-1570s to the late 1580s; this decline, however, was more moderate and gradual in nature. Taḥrir registers do not provide the sole evidence for this crisis, which also found expression in the ever-increasing desertion of the city by scholars and, we must assume, by householders as well. Some individuals relocated to Syrian and Egyptian Jewish centers, and others found homes elsewhere in Eretz-Israel, in Jerusalem and Hebron for example. Several of Safed's outstanding sages left the city during the century's last quarter, either relocating permanently or temporarily trying their

Table 3. Population of Safed in the Sixteenth Century According to Ottoman Survey Returns

		1525/26	1555/56	1567/68	1596/97
Muslims	Householders	693	1,093	986	1,179
	Bachelors	40	222	306	386
	Religious officials	26	63	42	53
	Disabled persons	9	9	5	
Jews	Householders	233	719	945	904
	Bachelors		63	12	93
	Religious officials				8
	Disabled persons				64

Sources: The data for 1525/26, 1555/56, and 1567/68 are based upon Cohen and Lewis, *Population and Revenue,* 161, and the final survey is based upon Hütteroth and Abdulfattah, *Historical Geography,* 52.

luck in other locations. Among them we must note: Elijah de Vidas, Gedaliah Cordovero, Ḥayyim Vital, Ḥiyya Rofe, Isaac Gershon, Israel Najara, Jacob Abulafia, Joseph Trani, Moses Alshekh, Moses Berab, Moses Najara, Solomon Adeni, Samson Back, and Yom Tov Ṣahalon.

As I have already noted, the extant statistical data do not enable us to arrive at an accurate estimate of Safed's Jewish population. They do however provide clear indication of demographic trends.

The population figures in Table 3 display Safed's obvious demographic superiority over the other centers in Eretz-Israel, Jerusalem included. If, as we have seen, the small Jerusalem kehillah was by no means homogeneous, this diversity was even more pronounced in the much larger Safed kehillah. As the prime target for sixteenth-century Jewish immigrants, Safed was home to a variety of congregations. These congregations and the balance of power between them are examined in the next chapters.

10 The Communities

The extant sources convey the impression that Safed's early-sixteenth-century Jewish community was divided into two main kehalim: Musta'rabs and Sefardim. This in no way implies that members of other kehalim were not represented in Safed at that time, simply that these two kehalim then constituted the leading groups. This picture alters in the early Ottoman period, when it appears that three kehalim played a central role in the larger Jewish community; we now find the Maghrebi kahal mentioned in conjunction with the Musta'rabs and Sefardim (see below). The more copious data available for Safed's Jewish community following the Ottoman conquest, the result of its popularity among immigrants to Eretz-Israel, broaden and change the picture. Taḥrir registers convey the distinct impression that beginning with the century's second quarter, Safed's Jewish community encompassed a much larger variety of kehalim, who were split according to country or region of origin,[1] an impression corroborated by additional sources. These autonomous congregations jockeyed for position within the larger communal structure, with an eye to gaining greater influence and a greater share of the communal budget. They also maintained close ties with congregations from their native lands elsewhere in the Diaspora; requests for financial assistance were a prime aspect of these contacts. Despite Safed's multiplicity of congregations, we must note the Sefardi kahal's dominant role. Safed's Sefardi component did not actually absorb the members of the other congregations as it did in Jerusalem; nonetheless, by virtue of its numerical superiority, economic know-how, outstanding leadership, and unique cultural achievements it succeeded in capturing the leading role in Safed's Jewish community for the better part of the century.

A. MUSTA'RABS (MORISCOS)

This kahal's roots in Eretz-Israel predate the Ottoman period. Its members, who derived mainly from Near Eastern countries, became almost totally integrated in Eretz-Israel's rural sector. Contemporary written sources retain only faint traces of this congregation[2] despite its preeminence in early-sixteenth-century Safed and Jerusalem; as we shall have occasion to see, it was overshadowed by the Sefardi kahal even at this early date. Nonetheless, Moses Basola's description of Safed's three synagogues in 1522—"a Sefardi one, a Morisco one, and a Maghrebi one"[3]—suggests that this congregation was still of central importance. The order in which the synagogues are listed may hint at each group's relative rank, making it likely that the Musta'rabs were then in second place, after the Sefardim.

Taḥrir registers rank the Musta'rabs as the largest group in the first census (1525/26). Nonetheless, it is safe to say that the Sefardim, who for reasons unknown were omitted from this census, certainly constituted the majority at that time.[4] Although subsequent censuses indicate that the Musta'rab kahal continued to constitute one of the largest congregations, we can discern a steady decline in its ranks over time. In 1525/26 it numbered 131 households; in 1555/56 it numbered 98 households with an additional 10 bachelors; and by 1567/68 it had declined to 70 households.[5]

Not a single sixteenth-century Musta'rab scholar in Safed left his mark on contemporary literature. Several individuals are named in an early-sixteenth-century appeal for parity with Sefardi ḥakhamim sent by representatives of the Musta'rab kahal to Nagid Isaac Sholal.[6] Among these personalities we find "R. Moses the dayyan," none other than Moses ben Isaac ha-Dayyan ha-Levi, who is known from several sources.[7] Another contemporary source, the letter concerning the fixing of the sabbatical year (1504) referred to earlier, mentions "Isaac b. R. Joseph Ẓoref, known as Ẓaig."[8] In the century's latter half we find a reference to the dayyan "R. Yeshua, may God preserve and protect him."[9]

The Musta'rabs did not readily surrender their seniority. Echoes of a Musta'rab/Sefardi power struggle for hegemony in the Safed kehillah were still evident in the mid-sixteenth century, in pointed disagreements that continued into the early seventeenth century over the liturgical rite to be followed in the synagogue.[10] Evidently, the small minority of Jews from Yemen and Kurdistan who resided in sixteenth-century Safed were counted as members of the Musta'rab community.[11]

B. SEFARDIM

As early as the century's first decade unmistakable signs of the preeminent status of Safed's Sefardim are in evidence. We have already noted that most of the signatories on a letter sent by Safed's sages to their counterparts in Jerusalem concerning the fixing of the sabbatical year (1504) were of Spanish origin.[12] Both this letter and the one sent by Safed's Musta'rab sages to Isaac Sholal in 1510[13] indicate that the Musta'rabs and the Sefardim were the main kehalim at the time. Only the latter, however, were beneficiaries of the nagid's assistance.[14]

With the marked increase in immigration following the Ottoman conquest, our knowledge of the various kehalim in Safed, including the Sefardi one, is enhanced. Only a few short years after the inception of Ottoman rule, the Sefardi kahal, composed of expellees from the Iberian Peninsula who reached Eretz-Israel from various points in the Sefardi diaspora—Turkey, the Balkans, North Africa, Egypt, and Syria—dominated Safed.[15] A responsum composed by Moses Trani in 1574 provides evidence for Sefardi numerical superiority. Notwithstanding the late date of its composition, the responsum refers to the state of affairs in 1525: "As the Sefardim who were expelled from Spain outnumber the other congregations, they require two synagogues which they call the 'Great Congregation' and the 'Congregation of Bet Yaakov.' . . . Fifty years have passed since I began to teach Torah in the Bet Yaakov congregation, from 1525 to 1574" [Moses Trani, *Responsa,* pt. 3, no. 48].

Moses Trani provides additional information on this kahal's original communal structure and its subsequent breakup. Although at first it functioned as a single group with a common treasury, internal discord later generated the formation of separate frameworks according to cities of origin in Spain. He stated: "At first, there was a single purse for all, for charity, taxes, and levies as all shared a common language. Later, due to discord they separated; each congregation has its own treasury for its poor and for other expenses" [Moses Trani, *Responsa,* pt. 3, no. 48].

The taḥrir registers disclose a progressive increase in the numbers of Safed's Sefardi component, whose members hailed from different cities and regions in Spain: Castile, Cordova, Aragon, Catalonia, and Seville.[16] The Safed Sefardim, like their Jerusalem counterparts, not only formed the majority group but also functioned as the city's dominant social element, the pacesetters for the other kehalim in the social and intellectual spheres. In brief, the reasons for this success do not lie just in the domain of numerical superiority. Additional factors are the presence of outstanding Spanish sages who took an active role in public and intellectual life and Sefardi business acumen.

Indeed, the thriving of Safed's textile industry, which was based mainly on woolen and silk dry goods but which also encompassed marketing and dyeing of fabrics, is largely attributable to the role played by Safed's Jews, its Sefardi component in particular. As we have already noted, Jews from the Iberian Peninsula were naturally drawn to this industry, as fully a third of the Castilian population engaged in wool manufacture, and weaving was a popular occupational choice among

Spanish Jews. Thus a direct link can be adduced between this industry's success and the presence of Spanish Jews.[17]

From the 1530s Safed was the center of a wide-branched spiritual-intellectual awakening whose influence was felt throughout the Jewish world. Scholars from the entire Diaspora were drawn to Safed by this activity, but we must note in particular the role played by Spanish Jews of the first, second, and third generations after the expulsion in the development of various schools of thought, both exoteric and esoteric. The leading figures in this unprecedented intellectual flowering were Sefardim. The century's last quarter saw Sefardi influence on the wane, the result of economic difficulties and the dying out of the generation of intellectual giants whose accomplishments will be surveyed below in the context of Safed's communal organization and centers of Jewish learning.

C. CONVERSOS

Signs of the longing of Spanish conversos to settle in Eretz-Israel and throw off the mask of Christianity are discernible as early as the mid-fifteenth century, sparked by messianic expectations that intensified following the Ottoman conquest of Constantinople in 1453. This event, perceived as a sign of impending redemption, stirred the imagination of Spanish conversos and Jews alike. Although scanty, the extant evidence for this phenomenon in contemporary Hebrew and Spanish sources suffices to verify its existence. The sources also attest to the presence of conversos in Jerusalem and Hebron during that period as well.[18]

Shortly after the expulsion from Spain, Don Isaac Abrabanel noted the increased number of conversos leaving Spain for Eretz-Israel.[19] Nonetheless, I find the lack of extant references attesting to the presence of conversos in Eretz-Israel over the ensuing forty-year period puzzling. This may indicate their total absorption by the Sefardi community; alternately, it may represent an attempt to obliterate the traces of the converso phenomenon itself. Whatever the explanation for their previous silence, from the 1530s our sources, Hebrew ones in the main, not only reflect the presence of conversos in Eretz-Israel but also describe the hardships they encountered. Safed in particular appears to have been a significant center for their absorption.[20] Logic dictates that most of these individuals were Portuguese conversos who fled Portugal in the 1530s with the founding of the Royal Inquisition.[21]

Messianic expectations seem to be the most convincing explanation for the flow of conversos to Eretz-Israel in general and to Safed in particular. The tragedy that befell Iberian Jewry in the late fifteenth century excited messianic longings and inspired the blossoming of hopes for redemption and the end of the exile. The rapid spread of apocalyptic doctrines throughout the Jewish world, both in Eretz-Israel and the Diaspora, brought many Iberian exiles to the gates of the land. That the conversos were affected by this messianic activity as well, both before and after the expulsion, is a phenomenon with traces that are only now being uncovered.[22] Safed played a considerable role in these messianic expectations, based upon an explicit tradition in the midrash and the Zohar that predicted the Messiah would initially reveal himself in Galilee. The well-known kabbalist Abraham ha-Levi referred to this tradition in his letter "On Martin Luther and the Falashas" (1525): "I fail to understand why you claim that redemption must necessarily occur in Jerusalem; is it not well known that true redemption will come when the Messiah appears in the Galilee, for he will proclaim liberty to all the inhabitants of the land and to those who return" [paraphrase of Lev. 25:10—TRANS.]. [Robinson, "Two Letters," 407].[23]

An ever-increasing number of conversos continued to arrive in Safed throughout the sixteenth century. A late-sixteenth-century Safed sage spoke of "the contemporary conversos . . . who come to our borders in order to repent [return to Judaism] in our lands."[24] Although conversos began to settle in Eretz-Israel as early as the sixteenth century's first quarter, only a minority then made their way to Safed. Again the primary factor that seems to have sparked aliyah by conversos to Safed was the founding of the Portuguese Royal Inquisition.[25] The eminent kabbalist Solomon Alkabetz voiced his admiration for their massive aliyah in a prayer for redemption composed following his arrival in Eretz-Israel in 1536:

> If there be among them those who abandoned their honor [converted] on a bitter day and prayed to a strange god, You alone know the heart of man, You know his hurt and the pain of his heart. . . . In distress they called upon You and some sanctified Your name in *auto-da-fés*, others chose suffocation, and sacrificed their sons and daughters so as not to desecrate Your honored name, and [there were] those who were sprinkled with the seething [baptismal] waters . . . yet nonetheless they kept Your Torah, neither leaving nor abandoning it. . . . Now their spirit moves them to go up to Mt. Zion, the Lord's mountain, to delight in its stones and to rebuild the dust of its ruins. All assemble to come to You; they take their lives in their hands and set forth by sea, they were swifter than eagles, they were stronger than lions [2 Sam. 1:23] to go up and bow before You in this land. They left all their property and their pleasant homes, they did not value silver or delight in gold [in their

desire] to come to the Land. [Werblowsky, "Solomon Alkabets," 152–53][26]

Virtually no information is extant on the communal life of the conversos in Safed as such, but some data exist for the Portuguese community. Censuses conducted by the Ottoman authorities indicate a significant rise in this group's population as the century progressed. In 1525/26 it numbered 21 households; in 1555/56 it numbered 143 households; and by 1567/68 it had reached a total of 200 households.[27] Caution is needed in interpreting the numbers, as I have noted elsewhere, because the taḥrir registers by no means reflect the demographic reality with any accuracy; they serve rather as indicators of trends and relative size. The statistics for the Portuguese congregation clearly reflect a dramatic increase in this kahal's size, far beyond what we would expect from natural increase alone. Indeed, in the space of some thirty years Safed's Portuguese population increased almost sevenfold. In the second census it ranked second after the Castilian congregation; by the third census it had attained equality with the Castilians. I believe that the Jews listed as Portuguese in the sixteenth-century Safed taḥrir registers must be identified as conversos who fled Portugal, as no practicing Jews remained in Portugal following their forcible conversion in 1497. The founding of the Portuguese Royal Inquisition provided second-generation conversos with a strong incentive to flee this land. In my view, this explains the sharp rise in the numbers of Safed's Portuguese community during the course of the sixteenth century.

If my conjecture concerning their origins is correct, the Portuguese congregation, having emerged from a unique social and political milieu, must then be singled out as distinct from the other kehalim in Safed.[28] These former conversos founded an independent kahal in Safed that boasted its own communal framework and institutions: for example, "The Portuguese Synagogue" mentioned as early as the 1530s or early 1540s and the "*Bet Din* of the Portuguese congregation."[29] This kahal also maintained a yeshivah, headed at one point by Moses Cordovero, himself of Portuguese origin,[30] as his disciple Mordecai Dato attests in his *Iggeret ha-Levanon:* "This alludes to the yeshivah of the Portuguese community in Safed which he [Moses Cordovero] headed."[31] Another institution that may reflect their unique situation is the "*Baaley Teshuvah* Society," whose members aspired to achieve forgiveness for their former deeds through sincere repentence.[32]

It is no simple matter to identify individual members of the converso community in Safed. Defined neither as conversos nor as forced converts and not referred to by their Christian names, their identification is further complicated by the fact that many had Spanish names, for Portugal was a convenient destination for Spanish Jews after the expulsion. Nonetheless, several individuals can definitely be singled out as former Portuguese conversos, including Solomon Ḥazan, who was involved in the 1538 ordination controversy; Joseph Podniero; Moses Atiyah; and members of the Oliveira and Gediliah families. One of the latter served as "physician to the queen." It is also possible that the Sagis family, whose members belonged to Safed's intellectual elite in the sixteenth and seventeenth centuries, originated from the Portuguese city of Sagres; similarly we can assume that the Deleiria family almost certainly originated from the Portuguese town of Leiria. Its representative in Safed was Moses Deleiria, who resided in Safed in the latter half of the sixteenth century. A member of the Portuguese Albotini family, Moses Albotini, resided in Safed in the century's first half. Let me reiterate the strong likelihood that these families were none other than Portuguese conversos who left Portugal either following the forcible mass conversion in 1497, or after the institution of the Royal Inquisition there.[33]

D. MAGHREBIS (MAARAVIM)

In 1522 Moses Basola mentioned three synagogues in Safed, which were divided along communal lines. In addition to noting their presence, he provided additional details about the Maghrebi synagogue: "There is a Sefardi one, a Morisco one, and a Maghrebi one known as 'Elijah of blessed memory's Synagogue,' for it is ancient, and they have a tradition that Elijah of blessed memory prayed there."[34] In 1533 we find these three kehalim listed in the same order in a decision (*pesak*) by Jacob Berab: "I found it necessary to gather all the kehalim, the Sefardim, the Musta'rabs, and the Maghrebis."[35] We have no knowledge of any individuals from the Maghrebi kahal prior to the Ottoman conquest, with the possible exception of Abraham Maaravi, who was the son-in-law of Joseph ben Abraham Iscandari, a leading member of the Safed Jewish community. Iscandari, who resided in Damascus in the sixteenth century's first decade, is known to have supported scholars in Safed.[36]

Taḥrir registers, their restricted ability to provide precise data notwithstanding, indicate that the Maghrebi congregation showed practically no growth in the sixteenth century. In 1525/26 this kahal numbered 33 families out of a total of 233 Jewish families; thirty years later it numbered 38 families out of a total Jewish population of 719 families; and twelve years hence its numbers rose to 52 out of a total of 945 households.[37] We see, then, that over a thirty-year period, or a generation, the Maghrebi component increased only by five families; and twelve years later, by fourteen. Taking natural increase into account, as well as the rapid growth of Safed's Jewish community in general during that period, indicates that not only did the Maghrebi kahal fail to show perceptible growth, but also its numbers actually declined. The underlying causes for this decline are unknown; I can only suggest that members of this kahal, whose ancestors had emigrated to the Maghreb from Spain, either now chose to merge with the large Sefardi kahal, or perhaps relocated elsewhere in Eretz-Israel or outside its borders.

Their small numbers notwithstanding, several important Maghrebi sages resided in Safed and took an active part in its intellectual life from the second third of the sixteenth until the early seventeenth century. Of these figures, the most prominent was Issachar ben Mordecai ha-Maaravi ibn Susan, a native of Fez, whom we encountered earlier in the section on Jerusalem. In the Hebrew introduction to his Arabic translation of the Bible, *Al-Sharḥ al-Susani,* he noted his origins and arrival in Safed: "The youth Issachar son of . . . the great sage R. Mordecai known as ben Susan of blessed memory, ha-Maaravi, came several years ago, in his youth, from the city of Fez . . . to the city . . . of Safed."[38] Issachar ibn Susan resided in Safed for several decades, beginning with the 1530s. He served as head of the Maghrebi community in that city, and most likely headed the Maghrebi yeshivah as well. He stated: "I am young and burdened by great poverty and my energies are largely devoted to feeding the children God has blessed your servant with . . . and the needs of the kahal, may God preserve and protect it, and the fixed periods of study with the ḥaverim, may God protect and preserve them, [which are] daily, morning and evening, as well as other Torah-related tasks" [MS. London Or. 14020a, p. 5]. Ibn Susan's intellectual inquiries in Safed are subsumed in his treatise *Tiqqun Yissakhar* (Constantinople, 1564).[39] This treatise's main focus is on calendrical matters and on the different customs of Safed's main kehalim—Sefardim, Musta'rabs, and Maghrebis. The emphasis is placed on their divergent practices, especially the ones related to the cycle of the weekly Pentateuchal reading in the synagogue.

The other contemporary Maghrebi sages active in Safed were kabbalists who either antedated Isaac Luria or belonged to the generation that followed. One noteworthy kabbalist of the pre-Lurianic era was Judah Ḥallewa, a native of Fez, who composed his kabbalistic work *Ṣafenat Paaneaḥ* in Safed in 1545. Late in life he evidently moved to Jerusalem. Another Maghrebi figure, Joseph ibn Tabul, known also as Joseph ha-Maaravi, or Joseph the Maghrebi, was one of Luria's leading disciples. The sparse information extant about Ibn Tabul and the small number of his kabbalistic works, most of which are still in manuscript, are incongruent with his position as one of the leading members of Isaac Luria's coterie. Additional members of Safed's Maghrebi community can be identified among the students of Isaac Luria's direct disciples: Abraham ha-Levi Berukhim (late sixteenth/early seventeenth centuries), also called Abraham the Maghrebi, known for his prominent role in folktales and for his personal, idiosyncratic customs; Masud Azulay, known also as Masud the Blind, or Masud Maaravi; and Suleiman Oḥana, also called Solomon Maaravi.[40]

Although scanty, the available data on Maghrebis in Eretz-Israel in the sixteenth and early seventeenth centuries disclose that the vast majority were of Moroccan origin. It is perhaps not coincidental that the outstanding Maghrebi figures of whom we have some knowledge were associated with the kabbalistic trends in Safed. Separate consideration must be given to the question of whether a mystic orientation linked the influential Moroccan kabbalistic centers in Fez and Dr'aa, of such great importance to the Jews of the Maghreb, with the kabbalistic center in Safed.[41] In any event, the notable contribution of Maghrebi sages confirms their position as a force to be reckoned with in Safed's intellectual life, a role that was enhanced in late century as Sefardi influence waned.

E. ITALIANS

In the sixteenth century's latter half, Safed boasted three congregations from various regions in Italy, two from the south—Apulia and Calabria—and one from central and northern Italy.[42] Contemporary sources relating to the "Italian kahal" in the last quarter of the sixteenth and early seventeenth centuries document a well-established congregation.[43] According to the taḥrir register from 1555/56, Safed's Italian Jewish component totaled seventy-four households; in 1567/68 it numbered eighty.[44]

Relatively little is known of Safed's sages of Italian origin. In the 1490s and early 1500s (prior to 1504), Peretz Colon, son of the eminent Italian-Jewish scholar Joseph Colon and father of the Jerusalemite sage Joseph Colon, headed a Safed yeshivah. In the early 1520s, Abraham Rafael ben Azriel, a member of the leading Italian-Jewish Trabot family, resided in Safed and corresponded with the nagid, Isaac Sholal.[45] In the sixteenth century's latter half we know of two kabbalists of Italian origin: Ḥayyim Vital (1543–1620), foremost disciple of Isaac Luria, known also as Ḥayyim Calabrese (that is, from Calabria, South Italy), who was born in Safed in 1543 and lived there for most of his life, and Samson Back (Bacchi), who arrived in Safed in 1582 and must be counted among the students of Isaac Luria's disciples. In 1584 Back moved to Jerusalem. Other Italian sages known to have resided in Safed in the sixteenth century's latter half include Moses Basola, a noted rabbi and posek who settled in Safed in 1560, the year of his demise, and whose travel book recording his visit to Eretz-Israel in the early

1520s has been frequently cited throughout this book; Elisha Gallico, a disciple of Joseph Caro; Abraham Gabriel, a disciple of Isaac Luria; and Isaac Gershon, a well-known proofreader in the Italian-Hebrew press, who lived in Safed in the last quarter of the sixteenth century, from whence he returned to his birthplace, Italy.

F. PROVENÇAL (FRANKISH) JEWS

The existence of a Provençal kahal in Safed is attested by a variety of sources that also testify to its strong ties with the Provençal congregations in Italy and in Provence. The congregation in Safed was evidently founded either by Jews expelled from Provence in the late fifteenth century, or by their descendants.

In the 1525/26 census Provençal Jews numbered forty-eight families.[46] Although the taḥrir registers refer to this kahal as Ifranjiye, it is certainly the Provençal congregation of southern France that is meant, as the Jews of northern and central France had last been expelled from that land in 1394. It seems doubtful that some 130 years later descendants of Jews from the last-named regions still maintained their congregational framework; it is more likely that they were absorbed into the local communities where they settled. Significant data concerning the Provençal kahal in Safed are extant in sources dating from the last third of the sixteenth to the first half of the seventeenth century. Of special interest are its close ties with the Provençal kehillah of Cuneo, in the Piedmont, during the sixteenth century's last quarter, which provided its compatriots in Safed with ample monetary aid.[47] In the latter part of the century, Joseph Caro promoted the founding of a yeshivah for the Provençal community in Safed, as seen from his letter (1575) to "the appointed officials, parnassim, and leaders of the Provençal congregation in the Piedmont" in northern Italy: "Now God has inspired us to found a yeshivah for the holy Provençal congregation, headed by one of my disciples, the perfect sage, R. Moses Galante, may God preserve him . . . in his coterie the ḥaverim study with young Provençal pupils" [David, "Community of Cuneo," 440].[48]

It appears that the heads of this congregational yeshivah were the Galante brothers, Moses and Abraham. Perhaps they themselves had Provençal origins, as the Galante family was eminent in medieval Provence.

G. ASHKENAZIM

As in Jerusalem, the Ashkenazi kahal, its numerical inferiority notwithstanding, was recognized as an exception within the larger communal structure. Whereas the individual Safed congregations exercised a fair degree of autonomy, the Ashkenazi kahal's independent status was of a different order, explicitly laid down in a takkanah. This regulation, issued jointly by the Safed and Jerusalem communities in the sixteenth century and renewed in 1623, recognized the Ashkenazi congregation's unique status and outlawed any attempts to coerce the Ashkenazi kahal into adopting customs or halakhot against its will.[49]

> As an earlier haskamah [agreement] signed by the Jerusalem sages . . . and by Safed's sages exists . . . [to the effect] that no individual or group shall split off from the community . . . in matters of Torah or in financial matters with the exception of the Ashkenazi congregation, nor shall [anyone] defame the communal leadership or the officials who tend to the city's needs in writing . . . we the undersigned have undertaken to ratify and renew this haskamah . . . on Thursday, 18 Iyyar 5383 years to the Creation [18 May 1623], here in the holy city, Jerusalem. [Luncz, "Issur laasot Peyrud," 147–48]

As compared to Safed's other congregations its Ashkenazi kahal was tiny, numbering twenty households in the 1555/56 census and forty-three in the 1567/68 census.[50] This represents a doubling in its ranks in the course of twelve years. Its small size notwithstanding, like its Jerusalemite counterpart, the Safed Ashkenazi community zealously guarded its singularity as seen from internal regulations issued in 1565 and renewed in 1576. Cited by Moses Trani, their contents indicate that "the officials, and some of the rabbis, and some individuals" made a concerted effort to impose their will on the entire Ashkenazi congregation; that is, without exception, its members were expected to remain within the Ashkenazi congregational structure and were forbidden to mix with other congregations for the purposes of prayer or study.[51]

Apart from two laconic references to the Ashkenazi yeshivah, one in a responsum from 1576 and the other in an early-seventeenth-century letter,[52] no details have survived regarding the Ashkenazi communal institutions. An additional late-sixteenth-century source indicates the existence of two Ashkenazi yeshivot.[53]

Little information has survived regarding Ashkenazi sages active in Safed, neither for its period of flowering nor its decline.[54] Some are identifiable by the appellation "Ashkenazi," which was appended to their names. Several of the most prominent Ashkenazi figures who resided but briefly in the city include: (1) Isaac Luria Ashkenazi, resident of Safed from 1569 until his demise in summer 1572; (2) Bezalel Ashkenazi, a rabbi in Egypt for most of his life, who spent his last years in Jerusalem but also resided in Safed for a very brief period during the mid-1570s when he headed a yeshivah together with Sefardi ḥakhamim; (3) Joseph Ashkenazi, an unusual figure nicknamed *Ha-Tanna ha-Elohi* or *He-Ḥasid,* who has recently aroused scholarly interest. Known for his zealous preservation of the talmudic tradition, he systematically opposed the partisans of philosophical education, going so far as to speak out strongly against Maimonides' philosophical writings. He is best known for his critical edition of the text of the Mishnah; (4) kabbalist Samson Back, mentioned earlier; (5) Zechariah Zaksel Frank, whose two sons David and Moses served as dayyanim in Safed.[55] In the sixteenth century's latter half, one of the Ashkenazi kahal's leading figures was (6) Judah Aberlin (Aberlein?). This scion of a leading wealthy Ashkenazi family in Salonika evidently arrived in Safed in the 1560s and became the head of the city's Ashkenazi kahal. Aberlin came into the public eye by virtue of his fierce opposition to the tax exemption for scholars issued by the nagid's court.[56]

H. HUNGARIANS

Evidence for the presence of a tiny Hungarian community in Safed is found in the Ottoman taḥrir registers. In 1555/56 this kahal numbered twelve households, and in 1567/68 it numbered fifteen.[57] A Hungarian kahal is also mentioned in a late-sixteenth/early-seventeenth-century responsum by Yom Tov Ṣahalon.[58] Despite its affinity with the Ashkenazi tradition, like Safed's other kehalim the Hungarian kahal apparently maintained its autonomy.[59]

Additional kehalim are known to have existed in Safed, perhaps as subdivisions of a larger kahal to which they were socially and culturally allied: for example, the Sicilian congregation,[60] and the "Romanian" congregation, which preserved the traditions of the Romaniot or Byzantine communities.[61] In addition, we know of the presence of Jews from Kurdistan,[62] and even from Bosnia.[63]

I. INTERCOMMUNAL RELATIONSHIPS

Unlike Jerusalem, where issues of communal hegemony were resolved with the recognition and perhaps even the acceptance of the Sefardi kahal's dominant position, in the Safed kehillah internal tensions were rife among the larger congregations especially, against the background of the struggle for preeminence within the larger communal framework. Each congregational leader had before him the primary goal of preserving his kahal's unique traditions; furthermore, each aspired to recruit members of other congregations to their ranks, whether of similar or different background, in order to enhance his kahal's

Table 4. Communities and Congregations in Safed According to Population Censuses

Congregations	1525/26	1555/56		1567/68		1596/97	
	H.	H.	B.	H.	B.	H.	B.
Musta'rab[2]	131	98	10	70			
French (Provençal)[1]	48						
Portuguese (Conversos)[1]	21	143	18	200			
Maghrebi[2]	33	38	7	52	3		
Spanish (Cordova)[2]		35	7	53	2		
Spanish (Castile)[2]		181	12	200			
Spanish (Aragon and Catalonia)[2]		51	3	72			
Spanish (Seville)[1]		67	4	160			
Ashkenazi[2]		20	1	43	7		
Hungarian[2]		12		15			
Italian[2]		29		35			
Italian (Apulia)[1]		21	1	25			
Italian (Calabria)[2]		24		20			
Sicilian[3]							
Bosnian[3]							
Romaniot[4]							
Kurdish[4]							
Yemenite[4]							
Total	233	719	63	915	12	904	93

Legend: H.=Households; B.=Bachelors

[1] Based on Cohen and Lewis, *Population and Revenue*

[2] Based on Cohen and Lewis, ibid., and Hütteroth and Abdulfattah, *Historical Geography.*

[3] Based on Hütteroth and Abdulfattah, ibid., only.

[4] Based on other sources.

Please note that the data for the 1525/26, 1555/56, and 1567/68 censuses are based on Cohen and Lewis, ibid., 161, while the data for the 1596/97 census come from Hütteroth and Abdulfattah, ibid., 52. (The final census contains no breakdown according to congregations or communities.)

power and influence within the larger communal framework. Earlier I noted one area of intercongregational friction, the Musta'rab kahal's objections to Sefardi dominance in the Safed kehillah, regarding the elimination of the Musta'rab prayer rite especially. In addition, we have noted that the Ashkenazi congregation sought to keep its membership intact by means of takkanot, stressing the obligatory nature of this congregational affiliation.

A glimpse of the nature of this power struggle within the larger communal structure, the battle for constituents, is found in a responsum by Moses Trani (1562).[64] The inquiry raised the question of how communal belonging was to be determined—from family origin or from geographical origin, which would take immigration patterns into account—against the background of an attempt to legislate affiliation by communal accord. An arrangement reached among the "congregations in a certain city," undoubtedly a reference to Safed where clear guidelines for determining communal affiliation were in effect, stipulated that a Jew born in the same land as his father but whose grandfather was born elsewhere would belong to the kahal of the land where he himself was born. If, however, his father's birthplace differed from his, he would then belong to his father's congregation. Trani was approached to rule on the validity of this accord in the context of a dispute that had broken out between the "Aragonese congregation" and the "Italian congregation." The Aragonese congregation argued that family origin was the deciding factor, that is, if the family originated from Aragon, both father and son should be counted as members of the Aragonese congregation even if the father was born in Italy. The opening argument stated:

> The congregations in a certain city made an agreement that whoever came to the city [Safed] if both he and his father were born in Italy, even though his grandfather came from Portugal or Castile or Aragon or some other kingdom, he should belong to the Italian congregation. And if his father was born in one of the forementioned kingdoms, though he himself was born in Italy he should belong to [his father's] kingdom, and the same principle applied to all the nations. Upon this haskamah's renewal, the Aragonese congregation raised objections, saying that it was not right that someone who is [really] Aragonese, or from another kingdom, should be considered Italian simply because he and his father were born in Italy. They argued further that one of the congregations had reached a compromise with the Italian congregation even prior to the haskamah, [to the effect] that if individuals came from Italy who had themselves been born in Italy as were their fathers, they would not be forced to abide by this agreement. Because of this compromise they did not join in the haskamah. They accepted the agreeement on a provisional basis only, for if they had protested, the upholding of the agreement between the representatives of the different congregations, may God protect and preserve them, would have been impossible. [Moses Trani, *Responsa,* pt. 1, no. 307]

In his reply, Trani recognized the Aragonese contention that they had not accepted the haskamah upon its renewal. He wrote:

> If this haskamah was not accepted by the Aragonese congregation, the other congregations do not have the power to force them to obey it. Therefore, whoever comes from Italy, even if [both] he and his father were born there, if his forebears were from the kingdom of Aragon, so-called by virtue of the Aragonese language, he shall belong to the Aragonese congregation according to the established practice that each person is assigned to the congregation to which he belongs according to linguistic criteria, and not to any other congregation. Thus says Moses Trani. [Moses Trani, *Responsa,* pt. 1, no. 307]

This greater congregational independence and variety influenced the pattern of Safed's communal organization, which will be considered in the next chapter. The larger size of the community certainly played a role in the greater autonomy demonstrated by the Safed congregations. Nonetheless, in Safed, as in Jerusalem, Sefardi dominance was the rule throughout most of the century. It appears, however, that this was on the wane from the sixteenth century's last quarter on, as the spiritual giants belonging to the first- and second-generation expellees from Spain died out, and with them the pure Spanish tradition. The third-generation Sefardim, less rooted in their Spanish heritage, were hard put to compete with the traditions imported by new arrivals in the sixteenth century's latter half. In addition, as was the case in Jerusalem, the severe economic crisis of the 1570s affected the status of the Safed Sefardim, depriving them of their sources of income.[65] We turn now to a consideration of the broader communal structure in sixteenth-century Safed.

11 Communal Organization

Unlike Jerusalem, where the Jewish community was administered under a dual system of leadership headed by two main officeholders (the dayyan and the shaykh al-yahud), in Safed, a different arrangement was in effect. Each congregation had its own separate administration, whose leaders handled its collective affairs. The individual congregations were joined together in an umbrella organization, the *kolel,* which administered the affairs of the kehillah as a whole. But the kolel was not the sole institution that served the entire community. Sixteenth-century Safed saw the development of a Council of Sages and of a supreme court, with influence that extended beyond Safed by virtue of the force of the influential personalities who stood at its head. Unfortunately, the extant sources provide no more than a glimpse of the internal workings of Safed's Jewish community and not much on the broader communal or the congregational level.

On the microcosmic level, each congregation had its own leaders, *memunim* ("officials"),[1] who exercised the following powers: issuing of regulations for their individual congregations (an example of which will be examined below);[2] fund-raising abroad for communal needs, generally via emissaries;[3] tax collection for communal needs and for payment of governmental taxes as well—the poll tax (jizya), for example.[4] Little information is available concerning the precise nature of the Safed congregations' internal structure. The extant material relates almost exclusively to the Ashkenazi congregation, which, as we have seen, had a special status and therefore cannot necessarily be regarded as a representative model for the city's other congregations. In 1576 the Ashkenazi kahal issued a series of haskamot to earlier regulations with the addition of new clauses. These regulations were preserved in a responsum by Moses Trani: "This is the synopsis of the haskamot made by the Ashkenazi congregation of Safed, may it be speedily rebuilt, as promulgated by the memunim, some of the sages and other individuals, effective for fifty years from the 12th of Shevat, in the year 5336 to the Creation [14 January 1576]" [Moses Trani, *Responsa,* pt. 3, no. 96].[5]

These haskamot represented the renewal of regulations first issued in 1565, which had a ten-year limit (par. 1); in addition, new regulations were now promulgated (pars. 2–10). Aimed primarily at preserving congregational solidarity, forbidding the individual to act on his own initiative at variance to the communal good, the takkanot placed particular emphasis on the handling of special and regular financial contributions received by the congregation:

> They agreed furthermore that no individual from the said holy congregation shall write to the Diaspora in such a way that the congregation incurs a loss; nor shall he write to any person requesting money for a yeshivah or for the poor. If an individual receives funds for disbursement, the said individual must hand them over to the treasurer of the abovementioned congregation. (par. 3)
>
> Furthermore, they agreed that no one shall make contributions on an individual basis. Even if a Sefardi or an Ashkenazi arrives from abroad and gives a sum of money to a particular individual to disburse as he sees fit, that individual must turn the money over to the treasurers. (par. 6)

Furthermore, members of the Ashkenazi congregation were forbidden to pray anywhere other than in their own synagogue: "They also agreed that no individual from the abovementioned congregation shall pray outside of the synagogue. Nor shall he pray elsewhere at any time during the year. At the very least, everyone is obligated to pray in the synagogue on the Sabbath" (par. 5). Similarly, the sole acceptable venue for study was the synagogue. "Scholars were to receive support only if they studied in the synagogue" (par. 4).

In its attempt to safeguard its singular character and its autonomy within the broad congregational spectrum in Safed, the Ashkenazi congregation explicitly obligated each and every member of the congregation to uphold the congregational regulations unfailingly:

> Furthermore they agreed that even if a rabbi instructs his disciple not to sign one of these agreements, nonetheless the disciple is obligated to sign. (par. 7)
>
> And if any sage, or sages, in the city rises up in opposition and comes to the assistance of someone who does not wish to sign, his words shall be null and void, as insubstantial as broken pottery. (par. 9)

This extreme resistance to possible influence by members of other Safed congregations conforms to my previous observations on the Ashkenazi congregation in Jerusalem, which, like its Safed counterpart, also zealously guarded its independence.[6] Moreover, the "holy Ashkenazi congregation" was explicitly excluded from a haskamah to an earlier regulation, aimed at preventing divisiveness and discord in these cities. Signed in 1623 by Jerusalem and Safed sages, of all the congregations the Ashkenazi one alone was recognized as possessing the right to organize independently.[7]

Most, but possibly not all, of the congregations maintained the standard institutions—a synagogue, a study house (bet midrash), and perhaps a yeshivah as well. Several of the larger congregations boasted more than one synagogue or yeshivah. A Turkish document dated November 1584 indicates a total presence of thirty-two synagogues in Safed,[8] while a Hebrew source dated 1607 attests to thirty-one.[9] As early as 1525, the Sefardi kahal boasted two synagogues,[10] but as its membership grew, so did the number of its synagogues. We also know that the small Ashkenazi congregation maintained two yeshivot in the sixteenth century; it therefore seems more than likely that the large Sefardi kahal had more than one yeshivah.[11] The leading congregations also maintained their own courts. Extant responsa literature cites rulings and deeds signed by Sefardi dayyanim.[12] But the Sefardim were not alone in possessing a bet din. The Ashkenazi congregation also boasted its own court, as did the Portuguese (converso) congregation.[13]

On the macrocosmic level, the Safed kehillah also had a collective leadership whose members were drawn from the memunim, the representatives of the different congregations.[14] Known as a "kolel,"[15] this umbrella organization's sphere of responsibility encompassed most public matters affecting the overall community. Not only did the kolel dispatch emissaries to the Diaspora, it also possessed the authority to set the communal tax and the manner of its collection.[16] It seems that in its role as the representative communal body, the kolel negotiated with the governmental authorities and promulgated regulations on matters affecting the entire Safed kehillah.

The kolel was not the sole institution that served the entire community. In addition, we know of the existence of a "Council of Sages" whose members were drawn from the congregational courts. Its sessions were held in what was termed the "Bet ha-Vaad" (Academy of Scholars).[17] A partial definition of this institution is found in a responsum by Moses Trani: "In previous years we gathered in the Bet ha-Vaad to see to the many breaches in the city [Isa. 22:9], and to hedge the vineyard of the Lord of Hosts, the God of Israel. Included in what we taught or took note of were some commandments that had been neglected by the people" [Moses Trani, *Responsa,* pt. 2, no. 115].

The Council of Sages numbered between ten and twenty members. Established by Jacob Berab long before the eruption of the ordination controversy in 1538, its members included rabbis ordained by Jacob Berab, his direct disciples, and their students. This scholarly forum also served as the pool for the different configurations of Safed's *Bet Din ha-Gadol* (Great Court), which was the venue for thorny legal problems. Initially, four judges sat on the panel; at a later date, five was the accepted composition of the court.[18]

The Bet ha-Vaad was chaired by the leading halakhic scholars of the day. Following Jacob Berab's death in 1541, Joseph Caro chaired the Bet ha-Vaad until his own demise in 1575. Caro was also head of the bet din, whose judges included two of the foremost contemporary halakhists, Moses Trani and Israel di Curiel. Shortly after 1564, they were joined by David ibn Abi Zimra, who relocated to Safed from Jerusalem in or just after that year.[19]

It was Joseph Caro who probed the character of this bet din in a responsum, awarding it the status of a Supreme Court for the Jewish world. In his reply to an inquiry "regarding someone who was handed down a decision and then asked the court, 'instruct me as to its basis,'" Joseph Caro broadly examined the very concept of a High Court, enunciating the principle that the court was not accountable to its litigants for its decisions. He also ruled in this context that the Safed court, which he chaired, possessed the standing of a Supreme Court. He stated: "Behold, in our day the bet din of this city is recognized as expert by many, as greater in wisdom and in number than any other in the known world. Queries are forwarded from the four corners of the earth, nor do any question its decisions. As this is the case, the court has the standing of a Supreme Court, especially as all the communities appointed them [its members]" [Joseph Caro, *Shu"t Avqat Rokhel,* no. 17].[20]

Undoubtedly, the court referred to in this responsum was the legal forum founded by Jacob Berab. Three of Berab's four closest disciples, whom he ordained in 1538 as part of his plan to establish a Sanhedrin in Safed, sat on this court. Following the aborted plan to establish a Sanhedrin, this small bet din evidently served as the supreme court for the entire Jewish world.

In conclusion, we must bear in mind the relationship between the Jewish courts and the civil authorities. Regarding Jerusalem, we saw that the appointment of the chief dayyan, and perhaps that of the entire bet din, required the local kadi's authorization. Moreover, we must remember that the Jerusalem court was empowered to exercise only limited powers of punishment. It seems logical to infer that the same procedure governed the appointment and status of dayyanim in Safed as well.

As indicated by this chapter's brevity, little substantive data are available regarding Safed's communal structure beyond the names of its major institutions—the kolel, the Bet ha-Vaad, and the Bet Din. Evidently, while autonomous in many spheres, maintaining their own synagogues, yeshivot, and even courts, the congregations did cooperate in matters affecting the community as a whole. Nonetheless, many areas remain to be elucidated: how the congregational and communal memunim were chosen and the length of their terms in office; the number of representatives from each congregation to the kolel; if the intercongregational tensions alluded to in the previous chapter found expression in their deliberations. What does emerge is a clear picture of the role played by Safed's noted sages, Berab, Caro, and others in two of the three communal institutions—the Bet ha-Vaad and the Bet Din ha-Gadol. The dominant role of these individuals in Safed's communal and more particularly its intellectual life will be further explored in the next chapter.

12 Centers of Jewish Learning—Structure and Program of Study

Sixteenth-century Safed witnessed the accelerated development of its intellectual-spiritual sphere. It was a center of learning not only for the greatest sages of the day, codifiers and mystics who left their lasting mark on the fields of halakhah, kabbalah, and textual study of the fundamental Jewish texts, but also for householders who attended daily study sessions in the synagogue. There have been great centers of Jewish learning throughout the ages; but in some respects sixteenth-century Safed represents a unique peak of accomplishment. Although intellectual trends are not within the purview of this volume and their examination is best left to specialists in the field, we cannot proceed without briefly mentioning some of the lasting achievements of the age: Lurianic kabbalah, Caro's legal code—the *Shulḥan Arukh,* textual examination and commentaries on the Mishnah, which represent but a fraction of the century's outstanding achievements. So great were the sages in that day and age that they even contemplated the renewal of ordination, the reinstatement of a Sanhedrin modeled on the one of Second Temple times, the supreme authority of its day. Let us now turn to an examination of the institutional settings in which this unusual degree of scholarship found its expression.

A. YESHIVOT: GENERAL SURVEY; FINANCIAL ARRANGEMENTS

In sixteenth-century Safed, intensive exoteric study of Torah was inextricably linked to the study of esoteric lore. Beginning with the 1520s, Safed experienced an intellectual-spiritual flowering that continued to intensify until the century's end, leaving a lasting mark on Jewish culture. Hebrew sources dating from the mid-sixteenth until the early-seventeenth century paint an idyllic picture of a broad-branched intellectual development in both halakhah and kabbalah. Joseph Caro gave apt expression to this phenomenon in a responsum embellished with flowery turns of phrase (1568 or 1569):[1]

> In the city of Safed, may it be speedily rebuilt . . . God's vineyard, the house of Israel, was handsome, beautiful indeed, the vale bud-

> ded, the vines blossomed [Cant. 1:16, 6:11]. Heads of yeshivot and their students study incessantly. . . . It was a tower of strength [Ps. 61:4] built with turrets [Cant. 4:4], devoted to the study of Torah. The wine press of Torah was hewn therein, the choice wine made from its grapes rises and falls in the wars of Torah. They rest in the depths of halakhah. For our vineyard is in blossom [Cant. 2:15], the mandrakes yield their fragrance, at our doors are all choice fruits [Cant. 7:14]. These are the students who grew lofty and bore fruits of wisdom. . . . From there instruction and light shall come forth to the entire Diaspora. There is a bowl above it and its seven lamps give light which reflects on its face [Zech. 4:2]. [Joseph Caro, *Shu"t Avqat Rokhel,* no. 1]

The same state of affairs is depicted in a letter sent in 1575 by Joseph Caro and his student, Moses Galante, to the Provençal congregations in the Piedmont, northern Italy: "It is well known everywhere, that God has enlarged our borders [Exod. 34:24] with students, who themselves have raised many disciples, for the earth shall be full of the knowledge of the Lord [Isa. 11:9], [that is, with] many yeshivot, each according to its own idiom" [David, "Community of Cuneo," 440].

Although relatively extensive data on Safed's kabbalists and sages are available, especially for the sixteenth century's latter half, Safed's scholarly institutions during that period—its yeshivot and houses of study (batei midrash)—still require further investigation. For data regarding Safed's yeshivot in the late 1560s we turn to Zechariah al-Ḍāhiri [Zacharia al-Dahri], whose *Sefer Hamussar,* composed in 1568–69, is an important source of information:[2] "Mordecai of Sidon [the author, Zechariah al-Ḍāhiri] related: I traveled from a city in Syria [either Hamath or Damascus] through the Upper Galilee to the city of Safed . . . and the presence of the *shekhinah* rests on Safed, which has a large community, and, without exaggeration, some fourteen thousand study Talmud in eighteen yeshivot" [Zechariah al-Ḍāhiri, *Sefer Hamussar,* 116].

Although the population figure cited by Al-Ḍāhiri is certainly exaggerated,[3] the number of yeshivot cited apparently was not. Later sources dating from the early seventeenth century confirm the existence of a similar number of yeshivot. Witness the letter sent in 1604 by the leaders of the Safed community to Ḥayyim Cansino in Oran (Algeria): "In this city, perfect in beauty, there are twelve synagogues and sixteen yeshivot, and a Talmud Torah for young children."[4] In a letter sent from Safed in 1607, Solomon Shlomil Meinstral of Dreznitz observed: "I found a holy community here in Safed, which is a large city of God [Jonah 3:3], a city full of wisdom with nearly three hundred great rabbis, all pious and men of deeds. I found eighteen yeshivot in

Safed, may it be speedily rebuilt, and twenty-one synagogues, and a large bet midrash" [Yaari, *Letters,* 197].

An additional source, dating from the early 1590s, attests to a hyperbolic number of yeshivot in Safed, some thirty-two.[5] Nonetheless, the sources cited above do corroborate the state of affairs described by Joseph Caro and Moses Galante, of a city devoted to intensive study of Torah. The statement "many yeshivot, each according to its own idiom" evidently refers to yeshivot associated with the individual congregations. No fewer than sixteen congregations of varying size are known to have existed in Safed at that time; we must assume, however, that some of the smaller congregations lacked the wherewithal to maintain either a yeshivah or a bet midrash, whereas, as we shall see below, some of the larger congregations, the Sefardi one, for example, maintained several yeshivot.

Another little-studied aspect of Safed's sixteenth-century yeshivot is the question of how the yeshivot were funded—their local and foreign sources of financing. Fairly extensive data are extant for the sixteenth century's latter half concerning various kehillot and individuals (in Europe, in Italy especially, and in the Ottoman Empire) who assumed the obligation of providing general financial support for Safed's Jewish community. Within the broader context of fund-raising activities initiated by the kolel or the congregations themselves, however, we find but scant reference to funds specifically designated for the yeshivot.[6] Joseph Sambari noted that Joseph Bagilar, a wealthy sixteenth-century Egyptian philanthropist,[7] "supported the ARI [Isaac Luria] of blessed memory's yeshivah in Safed, may it be speedily rebuilt, for ten years at his own expense."[8] We also have information concerning funding for the yeshivah in Ein Zitun near Safed. Founded by Moses ben Makhir in the latter half of the sixteenth century, this yeshivah functioned until close to the century's end.[9]

The yeshivot undoubtedly received a share of the communal budget; however, their needs were not always perceived as a top priority. Indeed, on at least one occasion, conditions of severe economic distress led the city fathers to divert funds destined for a "certain yeshivah in Safed" to general communal needs. Such an occurrence is documented in a late-sixteenth/early-seventeenth-century responsum:

> It happened that, prior to his death, the elderly honorable rabbi, Mordecai Dada [or Dede], a resident of Egypt, left instructions regarding the disposal of his property. In this will he endowed a sum of money to a yeshivah in Safed, may it be speedily rebuilt. . . . He also decreed that the promissory note held by R. Jacob Nazo, now [residing] in Venice, in the amount of 107,000 muayyadi . . . was to be disposed of absolutely as follows: a third to the yeshivah of the

perfect sage R. Abraham Monzon,[10] may God preserve and protect him, and another third to a yeshivah in the holy city of Jerusalem, may it be speedily rebuilt, and the remaining third to a yeshivah in Safed, may it be speedily rebuilt. These yeshivot were to benefit from the interest, leaving the capital untouched. . . . It now came to pass that the leaders of the city of Safed, may it be speedily rebuilt, upon perceiving the depths of poverty in the city and the debt owed to the nations, agreed to appropriate the abovementioned principal to pay their debts, saying that without a city, there can be no yeshivot. [Yom Tov Ṣahalon, *Responsa,* no. 158]

B. AN EARLY-SIXTEENTH-CENTURY YESHIVAH IN SAFED

Laconic references to institutionalized study of Torah are found in three sources dating from the sixteenth century's first decade:

1. The letter sent by Safed's Musta'rab sages to Isaac Sholal in Egypt in 1510 mentioned above contains oblique references to educational frameworks maintained by this congregation; for example: "But every day without exception we set apart hours for [studying] the Law,"[11] and, "The exalted Nagid assists everyone who studies Torah, and we were informed that he gave assistance to the Sefardim but has provided no aid for your servants, the Musta'rabs . . . nor do we cease at all to study the Talmud."[12] In addition, the "yeshivah" in Safed is explicitly mentioned.[13]

2. The first half of a letter from Egypt addressed to "the perfect sages, the rabbis who sit in the holy yeshivah in Safed" was found in the Cairo Geniza.[14] This letter imparted news of the death of the Safed emissary, Samuel Bahalul. As this emissary is known from other sources dated from 1500 to 1510, this letter may be attributed to the same period.

3. In other contexts, we have already mentioned "a letter sent by Safed's sages to the rabbis of the holy yeshivah in Jerusalem concerning the sabbatical year" in 1504, which was signed by fourteen sages.[15] It seems likely that most or all were associated with the Safed yeshivah, the absence of any explicit references to this institution notwithstanding.

C. HEADS OF YESHIVOT

Because of the paucity of detailed information on the course of study in the yeshivot, we must confine the discussion to a brief excursus on the eminent rabbis who served as their heads and set the tone for intellectual-spiritual activity in Safed. One point is clear, however.

The rabbis who headed the Safed yeshivot were heirs to the method of Isaac Canpanton (Campanton), the *gaon* of Castile.[16] Canpanton's disciples, themselves outstanding figures of the expulsion generation, bequeathed this speculative method to their students in the yeshivot they founded throughout the Ottoman Empire.[17] In the case of Safed, the train of transmission proceeded via Isaac Aboab who headed two Castilian yeshivot, in Buitrago and Guadalajaru,[18] and who was a direct disciple of Canpanton, to Jacob Berab, discussed below.[19]

Although in this context justice cannot be done to Isaac Canpanton's speculative method for talmudic study, it is impossible to proceed without briefly surveying some of its characteristics. This method incorporated close intellectual-didactic scrutiny of the talmudic text (*sugya*) with an eye to derivation of practical halakhah in matters of current relevance. This intensive textual study relied heavily on the commentaries of Rashi, the Tosafists, and Naḥmanides' novellae (*Ḥiddushey ha-Ramban*).[20] The students were apparently themselves eminent scholars; as we shall see below, this was certainly the case in Safed. In addition, the study of practical halakhah using Maimonides' *Mishneh Torah* as a text was an integral part of the program as practiced in Safed. This aspect of study, however, was not restricted to scholars alone; part of daily study sessions held immediately after prayer, it was open to scholars and laymen alike.[21]

Let us now turn to the practitioners of this method in sixteenth-century Safed.

1. Jacob Berab

Best known perhaps for his attempt to reinstate rabbinical ordination and the Sanhedrin, Jacob Berab arrived in Safed in the mid-1520s and gave Torah scholarship there a major impetus. Berab's domination of the city's intellectual scene until his death in 1541 cannot be overstated. Even though Berab first came to Safed in 1524, he did not immediately settle there permanently. He apparently relocated to Damascus in 1527, subsequently dividing his time between Egypt, Gaza, Jerusalem, Safed, and Egypt again, before settling permanently in Safed in 1535.[22]

Logic dictates that Jacob Berab founded a yeshivah in Safed during his first period of residence there. All the contemporary Safed scholars were evidently enrolled in this yeshivah, which essentially functioned as a forum for discussions of halakhic matters by the ḥaverim (rabbinic colleagues); the resulting halakhic decisions and responsa were based on majority resolutions reached by a representative quorum. In the belief that academic study of Torah alone was insufficient, Jacob Berab sought to instill in his disciples a level of mastery that would enable them to serve as dayyanim and teachers of the law in turn. Berab communicated this hope to Solomon ben Yaqar of Rhodes: "And the ḥaverim who hear my voice, who have hopes of succeeding in their studies, will give instruction in the law in Israel" [*Quntres ha-Semikhah* (ordination pamphlet)].[23] Somewhat similar sentiments were expressed by Jonathan Galante and Moses Parodis, the editors of Berab's responsa (Izmir, 1655):

> The remarkable gaon, the ordained rabbi, outstanding in his generation, the honored rabbi Jacob Berab of blessed memory . . . from whom the light of Torah went forth to all of Israel in the land of Israel from Safed, may it be speedily rebuilt. There the thrones of judgment stood [Ps. 122:5]. He undertook intensive efforts on behalf of the Torah and expanded its borders with students, all wise, chiefs of thousands sitting in judgment, all teachers of the law in Israel. [Jacob Berab, *Responsa,* editors' introduction][24]

Jacob Berab saw himself as heir to the method of academic study and speculation expounded by the greatest Spanish scholars of the pre-Expulsion era. The sources convey the distinct impression that the students engaged in study in the yeshivah were important scholars in their own right. Disputed issues were examined in-depth under the supervision of the head of the yeshivah, "to whose voice they attended" and whose decisions they accepted. In essence, there were two educational frameworks—one for the ḥaverim, the older students already proficient in Talmud and practical halakhah, and the other for neophytes just embarking on talmudic studies. At their sessions, the ḥaverim concentrated on selected knotty talmudic issues and difficult texts; they did not study the talmudic tractates in sequence. The heart of this method was the give and take of the debate between the ḥaverim, while the head of the yeshivah acted as the moderator of the discussion.[25]

Berab began to groom several of his finest students to serve as dayyanim and posekim as the initial step in his plan to establish a legislative body along the lines of the Sanhedrin from Second Temple times, with members who were ordained scholars. This plan began to assume practical form in 1536.[26] Among Berab's disciples five outstanding scholars must be noted: (1) Joseph Caro, the leading member of the circle, already a renowned scholar upon his arrival in Safed in 1536; (2) Moses Trani, who wrote in a letter to Joseph Caro pursuant to a disagreement between them: "I will remind him who set the tone for the discussion of the difficult cases which we learned in the yeshivah of our deceased teacher of blessed memory."[27] Both Joseph Caro and Moses Trani received ordination from Jacob Berab; (3) Abraham Shalom, a well-known ḥakham in Turkey prior to his arrival in Safed. Of him it was said that "this rabbi was a disciple-ḥaver to R. Jacob Berab of blessed memory."[28] He too was ordained by Berab; (4) Israel di Curiel, who later became one of Safed's most eminent dayyanim; and (5) Menaḥem ha-Bavli, who came to Safed from Greece in 1537.

Jacob Berab's yeshivah formed the model for the ones subsequently founded by his students, Joseph Caro and Moses Trani, and their disciples. In these yeshivot, the methodological principles of Isaac Canpanton as introduced and implemented by Berab continued to dominate the course of study.[29]

2. Joseph Caro

Following Jacob Berab's death in 1541, his disciple Joseph Caro inherited his position as the leading force shaping Safed's intellectual-spiritual life, a position he held for almost thirty-five years until his demise in 1575. Various sources portray him as an extraordinary leader who did not confine himself to the ivory tower of halakhic codification, but rather combined his function as a teacher and posek with the assumption of public duties. His multifaceted activities are reflected in several of his responsa: "I was burdened with teaching in the yeshivah, in addition to being burdened with the duties of the congregations, may God protect them."[30] Or as he states elsewhere: "I saw that his intentions were desirable and his deeds were for the sake of heaven while I was burdened with the battle of the commandments, whether in the form of study with the *ḥaverim maqshivim* in the yeshivah . . . or whether [in the form of] the burden of the holy congregations, may God protect and preserve them, the trouble, the burden, and the bickering [paraphrase of Deut. 1:12]" [Joseph Caro, *Shu"t Beit Yosef,* "Laws of Levirate Marriage," no. 3, p. 393].

In all probability these references to the congregations (kehillot, in the plural) are related to Joseph Caro's role in the overall kehillah administration, undoubtedly his duties on the Bet ha-Vaad.[31] Logic dictates that Caro chaired the "Council of Sages," which united all the congregations in Safed under its aegis and which served as the forum for discussion of issues affecting the community as a whole. On more than one occasion, difficult questions were put to this broad forum that necessitated a decision by its central judicial body, the bet din ha-gadol (supreme court), which Caro is definitely known to have chaired.[32]

As noted above, Joseph Caro also stressed that in addition to his communal duties he "was burdened with teaching in the yeshivah." Although Caro himself made several references to his yeshivah and to his role as instructor in his treatise *Maggid Mesharim,* little detailed information is extant regarding the Safed yeshivah he headed. A somewhat hyperbolic description was provided by the Yemenite traveler, Zechariah al-Ḍāhiri, who visited Safed in 1568: "In particular, the great luminary, the sage R. Joseph Caro, from whose yeshivah the sages of Safed do not depart . . . after he studied the Talmud for seven years apart."[33] Nor is any substantive information available concerning the course of study followed in Caro's yeshivah. The most feasible assumption is that it followed the Spanish tradition as crystallized earlier in Safed under his teacher and mentor, Jacob Berab.[34] We cannot entirely rule out the possibility that Caro may have introduced esoteric lore and Jewish philosophical thought into the curriculum, as Zechariah al-Ḍāhiri alludes to Caro's prowess in both realms: "For the Talmud dwells in his heart . . . exoteric and esoteric wisdom are sealed in his heart."[35]

Al-Ḍāhiri did not confine his description of the yeshivah and its head to this laconic observation; rather, he praised the system of instruction as he personally witnessed it on a Sabbath. Caro's homily, which was based on the "plain meaning and the kabbalah," was followed by a discourse on the philosophical question of "the soul and its attributes" presented by one of his students. Al-Ḍāhiri recapitulates these talks, using flowery language, as follows:

> One Sabbath I went to his yeshivah, to observe the splendid glory of his majesty. I sat in the entrance, near the doorpost . . . while the elderly sage sat on a seat [1 Sam. 4:13], speaking of the topic of the day . . . the verse "The law of the Lord is perfect, restoring the soul" [Ps. 19:8], which the honored exalted sage taught according to its plain meaning and the kabbalah. Some two hundred worthy students sat before him, seated on benches. When his words of wisdom were completed, he hinted to a student opposite him to speak about the soul, its attributes and its purpose, and in general. And he [the student] stood before him with his pleasant teaching, saying: "Our rabbi has taught us perfectly, it is not from our wisdom." [Zechariah al-Ḍāhiri, *Sefer Hamussar,* 117][36]

Although the discourse on psychology as presented by Zechariah al-Ḍāhiri is clearly a literary reworking of a contemporary medieval view, this account appears to contain more than just a modicum of historical truth;[37] it implies that in Caro's yeshivah halakhic studies were supplemented by philosophical and kabbalistic inquiries.[38] This attestation to Caro's interest in philosophy is surprising given the absence of philosophical inquiries in Caro's own works, even in contexts in which they would be germane; in Caro's commentary (*Kesef Mishneh)* to Maimonides' philosophical chapters in "The Book of Knowledge," for example. Perhaps al-Ḍāhiri's account reflects a change in attitude that occurred late in Caro's life. Whereas Caro refrained from introducing philosophical inquiries into his halakhic works, perhaps in his later years, for reasons unknown to us, he may have encouraged his students to devote time to philosophical study.

Several sources indicate that in his role as head of the overall communal administration, Caro also served as a patron of additional Safed yeshivot, apparently taking an active role in their founding, their administration, and their upkeep. These yeshivot, which were established within the various congregational contexts, were often headed by his close colleagues and disciples. As we saw earlier, Caro described the multitude of congregational yeshivot in a letter to the officials, parnassim, and leaders of the Provençal community in the Piedmont.[39] In this letter Caro related his role in establishing a Provençal yeshivah in Safed, to which he appointed his disciple Moses Galante as head. Joseph Caro appealed to the parnassim for monetary contributions toward the founding of the yeshivah, saying: "Now God has inspired us to found a yeshivah for the holy Provençal congregation, which is to be headed by one of my disciples, the perfect scholar, R. Moses Galante, may God preserve him."[40] In a different letter, Caro appealed directly to Moses da Rosa, also known as Moses Provençal (Provenẓali), an outstanding rabbinic figure in Mantua and one of the greatest contemporary rabbis in Italy,[41] for generous material assistance toward "the needs of five yeshivot" in Safed.[42]

An additional source, a copy of a pamphlet on ordination for teaching, indicates that Caro headed another yeshivah in Safed in conjunction with three other ḥakhamim. This pamphlet, sent from Safed by Jeremiah ben Levi Maurogonato (Mavrogonato) to his brother Eliezer Maurogonato who resided in Crete, notes: "We meticulously observed this matter in the yeshivah of the masters and sages R. Joseph Caro of blessed memory, and R. Bezalel Ashkenazi of blessed memory, and R. Solomon Sagis, and R. Z. ibn Ziza of blessed memory."[43] Clearly, Joseph Caro made a significant contribution toward the material and intellectual development of Safed's yeshivot. Despite the difficult economic conditions that led to a decline in Safed's Jewish population, his efforts were crowned with a large measure of success.

Caro was blessed with many disciples, not all of whom are known. Among his disciples, however, were some outstanding individuals who by virtue of their intellectual activity left their mark on Safed and other communities in Eretz-Israel. Naturally, certain disciples were closer to Caro than others; members of his select coterie sometimes cosigned decisions handed down by Caro and his court.[44] The following individuals are definitely known to have been students of Caro: the eminent kabbalist Moses Cordovero, Abraham ibn Asher, Baruch [of Tivoli], Moses Alshekh, and Moses Saadiah.[45] Caro ordained five disciples: Moses Alshekh, Elisha Gallico, Solomon Absaban, Jacob ben Abraham

Berab (whose grandfather had renewed ordination), and Moses Galante. Other known disciples included Jeremiah Maurogonato, Eleazar ibn Yoḥai,[46] Samuel ibn Verga,[47] Moses Baruch,[48] Moses Najara (father of poet Israel Najara), and Abraham Laniado.[49]

Caro was essentially the leading halakhist of his generation, and thus queries on cardinal issues were addressed to him and to his court by other prominent figures also well versed in halakhah. He received inquiries from the entire Jewish diaspora; we have responsa originating from Italy,[50] Egypt and Syria,[51] Turkey,[52] Greece,[53] Crete (Candia),[54] Provence,[55] and elsewhere as well.

3. Moses Trani

Moses Trani (also known by the acronym ha-Mabbit; d. 1580) was thoroughly immersed in the realm of halakhah. A contemporary and friend of Joseph Caro, he was also his fierce and outspoken rival. This mutual friction notwithstanding, Caro and Trani maintained a longstanding relationship; first as ordinees of Jacob Berab, then as members of the court chaired by Caro at least from the time of Berab's death in the early 1540s. Many responsa composed by both rabbis are extant; their opinions were often cosigned by other dayyanim and sages, including Israel di Curiel and David ibn Abi Zimra (from the mid-1560s on).[56] Moses Trani had difficulty coming to terms with Caro's absolute control of the Safed kehillah's central institutions and with his status and international renown as the outstanding scholar and posek of his time. On various occasions Trani availed himself of the opportunity to complain bitterly, in responsa and directly, about Caro's attitude toward him, criticizing him for his failure to recognize his eminence. In one instance, we find Trani asserting that his powers of instruction and legal decisions were in no way inferior to Caro's:

> Shall I fear the students who have become expert in halakhah under his [Caro's] tutelage, and partly under mine? The majority have equal need of me as of him, and in their modesty accept my words as they do his . . . for he has not the ability to contradict the plain law with idle remarks, and concerning more profound matters my pronouncements are in no way inferior to his. For he is aware, as was he who ordained us both, that my achievements equal his—that is, I have studied and taught and instructed the public just as he has, from my youth until reaching hoary maturity. [Dimitrovsky, "Dispute," 111–12]

Essentially, Moses Trani's remarks may be construed as a challenge to Caro's unquestioned status as the leading rabbinic authority of his day.[57]

Moses Trani expounded Torah for five decades in the Sefardi Bet

Yaakov congregation.[58] He also headed a yeshivah, allusions to which are found in several responsa; for example: "I taught thus to the ḥaverim in the yeshivah and to the sages close to me."[59] Elsewhere, he states: "For perhaps I will not be unencumbered after the holiday from the burden of king—who is the king but the rabbis?—and princes [Hosea 8:10]—who are the princes but the scholars?—from discussions of Torah matters and other questions addressed from abroad, and the encumbrance of the litigants—all these in addition to the appointed times of study in the yeshivah with the ḥakhamim and the students, may God preserve and protect them" [Moses Trani, *Responsa,* pt. 3, no. 15].[60]

Moses Trani undoubtedly trained many disciples, but only two of his students are known by name: Isaac Mishan and Moses ha-Levi.[61] It seems likely that Eleazar Azikri (Azkari) was also one of Trani's disciples.[62]

4. Heads of Yeshivot: The Disciples of Joseph Caro, Moses Trani, and Others

Sparse information is extant regarding those colleagues and students of Joseph Caro and Moses Trani who held positions as heads of yeshivot. Among them we must note schematically: (1) Israel di Curiel, for whom no specific yeshivah is mentioned; we are informed however that he had students: "for the ḥakham R. Israel Curiel . . . also used to go with his students";[63] (2) Moses Alshekh, who stated in his introduction to a treatise: "God has granted us two yeshivot with students";[64] (3) Elisha Gallico, referred to as "head of the yeshivah in Safed, may it be speedily rebuilt";[65] (4) Eleazar ibn Yoḥai;[66] (5) Yom Tov Ṣahalon, who remarked in a responsum: "We are burdened with studying with the students in the yeshivah";[67] (6) Ḥiyya Rofe, who mentioned his yeshivah numerous times;[68] (7) Samuel de Uceda, who remarked in the introduction to his *Iggeret Shemuel:* "I cannot endure the burden of the yeshivah";[69] and (8) possibly Joseph Sagis, for whom no direct references as the head of a yeshivah are found. Moses Galante and Eleazar Azikri were among Joseph Sagis' disciples,[70] as was Solomon Sagis, about whom his student Ḥiyya Rofe wrote: "I recall the days of my youth when I studied in the yeshivah of R. Solomon Sagis of blessed memory."[71] As we saw earlier, Jeremiah Maurogonato mentioned Solomon Sagis in conjunction with three additional sages as joint heads of a yeshivah.[72] Sagis' disciples included the following sages: Joseph Trani, Abraham Shalom, and Tuvia ben Abraham ha-Levi,[73] as well as Moses Galante, who headed the Provençal yeshivah in Safed.[74]

We also find Safed's eminent kabbalists teaching within the yeshivah framework. Some expounded exoteric Torah in conjunction with kabbalah; for example, Moses Cordovero, who, according to the testimony of his student Mordecai Dato, headed the Portuguese yeshivah in Safed.[75] Menaḥem Azariah Fano also alluded to Cordovero's yeshivah in his *Asis Rimmonim:* "Although he himself was a great talmudic scholar, he sat in the yeshivah all his life for the purpose of stimulating the students."[76] Concerning Isaac Luria (the ARI) scattered references throughout the various versions of the biographical treatise *Toledot ha-Ari* indicate his involvement in teaching exoteric Torah.[77] As we saw earlier, Luria's yeshivah benefited from the generosity of Egyptian philanthropist Joseph Bagilar for a decade.[78] Luria was succeeded by his disciple Ḥayyim Vital, who gave instruction in both exoteric and esoteric lore. We know of two additional kabbalists in Safed of the generation after Joseph Caro: Masud Azulay (or Masud the Blind) and Solomon Maaravi (or Suleiman Oḥana). Both figures are mentioned in an early-seventeenth-century letter written by Azulay's disciple, Solomon Shlomil Meinstral of Dreznitz: "Then the two heads of the yeshivot, great, wise, and pious men, men of deeds . . . went up on the podium. One was called the ḥakham R. Masud the Blind, and he was my teacher and rabbi, renowned among all Jews . . . and the second was called R. Solomon Maaravi, may God protect and preserve him" [Yaari, *Letters,* 198].[79]

This brief survey of Safed's yeshivot and their heads would be incomplete without mentioning the famous yeshivah in nearby Ein Zitun founded by Moses ben Makhir. Makhir's *Seder ha-Yom* (Venice, 1599) encapsulates the essentials of his method and teachings in exoteric and esoteric lore. The curriculum in this yeshivah encompassed study of Bible, Mishnah, Talmud with commentaries, Alfasi's Code, and Maimonides' Code. In addition, the students devoted a portion of their time to regular study of the *Zohar.*[80] The course of study in this institutional setting bears a large degree of similarity to the one followed in Safed's synagogues discussed below; nonetheless, I assume that the course of study in the yeshivah was on a higher level.

D. THE SYNAGOGUE AS A PLACE OF STUDY

Study was not restricted to the yeshivot—another framework for study, intended for laymen, could be found in the synagogue setting. Aimed at those who did not devote themselves to full-time study, the material studied was on a less demanding level. As in Jerusalem, classes were held following the morning and evening prayer services.[81] Two letters dating from the first decade of the seventeenth century, written by Solomon Shlomil Meinstral of Dreznitz, describe some of the available educational options. In his letter from 1607, he described the program of study at length:

> In all the synagogues, immediately after the evening and morning prayers, the entire congregation gathers to sit before the rabbis, some five or six classes in each synagogue. Each class studies before leaving the synagogue. One such class regularly studies Maimonides [*Mishneh Torah*], one class regularly studies *Ein Yaaqov,* one regularly studies tractate *Berakhot,* another regularly studies a chapter of the Mishnah with commentary, another learns halakhah [Talmud] with the commentaries of Rashi and the Tosafists, another regularly studies *Zohar,* and yet another regularly studies the books of the Bible—the Pentateuch, the Prophets, and the Writings. Thus no individual leaves for his work or his business in the morning without regularly devoting time to study of the Torah. The same holds true for the evenings following the prayers. On the Sabbath, everyone goes to hear the sermon delivered by the sages. [Yaari, *Letters,* 197–98]

A similar, shorter description is found in a second letter penned by Meinstral to his brother-in-law at approximately the same time:

> Following prayers the entire congregation studies regularly. They sit before the rabbis, and are divided into about six classes in each synagogue. Each class studies before leaving the synagogue. One class studies *Ein Yaaqov,* another studies the laws of the benedictions [possibly tractate *Berakhot*], another studies Maimonides, another studies Mishnah, another studies Talmud with Rashi and *Tosafot,* another studies *Zohar,* and another studies Bible. Consequently, no individual leaves for work or business in the morning without regularly devoting time to Torah, and in the evenings after prayers, they study at greater length. [Assaf, "Iggerot mi-Ṣefat," 126]

In his letters, the writer mentions six options for study available to laymen:

1. Maimonides: Referred to in other sources as pesak, "Maimonides" denotes the study of the *Mishneh Torah,* known to have been studied in the Jerusalem kehillah as early as the Mamluk period.[82] These sessions devoted to halakhah were attended by yeshivah students as well.[83]

2. *Ein Yaaqov:* Jacob ibn Ḥabib's compendium of the aggadic material found in the Talmud, organized according to the sequence of the tractates.

3. Halakhah [Talmud][84] with the commentaries of Rashi and the Tosafists: Study of Talmud with the above-mentioned commentaries.

4. *Zohar:* It seems that *Zohar* was studied in a group context. Another late-sixteenth-century source advocates studying kabbalah in a group, especially *Zohar* "by whose merit the Messiah will come."[85] It

should also be noted that kabbalistic studies had penetrated the course of study in Spanish yeshivot as early as the second half of the fifteenth century.[86] Concerning Safed, however, there is no evidence for such study prior to the sixteenth century's last quarter. Kabbalistic studies were evidently introduced into the curriculum of several of Safed's yeshivot only near the end of the sixteenth century.[87]

5. The Bible—Pentateuch, Prophets, and Writings: The centrality of biblical study as an important component of the curriculum in medieval oriental yeshivot is well documented in the Cairo Geniza.[88] In contrast, the study of Bible was not included in the framework of the yeshivot in Ashkenaz (Germany), Italy, and Spain; their curricula concentrated on Talmud and halakhah.[89] Nevertheless, it appears that in sixteenth-century Safed Bible was an important component of group study, particularly in the course of study for youths.[90] In the introduction to his *Al-Sharḥ al-Susani,* an Arabic translation of the Bible composed in Safed (1571–74), which is still in manuscript, Issachar ibn Susan explicitly emphasized the importance of Bible study.[91] As we shall see below, according to Moses ben Makhir both biblical and Mishnaic studies had an underlying kabbalistic rationale. Involvement with these realms was perceived as possessing the ability to prepare the ground for the unification of the shekhinah with God.[92]

6. A chapter of Mishnah with commentary: Before the late fifteenth century, Mishnah was not found in the curriculum of occidental or oriental yeshivot; in any event, there is no extant evidence for its inclusion.[93] For the sixteenth century, however, contemporary literature strongly reflects the great interest in Mishnaic study within the context of group study both in Jerusalem and in Safed,[94] from which we may adduce the high estimation for such study. In Safed, more so than in Jerusalem, Mishnah was a major component of the daily study program on all levels; it was a significant part of the *Tikkun Leil Shavuot* as well. Memorization of the Mishnah was encouraged. Even before Isaac Luria's arrival in the city, Safed's kabbalists ascribed intrinsic importance to its study, equating Mishnah with the exiled shekhinah, which had descended to the realm of Metatron, and with the kabbalistic *sefirah* of *malkhut* (kingdom). In the kabbalistic scheme, Mishnaic study conferred the ability to perceive the shekhinah. We can further infer that, in the kabbalists' view, the study of Mishnah possessed the ability to hasten redemption.[95] For Joseph Caro, Mishnah was the apotheosis of his *maggid* (an angel or sacred soul that made revelations to the kabbalists), the heavenly power that directed his actions. This conception found tangible expression in Caro's *Maggid Mesharim.*[96]

The growing interest in Mishnah also manifested itself in the close attention now paid to its text. In the latter half of the sixteenth century, various proofreaders among Safed's sages felt impelled to reexamine the Mishnaic text with an eye to establishing accurate readings based on early versions. These figures included Joseph Ashkenazi, known as *Ha-Tanna ha-Elohi*;[97] Bezalel Ashkenazi, who, as we have already seen, resided in Safed in the 1570s; his disciple, Solomon Adeni, an important commentator on the Mishnah who resided in Safed toward the century's end; and kabbalist Suleiman Oḥana.[98]

E. JERUSALEM-SAFED RIVALRY FOR SPIRITUAL HEGEMONY

The period of intense intellectual development in Safed dates from the late fifteenth or perhaps only from the early sixteenth century, when the city overtook Jerusalem as the preferred destination for Iberian exiles. In early-sixteenth-century Safed the Sefardic element emerged as the pacesetter for the kehillah as a whole. Although the Sefardim were soon to dominate Jerusalem as well, tensions were rife between the Safed and Jerusalem communities. As early as the century's start each kehillah claimed intellectual-spiritual hegemony in Eretz-Israel and viewed itself as the supreme authority for instruction and decision-making in the Law. The existence of these tensions may be inferred from a letter sent by Safed sages to the Jerusalem sages concerning the fixing of the sabbatical year (1504):[99] "If there is no wisdom here, then there is old age and maturity. . . . We too [who reside] in the cities of the Galilee [Safed] are not mere cutters of reeds [simple men]. . . . Each one [presides] in his bet midrash, one to a greater extent, one to a lesser extent" [Benayahu, "Teudah," 122–23].

One segment of scholarly opinion views this statement, in conjunction with other matters found in the letter, as a clear challenge to the Jerusalem sages for failing to consult them on this important matter.[100] Others adduce that this statement reflects a different tone, because according to a later source, the Jerusalem sages did explicitly include their Safed colleagues in their deliberations on the sabbatical year via special emissary.[101] Viewed in this light, the writers of this letter are actually stressing the merit of their opinions, in line with the statement found further on in the letter: "On matters great and small, prohibition and dispensation, or civil matters we gather with haste, clashing and debating in order to bring our judgments to light."[102] Accordingly, this school of thought maintains that this letter implies mutual contacts and exchanges of opinions between Safed and Jerusalem concerning questions of halakhah and *minhag* (custom). Nonetheless, careful reading between the lines provides evidence for the existence of tension between the two centers.

A more palpable expression of this intercommunal rivalry is found in the famous controversy over the renewal of ordination (1538), in which leading protagonists were Safed rabbi Jacob Berab and Jerusalem rabbi Levi ibn Ḥabib.[103] Upon settling in Safed in 1538, Berab, who had formerly headed a yeshivah in Jerusalem, decided to renew the ancient practice of rabbinic ordination as a prelude to the reestablishment of a Sanhedrin modeled on the Supreme Court of Second Temple times, whose members were all ordained rabbis. Although Berab's primary aim was to establish Safed as the leading intellectual-spiritual center in the Jewish world, it was not his sole intent. An additional aspect of his desire to reinstate the Sanhedrin was linked to the conversos problem. Many Spanish and Portuguese conversos, who had made their way to Eretz-Israel and to Safed in particular,[104] now sought expiation for their temporary lapse into Christianity. Flogging, the prescribed punishment, could be administered only on the authority of the Sanhedrin.[105] Nor can we discount the role of contemporary messianic expectations among the sages of Jerusalem and Safed on the desire to renew ordination.[106]

Jacob Berab sought to obtain the backing of the Jerusalem rabbinate for this radical step. His rationale was grounded in his interpretation of a Maimonidean statement that ordination could be renewed by the unanimous decision of all the rabbis in Eretz-Israel. The statement follows:

> It seems to me that if all the wise men in Palestine were to agree to appoint judges and to ordain them, the ordination would be valid, empowering the ordained to adjudicate cases involving fines and to ordain others. . . . If, however, there were one ordained by a man who had himself been ordained, no unanimity would be necessary. He would have the right to adjudicate cases involving fines because he would be an ordained judge. But this matter requires careful reflection. [Maimonides, *Code,* "The Book of Judges: Sanhedrin," chap. 4: 11. English translation cited from A. M. Hershman (New Haven, 1949), 15][107]

In Berab's view this statement meant that practically speaking, a majority decision was sufficient; unanimity was not required. Berab's chief antagonist, Jerusalem sage Levi ibn Ḥabib, was inflexibly opposed to the renewal of ordination. In his halakhically grounded arguments, Ibn Ḥabib contested Berab's interpretation of the selfsame Maimonidean passage.[108] Nonetheless, fear that Jerusalem would cede its spiritual-intellectual primacy to Safed also played a role in his opposition.[109] Although Ibn Ḥabib's fierce opposition prevented implementation of Berab's plan to renew the Sanhedrin, it did not prevent Berab from ordaining four of his disciples, who in turn ordained their students for two or three generations thereafter.[110]

His success in thwarting the plan to found a Sanhedrin and to re-institute ordination notwithstanding, Levi ibn Ḥabib's fears were realized—the balance of power did shift from Jerusalem to Safed in the latter half of the sixteenth century. Jerusalem was increasingly overshadowed in the intellectual-spiritual realm by dint of the convergence of outstanding scholars in the fields of halakhah, ethics, homiletics, and kabbalah on Safed. Even the presence in Jerusalem of so eminent a sage as Bezalel Ashkenazi in the late 1580s and early 1590s posed no threat to Safed's superior position, despite Safed's decidedly depressed economic situation at that time.

Safed's supremacy found further expression in the highly irregular step of intervention by the heads of its kehillah in matters related to the Jerusalem community's internal affairs. In the sixteenth century's third quarter, Joseph Caro himself was directly involved in raising funds to assist the Jerusalem community. This is borne out by a letter propagandizing for assistance for the said community signed by the Jewish notables of Mantua in 1575:

> We have marked the plight of the cherished sons of Zion and their moaning and have seen their distress, the hardships and straits that press on them. We have seen written in a letter that is before us, and as is the case for all truthful writings, it is signed and endorsed by all the notables . . . among them the most eminent among the rabbis of our people, Rabbi J[oseph] Caro, may he live long. They will surely testify to the needs of the inhabitants of Jerusalem, may it be speedily rebuilt. For almost all of them are poverty-stricken, miserable, and destitute by dint of their [financial] burdens. [David, "Emissaries' Letters from Jerusalem," 329–30]

We must note in this context that it was highly unusual for sages from one city to endorse the collection of funds for another city; indeed, both Jerusalem and Safed competed for the funds, targeting the same source. The fact that this text explicitly notes Joseph Caro's intervention on Jerusalem's behalf can only be seen as further proof of Jerusalem's dependence on the heads of the Safed kehillah at that juncture.

In this section on Safed, as in the section on Jerusalem, I attempted first to establish the location of the Jewish quarter and the century's demographic trends and then to delineate the makeup and structure of the community and its institutions. We have seen that Safed experienced a period of rapid growth in the sixteenth century and that its Jewish residents were a significant component of this trend, making a major contribution to the development of its textile industry. Jewish

Safed was home to a variety of congregations; once again, however, it was its Sefardi component that set the tone for the community as a whole. It was the outstanding leaders of Iberian extraction who led the community, playing an active role in its public life and institutions. Not only did they dominate economically, politically, and institutionally, but also these figures must be attributed with some of the outstanding intellectual achievements of the day. The very convergence of such an elite group of scholars upon a single city is in itself remarkable. No less remarkable is the evidence that intellectual inquiry was pursued by the Jewish population as a whole; that study was a fixed part of the daily routine of the entire community. As the century waned, the empire-wide severe economic crisis left its mark on Safed; nonetheless, the influence of sixteenth-century Safed on Jewish law and mysticism is inestimable.

13 Brief Biographies of Rabbinic Personalities in Eretz-Israel

Following this survey of the institutional structure of the sixteenth-century communities in Eretz-Israel, we now turn to brief biographies of the major rabbinic personalities active there during this period. As we have seen, many of the sages assumed dynamic roles in communal affairs, and it was the Spanish expellees and their descendants who, in the course of events, had the major share in shaping the intellectual character of the Jewish community in Eretz-Israel, in Safed and Jerusalem in particular. It is helpful to sketch the lives of these figures, as well as to survey succinctly their many-branched intellectual corpus, so significant for the study of the development of the halakhah and Jewish thought in the late Middle Ages. (Notice that the list is arranged in alphabetical order according to first names.)

1. **Abraham Abzardiel** (born in Spain, 1463; died in Jerusalem, 1523). Early-sixteenth-century sage active in Jerusalem. Abzardiel studied in Isaac de Leon's yeshivah in Toledo. The date of his arrival in Jerusalem is unknown;[1] however, in 1509 he was a signatory along with the other Jerusalemite sages on a tax exemption for scholars.[2] Many of the decisions and teachings he issued in Jerusalem are cited in *Quntres Ḥiddushey Dinim.*[3]
2. **Abraham ben Eliezer ha-Levi** (born c. 1450 in Spain; died 1530–35). Jerusalem sage and kabbalist active in the first third of the sixteenth century and intricately associated with the incipient early-sixteenth-century messianic expectations in Jerusalem.[4] Scholars have scrutinized ha-Levi's unusual personality and apocalyptic writings but have devoted less time to his kabbalistic works.[5] Like many Spanish exiles, ha-Levi did not immediately settle down following the expulsion. Along with other expellees, he may have first gone to Portugal; he subsequently made his way to Italy. In 1508 we find him in Greece, where he composed his apocalyptic treatise, *Mesharei Qitrin* (Untier of Knots), a commentary on Daniel. Two years later, Abraham was in Istanbul, where this treatise was published. He then proceeded to Egypt where he encountered Nagid Isaac Sholal. By 1513, perhaps earlier, ha-Levi had arrived in Jerusalem from Egypt, as evidenced by a letter written by his stepson Moses Castro in 1513 or early 1514, in which the latter commented that both ha-

Levi and his brother-in-law Abraham Zacuto "were the most impoverished and destitute persons found in Jerusalem."[6] Somewhat later we find ha-Levi as a member of one of the Jerusalem yeshivot, and by 1521 he must be counted among the senior members as his name tops the list of the signatories of the letter written by beney ha-yeshivot in that year.[7] A year later ha-Levi headed the Sefardi yeshivah in Jerusalem in conjunction with the Sefardi sage and physician David ibn Shoshan.[8] Ha-Levi engaged in apocalyptic reckonings of the end of days and even prescribed actions to be taken in order to hasten redemption.[9] Some of ha-Levi's works on redemption are extant, including his commentary on the thirteenth-century apocalyptic work *Nevuot ha-Yeled* ("The Child's Prophecies," completed in Jerusalem, 1517). Also extant are various letters on the imminent redemption sent to Italy, where they found a receptive audience.[10]

3. **Abraham ben Gedaliah ibn Asher** (dates unknown). Safed sage active in the latter half of the sixteenth century, also known by the acronym Aba. One of Joseph Caro's students, for part of his life Ibn Asher served in the rabbinate in Aleppo, Syria. Two of his responsa are extant in his teacher's responsa collections.[11] Ibn Asher wrote a commentary on *Midrash Rabbah* and the five biblical scrolls, titled *Or ha-Sekhel,* of which only the portion on Genesis, *Maadaney Melekh,* has been published (Venice, 1562).
4. **Abraham ben Mordecai Galante** (died prior to 1589[12]). Safed kabbalist active in the latter half of the sixteenth century, Galante belonged to a family of Spanish expellees who had settled in Rome. Galante himself came to Safed as a young man—the earliest known reference to his presence in Safed dates from 1559.[13] In Safed, he studied under Moses Cordovero, whom he mentions frequently in his writings as his mentor.[14] Galante headed the Safed Provençal yeshivah in conjunction with his older brother, Moses, also a highly esteemed scholar.[15] Several of Abraham Galante's kabbalistic works are extant. Two have been published: *Qinat Setarim,* a kabbalistic commentary to Lamentations (published in *Kol Bokhin,* [Venice, 1589]); and *Zekhut Avot,* a commentary to tractate *Avot* (Bilgoray, 1911). Among his extant unpublished works, we must note: (1) *Yareaḥ Yaqar,* a broad commentary on the *Zohar* to Exodus; and (2) an anthology of kabbalistic remarks and novellae on aggadah and midrash compiled from various manuscripts.[16] Pietistic *regimen vitae* practiced in Safed have also been attributed to Galante.[17]
5. **Abraham ben Samuel Zacuto** (born 1452 in Salamanca, Spain; died in Jerusalem, 1514).[18] A famed astronomer, Zacuto's astronomical tables are extant in several languages: in Spanish, *Almanach Perpetuum,* composed in Salamanca in 1473; and in Hebrew (Jerusalem, 1513). The tables also existed in an Arabic version, titled *Al*

Talikat.[19] Zacuto also evinced a strong interest in astrology and is known to have composed short astrological treatises, including *Mishpatey ha-Iṣtagnin* and *Maamar al ha-Qeṣ ve-ha-Iṣtagninut.*[20] He was a historian as well, the author of *Sefer Yuḥasin* (Book of Geneaology).[21] In Salamanca Zacuto held the post of professor of astronomy in the local university.[22] Following the expulsion, Zacuto relocated to Portugal, where he served as royal astronomer to John II, and his successor, Manuel I. Explorer Vasco da Gama relied on Zacuto's astronomical calculations in plotting his route to India.[23] After the forced conversions in Portugal in 1497, Zacuto found refuge in North Africa.[24] In 1504 he was in Tunis, where he completed his *Sefer Yuḥasin.*[25] Zacuto arrived in Jerusalem in 1513,[26] and he studied in a Jerusalem yeshivah until his death a year later. He was related to Abraham ha-Levi by marriage and was Moses Castro's maternal uncle.[27] As we saw in the section on Abraham ha-Levi, both Zacuto and his brother-in-law were impoverished.[28] Zacuto also engaged in talmudic studies; however, only a small portion of his *Iqqarey ha-Talmud,* a dictionary of difficult words in the Talmud, from the letter *quf,* is extant.[29] The surviving portion of this work bears great similarity to Nathan ben Yeḥiel of Rome's lexicon, *Sefer he-Arukh.*

6. **Abraham Besodo** (died 1509 in Ein Zeitim [Ein Zitun]).[30] Safed sage active in the early sixteenth century, of Spanish origin. Besodo's father can perhaps be identified as Isaac Besodo, who headed a yeshivah in Leon in the pre-Expulsion generation. Abraham Besodo was one of the signatories on the letter sent from Safed to Jerusalem (1504) concerning the sabbatical year.[31] His son, Isaac Besodo, must also be counted among the early-sixteenth-century sages in Safed.
7. **Abraham Castro** (died 1560, probably in Jerusalem). Of Spanish origin, perhaps himself an expellee, Castro was an outstanding figure in early Ottoman Egyptian-Jewish society. The discovery of documents that shed light on his biography and personality has further enhanced scholarly interest in this figure. Contemporary Hebrew and Muslim sources indicate that he moved in official government circles, especially in the financial realm. He leased duties on customs and trade in Alexandria, and from 1520 (and perhaps earlier) he served as master of the mint (muallim dar al ḍarb).[32] He was also renowned for his philanthropic activity on behalf of individuals and institutions in Egypt and Eretz-Israel.[33] Hebrew sources as well as Jerusalem sharia court documents indicate that Castro resided in Jerusalem from the late 1530s. Here, too, he played a central role in the city's Jewish society, primarily in its economic life, dealing in real estate and apparently tax farming as well. According to a seventeenth-century Hebrew source, "Sultan Suleiman built the walls

of Jerusalem through his agent, his excellency the Nagid, Abraham Castro."[34] During his residence in Jerusalem, Castro maintained close relationships with various sages, Joseph ibn Ṣayyaḥ in particular. Moreover, it seems that Castro evinced special interest in kabbalah.[35] A Jerusalem sharia court document from 1540 mentions his name as a convert to Islam. This, however, contradicts our knowledge of the man. Non-Jewish sources indicate that another Jew by the same name also resided in Jerusalem at that time, and it was this individual who converted.[36] Castro evidently remained in Jerusalem until his demise in 1560. Of his two sons, Moses and Jacob, the latter was one of the more important sages in late-sixteenth/early-seventeenth-century Egypt.[37]

8. **Abraham Gabriel** (dates unknown). Safed sage of probable Italian origin. In Safed, Gabriel studied under Isaac Luria and received ordination from Jacob Berab II in 1594. He also sat on the Safed bet din and in 1610 signed as head of the city's Italian congregation. In 1603 he accompanied Joseph Trani to Sidon as an emissary of the Safed community.[38]
9. **Abraham ha-Levi Berukhim** (died before 1600). Safed sage and kabbalist active in the latter half of the sixteenth century, a student of Moses Cordovero and Isaac Luria, also known as Abraham ha-Levi the Maghrebi, Abraham ha-Levi ha-Zaqen (the Elder), or Abraham ha-Levi, disciple of Isaac Luria.[39] Although authorship of the kabbalistic work *Galya Raza* has been attributed to Berukhim, this ascription has been proved erroneous.[40] We know of several pietistic regimen vitae prescribed by Berukhim in Safed.[41] In addition, Berukhim's fame rests on his moderately central role in Lurianic mythology.[42]
10. **Abraham Shalom** (born in Salonika?; died in the late 1560s). Safed rabbi and posek also known by the acronym Rosh. In his native city of Salonika, Shalom and his contemporary, Solomon Alkabetz, studied under Joseph Taitaẓak. Prior to his arrival in Safed (c. 1530) Shalom expounded Torah in his birthplace. In Safed he served as a dayyan and headed a yeshivah as well. He must be counted among Jacob Berab's closest disciples and was one of four sages ordained by this rabbi.[43] His grandson, Abraham ben Eliezer Shalom, was an eminent Safed sage in the late sixteenth century. In 1599 he accompanied Joseph ben Moses Trani to Istanbul as an emissary of the Safed kehillah.[44]
11. **Bezalel ben Abraham Ashkenazi** (died in Jerusalem between 1591 and 1595).[45] Rabbi and posek active in Jerusalem and Safed in the latter half of the sixteenth century, one of the more important sages in sixteenth-century Egypt. Neither the date nor place of his birth are known. In his youth, Ashkenazi resided in Safed, where he stud-

ied under Israel di Curiel.[46] At a later date, he moved to Egypt, where he studied under David ibn Abi Zimra. In Egypt, Ashkenazi headed a yeshivah, whose students included Isaac Luria, Abraham Monzon, and Ḥayyim Ḥevraya.[47] When David ibn Abi Zimra left Egypt for Jerusalem in 1553, Ashkenazi replaced him as the leading rabbi in the Egyptian-Jewish community. While serving in this position, Ashkenazi openly quarreled with one of the important communal leaders, Jacob Talmid. Pursuant to this quarrel, Jacob Talmid was dismissed from his position, and Ashkenazi was forced to leave Egypt.[48] By 1587 Ashkenazi already resided in Jerusalem,[49] where he remained until his death some four to eight years later. During his tenure in Jerusalem, Ashkenazi served as functional head of the entire community;[50] in addition, he headed a yeshivah where he expounded Torah.[51] Ashkenazi evidently spent some time in Safed before settling in Jerusalem, as revealed in paragraph 279 of his *Kelaley ha-Talmud:* "Tuesday, the weekly portion of *Va-yeṣe Yaaqov* [Gen. 28:10–32:2], the third of Kislev, in the year 5335 to the Creation [16 Nov. 1575], here in Safed, may it be speedily rebuilt."[52] While in Safed Ashkenazi headed a yeshivah under Joseph Caro's patronage, in conjunction with other sages.[53]

Bezalel Ashkenazi occupied himself with the copying of ancient manuscripts, for which purpose he even hired scribes to assist him. Ashkenazi copied geonic and rishonic novellae on the Babylonian Talmud, which served as the basis for his classic work, *Asefat Zeqenim,* better known as the *Shitah Mequbbeṣet,* in part a supplement to the *Tosafot.* The *Shitah Mequbbeṣet* has been published for several tractates only, and much remains in manuscript. Parts have been lost, and we are aware of their existence only from citations in the works of others.[54] In some instances, *Shitot* by different authors have been mistakenly attributed to Ashkenazi. Ashkenazi and his school laid the foundations for a critical approach to the talmudic text. Moreover, they worked to establish accurate texts of both the Mishnah and the Talmud and of Maimonides' Code and the code of Isaac Alfasi. Corrections made by Ashkenazi, his colleagues, and students can be found in the margins of the printed editions of the Talmud.[55] In his *Kelaley ha-Talmud,* Ashkenazi compiled general rules of talmudic methodology based on excerpts from the rishonim.[56] His sermons are extant in manuscript,[57] and his collected responsa were published in Venice in 1595.

12. **David ben Solomon ibn Abi Zimra (RaDBaZ)** (born Spain, c. 1480; died 1573, in Safed). Jerusalem and Safed sage. Following the expulsion from Spain, Abi Zimra settled in Egypt, where he served as dayyan and expounder of Torah for nearly forty years.[58] He headed a yeshivah in Cairo; at the same time, he engaged in commerce.[59]

By 1514, and perhaps earlier, he was a member of Nagid Isaac Sholal's court.[60] According to Isaac ben Abraham Akrish, who frequented Abi Zimra's home: "He [Abi Zimra] expounded Torah and ruled over the Jews in Egypt for forty years, and in Jerusalem and Safed, may they be speedily rebuilt, for twenty years."[61] His disciples included Bezalel Ashkenazi, Isaac Luria, and Jacob Castro, among others. The known chronology of his life enables us to determine the date of his arrival in Jerusalem. Abi Zimra died in Safed in 1573. In 1514 he already sat on the Nagid's court. In light of Akrish's testimony, it appears that Abi Zimra arrived in Jerusalem in 1553.[62]

Of Abi Zimra's activities in Jerusalem, little is known. During his first years in Jerusalem, he served as the "appointed dayyan" without the local kadi's approval; furthermore, he prescribed punishments outside the scope of those permitted to Jewish judges. In so doing, he exceeded his authority, consequently incurring the danger of harsh punishment, which was averted however. In 1560 his appointment as dayyan received official approval, and he retained this position until 1564 at least.[63] As the leading figure in the Jerusalem kehillah, Abi Zimra naturally addressed himself to the city's pressing social and economic problems. The Jerusalem kehillah was in dire financial straits; economic opportunities were scarce, and the tax burden extremely heavy. Abi Zimra attempted to arrive at a more equitable distribution of the tax burden by canceling the scholar's exemption from all taxes except the jizya promulgated by Nagid Isaac Sholal's court in 1509. In Abi Zimra's view, the community's dire economic situation required that scholars should pay their taxes in full, including the levy for protection against thieves, which the scholars refused to remit.[64] Abi Zimra's measures encountered the angry opposition of Jerusalem sage Joseph ibn Ṣayyaḥ, who harshly blamed him for the community's decline. Ibn Ṣayyaḥ wrote: "From that point on, Jerusalem declined rather than advanced";[65] this statement was a specific reference to the exodus of scholars from the city.

After 1564, against the background of friction with the authorities over taxes, Abi Zimra relocated to Safed,[66] as we learn from Isaac Akrish: "When he saw the people of the land who were not of our faith, and the burdensome taxes laid upon him, he had no desire to carry this evil [burden]. He said, 'Better to live on the corner of a roof than to live with contention.' And he went to Safed."[67] Abi Zimra resided in Safed until his death during an epidemic in 1573.[68] Little is known of his public activity in Safed, with the exception of halakhic decisions issued by Safed's sages that he cosigned.[69]

Abi Zimra's status as a halakhist remained unchallenged in his and later generations, and his halakhic decisions and teachings gained wide acceptance throughout the Jewish world. More than twenty-five hundred of his responsa sent to Jewish communities worldwide are extant.[70] Additional works by Abi Zimra are also known: in halakhah, *Yeqar Tiferet,* a commentary on those parts of Maimonides' Code for which Vidal Yom Tov of Tolosa's commentary *Maggid Mishneh* is not extant; *Kelaley ha-Gemara,* and *Peyrushim la-Miqra.*[71] His kabbalistic works include: *Magen David* (Amsterdam, 1713)—a kabbalistic commentary on the letters of the Hebrew alphabet; *Migdal David* (Lemberg, 1883)—a kabbalistic commentary on the Song of Songs; *Meṣudat David* (Zolkiew, 1862)—an explanation of the 613 commandments; and *Kelaley Qiṣur Sefer ha-Peliah* (Jerusalem, 1910–11)—a summary of the main ideas of *Sefer ha-Peliah.*[72] Several *piyyutim* composed by Abi Zimra have also been preserved, including the kabbalistic poem *"Keter Malkhut,"* found in the Sefardic rite for the Day of Atonement.[73]

13. **David ben Zechariah Frank** (dates unknown). Ashkenazi sage active in Safed and Jerusalem whose father, Zechariah, served as av bet din in Safed. David Frank resided in Safed until 1543 at least, before moving to Jerusalem sometime between 1543 and late 1547,[74] when we find him as a signatory on a haskamah to the tax exemption for scholars.[75] Frank almost certainly headed one of the Jerusalem Ashkenazi yeshivot. Two of his halakhic decisions are cited in Joseph Caro's responsa.[76]
14. **David ibn Shoshan** (dates unknown). Sage and physician who resided in Jerusalem in the first decade of the sixteenth century, one of the signatories on the haskamah to the tax exemption for scholars (1509).[77] In 1522 we find him heading the Sefardi yeshivah in conjunction with Abraham ha-Levi.[78] Ibn Shoshan served as a trustee of the communal *hekdeshot,* and he apparently held the office of dayyan as seen from the following responsum by Levi ibn Ḥabib (post-1525): "I assembled all the anshey maamad (officeholders) before the dayyan at that time, who was the perfect sage, R. David ibn Shoshan, may God preserve and protect him. . . . "[79] Before Isaac Sholal died in late 1524, he appointed Ibn Shoshan as one of four guardians for his young son Abraham.[80] Sermons delivered by Ibn Shoshan in the Jerusalem synagogue are extant in manuscript.[81]
15. **Eleazar ben Moses Azikri (Azkari)** (born 1533 in Eretz-Israel; died 1600 in Safed). Safed sage and kabbalist active in the latter half of the sixteenth century, a resident of that city from 1548, perhaps earlier.[82] In Safed, Joseph Sagis was his particular mentor.[83] Azikri headed two societies (*ḥavurot*) whose purpose was to enhance repentance through deeds: *Ḥavurat Sukkat Shalom,* which he founded in 1575, and *Ḥavurat Ḥaverim Maqshivim.*[84] In 1596 he received ordination at the hands of Jacob Berab II.[85] Azikri's fame rests on

his *Sefer Ḥaredim,* a systematic ethical-kabbalistic work (written in 1588 and published in Venice in 1601), which exhibits the strong influence of Moses Cordovero.[86] Azikri also commented extensively on the Talmud Yerushalmi. In Solomon Adeni's Mishnaic commentary, *Melekhet Shelomo,* we find citations from Azikri's commentaries to the following tractates of the Jerusalem Talmud: *Berakhot, Peah, Demai, Terumot,* and *Pesaḥim.* Only the commentaries to tractates *Berakhot* (Zhitomir, 1865) and *Beṣah* (New York, 1967) are extant and have been published.[87] Drafts of his commentary to some treatises of the Babylonian Talmud, as well as sermons on the weekly portion and rabbinic epigrams have also been preserved. His ethical teachings are reflected in his treatise *Milei De-Shemaya.*[88] Scattered among these works and in their margins are fragmented notations from Azikri's personal mystical diary written between 1564 and 1599, which shed additional light on Azikri's personality and inner spiritual life.[89] Azikri must also be credited with the authorship of the well-known poem "Yedid Nefesh" still recited by many communities during the *Qabbalat Shabbat* (Friday night) service.

16. **Eleazar ben Solomon ben Yoḥai** (died before 1572). Sage active in Safed and Tiberias in the latter half of the sixteenth century,[90] perhaps related to Samuel ben Benveniste ben Yoḥai, who served as Safed kehillah secretary in the early sixteenth century.[91] If this is indeed the case, Eleazar was of Spanish origin, as the name Benveniste attests. Eleazar was one of the founding fathers of the renewed settlement in Tiberias in the 1560s. He also headed a yeshivah there.[92]
17. **Elijah ben Moses de Vidas** (died in Hebron). Sage and kabbalist active in Safed and Hebron in the latter half of the sixteenth century, a close disciple of Moses Cordovero. Late in his life, he moved to Hebron where he died.[93] De Vidas is best known for his ethical-kabbalistic work *Reshit Ḥokhmah,* which, like *Ḥovot ha-Levavot,* must be considered one of the basic texts of Jewish ethical writing. *Reshit Ḥokhmah* has the distinction of being the first ethical-kabbalistic work and remains the epitome of this genre to the present.[94] In this treatise, Elijah de Vidas gave practical expression to the moral implications of Moses Cordovero's kabbalistic method. The book was first published in Venice in 1579, and its popularity is attested by the multiplicity of abridgements, reworkings, and translations into Yiddish and Ladino (partial translation), which numbered more than ten. Six have been issued in more than one edition. De Vidas himself wrote an abridged version of *Reshit Ḥokhmah* titled *Toṣot Ḥayyim* by the copyist (Prague, n.d.).
18. **Elisha ben Gabriel Gallico** (born in Italy in the 1520s; died in 1579 in Safed). Safed scholar active in the latter half of the sixteenth cen-

tury; his arrival in Safed can be dated to c. 1540.[95] One of Joseph Caro's close disciples, Gallico received ordination at Caro's hands.[96] In Safed Gallico headed a yeshivah; Samuel de Uceda and Joseph ben Moses de Segovia Benveniste were among his disciples.[97] Gallico composed a commentary to the five biblical scrolls, three of which have printed editions: Qohelet (Venice, 1578); Esther (Venice, 1583); Song of Songs (Venice, 1587). Excerpts from his other commentaries are cited by his disciple Samuel de Uceda—on Lamentations in the latter's *Leḥem Dimah* (Venice, 1606), and on Ruth in de Uceda's *Iggeret Shemuel* (Kuru-Chesme, 1597). Recently, fragments of Gallico's commentary on Ruth have been discovered in manuscript. Evidently, he also wrote a book of halakhic decisions, which is no longer extant.[98]

19. **Ephraim Fish ben Moses Judah** (dates unknown). Jerusalem sage active in the late sixteenth century. Of Polish extraction, he was the son-in-law of Solomon ben Yeḥiel Luria (Maharshal).[99] He held the post of av bet din in Brisk, where he studied under Joel Sirkes (known also by the acronym BaḤ). The date of his arrival in Jerusalem is not known; however, it appears that he played a central role in that kehillah's intellectual life. Hyperbolic praise for Ephraim is found in Yom Tov Ṣahalon's writings: "And I have heard that there were more than two hundred great scholars in his yeshivah."[100] In 1594 we find him among the Jerusalem signatories on an agreement to the nagid's regulation exempting scholars from taxes.[101] He wrote a commentary on the Mishnah, including on tractate *Avot,* as well as glosses on the Mishnaic text.[102]

20. **Gedaliah ben Moses Cordovero** (born in Safed, 1562; died in Jerusalem, 1625). Safed and Jerusalem sage active in the late sixteenth and early seventeenth centuries,[103] son of the famed kabbalist Moses Cordovero, and nephew (on his mother's side) of Solomon Alkabetz.[104] In his youth, Gedaliah studied in Safed under Solomon Sagis. Sometime prior to 1584, when he was already more than twenty years old, Gedaliah moved to Italy, where he became a book dealer. He also oversaw the publication of several of his father's works, in addition to the works of other Safed scholars. After 1590 Gedaliah returned to Eretz-Israel and settled in Jerusalem. At the century's end he was evidently appointed chief rabbi of the Jerusalem kehillah, and the Arabic title shaykh al-yahud was conferred on him, in addition to his position as av bet din. He served in these capacities until his death in Nisan (April) 1625. In 1607 Gedaliah became involved in a dispute with the well-known sage Menaḥem de Lonzano, who was forced to leave Jerusalem as a result. The two men were subsequently reconciled and de Lonzano was reinstated to his former communal posts.[105] In 1617 we find Gedaliah in Padua, Italy,

as an emissary of the Jerusalem community.[106] During the anti-Jewish disturbances fostered by Jerusalem governor Muḥammad ibn Farruk in 1625, Gedaliah's role as leader of the Jewish community was put to the test.[107] He died in the course of these events.

21. Ḥayyim ben Joseph Vital (born 1543, probably in Safed; died 1620 in Damascus). Sage and kabbalist active in Safed and Jerusalem in the latter half of the sixteenth century; Isaac Luria's most eminent disciple.[108] He was known also as Ḥayyim Calabrese, and this name attests to his family's probable origins in the Calabria region of southern Italy.[109] Vital almost certainly received his instruction in kabbalah from Moses Cordovero and in halakhah from Moses Alshekh, with whom he began to study in 1557 when he was fourteen years old.[110] Following Cordovero's death in 1570, Vital pursued kabbalistic studies with Isaac Luria. In Kislev (Nov/Dec) 1577, that is, less than six years after Luria's death, Vital left Safed for Jerusalem. In Jerusalem Vital headed a yeshivah, where Solomon Adeni was one of his students.[111] Vital remained in Jerusalem until no later than 1586, when he again returned to Safed. In 1590 he was ordained by his mentor, Moses Alshekh.[112] Following his ordination, Vital evidently returned to Jerusalem, where we find him as a signatory on the agreement to the regulation exempting scholars from taxes in 1594.[113] It is possible that Vital was summoned to Jerusalem to assume Bezalel Ashkenazi's position, as Ashkenazi died sometime between 1591 and 1595.[114] Vital apparently moved to Damascus prior to 1597, where he served as rabbi of the Sicilian congregation[115] until his death in 1620.

Vital's extant halakhic works include his novellae and comments on the Talmud, *Ḥayyim Shenayim,* and several responsa as well.[116] His known exegetical works on the Bible include: *Eṣ ha-Daat Tov al ha-Torah* (Zolkiew, 1871); *Eṣ ha-Daat Tov,* pt. 2, including glosses on rabbinic sayings for various occasions (Jerusalem, 1906); and a commentary on Psalms, *Eṣ ha-Daat Tov al Tehillim* (Piotrkow, 1926).[117] The bulk of Vital's literary legacy lies in the field of kabbalistic studies. Following the death of his teacher in 1572, as Luria's closest disciple, Vital wanted to exercise exclusive control over the former's legacy and demanded that Luria's other disciples bow to his authority. Vital forbade the further transmission of any of Luria's esoteric lore either previously or currently under study, a demand to which the other disciples acceded, signing a binding agreement in 1575 in which they granted Vital exclusive rights for a ten-year period.[118] Proceeding from his self-perception as the sole individual endowed with the ability to transmit Luria's legacy properly, Vital decided to edit and recast Luria's written kabbalistic teachings, basing this work also on Luria's oral teachings he personally had heard or on those reported by other disciples. Vital's attempt at exclusivity did not pass unopposed. One of his colleagues, Joseph ibn Tabul, also a member of Luria's select coterie, tried to compete with Vital in disseminating Luria's kabbalistic tradition. His works, however, never attained the popularity of Vital's. Vital intended to publish Luria's teachings in his treatise *Eṣ Ḥayyim;* however, this treatise did not appear during Vital's lifetime. Vital reworked his teacher's legacy—adapting Luria's written texts and oral teachings and arranging them in various editions. Following Vital's death, his writings, along with those of other disciples of Luria, were disseminated throughout the Orient and Italy,[119] where they received an enthusiastic reception. In the next generation, other kabbalists continued Vital's pursuit—collecting and explaining the tenets of Lurianic kabbalah. They included his son, Samuel Vital, who resided in Egypt; Jacob Ṣemaḥ of Jerusalem; and Ṣemaḥ's disciple, Meir Poppers, among others.[120]

22. **Ḥiyya Rofe** (born c. 1550, probably in Safed; died c. 1617 in Safed). Sage and kabbalist active in Safed, Tiberias, and Jerusalem in the latter half of the sixteenth and early seventeenth centuries,[121] a student of Solomon Sagis and Ḥayyim Vital.[122] In the late sixteenth century, Rofe was ordained by Jacob Berab II, along with another six Safed sages,[123] and he sat in judgment on Moses Galante's rabbinic court there. Sometime prior to 1587, Rofe moved to Tiberias, where he headed a yeshivah for a number of years. From 1607 until the early 1610s, he is known to have been living in Jerusalem; he then returned to Safed where he was considered a leading scholar. In 1613–14 we again find Rofe in Tiberias. He died c. 1617 in Safed. Several of Ḥiyya Rofe's responsa and decisions have been preserved in the works of his contemporaries. Also extant is his *Maaseh Ḥiyya* (Venice, 1652), published by his son Meir Rofe. This treatise consists primarily of novellae on talmudic tractates but includes some responsa as well.
23. **Isaac ben Mordecai Gershon** (dates unknown). Safed sage active in the sixteenth century's latter half, a disciple of Moses Alshekh.[124] At an unknown date he left Safed for a brief stay in Istanbul; he later lived in Ancona and Venice.[125] By 1578 he was a permanent resident of Venice, where he was employed as a proofreader in the Hebrew press and as a preacher. Isaac Gershon returned to Eretz-Israel in 1631, when he was about eighty years old.
24. **Isaac ben Solomon Ashkenazi (Isaac Luria; Ha-Ari)** (according to an unverified tradition, born 1534 in Jerusalem; died 1572 in Safed). Safed sage and outstanding kabbalist in the latter half of the sixteenth century,[126] founder of a major school of kabbalistic thought. According to an unauthenticated tradition, Luria's father was Solo-

mon Luria Ashkenazi, and his mother was a member of the Sefardi Frances family. In Jerusalem Luria evidently studied with Kalonymus, who headed one of the Ashkenazi yeshivot, as his disciple Ḥayyim Vital testified: "My teacher of blessed memory said that he heard [this] from a great contemporary sage named R. Kalonymus of blessed memory."[127] Sometime prior to 1554, Luria moved to Cairo, where he studied under David ibn Abi Zimra and teacher-colleague Bezalel Ashkenazi.[128] Luria sat in judgment on the Cairo Ashkenazi bet din with his teacher Bezalel Ashkenazi and Simeon Castellazzo.[129] Various sources, Geniza documents in particular, indicate that Luria engaged in commerce, both on the local and on the international level. His commercial activities encompassed culinary items (vegetables, grain, and wine) and hides.[130] We can also conjecture that Luria almost certainly undertook philanthropic activity on behalf of kehillot in Eretz-Israel and perhaps for individuals as well.[131] Luria immigrated to Safed in fall 1569. As his arrival preceded Moses Cordovero's death in that year, there is a strong likelihood that he attended sessions in Cordovero's bet midrash.[132] Luria headed a yeshivah in Safed whose curriculum focused on two areas: halakhic and kabbalistic studies, with the primary emphasis on the latter.[133] Of Luria's contribution to halakhah little is known. Like his teacher-colleague Bezalel Ashkenazi in Egypt, Luria and other disciples of David ibn Abi Zimra applied themselves to checking and correcting the text of the Talmud and of Alfasi's code, in addition to composing novellae and commentaries on various tractates. In his introduction to Tam ibn Yaḥya's *Sefer Tummat Yesharim* (Venice, 1622), Benjamin ben Abraham Motal notes that he received R. Abraham Monzon's "copy of Alfasi's code which he brought from Egypt, [which had been] proofread by the two great luminaries, the eminent rabbi Bezalel Ashkenazi of blessed memory and the divine rabbi Isaac Ashkenazi of blessed memory."[134] Nonetheless, Luria's intellectual interests rested preponderantly in the sphere of kabbalistic studies. From the scanty evidence at our disposal, it appears that Luria received his initial introduction to kabbalah in Egypt, under the tutelage of his mentor, David ibn Abi Zimra, himself the author of several kabbalistic treatises.[135]

Luria's kabbalistic doctrines, which reached the apex of their development in Safed between late 1569 and the 5th of Av (16 July) 1572, the date of Luria's death, represent a revolution in the realm of mystical thought. Luria gathered a select coterie of some thirty disciples with whom he examined and refined his theoretical-kabbalistic doctrine, which was largely grounded in earlier traditions current among Spanish and North African kabbalists. Luria himself recorded almost none of his ideas in writing; his known written works include only *Beyur Sifra di-Ṣeniuta* and some statements on *Zohar.*[136] In effect, almost the entire corpus of Lurianic kabbalah was transmitted orally to his disciples, first and foremost, to Ḥayyim Vital and Joseph ibn Tabul. These individuals and their students were instrumental in recording, interpreting, and disseminating Luria's doctrine, with variants in language and style, throughout the Jewish world both in manuscript and in printed editions.[137]

25. **Isaac ibn Ḥayyim** (dates unknown). Jerusalem sage active in the early sixteenth century, of either Spanish or North African origin. In 1504 he was a student at the Jerusalem yeshivah founded by Nagid Isaac Sholal.[138] In 1509 we find him among the signatories to the agreement to the nagid's regulation exempting scholars from taxes.[139] He later served as a dayyan in Damascus, and he lived there until 1537 at least.[140]
26. **Isaac Mar-Ḥayyim** (dates unknown). Jerusalem sage active in the early sixteenth century, an outstanding Spanish kabbalist of the expulsion generation. Having left Spain for Italy prior to the expulsion, Mar-Ḥayyim resided in Naples and Pisa, where he engaged in commercial activities.[141] By 1503 he was already in Jerusalem, having moved there from Salonika.[142] Mar-Ḥayyim has been mistakenly identified with another Jerusalem sage, Isaac ibn Ḥayyim.[143] Mar-Ḥayyim's period of residence in Jerusalem was brief, as he evidently died before 1509. It was his son, Jacob ben Isaac Mar-Ḥayyim the Sefardi, who signed the well-known agreement to the tax exemption for scholars in 1509.[144]
27. **Isaac Sholal (Shulal)** (died late 1524 in Jerusalem.) Last Egyptian nagid. Although of Spanish ancestry, by the early fifteenth century and perhaps even earlier Sholal's direct forebears were residing in Tlemcen, Algeria. During the latter half of the fifteenth century Sholal himself resided in Egypt,[145] where he actively engaged in the grain trade and other pursuits.[146] In 1502 he inherited the office of nagid from his uncle/brother-in-law Jonathan (Nathan) Sholal, and he served in this capacity until the Ottoman conquest in 1517, which saw the termination of the nagidate. Various sources indicate that Isaac Sholal was intensely involved in the affairs of the Jerusalem and Safed communities on a number of levels. During his tenure as nagid, and later, after 1517, when he moved to Jerusalem, Sholal made a significant contribution to intellectual life in that city in the form of massive material support for two Jerusalem yeshivot: one reopened at his initiative, and he founded the other. Sholal also supported the Sefardi yeshivah in Safed. In addition, by promulgating regulations through the agency of his court, Sholal took steps aimed at legislating social issues in the Jerusalem kehillah. In early 1517 Sholal came to Eretz-Israel and settled in Jerusalem, but he was

an impoverished man, no longer able to contribute financially to the upkeep of the yeshivot. Nonetheless, in Jerusalem Isaac Sholal continued to exercise spiritual influence. He belonged to a circle of individuals who engaged in pietistic practices aimed at hastening redemption. He himself prescribed vigils "to pray and undergo privation for the sake of all our brethren in the Diaspora."[147] Ever attuned to the incipient signs of the Messiah's approach, Sholal evinced particular interest in individuals who claimed descent from the Ten Tribes. Sources from the early 1520s indicate that he hosted individuals claiming such ancestry in Jerusalem and in Egypt as well, at an earlier date. Sholal's scholastic achievements and status among the Jerusalem halakhists are reflected in several of the halakhic decisions extant in *Quntres Ḥiddushey Dinim* and in his correspondence with his contemporaries in Egypt and Jerusalem.

28. **Israel ben Meir di Curiel** (died 1577 in Safed). One of the most outstanding sixteenth-century Safed sages. Neither the place nor the date of his birth is known; similarly, we have no precise idea as to the date of his arrival in Safed. Di Curiel studied under Joseph Fasi in Adrianople, and presumably he held a rabbinic office in one of the congregations there. He evidently spent some time in Istanbul as well.[148] In Safed, di Curiel studied under Jacob Berab and was one of the latter's ordinees.[149] In conjunction with Joseph Caro and Moses Trani, di Curiel sat on the Safed supreme court.[150] Among his disciples, we must note Bezalel Ashkenazi.[151] One of the outstanding preachers of his day, di Curiel's many-branched homiletic corpus is extant in manuscript, in addition to his *Or Ṣaddiqim* (Salonika, 1799), which was mistakenly attributed to Joseph Caro.[152] The noted poet Israel Najara was his grandson.[153]

29. **Israel ben Moses Najara** (born c. 1550 in Safed; died c. 1625 in Gaza). Greatest Jewish poet of the post-expulsion period. During his childhood in Safed, Najara studied with his grandfather, Israel di Curiel, among others. Najara also spent several years in Damascus where his father held a rabbinical post. In Damascus Najara was apparently a preacher and communal scribe, but he engaged in commerce for his livelihood. For many years Najara wandered among various Turkish towns before settling in Gaza late in his life. He expounded Torah in Gaza until his death, c. 1625, and his son Moses inherited his position there.[154] Najara's fame rests on his prolific output in the fields of rhetoric, poetry, and piyyut.

Hundreds of his poems, as well as rhetorical and parodic pieces composed extemporaneously, are extant in various collections. The stylistic and musical influence of the surrounding Muslim culture is clearly discernible in Najara's poetry. Although taken to task by his contemporaries for this use of Arabic poetic devices, nevertheless his poetry strongly influenced both his contemporaries and later generations of poets. Several of his poems found their way into the Karaite and Shabbatean rituals,[155] and others have been translated into Persian, Ladino, and German.[156] Additional literary works by Najara, in the realm of thought and homily, include: (1) *Piṣey Ohev*—a commentary on Job (Istanbul, 1597–98), of which only a few pages of the printed edition have been preserved. Additional portions have recently been published from manuscript;[157] (2) *Miqveh Yisrael*—forty sermons;[158] (3) *Maarkhot Yisrael*—a commentary on the Pentateuch;[159] (4) *Keli Maḥziq Berakhah*—on grace after meals (Venice, 1618); (5) *Shoḥatey ha-Yeladim*—the laws of ritual slaughter in poetic form;[160] (6) *Ketubbah le-Ḥag ha-Shavuot*—a poetic parody for Shavuot printed in the oriental prayer rite;[161] (7) *Zemirot Yisrael*—collected poems and hymns; (8) *Mesaḥeqet ba-Tevel*—moral instruction, both published in Safed in 1587;[162] (9) *Sheerit Yisrael*—a large manuscript collection of hundreds of Najara's poems.[163] Also extant are several responsa.[164]

30. **Israel ben Yeḥiel Ashkenazi** (dates unknown). Jerusalem sage and posek active in the first half of the sixteenth century. During the century's initial decades, Israel Ashkenazi held important rabbinic posts in Italy—in Padua, Perugia, Bologna, and Rome. In Padua he was a student-colleague of Judah Minz, while in the 1510s he headed a yeshivah in Rome. In 1520 Ashkenazi arrived in Jerusalem where he filled several key communal positions—he headed the Ashkenazi yeshivah in conjunction with Rabbi Peretz and served as the appointed dayyan.[165] Abraham ben Eliezer ha-Levi and Joseph ben Peretz Colon were the other judges who sat on his court.[166] Ashkenazi also oversaw the collection and distribution of funds to Jerusalem's poor.[167] Some of Ashkenazi's responsa, composed in Italy, are extant. Also extant is Ashkenazi's letter to the notable Abraham of Perugia (1522), in which he depicts the contemporary social and intellectual scene in Jerusalem.[168] This letter is the most comprehensive source for the history of the Jerusalem kehillah in the early Ottoman era.

31. **Issachar ben Mordecai ibn Susan** (born c. 1510 in Fez). Sage active in Jerusalem and Safed. Born in Fez, Morocco, Ibn Susan immigrated to Safed in his youth. During the 1530s (and perhaps earlier) Ibn Susan resided in Jerusalem, where he studied under Levi ibn Ḥabib. He evidently came to Safed by 1538 and remained there for several decades. During this period he also spent intervals in Damascus, Turkey, and Salonika. In Safed he was the leading member of the North African congregation and apparently the head of the congregational yeshivah as well.[169] Ibn Susan evinced particular interest in matters pertaining to the Jewish calendar and to the diver-

gent customs of the communities in Safed—Musta'rabs, Sefardim, and Maghrebis—especially the public Torah reading, the prophetic portions, and synagogue liturgy. This interest found literary expression in Ibn Susan's *Tiqqun Yissakhar,* which he completed in late 1539 in Damascus, as indicated by the colophon.[170] Ibn Susan updated this work before its publication in Istanbul in 1564 and again in the second edition (Venice, 1579), which was titled *Ibbur Shanim.* From 1571 to 1574, having reached the conclusion that Saadiah Gaon's translation of the Bible no longer met contemporary needs, Issachar was occupied with his own translation of the Bible into Arabic, *Al-Sharḥ al-Susani.*[171]

32. **Jacob Abulafia** (died c. 1600). Safed sage active in the latter half of the sixteenth century,[172] grandson of Jacob Berab I on his mother's side.[173] Abulafia studied under Solomon Absaban;[174] Yom Tov Ṣahalon was one of his fellow students.[175] In 1593 he was in Damascus. Following his return to Safed, Abulafia was ordained by his cousin, Jacob Berab II, and he remained there until 1599 at least. Abulafia in turn ordained two disciples: his son, Ḥayyim Abulafia, and Josiah Pinto.[176] Abulafia's name is linked to Lurianic myth.[177] It seems likely that his father can be identified as the Judah Abulafia who had a falling-out with his brother-in-law, Aaron Berab, son of Jacob Berab I, over the latter's estate.[178]

33. **Jacob Berab** (born 1474 in Maqueda; died 1541 in Safed). Jerusalem and Safed sage active in the first half of the sixteenth century, a member of the "Mimongil" family.[179] In Spain Berab studied under Isaac Aboab, most probably at the latter's yeshivah in Guadalajara.[180] Following the expulsion, Berab settled in Fez, Morocco. By 1493 he was residing in Tlemcen, Algeria. With the Spanish invasion of the Maghreb in 1510, Berab went to Egypt,[181] where he was a member of Nagid Isaac Sholal's court. At a certain point a dispute of uncertain nature erupted between the two, and Berab was temporarily deprived of this office until a reconciliation effected between the two men enabled his reinstatement.[182] Berab immigrated to Eretz-Israel prior to the Ottoman conquest in 1516,[183] and he headed a Jerusalem yeshivah from the late Mamluk period until late 1519, when difficult economic conditions forced him and his students to settle temporarily in Egypt.[184] During his stay in Egypt, Berab, like many of the contemporary sages in Egypt and Eretz-Israel, engaged in commerce.[185] From 1524 on (and perhaps somewhat earlier) Berab was in Safed, where he headed a yeshivah.[186] He dominated Safed's intellectual scene until his death in 1541. In 1538 Berab promoted the idea of the renewal of ordination as the first step in establishing a supreme court in Eretz-Israel, on the lines of the ancient Sanhedrin. Although the court was never founded, ordina-

tion was practiced for two or three generations thereafter.[187] Apart from responsa, most of which were collected and originally published in Venice in 1663, though others are scattered in the halakhic works of his contemporaries. Berab's extant works include a collection of novellae on tractates *Kiddushin* and *Ketubbot* (Venice, 1663);[188] a commentary on those parts of Maimonides' Code for which Vidal of Tolosa's commentary *Maggid Mishneh* is not extant;[189] sermons scattered in various treatises and collections;[190] and commentaries on aggadic material and rabbinic epigrams.[191]

34. **Jacob ben Abraham Berab II** (died Sukkot 1599[192]). Safed scholar active in the latter half of the sixteenth century, grandson of Jacob Berab I, student of Joseph Caro, and one of his five ordinees.[193] Jacob Berab II ordained seven of his disciples between 1596 and 1599: Moses Galante, Eleazar Azikri, Moses Berab (his brother), Abraham Gabriel, Yom Tov Ṣahalon, Ḥiyya Rofe, and Jacob Abulafia.[194] For some portion of his life Jacob Berab II evidently lived in Egypt.[195]

35. **Jacob of Triel** (dates unknown). Jerusalem sage active in the early sixteenth century.[196] In 1495 Triel may have been in Gaza.[197] His name appears among the Jerusalem sages mentioned in a letter sent by Safed's sages to their Jerusalem counterparts concerning the sabbatical year (1504). At a later date he moved to Egypt where we find him as a signatory on the nagid's regulation exempting scholars from taxes.[198] He subsequently returned to Jerusalem. Triel's halakhic decisions and teachings issued in Jerusalem are found in *Quntres Ḥiddushey Dinim.*[199]

36. **Jeremiah ben Levi Maurogonato (Mavrogonato)** (dates unknown). Safed sage active in the latter half of the sixteenth century,[200] of Cretan extraction.[201] Maurogonato studied under Joseph Caro and other Safed sages; he headed one of the Safed yeshivot. Maurogonato spent an unspecified amount of time in Istanbul. Two of his responsa are extant.[202]

37. **Joseph Ashkenazi** (born c. 1530 in Prague; died in Safed before 1582[203]). Safed scholar active in the latter half of the sixteenth century, also known as *Ha-Tanna ha-Elohi* (the divine tanna).[204] A native of Prague, Ashkenazi was son-in-law to Aaron ben Gershon Land, a local rabbi. In 1551, when Land left Prague for Posen to assume the office of av bet din there, Ashkenazi accompanied him. Both Land and Ashkenazi were in the forefront of the opposition to philosophical studies, even going so far as to launch an unbridled attack on Maimonides' philosophical treatises. After his father-in-law's death c. 1560, Ashkenazi moved to Verona, Italy, where he served as rabbi or dayyan of its dynamic Ashkenazi congregation. In Italy he further intensified his campaign against philosophy, singling out theoretical-philosophical kabbalah in particular. Mai-

monides was the target of Ashkenazi's most virulent attacks, which represented Maimonides as a heretic opposed to normative Jewish beliefs. Joseph Ashkenazi went so far as to voice objections to Maimonides' Code, which he challenged as an audacious halakhic work.[205] Ashkenazi's writings reflect a strong affinity to the works of *Ḥasidey Ashkenaz.*[206] We have no precise knowledge as to when Ashkenazi arrived in Safed. We do know that, before his arrival in Eretz-Israel, Ashkenazi lived in Egypt, where he may have encountered Bezalel Ashkenazi. In any event, by 1570 he was residing in Safed, where he remained until his death.[207] While in Safed he contested the opinion of Joseph Caro and other sages concerning tithes on grain grown by non-Jews in Eretz-Israel. Ashkenazi's stringent ruling conflicted with Caro's more lenient opinion, which was based on Maimonides.[208] Ashkenazi's renown also rests on his reputation as one of the greatest textual critics of the Mishnah. He based his accurate readings and interpretations on an ancient manuscript; in addition, Ashkenazi proofread talmudic and midrashic texts.[209] Perhaps the addition of the epithet "divine tanna" to Ashkenazi's name can be attributed to this outstanding expertise in textual criticism of the Mishnah.

38. **Joseph ben Abraham ibn Ṣayyaḥ (Ṣiyyaḥ)** (dates unknown). Sixteenth-century Musta'rab kabbalist and posek in Jerusalem and Damascus, known to have lived in Jerusalem from 1518 and perhaps from an earlier date.[210] In 1538 Ibn Ṣayyaḥ completed his kabbalistic work *Even ha-Shoham*—a commentary on the combination of letters (*ḥokhmat ha-ṣeruf*)[211]—in Jerusalem. He dedicated this work to Abraham Castro, a major personality in the contemporary Jerusalem kehillah.[212] Other known kabbalistic works by Ibn Ṣayyaḥ include *Ṣeror ha-Ḥayyim*—a curious commentary to Todros Abulafia's *Oṣar ha-Kavod;*[213] *Ṣafenat Paaneaḥ;*[214] and *Sheerit Yosef,* written in Jerusalem in 1549.[215] Sometime prior to 1560 Ibn Ṣayyaḥ moved to Damascus. He was regarded as an important posek, and many of his responsa, written in Jerusalem and Damascus, are extant. Some of his responsa are cited in the works of his eminent contemporaries, and others are found in a separate collection.[216]

39. **Joseph ben Abraham Saragossi** (died mid-1507 in Safed, buried in Ein Zitun). Rabbi and expounder of Torah; active in Safed in the early sixteenth century.[217] An anonymous traveler who reached Eretz-Israel in late 1495 noted that he encountered Saragossi in Beirut. He referred to him as "the honored rabbi, Joseph Saragossa the Sefardi."[218] As the name Saragossi indicates, Joseph came from Syracuse, Sicily. He probably left Sicily during the expulsion from that island in 1493, as by late 1495 he was in Beirut en route to Eretz-Israel. Upon his arrival in Sidon, the Jewish community's leadership tried in vain

to exercise its persuasive powers to keep him there.[219] In the late 1490s, David ibn Abi Zimra visited him in Safed.[220] From 1504 Saragossi resided in Damascus. He died in Safed in mid-1507 and was buried in Ein Zitun.

40. **Joseph ben Ephraim Caro (Maran, Mahariq)** (born 1488; died 1575 in Safed). Outstanding scholar in Eretz-Israel, of Safed in particular, Caro was born on the Iberian Peninsula, probably in Faro, southern Portugal. It appears likely that Caro's family left Portugal following the forced conversion in 1497 and stayed in various locations in the Mediterranean basin for unspecified lengths of time: Turkey, the Balkans, and Egypt, which all served as havens for the Iberian exiles.[221] Caro apparently resided in Egypt for approximately a decade, as his presence there between 1511 and 1519 can be documented.[222] From a Geniza document we learn that Caro earned his living as a pearl merchant.[223] In 1522 Caro was living in Adrianople, Turkey, where he commenced composition of his *Beit Yosef.* Somewhat later, Caro spent time in Nikopol and Salonika, prior to reaching Safed in 1536. From the early 1540s until his demise on the 13th of Nisan (24 March) 1575, Caro commanded a position of eminence in Safed and played a major role in that city's intellectual scene. In 1538 he was one of four individuals ordained by Jacob Berab, his teacher. Following Berab's death in 1541, Caro inherited his position as communal leader, and he himself later ordained several of his own students. Various sources portray Caro as an outstanding public leader who took an active role in communal affairs, in addition to his role as a pedagogue and posek. Several of Caro's responsa allude to his concern with communal affairs.[224] From the sources we can infer that Caro was active in Safed's overarching communal structure, Bet ha-Vaad, and functioned as its head. This forum's major institution was the court, or bet din ha-gadol, which was chaired by Caro himself.[225] Among the great scholars who sat on this court in conjunction with Caro, we must note Moses Trani, Israel di Curiel, and David ibn Abi Zimra (from 1564 on when he left Jerusalem for Safed). As a scholar of international repute, Caro received halakhic inquiries from the entire Jewish diaspora: for example, from Egypt, Italy, Turkey, Provence, Crete, Rhodes, and elsewhere, often on knotty halakhic problems. At times, his decisions emerged from the forum of the supreme court and were signed by Caro and two or three of his above-mentioned colleagues; alternately, we find replies to petitioners signed by Caro and his students.[226] Although Caro is known to have headed a yeshivah in Safed, few details about this institution are extant. In his role as communal leader, Caro also served as patron of other Safed yeshivot. He left

his mark on several yeshivot by dint of his involvement in their founding, administration, and upkeep, and by virtue of the fact that some of his closest disciples were appointed to head these congregational academies.[227]

Caro's fame rests chiefly on his comprehensive halakhic works, which were published during his lifetime: *Beit Yosef,* a compendium of the halakhah and its sources as they developed until his day, arranged according to the order found in Jacob ben Asher's *Arbaah Turim;*[228] *Kesef Mishneh,* a partial commentary on Maimonides' Code;[229] and *Shulḥan Arukh,* a halakhic code based on the *Beit Yosef,* three works that comprise the pillars of the codification of Jewish law to the present. Even in Caro's generation these treatises already exercised extensive influence, although some contemporary scholars refused to recognize either his authority or his legal decisions.[230] Caro's responsa have been published in two separate volumes: *Avqat Rokhel,* which covers *Oraḥ Ḥayyim, Yoreh Deah,* and *Ḥoshen Mishpat* (Salonika, 1791), and *Teshuvot Beit Yosef* on *Even ha-Ezer* (Salonika, 1598). Also extant is Caro's ethical-kabbalistic work *Maggid Mesharim,* a personal mystical diary in which he receives instruction from the angelic personification of the Mishnah, mainly in nocturnal visions.[231] Another known treatise by Caro is his *Kelaley ha-Talmud,* on talmudic methodology.[232]

41. Joseph ben Moses Trani (Maharit) (born 1569; died 1639). Safed sage active in the late sixteenth and early seventeenth centuries, the son of the eminent Safed sage, Moses Trani (Ha-Mabbit). In Safed, Joseph studied in the yeshivah of Solomon Sagis.[233] After his father's death in 1580 the family's financial situation deteriorated, as it had been dependent upon the generosity of an Egyptian-Jewish notable for financial support.[234] From his published autobiographical notes, it appears that Joseph Trani spent brief periods in various locations in Eretz-Israel and in Egypt as well (1587). In 1588, 1597, and 1600 he was in Damascus and Aleppo; in 1603 he was in Sidon; and from 1597 to 1598 he was in Ankara and Istanbul. Joseph Trani was almost certainly ordained by Jacob Berab II in the late sixteenth century, the lack of direct evidence notwithstanding.[235] In 1597 Joseph Trani served as an emissary of the Safed kehillah. His mission took him to Turkey, Ankara, and Istanbul, accompanied by Abraham Shalom. Upon his return to Safed in 1599, Trani undertook a similar mission to Damascus and Aleppo in that same year.[236] From Trani's autobiographical notes we learn further that he participated in yet another mission to Sidon in 1603, this time accompanied by Abraham Gabriel. From c. 1605, Trani headed a yeshivah in Istanbul, which had been founded by the notable Abraham ibn Yaish, a post he held for some "twenty years," until 1625. From that date until his death in 1639, Trani headed a different yeshivah, which had been founded by Jacob Ankawa.[237]

Joseph Trani's literary output was significant. His responsa appeared in three volumes after his death: Part One (Istanbul, 1641); Parts Two and Three (Venice, 1645). Additional collected responsa were recently published along with other of his works.[238] Other published works include: novellae on tractates *Kiddushin* and *Ketubbot* (appended to part three of his responsa);[239] collected homilies on the Pentateuch, titled *Ṣafenat Paaneaḥ* (Venice, 1648); the pamphlet *Ṣurat ha-Bayit,* which he composed in Jerusalem in 1595,[240] excerpts from which are found in Ḥayyim Alfandari's *Derekh ha-Kodesh* (appended to Alfandari's *Maggid mi-Reshit* [Istanbul, 1710]; and *Shemot Gittin.* Trani mentions four additional treatises, which are no longer extant: *Sefer ha-Miṣvot,* composed in 1593; *Nimmuqey Masekhet Negaim,* written in "Buqaia" (Peqiin) in 1596; *Ḥiddushey Sheviit,* composed in Kefar Kanna in 1602; and *Ḥiddushey Yebamot,* written in Jinin in the same year.[241]

42. **Joseph ben Peretz Colon** (dates unknown). Jerusalem sage active in the first half of the sixteenth century, son of Peretz Colon, and grandson of the eminent late-fifteenth-century Italian rabbi Joseph Colon (Mahariq). In 1512 Joseph ben Peretz Colon's economic situation was so grave that he was forced to appeal to Nagid Isaac Sholal for financial aid in order to provide for his family's needs.[242] In 1521 we find him among the signatories of a letter written by the students of the Jerusalem yeshivot.[243] In 1525 Colon served as a dayyan in conjunction with Abraham ha-Levi and Israel ben Yeḥiel [Ashkenazi].[244] After 1525 we find Colon mentioned as one of the *anshey ha-maamad* in Jerusalem.[245] Bearers of this honorific held key positions in the kehillah administration. Another sage with a similar name, Joseph Colon ben Moses Latif,[246] was also active in Jerusalem at that time. He belonged to the Spanish Latif family, some of whose members resided in Jerusalem in the latter half of the fifteenth and early sixteenth centuries.

43. **Joseph Corcos** (died before 1567). Jerusalem sage of probable Spanish origin as his name indicates. Perhaps a Spanish expellee, Corcos resided in Jerusalem as early as the 1510s or 1520s, where he headed a yeshivah for an unspecified period of time. In 1560 he was still living in Jerusalem. He did spend an interval in Egypt, however, where he studied under David ibn Abi Zimra. Evidently, he engaged in commerce for his livelihood.[247] Some of his responsa and decisions are scattered in the works of his contemporaries, with whom he corresponded on halakhic issues. Two of his treatises on Maimonides' Code have been published: his responsa to *Leshonot ha-*

Rambam and his commentary to Maimonides' "Book of Agriculture," completed in 1553 and published in Izmir in 1757.[248]

44. Joseph ibn Tabul (dates unknown). Safed kabbalist active in the latter half of the sixteenth century; known also as Joseph ha-Maaravi or Maghrebi, a clear indication of his North African origins, most probably Dr'aa, Morocco.[249] One of Isaac Luria's closest disciples, Ibn Tabul was second in importance to Ḥayyim Vital. Ibn Tabul, who contested Vital's primacy, himself transmitted Lurianic traditions to his students in defiance of the latter's ban. Many of his works are extant in manuscript; however, they never attained the immense popularity of his rival's.[250]

45. Joseph Iscandari (also written Ascandarani, Scandarani, Scandari); (dates unknown). Jerusalem and Safed scholar active in the late fifteenth and early sixteenth centuries; a colleague of Obadiah of Bertinoro in the 1490s and perhaps earlier.[251] Following an encounter with Iscandari during a visit to Safed when he was thirteen years old,[252] David ibn Abi Zimra noted that Iscandari was "very pious and God-fearing, as well as expert in Talmud and Midrash." In 1504 we find him among the Safed signatories on a letter to the Jerusalem sages concerning the sabbatical year.[253] Iscandari headed one of Safed's two Musta'rab yeshivot.[254] He also wrote a commentary on Jacob ben Asher's *Arbaah Turim.* References to Iscandari are found in the works of other eminent Safed sages.[255]

46. Joseph Sagis (died 1572). Safed sage. Evidently, he was a native of Salonika, where he studied under Joseph Taitaẓak, one of the greatest halakhists in that city in the first half of the sixteenth century.[256] According to an unsubstantiated tradition, Sagis was ordained by Jacob Berab.[257] In Safed, he headed a yeshivah and exercised particularly strong influence on two contemporary scholars: his disciple Eleazar Azikri and Moses ben Mordecai Galante. Sagis cosigned responsa with Joseph Caro and Moses Trani.[258]

47. Judah Albotini (died in the early 1520s, before 1522[259]). Jerusalem sage and kabbalist active in the first half of the sixteenth century, of Portuguese descent. His grandfather was Joseph Ḥayyun, one of the leading figures in the Lisbon Jewish community just prior to the mass forced conversion.[260] By the sixteenth century's first decade, Judah Albotini was living in Jerusalem, as seen from his presence as a signatory on the agreement of the Jerusalem sages to the nagid's tax exemption for scholars in 1509.[261] In Jerusalem, Albotini served as the officially appointed dayyan. His successor to this post, Israel Ashkenazi, wrote as follows: "What I wrote was that they put my chair next to that of the true dayyan. There was an outstanding scholar there, named R. Judah Albotini of blessed memory, and they appointed me in his place."[262] Two of his literary works are extant.

In halakhah, his *Yesod Mishneh Torah,* a commentary on Maimonides' Code, is still in manuscript.[263] Albotini's kabbalistic work, *Sullam ha-Aliyah,* has recently been published in its entirety.[264]

48. **Judah Ḥallewa** (dates unknown). Sage and kabbalist active in Safed and Jerusalem; a native of Fez, Morocco. The date of his arrival in Safed is unknown. He composed his kabbalistic work *Ṣafenat Paaneaḥ* in this city in 1545 before moving to Jerusalem, where he apparently died.[265] One of his halakhic decisions was cited by Joseph Caro.[266]

49. **Judah Mishan** (died after 1610). Safed sage and kabbalist, who studied under Isaac Luria; active in the sixteenth century's latter half. He was reputedly an extremely wealthy man.[267] In his kabbalistic treatises, Ḥayyim Vital cites many Lurianic traditions transmitted by Judah Mishan. Mishan compiled the kabbalistic traditions of Isaac Luria, Solomon Alkabetz, and Moses Cordovero.[268]

50. **Kalonymus** (dates unknown). Ashkenazi sage active in Jerusalem in the first half of the sixteenth century. In 1565 Joseph Caro expressed his admiration for this figure: "the elder, R. Kalonymus of blessed memory, used to be there [in the yeshivah] with the other Ashkenazi sages."[269] Kalonymus is to be identified with "Kalonymus ben R. Jacob," who, in conjunction with other Jerusalem sages, signed an agreement to a tax exemption for scholars in late 1547.[270] There is a strong likelihood that he was none other than the "R. Kalman" who headed one of the mid-sixteenth-century Jerusalem Ashkenazi yeshivot.[271] Isaac Luria was his student.[272] Some scholars have identified this figure with Kalonymus Baal ha-Nes (the wonder worker),[273] while others have suggested that he was Kalonymus Kalman Haberkasten of Lvov, Solomon Luria (Maharshal)'s father-in-law, who held rabbinical posts in Ostrog and Brisk (Lithuania) before settling in Jerusalem.[274] These proposals require further investigation.

51. **Levi ben Jacob ibn Ḥabib (Ralbaḥ)** (born c. 1480 in Zamora, Spain; died in the 1540s in Jerusalem). One of the most important Jerusalem sages in the first half of the sixteenth century. Following the expulsion from Spain, Ibn Ḥabib's family fled to Portugal, where some six years later, in 1498, Ibn Ḥabib was forcibly converted to Christianity at the age of eighteen. A year later, the Ibn Ḥabib family relocated in Salonika, where its members openly returned to Judaism.[275] In Salonika, Levi studied with the greatest contemporary scholars, including his father, Jacob ibn Ḥabib.[276] As early as 1504–1509, we find Levi composing responsa in Salonika.[277] In 1513 he was in Jerusalem; he returned to Salonika shortly thereafter, where he completed his father's *Ein Yaakov,* the second part of which was published in Salonika then or in the following year. Ibn Ḥabib again

stayed in Jerusalem briefly in 1522/23, subsequently alternating between Damascus and Safed (1525), before taking up permanent residence in Jerusalem in 1525. In Jerusalem, Ibn Ḥabib was the leading communal figure until his death sometime in the 1540s. He is best known for his adamant opposition to the plan formulated by Jacob Berab in 1538 calling for the revival of ordination and the founding of a Sanhedrin.[278] In addition to his unofficial position as teacher, halakhist, and leading scholar, Ibn Ḥabib also held the post of dayyan (*dayyan ha-memuneh*[279]), effectively making him head of the Jerusalem kehillah. Among his students, we must note Moses Castro and Issachar ibn Susan.[280] Ibn Ḥabib's collected responsa were published some twenty years after his death (Venice, 1565), along with his commentary on Maimonides' "Sanctification of the New Moon."[281] Several of his extant sermons contain philosophical elements.[282]

52. **Malkiel Ashkenazi** (dates unknown). Kabbalist and sage active in Hebron, a leading member of the Hebron kehillah in the latter half of the sixteenth century and perhaps earlier. Concerning Ashkenazi, Ḥayyim Joseph David Azulay (Ha-Ḥida) wrote: "I heard from the city elders that the rabbi of blessed memory was the reason why Jews resided in Hebron."[283] Relying on hearsay, Azulay attributed the founding of the Hebron kehillah to Malkiel Ashkenazi, while in actual fact Jewish travelers reported the existence of a tiny Jewish community in Hebron two or three generations earlier in the 1480s.[284] Evidently, what Azulay noted was the infusion of new life into this community by this sage; in Ashkenazi's day and the following generation, some of Safed's outstanding sages lived in Hebron.[285] Several treatises written by Malkiel Ashkenazi on Lurianic kabbalah as found in Ḥayyim Vital's writings are extant in manuscript.[286] He also compiled a collection of "the practices (*minhag*) of the holy congregation of Hebron," which reflects various kabbalistic practices.[287] Also extant in manuscript are Ashkenazi's textual notations on the Talmud, as well as some of his halakhic decisions.[288]

53. **Meir ben Samuel Back Ashkenazi** (dates unknown). Jerusalem sage active in the latter half of the sixteenth century. He served as one of the arbitrators in a late-sixteenth-century dispute between the Sefardi and Ashkenazi kehalim.[289] I believe he can be identified as the Jerusalem sage "Moses Meir ben Samuel Back Ashkenazi" who signed the agreement to the tax exemption for scholars in 1594.[290] The latter was also among the signatories on a letter sent by the Jerusalem sages to Monastir (present-day Bitola, Macedonia) in 1591.[291]

54. **Menaḥem ben Moses ha-Bavli** (dates unknown). Safed and Hebron sage active in the first half of the sixteenth century. The appellation

"the Babylonian" notwithstanding, it appears that Menaḥem originally came from Italy, perhaps from Rome. Until 1525 he served as dayyan in the city of Trikkola, Greece.[292] By 1537 ha-Bavli and his family were already residing in Safed, where he and his brother Reuben were actively engaged in the wool-dying business.[293] After 1546 ha-Bavli relocated to Hebron, evidently part of a group of Safed rabbis who settled in this city for the purpose of strengthening the Jewish community there. One of his responsa, on divorce, is extant.[294] While in Hebron, ha-Bavli wrote a brief excursus on the reasons underlying the commandments, *Taamey ha-Miṣvot* (Lublin, 1571). In the introduction to this treatise he mentions a longer work he composed on the same subject called *Taamey Miṣvot ha-Arukot.*

55. **Menaḥem de Lonzano** (born c. 1550, in Istanbul; died before 1626). Kabbalist, poet, and grammarian active in Jerusalem in the late sixteenth and early seventeenth centuries. At the age of twenty-five (c. 1575), de Lonzano moved to Jerusalem where he held the posts of communal cantor and scribe until the early seventeenth century. In 1607, after an acrimonious dispute with Gedaliah Cordovero, de Lonzano was forced to leave Jerusalem; however, only a year or so passed before his reinstatement as a communal official. The dispute was evidently grounded in Menahem's sharp criticism of Gedaliah Cordovero for his support of elements among the communal officials whom the former dubbed "evildoers."[295] Many literary works by de Lonzano are extant, including treatises in the fields of poetics, linguistics, and kabbalah. He also edited several midrashic collections.[296] Some of his works are found in his anthology, *Shtey Yadot* (Venice, 1618). In his *Derekh Ḥayyim,* first published in Istanbul in 1575, de Lonzano fiercely attacked scholars who were attracted to philosophy, particularly those from his native city.[297]

56. **Moses ben Abraham Berab** (dates unknown). Safed sage active in the latter half of the sixteenth century; grandson of Jacob Berab I and brother to Jacob Berab II, who ordained him in the late 1590s.[298] Moses Berab was involved in the Safed wool business. Prior to 1580, Moses resided in Egypt for a time, where he was involved in leasing.[299] Portions of his halakhic decisions are extant in the Cairo Geniza.[300]

57. **Moses ben Ḥayyim Alshekh** (born c. 1520 in Adrianople or Salonika; died 1593 in Damascus?). Safed sage active in the latter half of the sixteenth century. Alshekh pursued his studies mainly in Salonika, under Joseph Taitaẓak's tutelage. The date of Alshekh's arrival in Safed is unknown; however, in 1557 Ḥayyim Vital was his student in that city.[301] In Safed, Alshekh studied under Joseph Caro, became one of Caro's ordinees, and sat in judgment on his court.[302] Alshekh headed two yeshivot,[303] and in 1590 he ordained his disci-

ple, Ḥayyim Vital.[304] From 1591 to 1592 Alshekh traveled to Istanbul as an emissary of the Safed kehillah. On the journey, during which he passed through Damascus and perhaps other Syrian cities, Alshekh composed his letter "Ḥazut Kasha" in which he graphically described the dire economic distress of Safed's Jews. He evidently intended to publish this letter in Venice and distribute it among Italian Jewry.[305] On his return trip to Eretz-Israel in 1593,[306] Alshekh stopped in Damascus, where he may have died in Elul (September) of that year. Alshekh was a prolific writer, particularly in the realm of biblical homiletics and exegesis. This is not to say, however, that he ignored the realm of kabbalah; indeed, his *weltanschauung* derived from this realm.[307] He composed commentaries on nearly all the biblical books, which have been printed repeatedly.[308] His collected responsa and halakhic rulings were first published in Venice in 1605. There is evidence that he wrote other treatises no longer extant: *Shearim,* a commentary on *Midrash Rabbah;* and *Sugyot me-ha-Gemara.*[309] He was a genuinely admired figure, and this high regard found expression in the repeated printings of Alshekh's works along with excerpts and abridgements of the same works and in the addition of the epithet *ha-Kadosh* (the holy) to his name.

58. **Moses ben Isaac Alashkar** (born 1466 or 1467 in Spain; died 1542 in Jerusalem). Jerusalem sage active in the first half of the sixteenth century. Born in Spain, he studied under Samuel Valensi in Zamora. After the expulsion, he apparently wandered in North Africa, spending some time in Tunis.[310] He next passed through Tripoli and Patras, Greece, before taking up long-term residence in Egypt, where he acquired a reputation as an eminent posek. In 1539 he immigrated to Jerusalem where he remained until his death.[311] Contemporary sources barely reflect his presence in Jerusalem. A friendly letter sent to Alashkar by "R. Elijah ha-Levi" (Elijah ben Benjamin ha-Levi of Istanbul) mentions that "his patronage extends over Jerusalem," which can perhaps be understood as a reference to Alashkar's high standing in the community.[312] In addition to his selected responsa and halakhic decisions, published in Sabbioneta in 1554, Alashkar wrote a commentary on Jacob ben Asher's *Arbaah Turim,* titled *Geon Yaaqov.*[313] Also extant are liturgical poems and prayers composed by Alashkar.[314] Alashkar also evinced an interest in philosophy. His harsh critique of Shem Tov ibn Shem Tov's *Sefer ha-Emunot,* an attack on Maimonides, exemplifies this interest.[315]

59. **Moses ben Jacob Cordovero (RaMaK)** (born c. 1522, location unknown, perhaps in Salonika; died 23 Tammuz [27 June] 1570). Safed sage and kabbalist, the most prominent kabbalist in the generation preceding Isaac Luria. Cordovero's family apparently originated from

Portugal. After his arrival in Safed at the age of twenty,[316] Cordovero began to study esoteric Torah under his brother-in-law, Solomon Alkabetz, and exoteric Torah under Joseph Caro.[317] From the early 1560s and perhaps earlier Cordovero served as dayyan and av bet din in Safed and headed a yeshivah sponsored by the Portuguese community.[318] Several of Cordovero's responsa have been preserved in the collected responsa of his mentor, Joseph Caro.[319] Cordovero himself raised many disciples both in esoteric and exoteric Torah. Among them we must note: Mordecai Dato (the well-known Italian kabbalist), Abraham Galante, Moses Galante, Isaac Luria, Samuel Gallico, and Elijah de Vidas.[320] Cordovero developed a coherent kabbalistic doctrine with roots that were grounded in the Spanish kabbalistic tradition. Although displaced by Lurianic kabbalah in Safed itself, this tradition had many followers elsewhere, mainly in Italy, where Cordovero's writings were widely distributed in manuscript and printed versions, in some instances with commentary.[321] Cordovero's *Tomer Devorah* also laid the foundation for the creation of ethical-kabbalistic literature in Safed.[322] Certain pietistic regimen vitae practiced in Safed have been attributed to Cordovero.[323]

60. **Moses ben Joseph Trani (Ha-Mabbit)** (born 1500 in Salonika; died 1580). Rabbi and posek, one of the outstanding figures in the Safed community. Trani's immediate family came from Castile, Spain; nonetheless, the family surname seems to indicate former Italian origins (Trani, Italy). With the expulsion from Spain, Trani's father Joseph first went to Portugal; in 1497 he fled to Salonika where Moses was born in 1500. During Moses' childhood his family relocated to Adrianople where he studied under Joseph Fasi.[324] In 1518, at the age of eighteen, Trani settled in Safed. After Jacob Berab's arrival in Safed in 1524, Trani became his disciple,[325] and Trani was one of four disciples ordained by Berab in 1538; Joseph Caro was another.[326] Trani publicly expounded Torah for decades; in one responsum he mentions his five-decade-long role as a teacher in the Bet Yaakov congregation. He alludes to his position as head of a yeshivah in several responsa.[327] Although Trani certainly had many disciples, only two or three can be identified by name: Isaac Mishan, Moses ha-Levi, and perhaps Joḥanan Kaṣin as well.[328]

In addition to his role as pedagogue, as a member of the Bet ha-Vaad Moses Trani was actively involved in communal affairs.[329] This council of sages, whose members represented the different congregations, was the umbrella organization that oversaw matters affecting the Safed community as a whole. On more than one occasion, problems arose that required a hearing before this august body.[330] Trani almost certainly inherited Joseph Caro's position as communal leader after the latter's death in mid-1575, effectively making him the leading halakhic authority and public figure in Safed. In 1565 Trani was in Damascus; in 1577 he was in Istanbul. He died in 1580, having fathered four sons. In addition to his son Joseph (Maharit), we know of Solomon, Nathan (who died during his father's lifetime), and Yom Tov. After their father's death, Trani's sons found themselves in economic straits and required financial aid.[331]

Several treatises by Moses Trani are extant. In addition to his collected responsa in three parts (Venice, 1629–30), Trani also wrote a work aimed at supplementing Maimonides' Code, titled *Kiryat Sefer* (Venice, 1641). Its title page bears witness to the author's intentions: "In order to know the source of each and every law, whether prescribed by biblical law, or derived from [one of] the thirteen principles of hermeneutics, whether it is a tradition ascribed to Moses, or was decreed by the sages." Trani's goal was to furnish what Maimonides omitted, that is, the sources for each law.[332] Two of Trani's ethical works also saw publication: *Iggeret Derekh ha-Shem,* written in 1545 and published eight years later (Venice, 1553);[333] *Bet Elohim,* a comprehensive, systematic exposition of ethics according to philosophical principles (Venice, 1576).[334] To the printed editions of the latter, an additional treatise by Trani was appended—*Peyrush le-Pereq Shirah,* a rationalistic commentary to this midrashic work that exhibits a unique critical approach.[335] In his *Bet Elohim,* Trani mentions a treatise he wrote on redemption, *Iggeret Geulat Olam,* composed in 1535.[336] This treatise's whereabouts are unknown. Trani differs from other contemporary halakhists in that no conclusive evidence that he belonged to kabbalistic circles exists either in Trani's own writings or in those of his contemporaries. The fact that Moses Trani occasionally relied on kabbalistic sources is in and of itself insufficient to reach conclusions regarding his attitude toward kabbalah in general, as he in no way differed in this respect from the fifteenth-century philosophers Abraham Shalom, Abraham Bibago, Joseph Albo, and others.[337] Indeed, Trani sharply criticized certain ascetic practices introduced by pietistic circles as a sign of repentance and mourning for the destruction of the Temple, viewing them as lacking a halakhic basis. In his opinion, these practices were moreover intrinsically harmful to the fabric of society.[338]

61. Moses ben Levi Najara (born c. 1510; died 1581 in Damascus). Sage and kabbalist active in Safed, scion of a Spanish family. Najara arrived in Safed c. 1530, where he married Israel di Curiel's daughter and studied under Isaac Luria, and probably under Joseph Caro as well.[339] At a later date, he moved to Damascus where he headed a yeshivah until his death in 1581. Of his written works, only *Leqaḥ Tov,* a homiletic commentary to the Pentateuch, has been published (Istanbul, 1571). The noted poet Israel Najara was his son.[340]

62. **Moses ben Mordecai Basola** (died 1560 in Safed). Member of a family of French extraction, Moses Basola was one of the outstanding sages in sixteenth-century Italy. Basola held rabbinic posts in several Italian cities: Fano, Pesaro, and Ancona, where he settled before 1540.[341] In 1521–23 he journeyed to Eretz-Israel and kept a written diary of his experiences.[342] In 1560, the year of his death at the age of eighty, Basola settled in Safed. Moses Basola was a frequent participant in the halakhic debates of his day. His halakhic decisions have been preserved in the works of his contemporaries. Also extant are some letters and sermons.[343]

63. **Moses ben Mordecai Galante** (died c. 1614). Halakhic authority (posek) and kabbalist active in Safed in the latter half of the sixteenth and early seventeenth centuries; member of a family of Spanish expellees who had settled in Rome. In his youth, he immigrated to Eretz-Israel and settled in Safed, where he studied under Joseph Sagis. One of Joseph Caro's closest disciples, Galante sat in judgment on the Safed bet din, which was composed of Caro's disciples, and pursued kabbalistic studies under the tutelage of Moses Cordovero. Sometime between 1596 and 1599 Galante received ordination from Jacob Berab II.[344] Moses Galante headed the Provençal yeshivah in Safed, which was under the direct aegis of his mentor, Joseph Caro.[345] After Caro's death on the 13th of Nisan (25 March) 1575, Moses continued in this capacity, now in conjunction with his brother, Abraham Galante.[346] In addition to his responsa, collected and published by his son Yedidiah (Venice, 1608) along with novellae on several talmudic tractates, Moses wrote a commentary on Qohelet, titled *Qohelet Yaaqov* (published in Safed in 1578). Mainly homiletic in nature, this commentary also contains some kabbalistic interpretations.[347] He also composed *Mafteaḥ ha-Zohar* (published in Venice in 1566), an index of biblical references in the *Zohar.*[348] Some of his sermons were preserved in Obadiah Hamon of Bertinoro's commentary on Ruth (Venice, 1585).[349]

64. **Moses ben Shem Tov Alfaranji** (born c. 1431 or 1441 in Spain; died 1511, "aged 70 or 80."). Safed and Jerusalem sage active in the early sixteenth century.[350] Born in Spain, he studied under Isaac Canpanton,[351] and he headed a yeshivah in the city of Valladolid.[352] Alfaranji was evidently among the Spanish expellees, and he arrived in Safed after 1499, following a stay in Bursa, Turkey. In 1504 Alfaranji was already a leading figure in the Safed kehillah; in that year, his name headed the list of signatories on a letter sent by the Safed sages to their Jerusalem counterparts concerning the sabbatical year.[353] Subsequently, he moved to Jerusalem, where he died in 1511 at the age of seventy or eighty. A laconic reference to his presence in Jerusalem in his old age is found in a letter sent by Nagid Isaac Sholal to "the

sages in the holy yeshivah in Jerusalem."[354] His son, Shem Tov Alfaranji, was also among the signatories on the above-mentioned letter. Shem Tov accompanied his father to Jerusalem and later served as head of the Musta'rab congregation in Damascus.[355]

65. **Moses ben Ẓaddik Castro** (died in the 1540s, before 1547, in Jerusalem). Jerusalem sage active in the first half of the sixteenth century; member of the Spanish Castro family, a branch of which had settled in Egypt in the late fifteenth century. Abraham Zacuto was Castro's maternal uncle; his stepfather was Abraham ben Eliezer ha-Levi, who had married Castro's mother in Spain, prior to the expulsion.[356] A letter sent by Moses Castro from Jerusalem to Egypt in 1513 indicates that early in that decade, he was already actively involved in the leadership of the Jerusalem kehillah. In Jerusalem,[357] he studied under Levi ibn Ḥabib and David ibn Shoshan; at a later date, he studied under Jacob Berab as well. Little is known, however, of Castro's spiritual or intellectual nature. In 1521 we find his name, "Moses ben Ẓaddik de Castro," among those of other sages, as a signatory on the letter of beney ha-yeshivot (members of the rabbinical academy).[358] In the celebrated ordination controversy (1538) between Levi ibn Ḥabib and Jacob Berab, Castro sided with the former, outlining the reasons for his disagreement with his teacher, Jacob Berab, in a detailed responsum. Berab, for his part, bitterly resented his former student's opposition.[359]

66. **Moses Deleiria** (dates unknown). Safed sage active in the latter half of the sixteenth century, of Portuguese origin, evidently from the city of Leiria.[360] Various late-sixteenth-century regimen vitae have been attributed to Deleiria.[361] Several sources indicate that he was an international trader whose business dealings extended to Egypt, Syria, and perhaps the Balkans as well.[362] The early-seventeenth-century Safed sage, Yehosef Deleiria, was probably one of his descendants.[363]

67. **Moses ibn Makhir** (dates unknown). Safed sage active in the latter half of the sixteenth and the early seventeenth centuries; founder of the yeshivah in Ein Zeitim (Ein Zitun). This yeshivah functioned for only a few years before closing in 1599, when hostile raids by Muslim marauders forced its students to relocate to Safed.[364] One of the emissaries dispatched by the yeshivah to raise funds in Italy in 1599 was none other than Solomon Mor David, Ibn Makhir's son-in-law.[365] In his treatise *Seder ha-Yom* (published by his son-in-law, Solomon Mor David, Venice, 1599), Ibn Makhir elucidated the pedagogical principles that guided the course of study and the curriculum as pursued in Ein Zeitim in the fields of halakhah and kabbalah.[366]

68. **Peretz ben Joseph Colon** (died c. 1504). Safed and Jerusalem sage

active in the late fifteenth and early sixteenth centuries; son of the renowned Italian rabbi Joseph Colon (Mahariq), and father of Joseph Colon. In the 1490s Peretz Colon resided in Safed, where he was evidently one of the communal leaders according to the letter of an anonymous traveler (late 1495): "R. Peretz Colombo [Colon], may he have a long life and many descendants, is a leader and a captain in that city . . . in order to earn a living he also has a grocery store."[367] Sometime before 1504, Peretz Colon settled in Jerusalem and was the leading rabbi there. He died during the first decade of the sixteenth century, sometime after 1504.[368]

69. **Samson Bacchi (Back)** (dates unknown). Safed and Jerusalem sage and kabbalist active in the latter half of the sixteenth century. Probably a native of Italy,[369] Bacchi moved to Safed in 1582, perhaps shortly earlier, where he studied under Joseph ibn Tabul,[370] himself a direct disciple of Isaac Luria. Shortly thereafter, in 1583 or 1584, Bacchi moved to Jerusalem.[371] While in Jerusalem, Bacchi came in contact with Ḥayyim Vital, who then held the post of rabbi and dayyan in that city.[372] In 1585 Bacchi sent a short treatise composed by Ḥayyim Vital, titled *Seder ha-Aṣilut be-Qiṣur Muflag*, to Italy.[373] From one of its copies, where an explicit reference to "the honored Rabbi Samson Back of blessed memory, head of a Jerusalem yeshivah" is made, it appears that Bacchi headed one of the Jerusalem yeshivot.[374]

70. **Samuel ben Isaac de Uceda** (died between 1602 and 1604 in Safed). Safed scholar active in the latter half of the sixteenth century, whose birthplace and birthdate are not known. We do know, however, that by the 1550s he was already residing in Safed, as he noted in the introduction to his *Iggeret Shemuel* (Kuru-Chesme, 1597), "I have been living in Safed for the past forty years." De Uceda evidently received his education in the academies there. Elisha Gallico was his mentor in the field of halakhah, and Isaac Luria instructed him in kabbalah. Following Luria's death in 1572, de Uceda studied in Ḥayyim Vital's yeshivah.[375] De Uceda himself headed a yeshivah in Safed and undertook a fund-raising mission to Istanbul on its behalf, as he stated in his introduction to *Iggeret Shemuel:* "I cannot endure the burden of the yeshivah, and I was forced to approach the donors, may God preserve and protect them, here in Istanbul, may the Lord found it well, for donations to ensure its continued functioning." Among his disciples, we must note Joseph de Segovia.[376] Samuel de Uceda was a prolific writer whose main sphere of interest was homiletic exegesis. His collected works have appeared in several printed editions: *Midrash Shemuel*—selected homilies and commentaries on tractate *Avot* (Venice, 1579); *Leḥem Dimah*—a commentary on Lamentations (Venice, 1606); and *Iggeret Shemuel*—a

commentary on Ruth (Kuru-Chesme, 1597).[377] Also extant in manuscript are his commentary on Esther,[378] and his sermons.[379] One of his responsa has also been published.[380]

71. **Samuel Masud** (dates unknown). Safed and Jerusalem sage active in the first quarter of the sixteenth century. Masud's arrival in Safed, most probably from Egypt, took place before 1504. He subsequently moved to Jerusalem,[381] where we find him among the signatories on an agreement to a tax exemption for scholars in 1509.[382] By 1512, and perhaps somewhat earlier, Masud headed a yeshivah, one almost certainly founded by Isaac Sholal, and he continued to hold this position at least until 1521, when his name appeared as head of one of the two academies in the letter sent by beney ha-yeshivot.[383] In that year he either resigned this position or died, as his name does not appear in two sources dating from 1522 concerning the heads of the Jerusalem yeshivot. Masud can perhaps be identified as the author of a halakhic decision cited in *Quntres Ḥiddushey Dinim* attributed to the "honored rabbi S—— M——."[384]

72. **Simeon ben Isaac Eshenberg ha-Levi** (dates unknown). Jerusalem sage active in the second half of the sixteenth century. A native of Frankfort on the Main, he moved to Jerusalem after 1588. In 1588 his treatise *Deveq Tov,* a supercommentary on Rashi to the Pentatuech, was published in Venice. He also wrote *Sefer Masoret ha-Miqra,* an index to all the biblical references in the Talmud (Lublin, 1572). In 1591 we find his name as a signatory, in conjunction with other Jerusalem rabbis, on a letter sent to Monastir: "Samson [should read—Simeon] b. R. Isaac ha-Levi of blessed memory, the Ashkenazi."[385] In his list of several Ashkenazi sages active in late-sixteenth-century Jerusalem, Yom Tov Ṣahalon praised Eshenberg effusively: "They said of the honored rabbi Simeon that he was a great man, author of a book."[386]

73. **Solomon Absaban** (died 1592). Safed sage active in the sixteenth century's latter half, a student of Rabbis Joseph Caro and Isaac Luria. Some of his halakhic rulings and haskamot, cosigned with the most eminent rabbis in Safed, are extant. He headed a yeshivah in Safed, where Jacob Abulafia was one of his disciples.[387]

74. **Solomon ben Jeshua Adeni (Adani)** (born 1567 in San'a, Yemen). Jerusalem and Hebron sage active in the latter half of the sixteenth century. After a difficult journey, Adeni arrived in Safed with his father when he was four years old. Several years later he moved to Jerusalem, where he studied under Bezalel Ashkenazi and Ḥayyim Vital. In his youth Adeni endured difficult circumstances until the notable Moses ben Jacob Alḥami undertook to provide for his needs. Adeni spent his last years in Hebron,[388] where he completed his commentary on the Mishnah, *Melekhet Shelomo.* Adeni's commen-

tary on the Mishnah, which he started at the age of twenty-two, is characterized by careful examination of Mishnaic and talmudic texts and comparison of variants, a method evidently attributable to the influence of his teacher Bezalel Ashkenazi. Adeni based the commentary on glosses and annotations that he recorded in his personal copy of the Mishnah as derived from Bezalel Ashkenazi's readings and his own examination of the text. Subsequently, Adeni collated these notes and arranged them as an independent commentary, which he completed in 1624.[389] In addition to this text-critical commentary on the Mishnah, Adeni also edited the glosses of his teacher, Bezalel Ashkenazi, to *Seder Kodashim* and other talmudic tractates, in a treatise titled *Binyan Shelomo le-Ḥokhmat Beṣalel.*[390]

75. **Solomon ben Joseph Sirillo** (Spain; died c. 1553–55 in Jerusalem). Rabbi and posek active in Safed and Jerusalem. Born in Spain, following the expulsion he lived in Istanbul, Salonika, and Adrianople, before arriving in Safed prior to 1542.[391] In Safed he expounded Torah.[392] In the mid-1540s (sometime before 1548), he moved to Jerusalem where he resided until his death. His halakhic decisions are cited in the responsa of his eminent rabbinic contemporaries.[393] A chance remark concerning his family's indigence is found in a letter sent from Safed by Joseph Caro to the notable "R. Jacob Villareal" in Egypt requesting financial aid for Sirillo's widow and children "who are in desperate straits, and totally destitute."[394] Sirillo's renown rests on his commentary to *Seder Zeraim* of the Jerusalem Talmud,[395] and to tractate *Sheqalim* (Jerusalem, 1958), considered one of the best commentaries on the Jerusalem Talmud.[396] Sirillo also compiled a commentary to the Mishnaic tractate *Eduyyot* in the form of a talmudic tractate, based on excerpts from both the Babylonian and Jerusalem Talmuds.[397]

76. **Solomon ben Moses ha-Levi Alkabetz** (born c. 1500 in Salonika; died 1576). Outstanding kabbalist active in Safed in the generation preceding Isaac Luria. Alkabetz came from a family of Spanish expellees and was himself probably born in Salonika where he studied under Joseph Taitaẓak and Moses Albilda. In summer 1534 Alkabetz left Salonika for Eretz-Israel; however, he arrived at his destination only two years later. He spent the intervening period in Greece, in Nikopol, where he studied under Joseph Caro, and in Adrianople.[398] During this period in the Diaspora, Alkabetz devoted much time and effort to the impassioned promotion of aliyah to Eretz-Israel.[399] Little is known of Alkabetz's role in public affairs in Safed. Apparently, Alkabetz and his brother-in-law/disciple, Moses Cordovero, sought to make kabbalistic studies a priority, in the belief that, by this means, redemption could be hastened.[400] Alkabetz and Cordovero spearheaded a school of kabbalistic speculation that was

largely grounded in the Spanish kabbalistic tradition. Both men taught many disciples, and the true extent of their rich literary corpus has yet to be fully gauged. Most of Alkabetz's treatises have appeared in printed editions, some during his lifetime.[401] Alkabetz's fame also rests on his renown as the composer of the "Lekha Dodi" hymn, still recited in the present-day *Qabbalat Shabbat* (Friday night) ritual.[402] Virtually no information is available regarding Alkabetz's halakhic interests or pursuits, with the exception of his signature on a single halakhic decision.[403]

77. **Solomon Sagis** (died 1587). Safed sage active in the second half of the sixteenth century.[404] From his son Moses' remarks, it appears that Sagis was Isaac Luria's son-in-law,[405] perhaps his disciple as well. Solomon Sagis headed a yeshivah in Safed, where Joseph ben Moses Trani, Ḥiyya Rofe, Abraham Shalom, and Tuvia ben Abraham ha-Levi were among his students.[406] Sagis' novellae were cited by his student, Tuvia ha-Levi, in the latter's work *Ḥen Tov* (Venice, 1605). Evidently, Solomon Sagis had contact with Ḥayyim Vital. Indeed, when Vital came to Jerusalem, he presented Sagis with one of his kabbalistic homilies.[407]

78. **Yeḥiel Ashkenazi Castellazzo** (died 1565–70 in Jerusalem). Jerusalem sage known as Yeḥiel Ashkenazi, to be identified as Yeḥiel ben Moses Saks da Castellazzo, who, as the addition of Saks to his name indicates, evidently originated from Saxony, Germany. In 1529 Castellazzo was still in Austria. At a later date he went to Salonika and then to Jerusalem. He also spent a brief period in Safed.[408] During his time in Jerusalem, Castellazzo coheaded one of the Ashkenazi yeshivot there in conjunction with Abraham Pollack.[409] Several of his halakhic decisions are extant, and these reflect exchanges of views between Castellazo and Joseph Caro, and other contemporaries as well. In one pesak, related to bigamy, Castellazzo strenuously objected to Caro's ruling on this matter, even going so far as to question the authority of Caro's Safed court.[410]

79. **Yom Tov ben Moses Ṣahalon (Maharitṣ)** (born c. 1559/60 in Safed; died c. 1620, probably in Safed). Safed sage active in the latter half of the sixteenth and early seventeenth centuries; scion of a Spanish family whose members served in the rabbinate in Italy and the Orient during that period. Ṣahalon must be considered one of the outstanding sages and posekim of the last quarter of the sixteenth to the first quarter of the seventeenth century. It seems likely that Ṣahalon was a native of Safed, where he studied under Moses Besodo,[411] and he received ordination from Jacob Berab II in the late sixteenth century.[412] Increased evidence indicates that from 1585 Ṣahalon lived in various locations outside the borders of Eretz-Israel; nonetheless, he did spend intervals in Safed. In the late sixteenth century, due

to Safed's worsened economic conditions, Ṣahalon served as the community's emissary to Egypt and Turkey. Ṣahalon evidently returned to Safed prior to 1608 and remained there until his death in 1620. His literary works include *Magen Avot*—a commentary on *Avot de-Rabbi Nathan;*[413] *Leqaḥ Tov*—a commentary on the plain and homiletic meaning of the scroll of Esther (Safed, 1577).[414] Ṣahalon's main area of intellectual interest rested in the halakhic sphere, and he answered hundreds of responsa sent from the Jewish diaspora worldwide. Three hundred of his collected responsa were published in Venice in 1694. An additional two hundred and forty responsa were published in Jerusalem, 1980–81.[415] The responsa reflect Ṣahalon's strong personality and intellectual prowess, his unwavering certainty in the aptness of his decisions.[416]

The sixteenth century witnessed an intense flowering of Jewish settlement in Eretz-Israel. With the Ottoman overthrow of the despotic Mamluk regime, new peace and prosperity came to the land, greatly benefiting its Jewish population, bringing waves of immigration, from among the Iberian expellees in particular. *To Come to the Land* sums up this significant chapter in the history of Eretz-Israel, summarizes the patterns of aliyah and settlement in the land, and explores some of the factors that brought to it the best minds of the age, mystics and codifiers alike, intensively examining the underlying institutional infrastructure in the major centers where they were active. The burst of glory was brief, cut short by the development of an empire-wide economic crisis, which peaked in late century.

Based on examination of a broad variety of Hebrew, Muslim, and Christian primary sources and on the existing secondary literature as well, this foray into sixteenth-century Jewish life in Eretz-Israel has outlined how Jews reached the Land, the distribution of settlement, areas of economic endeavor, and the attitude of the Muslim authorities toward the Jewish minority in Eretz-Israel. Its main focus has been on the major centers of Jerusalem and Safed: the location of their Jewish quarters, demographic trends, communal composition, institutional structure, and the educational infrastructure that brought together a confluence of seminal figures, whose lives and literary output are summarized in the final chapter of brief biographies.

I have written this volume with scholars and students of late medieval Jewish history and of the Middle East in mind. It is, however, for those with an interest in intellectual history that *To Come to the Land* will prove an essential companion volume, providing background crucial to understanding the intellectual flourishing of the age and rich detail on the lives of major scholars of halakhah and kabbalah active in Eretz-Israel during its brief burst of sixteenth-century splendor.

Notes

Translator's note: Full information has been provided for each reference at its first appearance. Henceforth, short titles (indicated in bold typeface in the bibliography) have been used for works referred to frequently. Where English title pages are available for the Hebrew sources, these have been cited with the word "Hebrew" in parentheses. Where no such title page was available, the references to Hebrew works have been provided in transliteration. (In the bibliography all references to Hebrew works appear in transliteration without the English titles.)

INTRODUCTION

1. M. A. Cook, ed., *A History of the Ottoman Empire to 1730* (Cambridge, 1976), 1–78.

2. For the progression of battles and the final conquest, see J. von Hammer Purgstall, *Histoire de l'Empire Ottoman,* trans. J. J. Hellert (Paris, 1836), 4:261ff; the English translation of Muslim historian Ibn Iyas's account of the conquest in W. H. Salmon, *An Account of the Ottoman Conquest of Egypt in the Year A. H. 922 (1516)* (London, 1921). For additional substantive information on the conquest, see Elijah Capsali, *Seder Eliyahu Zuta* (History of the Ottomans and of Venice and that of the Jews in Turkey, Spain and Venice), ed. A. Shmuelevitz, S. Simonsohn, and M. Benayahu (Jerusalem, 1976–77), chaps. 109–33, pp. 312–65. See also D. Ayalon, "The Mamluk Army of the Ottoman Conquest" (Hebrew), *Tarbiẓ* 23 (1952): 221–26; I. Ben-Zvi, *Eretz-Israel under Ottoman Rule: Four Centuries of History* (Hebrew; Jerusalem, 1967), 4–14; P. M. Holt, *Egypt and the Fertile Crescent* (London, 1966), 33–41.

3. See n. 4 below.

4. See Ben-Zvi, *Eretz-Israel under Ottoman Rule,* 92–95; A. Cohen and B. Lewis, *Population and Revenue in the Towns of Palestine in the Sixteenth Century* (Princeton, 1978), 9–10; W. D. Hütteroth and K. Abdulfattah, *Historical Geography of Palestine, Transjordan, and Southern Syria in the Late Sixteenth Century* (Erlangen, 1977), 17–20. For further treatment of the sanjaks of Jerusalem and Safed, see E. Toledano, "The Sanjaq of Jerusalem in the Sixteenth Century: Aspects of Topography and Population," *Archivum Ottomanicum* 9 (1977): 279–319; A. Singer, *Palestinian Peasants and Ottoman Officials* (Cambridge, 1994); 35–42; H. Rhode, "The Geography of the Sixteenth Century Sancak of Safed," *Archivum Ottomanicum* 10 (1985–1987): 179–218.

5. This topic has been extensively studied by Bernard Lewis. See B. Lewis,

Notes and Documents from the Turkish Archives (Jerusalem, 1952), 5–22; idem, "Studies in the Ottoman Archives—1," *BSOAS* 16 (1954): 479–501; idem, "Palestine: On the History and Geography of a Name," *International History Review* 2, no. 1 (Jan. 1980): 1–12; idem, "Some Statistical Surveys of 16th Century Palestine," in *A Felicitation Volume for Professor J. D. Pearson,* ed. B. C. Bloomfield (London, 1980), 115–22; idem, "Nazareth in the Sixteenth Century According to the Ottoman *Tapu* Registers," in *Studies in Classical and Ottoman Islam,* ed. B. Lewis (London, 1976), 17:416–25; idem, "Jaffa in the Sixteenth Century According to Ottoman Tahrir Registers," ibid., 18:435–46; idem, "Acre in the Sixteenth Century According to the Ottoman *Tapu* Registers," in *Mémorial Ömer Lûtfi Barkan,* ed. O. Komlós (Paris, 1980), 135–39; Cohen and Lewis, *Population and Revenue.* See also Hütteroth and Abdulfattah, *Historical Geography,* 36–63.

6. See Lewis, *Notes and Documents,* 10; idem, "The Population and Tax Revenue of Eretz-Israel in the Sixteenth Century" (Hebrew), *Yerushalayim (Review)* 4 (1953): 136. (For a more detailed study, see idem, "The Ottoman Archives as a Source for the History of Palestine," *JRAS,* Oct. 1951: 139–55.)

7. On the difficulties involved in estimating general and Jewish population based on taxpayers' lists, see A. Cohen, "Demographic Changes in the Jewish Community of Jerusalem in the Sixteenth Century on the Basis of Turkish and Arabic Sources" (Hebrew), in *Jerusalem in the Early Ottoman Period,* ed. A. Cohen (Hebrew; Jerusalem, 1979), 104–7; idem, *Jewish Life under Islam* (Cambridge, Mass., 1984), 14–17. See also J. R. Hacker, "The Payment of *Djizya* by Scholars in Palestine in the Sixteenth Century" (Hebrew), *Shalem* 4 (1984): 90–98; A. David, "Demographic Changes in the Safed Jewish Community of the Sixteenth Century," in *Occident and Orient: A Tribute to the Memory of A. Scheiber,* ed. R. Dan (Budapest, 1988), 84–86.

8. See Lewis, "Studies in the Ottoman Archives—1," 487.

9. See Lewis' studies, n. 5 above.

10. For Suleiman's path of conquest, see R. B. Merriman, *Suleiman the Magnificent* (Cambridge, Mass., 1944). On Suleiman's economic projects, see Cohen and Lewis, *Population and Revenue,* 42–75; A. Cohen, "Development Projects in Jerusalem under Early Ottoman Rule" (Hebrew), *Cathedra* 8 (1978): 184–87; idem, "Ha-Mishar shel Ereẓ-Yisrael ba-Tequfah ha-Ottmanit," in *Commerce in Palestine Throughout the Ages,* ed. B. Z. Kedar, T. Dothan, and S. Safrai (Hebrew; Jerusalem, 1990), 300–308; idem, "Local Trade, International Trade and Government Involvement in Jerusalem during the Early Ottoman Period," *AAS* 12 (1978): 5–12.

11. This is attested to by inscriptions on the city gates. See Z. Vilnay, *Yerushalayim: Ha-Ir ha-Atiqah* (Jerusalem, 1971), 671ff. For the building of the wall and its rationale, see A. Cohen, "The Walls of Jerusalem," in *The Islamic World from Classical to Modern Times: Essays in Honor of Bernard Lewis,* ed. C. E. Bosworth (Princeton, 1989), 467–77; idem, "The Fortifications of Suleiman the Magnificent in Jerusalem" (Hebrew), *Cathedra* 57 (1990): 32–42; idem, "The Walls of Jerusalem—The European Connection" (Hebrew), *Cathedra* 63 (1992): 52–64.

12. In his *Divrei Yosef,* Joseph Sambari notes that "Sultan Suleiman built the walls of Jerusalem through his agent, his excellency the *Nagid,* Abraham Castro." Yosef ben Yitzhak Sambari, *Sefer Divrei Yosef,* ed. S. Shtober (Jerusalem, 1994), 285. See also A. David, "The Termination of the Office of *Nagid*

in Egypt and Biographical Data Concerning the Life of Abraham Castro" (Hebrew), *Tarbiẓ* 41 (1972): 334. Cohen questions the veracity of this report. See A. Cohen, "Were the Walls of Jerusalem Built by Abraham Castro?" (Hebrew), *Zion* 47 (1982): 407–18. See also A. David, "New Data about Abraham Qastro in Some Cairo Genizah Documents" (Hebrew), *Michael* 9 (1985): 149.

13. On the construction of the perimeter wall, see David ibn Abi Zimra, *Responsa*, no. 25. On the khan, see I. Ben-Zvi, "The Jewish Fortress of the 16th Century and the Qaisariya in Safed" (Hebrew), *BJPES* 10 (1942–43): 113–16 (=idem, *Studies and Documents* [Hebrew; Jerusalem, 1967], 26–29). See chap. 9 below.

14. See separate discussion below, chap. 2, "Tiberias."

15. See Cohen, "Development Projects," 179–87; idem, "The Fortifications of Suleiman in Jerusalem," 52–64. A brief discussion of this issue is found in Cohen's book, *Economic Life in Ottoman Jerusalem* (Cambridge, 1989), 3–4.

16. See Cohen, "Development Projects," 179–87; idem, "A Soap Factory in Ottoman Jerusalem" (Hebrew), *Cathedra* 52 (1989): 120–24; idem, *Economic Life.*

17. Various sources verify this trend. See Cohen and Lewis, *Population and Revenue,* 42ff. This topic will be dealt with at length below, chap. 3, sec. B.

18. For a general survey of this topic, see B. Lewis, *The Emergence of Modern Turkey,* 2d ed. (London, 1968), 21ff.; O. L. Barkan, "The Price Revolution of the Sixteenth Century: A Turning Point in the Economic History of the Near East," *IJMES* 6 (1975): 3–28; E. Bashan, "The Political and Economic Crisis in the Ottoman Empire from the End of the 16th Century as Reflected in the Responsa Literature" (Hebrew), *Proceedings of the Sixth World Congress of Jewish Studies* (Jerusalem, 1975), 2:107–15.

19. See Cohen and Lewis, *Population and Revenue,* 28–30, and passim. On Jerusalem, see Cohen, *Jewish Life under Islam,* 12–35; idem, "Demographic Changes," 93–111.

20. See my previous comments.

21. See the expanded discussion below, chap. 6, sec. B; chap. 10, sec. B.

22. M. Rozen, "The Position of the Musta'rabs in the Inter-Community Relationships in Eretz Israel from the End of the 15th Century to the End of the 17th Century" (Hebrew), *Cathedra* 17 (1980): 90.

23. For a general survey, see U. Heyd, "Jerusalem under the Mamluks and Turks" (Hebrew), in *Jerusalem Through the Ages,* ed. Y. Aviram (Hebrew; Jerusalem, 1968), 194–96; M. Sharon, "Processes of Destruction and Nomadisation in Palestine under Islamic Rule (633–1517)" (Hebrew), in *Notes and Studies on the History of the Holy Land under Islamic Rule,* ed. M. Sharon (Hebrew; Jerusalem, 1976), 9–32.

24. See expanded treatment below, chap. 3, secs. B and C.

25. D. Tamar, *Meḥqarim be-Toledot ha-Yehudim be-Ereẓ Yisrael u-ve-Arṣot ha-Mizraḥ* (Jerusalem, 1981), 12–16.

26. Responsa and rabbinical rulings from the period have been compiled by I. Schepansky, *Eretz-Israel in the Responsa Literature,* vols. 1–2 (Hebrew; Jerusalem, 1966–68).

27. On Geniza documents as a historical source for the study of Jewish settlement in Eretz-Israel during that period, see R. Gottheil and W. H. Worrell, *Fragments from the Cairo Genizah in the Freer Collection* (New York, 1927),

246–65; Ch. Turniansky, "A Correspondence in Yiddish from Jerusalem, Dating from the 1560s" (Hebrew), *Shalem* 4 (1984): 149–209; A. David, "New Information on Some Personalities in Jerusalem in the 16th Century" (Hebrew), *Shalem* 5 (1987): 229–49; idem, "New Genizah Documents: Ties of Egyptian Jewry with Eretz-Israel in the Sixteenth Century" (Hebrew), *Cathedra* 59 (1991): 19–55; idem, "The Genizah Sources and the Study of Jews of Egypt and the Land of Israel at the End of the Middle Ages" (Hebrew), *Zemanim* 38 (1991): 62–69; idem, "New Sources on the History of the Jews of Egypt and Their Ties with the Land of Israel in the Sixteenth Century," *Bulletin of the Israeli Academic Center in Cairo* 13 (1990): 10–15; idem, "A New Document Referring to the Yeshiva in Jerusalem in the Sixteenth Century" (Hebrew), *Cathedra* 68 (1993): 43–48.

28. The Christian sources relate mainly to Jerusalem. See the summaries in M. Ish-Shalom, *Christian Travels in the Holy Land* (Hebrew; Tel Aviv, 1979); and in N. Schur's studies, including his survey, "The Jewish Community of Jerusalem in the 16th–18th Centuries According to Christian Chronicles and Travel Descriptions" (Hebrew), in *Jerusalem in the Early Ottoman Period,* ed. A. Cohen, 343–434, and his book, *Jerusalem in Pilgrims and Travellers' Accounts: A Thematic Bibliography of Western Christian Itineraries, 1300–1917* (Jerusalem, 1980).

29. For the data available from Ottoman archives, see the studies by Lewis (n. 5 above); Cohen and Lewis, *Population and Revenue,* and Lewis's article, "The Ottoman Archives as a Source for Jewish History," in *Studies in Classical and Ottoman Islam,* ed. B. Lewis (reprint, London, 1976), article 20: 1–52; U. Heyd, *Ottoman Documents on Palestine, 1522–1615* (Oxford, 1960). For sharia documents from Jerusalem as a historical source for the city's Jewish population, see A. Cohen, *Ottoman Documents on the Jewish Community of Jerusalem in the Sixteenth Century* (Hebrew; Jerusalem, 1976); idem, *Jewish Life under Islam;* idem, *Economic Life;* idem, *A World Within: Jewish Life as Reflected in Muslim Court Documents from the Sijill of Jerusalem* (Philadelphia, 1994); and A. Cohen and E. Simon-Pikali, *Jews in the Moslem Religious Court* (Hebrew; Jerusalem, 1993). For further information on Muslim sources, see Cohen, "Turkish and Arabic Archives as a Source for the History of Jews in Palestine during the Ottoman Period" (Hebrew), in *Miqqedem umiyyam: Studies in the Jewry of Islamic Countries* 1 (1981): 39–48. On the importance of Arabic sources for Jewish history, see idem, "Ottoman Sources for the History of Ottoman Jews: How Important?" in *The Jews of the Ottoman Empire,* ed. A. Levy (Princeton, 1994), 687–704. For additional information, see J. W. Hirschberg, "Ottoman Rule in the Light of Firmans and Sharia Documents, Preliminary Note," *IEJ* 2 (1952): 237–48.

CHAPTER 1. IMMIGRATION TO ERETZ-ISRAEL

1. On the holiness of Jerusalem, see I. Ḥason, "Shivḥey Yerushalayim ba-Islam," in *Notes and Studies on the History of the Holy Land under Islamic Rule,* ed. M. Sharon (Hebrew; Jerusalem, 1976), 33–75. For Jerusalem's unique religious importance during the Mamluk period, see E. Ashtor, "Jerusalem in the Late Middle Ages" (Hebrew), *Yerushalayim (Review)* 2/5 (1955): 76ff; J. Drory, "Jerusalem in the Mamluk Period" (Hebrew), in *Jerusalem in the Middle Ages: Selected Papers,* ed. B. Z. Kedar (Hebrew; Jerusalem, 1979), 156–

66; A. Elad, *Medieval Jerusalem and Islamic Worship: Holy Places, Ceremonies, Pilgrimage* (Leiden, 1995). For the Mamluk regime's disinterest in developing Eretz-Israel, see J. Parkes, *A History of Palestine from 135 to Modern Times* (New York, 1949), 83–103, 130–70; Sharon, "Processes of Destruction," 9–32.

2. This issue has been recently examined by several scholars. See Cohen and Lewis, *Population and Revenue.* On Jerusalem specifically, see Cohen, "Demographic Changes," 93–111; A. David, "A Letter from Jerusalem from the Early Ottoman Period in Eretz-Yisrael" (Hebrew), in *Jerusalem in the Early Ottoman Period,* ed. A. Cohen, 39–60.

3. This topic, which merits independent study, has been dealt with from the vantage of Spanish Jewry. See J. R. Hacker, "Links between Spanish Jewry and Palestine, 1391–1492," in *Vision and Conflict in the Holy Land,* ed. R. I. Cohen (Jerusalem, 1985), 111–39.

4. See A. Grossman, "A Fourteenth Century Ashkenazi Letter of Vision and Chastisement (Concerning the Link of Ashkenazi Jewry with Eretz Israel)" (Hebrew), *Cathedra* 4 (1977): 191.

5. See A. David, "The Historical Significance of the 'Elders' Mentioned in the Letters of R. Obadia of Bertinoro" (Hebrew), in *Jerusalem in the Middle Ages,* ed. B. Z. Kedar (Hebrew; Jerusalem, 1979), 221–43; E. Reiner, "Jewish Community Leadership in Late Mameluke Jerusalem" (Hebrew), *Shalem* 6 (1992): 23ff.

6. See A. David, ed., "The Letter of R. Israel Ashkenazi of Jerusalem to R. Abraham of Perugia" (Hebrew), *Alei Sefer* 16 (1990): 113–14. This relocation apparently occurred before mid-1519. See A. David, "A Letter from Jerusalem," 51; H. Z. Dimitrovsky, "An Unknown Chapter in the Relations Between the *Nagid* Isaac Sholal and Rabbi Jacob Berab" (Hebrew), *Shalem* 6 (1992): 114–19.

7. Obadiah of Bertinoro's encounter with the "elders" of Jerusalem in the late 1480s illustrates this point. See David, "Historical Significance," 221–43; Reiner, "Jewish Community Leadership," 23–81. A somewhat different slant is found in an anonymous sixteenth-century letter sent from points unknown (Italy?) to an unknown addressee; the writer attempted to dissuade his correspondent from making aliyah to Eretz-Israel after learning of Sefardi aloofness and condescension toward members of other communities. See A. David, "New Sources Describing Travel from Venice to the Orient and Eretz Israel (Palestine) in the Fifteenth to the Seventeenth Centuries" (Hebrew), *Shalem* 6 (1992): 333.

8. For example, in the first half of the fifteenth century relations between *maarabim* (Jews of North African origin) and Ashkenazim in Jerusalem were so acrimonious that, coupled with other factors, they deterred one of the greatest contemporary Ashkenazi sages, Israel ben Petaḥiah Isserlein, from the very idea of emigrating to Eretz-Israel. Cf. Israel Isserlein, *Pesaqim u-Khetavim* (Venice, 1519), no. 88. For waves of immigration to Eretz-Israel during the Crusader and Mamluk periods and the problems experienced by the immigrants, see E. Reiner, "Pilgrims and Pilgrimage to Eretz Yisrael, 1099–1517" (Hebrew; Ph.D. diss., Jerusalem, 1988).

9. Naḥmanides' aliyah to Jerusalem and his role in the Jewish community there has been reexamined by B. Z. Kedar. See Kedar, "The Jews of Jerusalem, 1187–1267, and the Role of Naḥmanides in the Re-establishment of Their Community" (Hebrew), in *Jerusalem in the Middle Ages,* ed. B. Z. Kedar,

122–36. For Obadiah of Bertinoro's part in advancing the Jewish community in Jerusalem in the late 1480s, see David, "Historical Significance," 221–43; M. E. Artom and A. David, "R. Obadiah Yare mi-Bertinoro ve-Igrotav me-Ereẓ Yisrael," in *Jews In Italy: Studies Dedicated to the Memory of U. Cassuto,* ed. H. Beinart (Jerusalem, 1988), 29–33. (Reprint: *From Italy to Jerusalem: The Letters of Rabbi Obadiah of Bertinoro from the Land of Israel* [Hebrew; Ramat Gan, 1997]. All references to these letters are to the earlier edition.) See also Reiner, "Jewish Community Leadership," 23ff. On David ibn Abi Zimra's focal position in the Jerusalem Jewish community shortly following his aliyah, see Cohen, *Jewish Life under Islam,* 44, 234, and the discussion below, chap. 7, "the dayyan." For the seventeenth-century figure of Isaiah Horowitz, see A. L. Frumkin and E. Rivlin, *Toledot Ḥakhmey Yerushalayim* (Jerusalem, 1928), 1:146–58; M. Rozen, *The Jewish Community of Jerusalem in the Seventeenth Century* (Hebrew; Tel Aviv, 1984), 149–50.

10. On immigration from Spain, see Hacker, "Links," 112–20; A. David, "An Epistle Regarding Aliya to the Land of Israel from Spain" (Hebrew), *Tarbiẓ* 52 (1983): 655–59. On Ashkenaz, see Grossman, "A Fourteenth Century Ashkenazi Letter," 190–98; E. Reiner, "Between Ashkenaz and Jerusalem" (Hebrew), *Shalem* 4 (1984): 27–62.

11. On immigration from western Europe, see J. Braslvsky, *Studies in Our Country: Its Past and Remains* (Hebrew; Tel Aviv, 1954), 231–33. On immigration from Spain, see Hacker, "Links." Much can be learned about the relationship between Italian Jewry and Eretz-Israel from letters written by Italian immigrants to Eretz-Israel; for example, Elijah of Massa Lombarda's letter from 1438, reprinted by J. R. Hacker, "R. Elija of Massa Lombarda in Jerusalem" (Hebrew), *Zion* 50 (1985): 241–63; Joseph Montagna's letter from Jerusalem in 1481, recently published by A. Yaari, *Letters from the Land of Israel* (Hebrew; Ramat Gan, 1971), 89–93; Isaac b. Meir Latif, second half of the fifteenth century, in Yaari, ibid., 94–98; and according to a different MS, published by N. Ben-Menaḥem, "Iggeret R. Yiṣḥak b. R. Meir Latif mi-Yerushalayim," *Sinai* 53 (1963): 258–62. See also three letters by Obadiah of Bertinoro in Artom and David, "Obadiah mi-Bertinoro," 24–108 (abridged English version, E. N. Adler, *Jewish Travellers,* 2d ed. [New York, 1966], 209–50); or the letter composed by an anonymous traveler in late 1495. See Yaari, *Letters,* 144–60. An additional section of the conclusion of this letter has been recently discovered and published. See David, "New Sources Describing Travel," 323–26. On immigration from North Africa, see A. David, "Relations between North African Jewry and Eretz Israel in the Fifteenth and Sixteenth Centuries" (Hebrew), *Pe'amim* 24 (1985): 74–86.

12. For a comprehensive discussion, see E. Strauss-Ashtor, *History of the Jews in Egypt and Syria under the Rule of the Mamluks* (Hebrew; Jerusalem, 1951), 2:204–36.

13. Particularly calls from Spain. See H. Beinart, "A 15th Century Formulary from Spain" (Hebrew), *Sefunot* 5 (1961): 81–82, 88–91, 116–17, 120–21; Hacker, "Links"; Ch. Merchavia, *The Call to Zion* (Hebrew; Jerusalem, 1980), 54–58.

14. See Ashtor, "Jerusalem in the Late Middle Ages," 71–116; Drory, "Jerusalem in the Mamluk Period," 148–77; Y. Friedman, "Eretz-Yisrael and Jerusalem on the Eve of the Ottoman Period" (Hebrew), in *Jerusalem in the Early Ottoman Period,* ed. A. Cohen, 7–38.

15. Lewis, "Studies in the Ottoman Archives," 469–501; Ben-Zvi, *Eretz-Israel under Ottoman Rule,* 48ff.; Cohen and Lewis, *Population and Revenue,* 19ff.; Cohen, "Development Projects," 179–87; idem, "Demographic Changes," 93–111; idem, *Jewish Life under Islam,* 12–35; A. David, "The Spanish Exiles in the Holy Land," in *The Sephardi Legacy,* ed. H. Beinart (Jerusalem, 1992), 2:82ff.

16. For a summary of the reasons underlying Safed's ascendancy over Jerusalem in the sixteenth century, see Tamar, *Ha-Yehudim be-Ereẓ Yisrael u-ve-Arṣot ha-Mizraḥ,* 10–16. On settlement in the Galilee, see chap. 2 below.

17. For a summation, see David, "Spanish Exiles," 82ff.; idem, "Personalities in Jerusalem," 229–49; J. R. Hacker, "On the Intellectual Character and Self-Perception of Spanish Jewry in the Late Fifteenth Century" (Hebrew), *Sefunot* 17 (n.s. 2) (1983): 42–43.

18. For the role of Spanish exiles in Jerusalem, see David, "Personalities in Jerusalem," 229–40; M. Benayahu, "The Sermons of R. Yosef b. Meir Garson as a Source for the History of the Expulsion from Spain and Sephardi Diaspora" (Hebrew), *Michael* 7 (1981): 81–98. On their role in Safed, see M. Benayahu, "Teudah min ha-Dor ha-Rishon shel Megorashey Sefarad bi-Ṣefat," *Sefer Assaf,* ed. M. D. Cassuto, J. Klausner, and J. Gutman (Jerusalem, 1953), 109–25; idem, "Yosef Garson," 98–103.

19. For primary and secondary material on sea routes from European ports to the Middle East, see n. 22 below.

20. This land route was in use for years following 1428. European Jews sought alternate routes when the Venetian authorities banned transportation of Jews by sea vessels embarking from their ports. This edict has been treated in detail by J. Prawer, who believes it was enacted twice and remained in force until shortly before 1487. See J. Prawer, "The Friars of Mount Zion and the Jews of Jerusalem in the 15th Century" (Hebrew), *BJPES* 14 (1947): 15–24. See also the renewed discussion by D. Jacoby, "The Franciscans, the Jews, and the Issue of Mount Zion in the Fifteenth Century: A Reconsideration" (Hebrew), *Cathedra* 39 (1986): 51–70, where he presents a case for there having been only a single decree, in effect for some years after 1428. See also S. Simonsohn, "Divieto di trasportare ebrei in Palestina," *Italia Judaica* 2 (1986): 39–53.

21. We possess no precise information regarding the route through the Atlas Mountains used by travelers and pilgrims, but from other contexts it seems clear that Spanish Jews reached the Maghreb and proceeded east from there, overland through Egypt. For example, Abraham Zacuto, a famous Spanish scholar and astronomer of the expulsion generation, reached Jerusalem in 1513 via North Africa (Tunisia) and Egypt. See David, "North African Jewry," 76; idem, "New Sources Describing Travel," 322 n. 19.

22. For sea routes from European ports to the Middle East, see *Massa Meshullam mi-Volterra be-Ereẓ Yisrael,* ed. A. Yaari (Jerusalem, 1949), 39–45 (Adler, *Jewish Travellers,* 156–79); Artom and David, "Obadiah mi-Bertinoro," 54–64 (abridged English translation in Adler, *Jewish Travellers,* 209–19); an anonymous traveler's letter from late 1495 in Yaari, *Letters,* 146–48; A. David, "Fifteenth and Sixteenth Century Pilgrim and Immigrant Journey Routes to the Land of Israel," in *Jewish Studies in a New Europe: Proceedings of the Fifth Congress of Jewish Studies in Copenhagen 1994* (Copenhagen, 1998), 163–74. See also the itinerary, "Lalekhet mi-Veneṣiyah le-Ereẓ Yisrael u-le-Miṣrayim" (How to Go from Venice to Eretz-Israel and Egypt), MS. Cambridge Ad. 10.46

(Institute of Microfilmed Hebrew Manuscripts, Hebrew University, Jerusalem, no. 5929), fol. 6r, published by A. Neubauer, *Hebräische Bibliographie* 21 (1881–82): 136, and analyzed by M. E. Artom, "An Italian-Hebrew Itinerary of the Fifteenth Century" (Hebrew), *Italy,* ed. M. A. Szulwas, vol. 1 (1945): 21–23. For further studies on this itinerary, see M. A. Szulwas, "On the Italian Itinerary" (Hebrew), *Kiryat Sefer* 23 (1946–47): 73–74.

23. For Meshullam's itinerary, see n. 22 above. Obadiah of Bertinoro described his journey to Eretz-Israel in his first letter from Jerusalem (1488). See Artom and David, "Obadiah mi-Bertinoro," 54–81 (Adler, *Jewish Travellers,* 209–34).

24. Meshullam sailed from Naples to Venice, and from there to Rhodes. See Yaari, *Massa Meshullam,* 88 (Adler, *Jewish Travellers,* 208). Obadiah sailed East via Sicily. See Artom and David, "Obadiah mi-Bertinoro," 54–59 (Adler, ibid., 209–15). It seems that Meshullam's second trip to the East followed a route identical to that of Obadiah, i.e., via Sicily, as both men sailed together from Messina to Rhodes. See Artom and David, "Obadiah mi-Bertinoro," 59–60 (Adler, ibid., 214–16).

25. Yaari, *Massa Meshullam,* 45 (Adler, *Jewish Travellers,* 158).

26. Artom and David, "Obadiah mi-Bertinoro," 63–64 (Adler, *Jewish Travellers,* 217–19).

27. Yaari, *Massa Meshullam,* 49–71 (Adler, *Jewish Travellers,* 162–89); Artom and David, "Obadiah mi-Bertinoro," 68–81 (Adler, ibid., 223–34).

28. See Yaari, *Massa Meshullam,* 57 (Adler, *Jewish Travellers,* 171–72); Artom and David, "Obadiah mi-Bertinoro," 71–73 (Adler, ibid., 225–28).

29. On the supremacy of the Venetian Republic in fifteenth- and sixteenth-century Mediterranean trade, see F. C. Lane, *Venice: A Maritime Republic* (Baltimore, 1977). E. Ashtor has explored this topic in archival material from Venice and other locations in the Mediterranean basin. See E. Ashtor, "The Venetian Supremacy in Levantine Trade: Monopoly or Pre-Colonialism?" *Journal of European Economic History* 3 (1974): 5–53 (reprinted in Ashtor's collected articles, *Studies on the Levantine Trade in the Middle Ages* [London, 1978], article no. 6); A. David, "The Involvement of Egyptian Jews in the Trade with Venice, as Reflected from the Genizah Documents and Other Sources" (Hebrew), *PAAJR* 60 (1994): 1–29. For additional bibliography, see ibid., 4 n. 17.

30. For the medieval popularity of Venice as a main embarkation point for travel to the Orient, see E. Ashtor, "Venezia e il pellegrinaggio in Terrasanta nell basso Medioevo," *Archivio Storico Italiano* 143 (1985): 197–223; A. Grabois, "From Passengers on Board to the 'Passenger Vessel': Changes in the Maritime Transportation of Holy Land Pilgrims in the Middle Ages" (Hebrew), *Israel—People and Land* 5–6 (1987–89): 160–64. Many Jews bound for Eretz-Israel also sailed from Venice. See David, "New Sources Describing Travel," 319–33.

31. See Grabois, "Passengers," 160–64.

32. Artom and David, "Obadiah mi-Bertinoro," 99 (Adler, *Jewish Travellers,* 243).

33. Yaari, *Letters,* 148.

34. Moses Basola, *Masot Ereẓ-Yisrael,* ed. I. Ben-Zvi (Jerusalem, 1938), 92–93.

35. See A. Yaari, *Masot Ereẓ-Yisrael shel Olim Yehudim* (Ramat Gan, 1976), 169–96. On Elijah of Pesaro's journey, see J. Shatzmiller, "Travelling in

the Mediterranean in 1563; The Testimony of Eliahu of Pesaro," in *The Mediterranean and the Jews . . . 16th–18th Centuries,* ed. A. Toaff and S. Schwarzfuchs (Ramat Gan, 1989), 237–48.

36. Yaari, *Masot,* 168.

37. Beginning with the second half of the fifteenth century, Christian pilgrim literature contains guides for sailing to Eretz-Israel. For surveys of this genre, see E. G. Duff, ed., *Information for Pilgrims unto the Holy Land* (London, 1893). (My thanks to Dr. Oded Irshai for bringing this source to my attention.) See also M. M. Newett, introduction to *Canon Pietro Casola's Pilgrimage to Jerusalem in the Year 1494* (Manchester, 1907), 1–113; Ashtor, "Venezia"; Grabois, "Passengers," 155–64.

38. On this itinerary, see n. 22 above.

39. See *Canon Pietro Casola's Pilgrimage,* ed. M. M. Newett.

40. See David, "New Sources Describing Travel," 319–29.

41. See Yaari, *Letters,* 144–60.

42. See Basola, *Masot,* 28–42.

43. See Yaari, *Masot,* 165–96. For the specifics of the sea journey, see ibid., 168–84. For further details on him and his journey, see Shatzmiller, "Eliahu of Pesaro."

44. His letter has been published by David, "New Sources Describing Travel," 329–32.

45. On these pirates, see F. Braudel, *The Mediterranean and the Mediterranean World in the Age of Philip II,* 4th ed. (London, 1981), 2:877–82; E. Bashan, *Captivity and Ransom in Mediterranean Jewish Society (1391–1830)* (Hebrew; Jerusalem, 1980), 109–35.

46. On this scandal, which lasted for several years, see n. 20 above.

47. See Braslvsky, *Studies in Our Country,* 140–44.

48. An incomplete text of this letter was published by A. Yellinek, *Quntres Gezeyrot Tatnu* (Hebrew; Leipzig, 1854), 14–25. On the historical significance of this source, see H. Graetz, *History of the Jews* (Philadelphia, 1956), 4:271–73; Braslvsky, *Studies in Our Country,* 139–43; Prawer, "The Friars of Mount Zion," 15–24; Jacoby, "The Franciscans, the Jews and Mt. Zion," 68–70; Simonsohn, "Divieto di trasportare ebrei," 51–52; J. R. Hacker, "The Jewish Community of Salonica from the Fifteenth to the Sixteenth Century" (Hebrew; Ph.D. diss., Jerusalem, 1978), appendix 1, 1–12.

49. See R. Röhricht and H. Meisner, *Deutsche Pilgerreisen nach dem heiligen Lande* (Berlin, 1880), 111–14.

50. Ibid., 112–13. The translation of this paragraph is based on the Hebrew version published by Braslvsky, *Studies in Our Country,* 142–43.

51. This impression is based on biographical allusions by R. Eliezer Eilenburg from Braunschweig (Germany). See his introduction to a Hebrew treatise written in 1554, MS. New York, Jewish Theological Seminary of America, Mic. 2324 (Acc. 3637) (IMHM, no. 28577), fols. 89r–94r. Following their expulsion from Braunschweig in 1547, the author and some close family members relocated in Posen (Poland), later proceeding to Safed and Jerusalem. I intend to publish this text in the near future. For additional evidence, see the section on central Europe below.

52. This letter has been published by J. M. Toledano, "Documents from Manuscripts" (Hebrew), *HUCA* 4 (1927): 458–63. See also, David, "North African Jewry," 77.

53. On the Barbary Corsairs, see G. Fisher, *Barbary Legend: War, Trade, and Piracy in North Africa (1415–1830)* (Oxford, 1957). On their Jewish captives, see Bashan, *Captivity and Ransom,* 44–67.

54. See Artom and David, "Obadiah mi-Bertinoro," 60 (Adler, *Jewish Travellers,* 215).

55. See Artom and David, "Obadiah mi-Bertinoro," 59 (Adler, *Jewish Travellers,* 215).

56. Yaari, *Masot,* 180.

57. See David, "New Sources Describing Travel," 331.

58. On this topic, see H. H. Ben-Sasson, "Exile and Redemption Through the Eyes of the Spanish Exiles" (Hebrew), in *The Yitzhak F. Baer Jubilee Volume,* ed. S. W. Baron et al. (Jerusalem, 1960), 216–19; and in greater detail in J. R. Hacker, "Pride and Depression—Polarity of the Spiritual and Social Experience of the Iberian Exiles in the Ottoman Empire" (Hebrew), in *Culture and Society in Medieval Jewry: Studies Dedicated to the Memory of H. H. Ben-Sasson,* ed. M. Ben-Sasson, R. Bonfil, and J. R. Hacker (Jerusalem, 1989), 541–86.

59. See David, "Spanish Exiles," 82ff.

60. In the introduction to his commentary on Psalms (Venice, 1549), Solomon Atiyah mentions several sages who "went from Salonika to Eretz-Israel." One such sage was "Rabbi Isaac Mar-Ḥayyim" the Sefardi whom we know resided in Jerusalem by 1503. The temporary sojourn of Jewish exiles from Spain in Greece prior to aliyah to Eretz-Israel merits independent study. For a general survey, see E. Bashan, "*'Aliyoth'* from Salonica to the Holy Land during the Sixteenth to Eighteenth Centuries" (Hebrew), in *Then and Now: Annual Lectures on the Jews of Greece,* ed. Z. Ankori (Hebrew; Tel Aviv, 1984), 73–83.

61. On this letter and its author, see J. Prawer, "On the Text of the 'Jerusalem Letters' in the 15th and 16th Centuries" (Hebrew), *Jerusalem: Quarterly Devoted to the Study of Jerusalem and Its History* 1 (1948): 143–44; M. D. U. Cassuto, "Who Was David Reubeni?" (Hebrew), *Tarbiẓ* 32 (1963): 342–43, 354–56.

62. For the activity of the Knights of St. John on Malta from the mid-sixteenth century on, see Braudel, and Bashan, n. 45 above. On the capture of Jewish immigrants bound for Eretz-Israel specifically, see Bashan, 116–18.

63. This excerpt has been cited by Bashan, *Captivity and Ransom,* 116. In his works *Divrey ha-Yamim le-Malkhey Ṣorfat u-Malkhey beyt Ottoman ha-Tugar* (Sabbioneta, 1554), fol. 323v, and *Emeq ha-Bakha,* ed. K. Almbladh (Uppsala, 1981), 80, Joseph ha-Kohen mentions that in 5312 (1552) seventy Jews were taken prisoner by "ships of the monks of Rhodes" based on Malta (English translation, H. S. May, *The Vale of Tears* [The Hague, 1971], 86). Despite the numerical discrepancy and the absence of any reference to Eretz-Israel as the intended destination, evidently ha-Kohen was referring to the same event. Bashan, *Captivity and Ransom,* 116–17, concurs with this conjecture. From Joshua Ṣunṣin's collection of responsa, *Naḥalah li-Yehoshua* (Istanbul, 1731), no. 40, we learn that Moses Basola of Ancona was involved in the efforts to ransom the "Safed captives." See R. Lamdan, "'The Boycott of Ancona'—viewing the Other Side of the Coin" (Hebrew), in *From Lisbon to Salonica and Constantinople,* ed. Z. Ankori (Hebrew; Tel Aviv, 1988), 153–54.

64. In another letter concerning captives of the Knights of St. John, which does not mention their point of origin, the writer stressed the prisoners' distress: "Shackled prisoners went into captivity before the enemy—[there was]

distressing darkness with light: darkness in its lowering clouds—as they traveled from an unnamed district to go to Eretz-Israel, may it be speedily rebuilt. With sorrow and sighing . . . they went in captivity to the city of Malta" (MS. London, Montefiore Collection 488; IMHM, no. 6114). Additional letters treating the ransom of prisoners held in Malta, including those bound for Eretz-Israel, have been published by S. Assaf, *Be-Ohaley Yaaqov* (Jerusalem, 1943), 111–14. Two letters on Jews bound for Eretz-Israel who were captured at sea by the Knights of St. John appeared in the Hebrew version of this book, 222–24.

65. Published by U. Heyd in Hebrew translation. See his "Turkish Documents from Ottoman Archives Concerning Safed Jews in the 16th Century C.E." (Hebrew), *Yerushalayim (Review)* 2/5 (1955): 131–32.

66. For documents on the expulsion of Jews from Safed, see Lewis, *Notes and Documents,* 28–34. For an English translation of the firman cancelling the expulsion order, see Heyd, *Ottoman Documents,* 167–68. On this episode specifically, see J. R. Hacker, "The Ottoman System of Sürgün and Its Influence on the Jewish Society in the Ottoman Empire" (Hebrew), *Zion* 55 (1990): 65–66.

67. We can assume that they originated in Salonika, which boasted a large concentration of conversos. This topic merits in-depth study in its own right. At present, see Hacker, "Self-Perception of Spanish Jewry," 37–38; and the collected articles in *From Lisbon to Salonica and Constantinople: Annual Conference on Jews in Greece* (1986), ed. Z. Ankori (Hebrew; Tel Aviv, 1988).

68. This prayer has been published by R. J. Z. Werblowsky, "A Collection of Prayers and Devotional Compositions by Solomon Alkabets" (Hebrew), *Sefunot* 6 (1962): 148–53. For additional studies, see A. David, "Safed, foyer de retour au judaïsme de *conversos* au XVIe siècle," *REJ* 146 (1987): 68–69; idem, "Ṣefat ke-Merkaz le-Shivat Anusim ba-Meah ha-16," in *Society and Community,* ed. A. Haim (Jerusalem, 1991), Hebrew section, 188–89.

69. For descriptions of journeys by both Jewish and non-Jewish pilgrims who embarked from Venice, see n. 30 above.

70. See D. Kaufmann, "Contributions à l'histoire des Juifs en Italie," *REJ* 20 (1890): 39–44; N. Ferorelli, *Gli ebrei nell Italia meridionale* (Torino, 1915), 220–40; I. Sonne, *Mi-Paulus ha-Revii ad Pius ha-Ḥamishi* (Jerusalem, 1954): 91–92.

71. See M. Stern, *Urkundliche beiträge über die Stellung der Päpste zu den Juden* (Kiel, 1893), 93. The contents of the bull have been cited by M. A. Shulvass, *Roma vi-Yerushalayim* (Jerusalem, 1944), 69.

72. Isaac de Lattes, *Responsa* (Vienna, 1860), fol. 64.

73. This letter has been published by D. Kaufmann in "Don Joseph Nassi, Founder of Colonies in the Holy Land, and the Community of Cori in the Campagna," *JQR* 2 (1890): 305–10, and cited in Sonne, *Mi-Paulus ad Pius,* 176–77.

74. On the expulsion and its consequences, see Sonne, *Mi-Paulus ad Pius,* 175–79, 204–30 (on the allusion to the situation of Italian Jews in the letter, see 176–77); D. Carpi, "Geyrush ha-Yehudim mi-Medinat ha-Keneysiyyah bi-Yemey ha-Afifyor Pius ha-Ḥamishi u-Mishpatey ha-Ḥaqirah neged Yehudey Bologna (1566–1569)," in *Scritti in Memoria di Enzo Sereni,* ed. D. Carpi, A. Milano, and U. Nahon (Jerusalem, 1970), 145–65; A. David, "New Documents Concerning the History of Italian Jewry under the Shadow of Sixteenth Century Catholic Reaction" (Hebrew), *Tarbiẓ* 49 (1979–80): 376–83; idem, "Teudot Ḥadashot al Megorashey Medinat ha-Keneysiyyah bi-Shnat 1569 ve-ha-Gezeyrot she-kadmu la-Geyrush," *Italia* 10 (1993): 17–36; Y. Boksenboim,

ed., *Letters of Jewish Teachers in Renaissance Italy (1555–1591)* (Hebrew; Tel Aviv, 1985), nos. 144–46, pp. 272–79. Regarding the dating of this epistle, see Sonne, *Mi-Paulus ad Pius,* 175.

75. MS. Oxford, Bodleian Library, Mich. Add. 67 (2317); IMHM, no. 21009, fols. 14v–16v.

76. For the earlier period, see Reiner, "Ashkenaz and Jerusalem," 27–62; Braslvsky, *Studies in Our Country,* 129–53. On the sixteenth-century Ashkenazi communities in Jerusalem and Safed, see below, chap. 6, sec. A; chap. 10, sec. G.

77. See Braslvsky, *Studies in Our Country,* 137–49, and above.

78. Moses Trani (Ha-Mabbit), *Responsa,* pt. 3, no. 131. In this context France evidently refers to Provence inasmuch as no Jews were living in France at that time.

79. Ibid., pt. 1, no. 307.

80. For a superior version of the text, see I. Robinson, "Two Letters of Abraham ben Eliezer Halevi," in *Studies in Medieval Jewish History and Literature,* ed. I. Twersky (Cambridge, Mass., 1984), 2:408.

81. See Ṣemah and Simeon Duran (sons of Rashbash Duran), *Responsa, Shu"t Yakhin u-Boaz* (Leghorn, 1782), pt. 1, no. 58. See S. H. Kook, *Iyyunim u-Meḥqarim* (Jerusalem, 1963), 2:146–49; R. Elior, "The Kabbalists of Dr'aa" (Hebrew), *Pe'amim* 24 (1985): 59.

82. See Elior, ibid. The data on Solomon Ḥalafta dates from the early 1480s to the early 1520s, and on Samuel Ḥalafta from the second decade of the sixteenth century. See David, "North African Jewry," 75; idem, "Personalities in Jerusalem," 233–34; idem, "On the History of the Sholal Family in Egypt and Eretz Israel at the End of the Mameluke Period and the Beginning of the Ottoman Period, in the Light of New Documents from the Geniza" (Hebrew), in *Exile and Diaspora: Studies . . . Presented to Professor Haim Beinart,* ed. A. Mirsky, A. Grossman, and Y. Kaplan (Jerusalem, 1988), 383–84, 397–98; idem, "New Genizah Documents," 30–31.

83. See Elior, "Kabbalists of Dr'aa," 40–41. Elior rejects J. M. Toledano's unsubstantiated contention that a group of kabbalists emigrated from Dr'aa to Safed. Nevertheless, this does not rule out the presence in Safed of kabbalists from Dr'aa or other regions in North Africa. See David, "North African Jewry," 80–81.

84. See n. 52 above.

85. Contemporary responsa literature is relatively expansive on aliyah from Egypt to Eretz-Israel, whether with the intent of permanent settlement, pilgrimage, or other purposes. See, for example, David ibn Abi Zimra, *Responsa,* nos. 454, 1137, 1149, 1180; Yom Tov Ṣahalon, *Responsa,* nos. 227, 259; Jacob Castro, *Shu"t Ohaley Yaakov,* no. 51. See also M. Littman, "'*Aliyot*' (Immigrations) from Egypt to Eretz Israel in the Late Mamluk-Early Ottoman Period" (Hebrew), *Cathedra* 23 (1982): 47–56; J. R. Hacker, "Spiritual and Material Links between Egyptian and Palestinian Jewry in the Sixteenth Century," in *Egypt and Palestine,* ed. A. Cohen and G. Baer (Jerusalem, 1984), 241–51.

86. On the sea route, see nn. 22–23 above. On the North African route, see sec. D above. Considerable attention has been devoted to the lands of the Maghreb as a center of absorption for Iberian exiles. See H. Beinart, "Fez—A Centre of Return to Judaism in the 16th Century" (Hebrew), *Sefunot* 8 (1964): 319–34; D. Corcos, "Moroccan Jewry in the First Half of the 16th Century"

(Hebrew), *Sefunot* 10 (1966): 53–111; H. Z. (J. W.) Hirschberg, *A History of the Jews in North Africa* (Leiden, 1974), 1:403–15; J. R. Hacker, "The 'Nagidate' in North Africa at the End of the Fifteenth Century" (Hebrew), *Zion* 45 (1980): 118–32; I. Tishby, *Messianism in the Time of the Expulsion from Spain and Portugal* (Hebrew; Jerusalem, 1985), 38–39 n. 89. On aliyah from North Africa to Eretz-Israel in the fifteenth and sixteenth centuries, see David, "North African Jewry," 74–86.

87. See David ibn Abi Zimra, *Responsa,* nos. 957, 1165.

88. Abraham Raphael Trabot's letter was published by A. Neubauer, "Qibuṣim al Inyaney Aseret ha-Shevatim u-Veney Moshe," *Kobeẓ al Yad* 4 (1888): 33.

89. David ibn Abi Zimra, *Responsa,* no. 1329.

90. See Littman, "Aliyot from Egypt," 55; M. Rozen, "The Relations between Egyptian Jewry and the Jewish Community of Jerusalem in the Seventeenth Century," in *Egypt and Palestine,* ed. A. Cohen and G. Baer, 253–54; David, "New Genizah Documents," 38–39.

CHAPTER 2. DISTRIBUTION OF SETTLEMENT

1. See Artom and David, "Obadiah mi-Bertinoro," 81 (Adler, *Jewish Travellers,* 234).

2. See A. Yaari, "Toledot ha-Yishuv ha-Yehudi be-Ḥevron," *Maḥanayim* 72 (1962): 84.

3. Basola, *Masot,* 58.

4. Cohen and Lewis, *Population and Revenue,* 108–11; Hütteroth and Abdulfattah, *Historical Geography,* 53.

5. Cohen and Lewis, *Population and Revenue,* 108.

6. Yaari, "Toledot ha-Yishuv be-Ḥevron," 84–88.

7. See Trani's diary, published by H. Bentov, "Autobiographical and Historical Register of Rabbi Josef Trani" (Hebrew), *Shalem* 1 (1974): 219.

8. See I. Ben-Zvi, *Remnants of Ancient Jewish Communities in the Land of Israel* (Hebrew; Jerusalem, 1967), 221–22.

9. See J. Kena'ani, "The Jewish Population of Gaza in the Middle Ages" (Hebrew), *BJPES* 5 (1937–38): 33–41; Cohen and Lewis, *Population and Revenue,* 120; N. Schur, "History of the Jews of Gaza in the Mameluk and Ottoman Periods" (Hebrew), *Israel—People and Land* 5–6 (1987–89): 202–7. On the related Geniza documents, see A. David, "Aza—Merkaz le-Saḥar beyn Miṣrayim le-Ereẓ Yisrael ba-Meah ha-16," *Maḥanayim,* n.s., 2 (1992): 184–91.

10. On Jewish involvement in the working of precious metals, see Kena'ani, "Jewish Population of Gaza," 36–37. On Jews in agriculture, see ibid., 35; Braslvsky, *Studies in Our Country,* 162.

11. Cohen and Lewis, *Population and Revenue,* 128; Hütteroth and Abdulfattah, *Historical Geography,* 52.

12. In Turkish: *gurûs.* See Bashan, *Captivity and Ransom,* 317.

13. Cohen and Lewis, *Population and Revenue,* 120 n. 15.

14. Safed also boasted a Provençal community at that time. See A. David, "The Assistance of the Community of Cuneo to the Yeshiva of the Provencal Community in Safed" (Hebrew), *Shalem* 4 (1984): 429–44. See also below, chap. 10, sec. F.

15. On the Sefardim in Jerusalem and Safed during that period, see David, "Spanish Exiles," 77–108. See below, chap. 6, sec. B; chap. 10, sec. B.

16. Moses of Prague was mentioned in Obadiah of Bertinoro's first letter from Jerusalem (1488). See Artom and David, "Obadiah mi-Bertinoro," 79 (Adler, *Jewish Travellers*, 232).

17. Yaari, *Massa Meshullam*, 64.

18. Jacob Castro, *Shu"t Ohaley Yaaqov*, no. 119. He can perhaps be identified as Isaac Arḥa, a Safed scholar mentioned by contemporary posekim. See Moses Trani, *Responsa*, pt. 2, no. 128; Moses Galante, *Responsa*, no. 13; Elijah Mizraḥi and Elijah ibn Ḥayyim, *Shu"t Mayim Amuqim*, no. 54; as well as a letter sent from Safed to Avignon (1562), published as an appendix to Joseph Caro's *Beit Yosef*, p. 426.

19. David ibn Abi Zimra, *Responsa*, no. 657.

20. Cited in Hebrew translation by Ish-Shalom, *Christian Travels*, 304.

21. See Basola, *Masot*, 52. On the sixteenth-century Jewish settlement in Nablus, see A. Yaari, "Toledot ha-Yishuv ha-Yehudi bi-Shekhem," *Sinai* 36 (1955): 166–70; Schur, "The Jews of Shechem in the Middle Ages and Recent Times" (Hebrew), in *Shomron Studies*, ed. S. Dar and Z. Safrai (Hebrew; Tel Aviv, 1986), 229–301.

22. See Cohen and Lewis, *Population and Revenue*, 145–49.

23. Ibid.; Hütteroth and Abdulfattah, *Historical Geography*, 53.

24. Cited in Hebrew translation by Ish-Shalom, *Christian Travels*, 295–96.

25. The pertinent sources have been compiled by Y. Kena'ani, "The Jewish Population in Acre in the 16th and the First Half of the 17th Century" (Hebrew), *BJPES* 2 (1935): 29–31. On trade with Egypt, see Yom Tov Ṣahalon, *Shu"t Maharit ha-Ḥadashot*, no. 223.

26. See Ben-Zvi, *Remnants of Ancient Jewish Communities*, 41–42; Y. Kena'ani, "Ha-Ḥayyim ha-Kalkaliyyim bi-Ṣefat u-ve-sevivoteha ba-Meah ha-16 ve-ḥasi ha-Meah ha-17," *Zion (Me'asef)* 6 (1934): 217; Braslvsky, *Studies in Our Country*, 172–79.

27. Lewis, *Notes and Documents*, 9.

28. See Bentov, "Josef Trani," 204, 221–22.

29. See Braslvsky, *Studies in Our Country*, 171.

30. Lewis, *Notes and Documents*, 9.

31. Gottheil and Worrell, *Fragments from the Genizah*, 262–63.

32. Lewis, *Notes and Documents*, 9.

33. Ibid.

34. Ibid.

35. On Jews in Ein Zeitim, see Gottheil and Worrell, *Fragments from the Genizah*, 262–63, 264–65. On Moses Besodo's demise in Ein Zeitim, see Benayahu, "Yosef Garson," 100, 167.

36. See Basola, *Masot*, 45. For further information on the Jewish settlement in Ein Zeitim, see Ben-Zvi, *Remnants of Ancient Jewish Communities*, 73–75; Kena'ani, "Ha-Ḥayyim ha-Kalkaliyyim," 210–13.

37. Lewis, *Notes and Documents*, 9.

38. On the yeshivah in Ein Zeitim and the assistance it received from the Diaspora, see I. Sonne, "Teudot al Shadarim Aḥadim be-Italyah," *Kobeẓ al Yad* 5 (1951): 214–17; A. Yaari, *Sheluḥey Ereẓ-Yisrael* (Jerusalem, 1951), 844–45; D. Tamar, *Studies in the History of the Jewish People in Eretz Israel and in*

Italy (Hebrew; Jerusalem, 1970), 160–62; idem, *Ha-Yehudim be-Ereẓ Yisrael u-ve-Arṣot ha-Mizraḥ*, 194–96; Y. Boksenboim, ed., *Letters of Rabbi Leon Modena* (Hebrew; Tel Aviv, 1984), 29–30, 208; R. Meroz, "The Circle of R. Moshe ben Makhir and Its Regulations" (Hebrew), *Pe'amim* 31 (1987): 40–61. In the early 1580s Joseph Trani attended Moses ben Makhir's yeshivah in Ein Zeitim. See Bentov, "Josef Trani," 205, 218.

39. For a brief summary of the situation of the Jews under the regime of Faḥr ed-Din II, see M. Rozen, "Jews in the Service of Faḥr ed-Din II of Lebanon" (Hebrew), *Pe'amim* 14 (1982): 32–44 and the bibliography cited there.

40. Yaari, *Letters*, 199.

41. Gottheil and Worrell, *Fragments from the Genizah*, 262–63.

42. Lewis, *Notes and Documents*, 9.

43. See Ben-Zvi, *Remnants of Ancient Jewish Communities*, 69–73; Kena'ani, "Ha-Ḥayyim ha-Kalkaliyyim," 213–14; H. Y. Peles, "Birya ha-Atiqah mitokh ha-Meqorot," *Morasha* 2 (1972): 41–43; Bentov, "Josef Trani," 205, 217.

44. See Kena'ani, "Ha-Ḥayyim ha-Kalkaliyyim," 215–16; Braslvsky, *Studies in Our Country*, 271–73 (see index as well); Ben-Zvi, *Remnants of Ancient Jewish Communities*, 123–25.

45. Basola, *Masot*, 69.

46. Lewis, *Notes and Documents*, 9.

47. See Ben-Zvi, *Remnants of Ancient Jewish Communities*, 83–89; Kena'ani, "Ha-Ḥayyim ha-Kalkaliyyim," 214–15.

48. Basola, *Masot*, 48.

49. Lewis, *Notes and Documents*, 9.

50. Ben-Zvi, *Remnants of Ancient Jewish Communities*, 63–69.

51. On the festivities at the tomb of Simeon bar Yoḥai at Meron, see Braslvsky, *Studies in Our Country*, 342–52; A. Yaari, "History of the Pilgrimage to Meron" (Hebrew), *Tarbiẓ* 31 (1961): 72–101; M. Benayahu, "Devotion Practices of the Kabbalists of Safed in Meron" (Hebrew), *Sefunot* 6 (1962): 9–40.

52. See H. D. Azulay, *Shem ha-Gedolim: Maarekhet ha-Gedolim* (Jerusalem, 1960), s.v. "Abraham Galante."

53. Basola, *Masot*, 46.

54. Ben-Zvi, *Remnants of Ancient Jewish Communities*, 343–45.

55. Ibid., 94.

56. Ibid., 453–55; Strauss-Ashtor, *The Jews in Egypt and Syria*, 2:123; Z. Vilnay, *Derom Levanon* (Tel Aviv, 1982), 48–52.

57. Yom Tov Ṣahalon, *Shu"t Maharit Ṣahalon ha-Ḥadashot*, pt. 2, no. 176. This responsum was published by I. Nissim, "Responsa of R. Yom Tob Sahalon on Questions of Farming in Haṣbeyah and Galilee" (Hebrew), *Sefunot* 9 (Ben-Zvi Memorial Volume 2, 1964): 9–16. Christian sources also shed light on Jews in Ḥaṣbayah. See N. Schur, "The Jews of Lebanon" (Hebrew), *Pe'amim* 24 (1985): 119. A mid-sixteenth-century letter sent by a merchant, one Mattathias Ashkenazi, to his son (MS. Cambridge, University Library, Geniza Collection, T–S 13J 24, 25), mentions another son living in "Ḥaṣba[yah]."

58. Basola, *Masot*, 73. English translation cited from C. Roth, *The House of Nasi: The Duke of Naxos* (Philadelphia, 1948), 104.

59. Braslvsky, *Studies in Our Country*, 191–98.

60. Ibid., 180–215.

61. Joseph ha-Kohen, *Emeq ha-Bakha*, 93–94 (May, *Vale of Tears*, 100–101); E. Charriere, *Negociations de La France dans le Levant* (Paris, n.d.).

62. Turkish firmans mention "Ḥakim Daud" or "David ha-Rofe" as responsible for overseeing the building of the wall in Tiberias. See U. Heyd, "Turkish Documents on the Rebuilding of Tiberias in the Sixteenth Century" (Hebrew), *Sefunot* 10 (1966): 199–200, 204–6.

63. For Christian accounts, see Braslvsky, *Studies in Our Country,* 184, 190, 196–201; Ish-Shalom, *Christian Travels,* 309. For the related Ottoman firmans, see Heyd, "Turkish Documents on Tiberias," 193–210.

64. Published by Heyd, "Turkish Documents on Tiberias," 196–202.

65. This letter has been published by Kaufmann, "Don Joseph Nassi," 291–310. Excerpts were cited above, chap. 1, sec. B. Regarding the dating of the letter, see Sonne, *Mi-Paulus ad Pius,* 175. For additional appeals to Italian Jews to settle in Tiberias, see A. David, "Meqorot Ḥadashim le-Ḥiddush ha-Yishuv ha-Yehudi bi-Teveryah ba-Meah ha-16," *Ariel* 105–6 (1994): 81–86.

66. Ibid.

67. Braslvsky, *Studies in Our Country,* 192–93.

68. On commerce, see Moses Trani, *Responsa,* pt. 3, no. 220; Braslvsky, *Studies in Our Country,* 188–89. On agriculture, see ibid., 187–88. For a report by the Portuguese pilgrim Pantaleo de Aviero that Jews cultivated oranges, see ibid., 196–97. For beekeeping, see ibid., 160, 188.

69. Joseph ha-Kohen, *Emeq ha-Bakha,* 94 (May, *Vale of Tears,* 101). See also Braslvsky, *Studies in Our Country,* 213, on the cultivation of mulberry trees. The plan to cultivate mulberry trees for the silk industry in Tiberias was mentioned earlier in a firman from 1560. See Heyd, "Turkish Documents on Tiberias," 196, 202–3.

70. Braslvsky, *Studies in Our Country,* 188–89, 213–14. Braslvsky argues that Don Joseph Nasi was partly responsible for the plan's failure (ibid., 190); however, this claim requires further substantiation.

71. See N. Schur, "Ha-Nisayon le-Haqamat 'Medinah Yehudit' bi-Teveryah al-yedey Dona Gracia Mendes ve-Don Yosef Nasi ve-Hakhshalato bi-yedey ha-Franṣisqanim," *Ariel* 53–54 (1988): 44–50.

72. Bonifacio Stefani Ragusino, *Liber de Perenni Cultu Terrae Sanctae* (Venetiis, 1875), 268. English version based on the Hebrew translation found in Schur, "Ha-Nisayon le-Haqamat 'Medinah Yehudit' bi-Teveryah," 47.

73. For Dona Gracia's role, see Zacharia al-Dahri, *Sefer Hammusar,* ed. Y. Ratzaby (Jerusalem, 1965), 277–78; Braslvsky, *Studies in Our Country,* 207–9. References to the yeshivah are found in responsa literature as well as other sources. See ibid., 210–13; Yaari, *Sheluḥey Ereẓ-Yisrael,* 256–61.

74. See al-Dahri, *Sefer Hammusar,* 261; Braslvsky, *Studies in Our Country,* 208–9.

75. See J. Braslavi (Braslvsky), "The Land of Israel in the Hebrew Translation of Basnage's 'Histoire des Juifs'" (Hebrew), *Eretz-Israel* 6 (1960): 172.

76. For treatments of Solomon ibn Yaish and his son Jacob, see A. Galanté, *Don Salomon Aben Yaèch: Duc de Mételin* (Istanbul, 1936); Braslvsky, *Studies in Our Country,* 213–15; S. W. Baron, "Solomon Ibn Yaish and Sultan Suleiman the Magnificent," *Joshua Finkel Festschrift* (New York, 1974), 29–36.

77. See Ben-Zvi, *Remnants of Ancient Jewish Communities,* 347. Kefar Kanna is also mentioned in a letter from the Geniza, sent in the late fifteenth/early sixteenth century by Shalom ben Jacob of Damascus to the nagid, Nathan Sholal; however, this does not necessarily imply that Jews resided there. See David, "Sholal Family," 403–5.

78. Basola, *Masot,* 50–51.

79. Lewis, *Notes and Documents,* 9.

80. See Ben-Zvi, *Remnants of Ancient Jewish Communities,* 347–48; Kena'ani, "Ha-Ḥayyim ha-Kalkaliyyim," 216–17. A few pages of a rhymed prose composition written by a Jewish pilgrim who passed through Kefar Kanna while traveling from Gaza to Safed via the western route (via Maris) at the turn of the fifteenth to sixteenth centuries, have survived in the Cairo Geniza. "To Kefar Kanna—May God establish it and restore it to its former state." Naturally this wish to see Kefar Kanna restored to its former glory refers to the Jewish settlement. These fragments have been published by A. David, "Remains of Pages from the Genizah Tale of the Journey of a Jewish Traveler in the Land of Israel at the Turn of the Sixteenth Century" (Hebrew), *Israel—People and Land* 7–8 (1990–93): 223–30.

81. Bentov, "Josef Trani," 205, 222–23.

82. See Ben-Zvi, *Remnants of Ancient Jewish Communities,* 345–47.

83. Braslvsky, *Studies in Our Country,* 171–72, cites two bits of evidence, one Jewish and one Christian, provided by this pilgrim. Surprisingly, Ish-Shalom, *Christian Travels,* 305 n. 4, rejects Braslvsky's contention that the reference is to Jinin. For Trani's visits to Jinin, see Bentov, "Josef Trani," 205, 221–23.

84. Braslvsky, *Studies in Our Country,* 170–71.

CHAPTER 3. ECONOMIC LIFE

1. Important occupational data are found in the taḥrir registers of taxpayers and revenues drawn up at several-year intervals by the Ottoman regime, discovered and published by B. Lewis and A. Cohen. See Lewis, *Notes and Documents,* 14–22; idem, "Studies in the Ottoman Archives," 469–501; Cohen and Lewis, *Population and Revenue.* Christian pilgrims provide information on agriculture in Eretz-Israel. See N. Schur, "Madrikh Bibliografi: Aṣey ha-Pri ve-Giduley ha-Sadeh she-be-Ereẓ-Yisrael . . . ," *Nofim* 11–12 (1979): 138–60; Z. Ammar, "Notes on Flora and Agriculture in Mamluk Palestine" (Hebrew), in *Palestine in the Mamluk Period,* ed. J. Drory (Hebrew: Jerusalem, 1992), 220–36.

2. Lewis, "Studies in the Ottoman Archives," 469.

3. Ibid., 469–71; Cohen and Lewis, *Population and Revenue,* 64–68.

4. For a comprehensive discussion of this issue, see Kena'ani, "Ha-Ḥayyim ha-Kalkaliyyim," 208–17; Braslvsky, *Studies in Our Country,* 154–75; Cohen, *Jewish Life under Islam,* 209–10.

5. For a treatment of the textile industry in Safed, see Kena'ani, "Ha-Ḥayyim ha-Kalkaliyyim," 195–201; S. Avitsur, "Safed—Center of the Manufacture of Woven Woolens in the Fifteenth Century" (Hebrew), *Sefunot* 6 (1962): 41–69; Cohen and Lewis, *Population and Revenue,* 59–62; A. David, "The Integration of the Jews of the Land of Israel in Mediterranean Trade in the Early Ottoman Period" (Hebrew), in *The Mediterranean and the Jews,* ed. A. Toaff and S. Schwarzfuchs (Ramat Gan, 1989), Hebrew section, 25. For a discussion of Don Joseph Nasi's plan to rebuild and develop Tiberias into an important Jewish center, see chap. 2, "Tiberias." On Nablus, see Cohen and Lewis, *Population and Revenue,* 61–62.

6. See Braslvsky, *Studies in Our Country,* 160; David, "Jews in Mediterranean Trade," 25.

7. Joseph ha-Kohen, *Emeq ha-Bakha,* 93–94. See also Avitsur, "Safed," 55; David, "Jews in Mediterranean Trade," 21.

8. For the Safed-based dyeing center, see Avitsur, "Safed," 58–61. On dyeing in other locales, see Cohen and Lewis, *Population and Revenue,* 62.

9. Avitsur, "Safed," 43–45.

10. A type of fine woolen cloth. See Cohen and Lewis, *Population and Revenue,* 60 n. 45; Avitsur, "Safed," 62. See also E. Ashtor, "Die Verbreitung des englischen Wolltuches in den Mittelmeerländern im Spätmittelalter," *Vierteljahrschrift für Sozial und Wirtschaftgeschichte* 71 (1984): 23–25.

11. According to Avitsur, "Safed," 62, the Hebrew expression *begadim gevohim* here translated as "fancy suits," refers to broadcloth—TRANS.

12. On the crisis in the wool industry, see B. Braude, "International Competition and Domestic Cloth in the Ottoman Empire, 1500–1650: A Study in Undevelopment," *Review* 2 (1979): 437–51. For its effect on Safed, see Avitsur, "Safed," 67–69; S. Schwarzfuchs, "La décadence de la Galilée Juive du XVIe siècle et la crise du textile au Proche-orient," *REJ* 121 (1962): 171–79.

13. See Lewis, "Studies in the Ottoman Archives," 471; Cohen and Lewis, *Population and Revenue,* 62–63; Cohen, *Economic Life,* 61–97; idem, "Soap Factory," 120–24; idem, *World Within,* index, s.v. "soap"; Cohen and Simon-Pikali, *Jews in the Moslem Religious Court,* 219–31.

14. Cohen, *Jewish Life under Islam,* 192–95. In a letter sent from Jerusalem in 1522, Israel Ashkenazi noted the availability of soap in Jerusalem: "Many stores here sell oil and soap." See David, "Letter of Israel Ashkenazi," 112.

15. Muslim documents are a fruitful source of data on Jewish occupations. See Cohen, *Jewish Life under Islam,* 175–89; idem, *World Within,* index, s.v. "wine," "slaughterer," "bakery," "cheese," "indigo"; Cohen and Simon-Pikali, *Jews in the Moslem Religious Court,* 173–76, 252–66. Certainly, Jews in Safed and elsewhere pursued these occupations.

16. Relatively extensive data are available. See "Iggeret Samuel Figo," in Yaari, *Letters,* 181; David, "Letter of Israel Ashkenazi," 112; Basola, *Masot,* 44; Cohen, *Jewish Life under Islam,* 160–70; idem, *World Within,* index, s.v. "silversmith," "blacksmiths guild," "indigo," "tailor," "carpenter," "doctor," and pp. 60, 69, 74, 81, 99, 103, 118; Cohen and Simon-Pikali, *Jews in the Moslem Religious Court,* 209–18, 235–41, 265–77; Kena'ani, "Ha-Ḥayyim ha-Kalkaliyyim," 205–7.

17. On local and international trade in Eretz-Israel in the late Middle Ages, see Cohen and Lewis, *Population and Revenue,* 46–59; Cohen, *Economic Life;* idem, "Ha-Misḥar shel Ereẓ Yisrael," 300–308; idem, "Local Trade, International Trade and Government Involvement," 5–12; E. Ashtor, "Europäischer Handel im spätmittelalterlichen Palästina," in *Das Heilige Land im Mittelalter,* ed. W. Fischer and J. Schneider (Neustadt a. d. Aisch, 1982), 107–26.

18. Kena'ani, "Ha-Ḥayyim ha-Kalkaliyyim," 181–204; idem, Jewish Population of Gaza," 33–41; idem, "Jewish Population in Acre," 29–31; Cohen, *Jewish Life under Islam,* 192–98; idem, *World Within,* index, s.v. "markets," and the pages cited in n. 16 above; Cohen and Simon-Pikali, *Jews in the Moslem Religious Court,* 187–202, 272–77. Additional sources are cited below.

19. Basola, *Masot,* 59.

20. Cohen, *Jewish Life under Islam,* 197; idem, *World Within,* index, s.v. "markets"; Cohen and Simon-Pikali, *Jews in the Moslem Religious Court,* 187ff.

21. See Basola, *Masot,* 43–44; Kena'ani, "Ha-Ḥayyim ha-Kalkaliyyim," 184–95.

22. Ibid., 195–204; David, "Jews in Mediterranean Trade," 19–28.

23. See Kena'ani, "Jewish Population of Gaza," 36–37. Geniza documents from the sixteenth and seventeenth centuries indicate involvement by Gaza Jews in trade. See David, "Aza," 184–91. A source from the sixteenth century's second half provides data on export of local goods from Safed to Venice via one of the Egyptian commercial centers. See David, "Jews in Mediterranean Trade," 23–28. We cannot rule out the possibility that these goods were sent from Gaza's commercial center. See the end of this section, below.

24. See David, "Letter of Israel Ashkenazi," 112; Basola, *Masot,* 43; Cohen, *Jewish Life under Islam,* 195–98.

25. This takkanah is found in the context of a query addressed to Elijah Mizraḥi by Abraham Solomon Trèves. See Elijah Mizraḥi (Ha-Re'em), *Responsa,* no. 45. The query was sent on Wednesday, the 15th of Shevat, the weekly portion "let them bring every major dispute to you" (Exod. 18:22). According to the day of the week and date, the responsa could have been written in either 1505 or 1519. It is not possible to reach a definitive conclusion regarding the year. For a discussion of this takkanah, see A. Ovadya, "Rabbi Eliyahu Mizraḥi," *Sinai* 6 (1940): 511–15. Ovadya's claim that the takkanah was issued in the Ottoman period is unsubstantiated. Some scholars have proposed that the locations in the query are fictitious [Yaari, "Toledot ha-Yishuv be-Ḥevron," 90; idem, "Tiveryah ve-Ṣippori ki-Reuven ve-Shimon," *Tarbiẓ* 18 (1947): 64; E. Bashan, "The Names of Towns in Eretz Israel as Appellations of Foreign Towns in the Responsa Literature of the Ottoman Period" (Hebrew), *Bar-Ilan* 12 (1974): 137–65; N. Fried, "Le-Toledot ha-Yishuv ha-Yehudi be-Ḥevron," *Sinai* 53 (1963): 108 n. 8], but there is no reason to doubt either the authenticity of the case at hand or its geographical reference. This takkanah is referred to in a sixteenth-century collection of takkanot concerning Jerusalem. No. 14 states: "It has been agreed to purchase coal or wood only from fellahin or from stores." See A. H. Freimann, "Taqqanot Yerushalayim," in *Sefer Dinaburg,* ed. Y. Baer, J. Gutman, and M. Schwabe (Jerusalem, 1949), 209.

26. Spun cotton was a common product in Eretz-Israel from an earlier period as well.

27. The medicinal plant known as scammony, native to Syria and southern Turkey, was in great demand in Europe. On its marketing from Safed in the latter half of the sixteenth century, see David, "Jews in Mediterranean Trade," 23–28.

28. An excerpt is discussed in David, "Jews in Mediterranean Trade," 21.

29. Cohen and Lewis, *Population and Revenue,* 55–59.

30. On importation of wool to Safed, see Moses Trani (Ha-Mabbit), *Responsa,* pt. 1, nos. 32, 271; pt. 3, nos. 103, 107; Elijah ibn Ḥayyim (Ra'anaḥ), *Responsa,* no. 77; Jacob Berab, *Responsa,* no. 22, which also treats importation from Rhodes. On the role of Adrianople and shipping to Sidon, see Avitsur, "Safed," 55. The Hebrew sources contain no explicit references to Acre in the context of wool importation. See Kena'ani, "Jewish Population in Acre," 29–31; Cohen and Lewis, *Population and Revenue,* 30, where both Acre and Sidon are mentioned as ports supplying Safed's wool industry.

31. On export trade to Damascus, see Moses Trani, *Responsa,* pt. 1, no. 207. On trade with Egypt, see David ibn Abi Zimra, *Responsa,* no. 638; Joseph

Caro, *Shu"t Avqat Rokhel,* no. 140. On this topic and on silk exports in the sixteenth century's latter half, see David, "Jews in Mediterranean Trade," 21–28; idem, "Jewish Involvement in the Economic Life of Eretz-Israel during the 15th and 16th Centuries" (Hebrew), *Judea and Samaria Research Studies: Proceedings of the Seventh Annual Meeting, 1997* (Kedumin-Ariel, 1998), pp. 277–78. On cotton exports to Venice, see Moses Trani, *Responsa,* pt. 3, no. 203.

32. Basola, *Masot,* 43.

33. See David de Rossi's letter in Yaari, *Letters,* 187, cited above.

34. See David, "Jews in Mediterranean Trade," 21–28; idem, "Trade with Venice," 1–29.

35. On soap, see sec. B above. See also Cohen, *Jewish Life under Islam,* 192–95; idem, "Damascus and Jerusalem" (Hebrew), *Sefunot* 17 (1983): 98–99; idem, *World Within,* index, s.v. "soap"; Cohen and Simon-Pikali, *Jews in the Moslem Religious Court,* 219–31.

36. On trade with Syria, see Cohen, "Damascus and Jerusalem," 98. On the importation of rice from Egypt, see Cohen, *Jewish Life under Islam,* 195. From a responsum, we learn that imported rice destined for Sidon reached Acre instead and was sold there. See Yom Tov Ṣahalon, *Responsa,* no. 285.

37. See Kena'ani, "Jewish Population of Gaza," 33–41; idem, "Jewish Population in Acre," 29–31; David, "Aza," 184–91.

38. On the *fattoria* and *fattores* ("factors"), mentioned as a type of trade in sixteenth-century Hebrew sources, see H. Gerber, "Enterprise and International Commerce in the Economic Activity of the Jews of the Ottoman Empire in the 16th–17th Centuries" (Hebrew), *Zion* 43 (1978): 54–55; M. Rozen, "The Fattoria—A Chapter in the History of Mediterranean Commerce in the 16th and 17th Centuries" (Hebrew), *Miqqedem umiyyam: Studies in the Jewry of Islamic Countries* 1 (1981): 101–31; E. Bashan, "Economic Life from the 16th to the 18th Century" (Hebrew), in *The Jews in Ottoman Egypt,* ed. J. M. Landau (Hebrew; Jerusalem, 1988), 74–75. For information on the *fattoria* system in Eretz-Israel (Tiberias) in 1578, see Moses Trani, *Responsa,* pt. 3, no. 220.

39. On the subject of Jewish financial activity, see H. Gerber, *Economic and Social Life of the Jews in the Ottoman Empire in the 16th and 17th Centuries* (Hebrew: Jerusalem, 1982), 49–77.

40. Cohen, *Jewish Life under Islam,* 140–45; idem, *World Within,* index, s.v. "tax collector"; Cohen and Simon-Pikali, *Jews in the Moslem Religious Court,* 131–42.

41. See also Moses Trani, *Responsa,* pt. 3, nos. 207–8. On Jewish tax-farmers in Egypt, see S. Shtober, "'On the Issue of Customs Collectors in Egypt'—Jews as Tax Farmers in Ottoman Egypt" (Hebrew), *Pe'amim* 38 (1989): 68–94.

42. Cohen, *Jewish Life under Islam,* 144–45.

43. Ibid., 145–47; Cohen, *World Within,* index, s.v. "moneychanger"; Cohen and Simon-Pikali, *Jews in the Moslem Religious Court,* 203–8. On a Jewish moneychanger in Safed, see Heyd, *Ottoman Documents,* 164–66.

44. The Hebrew sources include: Elijah ibn Ḥayyim, *Responsa,* no. 45; David de Rossi, letter, in Yaari, *Letters,* 187; Joseph Trani, *Responsa,* pt. 2, *Yoreh Deah,* no. 39. For the Muslim sources, see Cohen, *Jewish Life under Islam,* 63–64, 214; idem, "Damascus and Jerusalem," 99–100; idem, *World Within,* 93, 107, 115, 135, 144; Cohen and Simon-Pikali, *Jews in the Moslem Religious Court,* 283–85.

45. This biblical quotation (Isa. 6:13) alludes to an interest rate of 10 percent, the maximum allowed under Sultan Suleiman's regime. See Cohen, *Jewish Life under Islam,* 69; Schur, "Christian Chronicles," 382.

46. Meir Gavison and other rabbis permitted the lending of money to Church institutions. Aaron ben Ḥayyim and Eleazar ben Arḥa cited the severe economic conditions in Jerusalem as a rationale for permitting this activity. For a general survey of this issue, see M. Benayahu, "Moneylending with Interest to the Jerusalem Monasteries" (Hebrew), *Jerusalem (Quarterly)* 1 (1948): 86–88, 221; E. Bashan, "A Document Dated 5384 (1624) Concerning a Dispute on Lending Money to Christians in Jerusalem" (Hebrew), in *Chapters in the History of the Jewish Community in Jerusalem* (Hebrew; Jerusalem, 1976), 2:77–96; E. Shochetman, introduction to Meir Gavison, *Responsa,* pp. 46–48.

47. The sources are cited by David, "A Letter from Jerusalem," 49 n. 47.

48. See Ashtor, "Jerusalem in the Late Middle Ages," 94–95.

49. See David, "A Letter from Jerusalem," 48–50.

50. MS. Jerusalem, Jewish National and University Library, Heb. 8° 1783, which forms the basis for Ben-Zvi's edition of Basola's *Masot,* contains two nearly indecipherable letters at this point. Ben-Zvi read them as the equivalent of five hundred, noting at the same time the logical difficulty involved. On fol. 72r of the MS two different, also unclear, letters appear. These may be read as equivalent to eighty-eight, which makes more sense in this context.

51. Similar comments are found in Levi ibn Ḥabib, *Responsa,* no. 103.

52. Documentary evidence has been compiled by Yaari, *Sheluḥey Ereẓ-Yisrael,* 221–23. See also David, "Two Sixteenth Century Emissaries' Letters from Jerusalem" (Hebrew), *Shalem* 3 (1981): 325–32. For additional bibliography, see ibid., 326 nn. 3–4.

53. See Y. Z. Kahane, *Meḥqarim be-Sifrut ha-Teshuvot* (Jerusalem, 1973), 206ff.; Yaari, *Sheluḥey Ereẓ-Yisrael,* 221–23.

54. The sources on emissaries and their missions have been collected by Yaari, *Sheluḥey Ereẓ-Yisrael,* 221–61. Sparse data have survived in the Geniza regarding a delegation from Hebron in the sixteenth or early seventeenth century. See David, "New Genizah Documents," 40–44. On the economic crisis in late century and its effect on Safed in particular, see Yaari, *Sheluḥey Ereẓ-Yisrael,* 233–61. More recent studies are cited in David, "Community of Cuneo," 429–44, and nn. 4–5, 14; idem, "New Sources on the History of the Jews During the Middle Ages" (Hebrew), in *Zev Vilnay's Jubilee Volume,* ed. E. Schiller (Jerusalem, 1984), 1:291–92.

55. Beginning with the sixteenth century, many extant sources relate to philanthropic activity by various Italian-Jewish communites on behalf of their coreligionists in Eretz-Israel. See Yaari, *Sheluḥey Ereẓ-Yisrael,* index; Sonne, "Shadarim," 197–218; D. Carpi, *Between Renaissance and Ghetto* (Tel Aviv, 1989), 131–47, 217–81; David, "Emissaries' Letters from Jerusalem," 325–32; idem, "Community of Cuneo," 429–44. Additional pertinent sources will be referred to below.

56. See Yaari, *Sheluḥey Ereẓ-Yisrael,* 65; Carpi, *Between Renaissance and Ghetto,* 231–81; Sonne, "Shadarim," 197–218; David, "Emissaries' Letters from Jerusalem," 331–32.

57. See Basola, *Masot,* 62.

58. See David, "Personalities in Jerusalem," 229–49; idem, "New Genizah Documents," 19–55; idem, "New Sources on the History of the Jews of Egypt," 10–15.

59. See A. David, "The History of the Jerusalem Academies in the 15th and 16th Centuries" (Hebrew), *Iyyunim be-Ḥinukh* 34 (1982): 148; idem, "Sholal Family," 378; Dimitrovsky, "Unknown Chapter," 106.

60. See Gottheil and Worrell, *Fragments from the Genizah,* 246–65.

61. For the takkanot issued by his court in Egypt, see David, "Sholal Family," 377–79, and the beginning of chap. 7 below.

62. See David, "The Office of *Nagid* in Egypt," 325–37.

63. See David, "Jerusalem Academies," 148–49.

64. For the halakhic and other material, see, for example, David ibn Abi Zimra, *Responsa,* nos. 698, 2248; Jacob Castro, *Shu"t Oholey Yaaqov,* no. 1; Yom Tov Ṣahalon, *Responsa,* nos. 29, 158, 160; Meir Gavison, *Responsa,* 322–23. See also Basola, *Masot,* 62, where he notes regarding the Jerusalem community: "More than 200 persons receive charity. Many contributions come from Egypt, Turkey, and elsewhere." In his chronicle *Divrei Yosef,* Joseph Sambari notes that "the *gabbai* and esteemed rabbi Joseph Bagilar supported the ARI [Isaac Luria] of blessed memory's yeshivah in Safed, may it be speedily rebuilt, for ten years" (Sambari, *Divrei Yosef,* 416). For the Geniza material, see Gottheil and Worrell, *Fragments from the Genizah,* 246–65; A. David, "On the Ashkenazic Comunity in Jerusalem in the 16th Century" (Hebrew), in *Vatiqin (Y. Y. Rivlin Memorial Volume),* ed. H. Z. Hirschberg with Y. Kaniel (Ramat Gan, 1975), 25–32; idem, "Personalities in Jerusalem," 243–49; idem, "New Genizah Documents," 19–55; idem, "The Yeshivah in Jerusalem," 43–48.

65. This event was referred to by Joseph Garson in a homily delivered in Damascus (1517). Cited by A. David, "Further Data on the Pogrom of 1517 Against the Jews of Safed" (Hebrew), *Cathedra* 8 (1978): 190–94.

66. For further details, see David, "A Letter from Jerusalem," 50–51. The writer stresses that it occurred "in this year"—namely, the year of the letter's composition, 1520. See ibid., 44–45.

67. The muayyadi was named for Mamluk sultan al-Muayyad Shaykh. See F. Balog, *The Coinage of the Mamluk Sultans of Egypt and Syria* (New York, 1964), 9–10, 47.

68. See n. 64 above. The majority of the letters cited therein deal with financial aid for the Jews of Eretz-Israel.

69. Abraham Castro has aroused much scholarly interest. In recent years, important documents concerning his life in Egypt and in Jerusalem (first half of the sixteenth century) have come to light. For details, see chap. 13, no. 7 below. For his philanthropic works, including his support of individuals (and perhaps institutions) in Eretz-Israel, see David, "The Office of *Nagid* in Egypt," 334–36; idem, "Abraham Qastro," 148.

70. See David, "The Office of *Nagid* in Egypt," 334–36; Cohen, *Jewish Life under Islam,* 20, 77; idem, "Abraham Castro."

71. See A. David, "Additional Biographical Data Concerning R. Moses Castro from a Genizah Fragment" (Hebrew), *Te'udah* 7 (1991): 349–50.

72. See David ibn Abi Zimra, *Responsa,* no. 638; Joseph Caro, *Avqat Rokhel,* no. 140. Several Geniza documents mention Ibn Sanji in connection with commerce. See MS. Cambridge, University Library, T–S 6J 10, 6; T–S AS 145,

313; T–S Misc. 28, 168; MS. New York, Jewish Theological Seminary of America Library, ENA NS 52, 13.

73. In one letter, sent in 1512 by Joseph ben Pereẓ Colon to Rabbi Nissim—the dayyan in Nagid Isaac Sholal's court—asking him to intercede with the nagid for additional financial aid, we find the following: "For no one has promised me money, except for R. Abraham ibn Sanji [who owes] 37 ducats, and it is doubtful whether they will be paid. He sends me neither payment nor interest." The second letter, sent to him in 1513/early 1514 by Moses di Castro, requested additional funding for the Jerusalem kehillah. Both letters have been published by David, "Personalities in Jerusalem," 230–43.

74. A letter found in the Geniza collection, MS. Cambridge, University Library, T–S AS 145, 313, dealing with commercial matters, was sent to both Alashkar and Ibn Sanji. On Alashkar's philanthropic activity in Eretz-Israel, see A. Scheiber and M. Benayahu, "Communication of Rabbis of Egypt to *Radbaz*" (Hebrew), *Sefunot* 6 (1962): 132–33. Contributions made by "the honorable R. Solomon Alashkar" are mentioned in a letter sent from Jerusalem by [Abraha]m Sagis to Jerusalem scholar Joseph Corcos, who resided in Egypt. The letter has been published by David, "Personalities in Jerusalem," 243–48. For the reference to Alashkar, see p. 247.

75. Gedaliah ibn Yaḥya, *Shalshelet ha-Qabbalah,* MS. Russian State Library, Günzburg 652, fol. 130r; and the printed edition (Venice, 1587), 65r. See below for more on Solomon Alashkar's support of yeshivot in Eretz-Israel.

CHAPTER 4. GOVERNMENTAL POLICY TOWARD THE JEWS

1. See E. Strauss, "The Social Isolation of Ahl-Adh-Dhimma," in *Etudes Orientales à la Mémoire de Paul Hirschler,* ed. O. Komlós (Budapest, 1950), 73–94; Strauss-Ashtor, *The Jews in Egypt and Syria,* 2:204–36; Bat-Yeor, *The Dhimmi: Jews and Christians under Islam* (Rutherford, New Jersey, 1985); M. R. Cohen, *Under Crescent and Cross* (Princeton, 1994).

2. See the preceding note, as well as Cohen and Lewis, *Population and Revenue,* 70–72; Cohen, *Jewish Life under Islam,* 137–39.

3. On the attitude of the Ottoman sultans toward the Jews in the early years of their regime, see Cohen, *Ottoman Documents on Jerusalem,* and below.

4. See chap. 3, sec. D, 1 for the earlier citation from Yaari, *Letters,* 186–87. English translation, Stillman, *Jews of Arab Lands,* 291–92.

5. On these taxes in the Mamluk period, see Strauss-Ashtor, *The Jews in Egypt and Syria,* 2:259–311. For the Ottoman period, see Cohen and Lewis, *Population and Revenue,* 70–72; Cohen, *Jewish Life under Islam,* 20–24, 105–7; idem, *World Within,* index, s.v. "poll tax"; Cohen and Simon-Pikali, *Jews in the Moslem Religious Court,* 37–52. Various Hebrew sources mention these taxes as well. See, for example, David, "Letter of Israel Ashkenazi," 118; David ibn Abi Zimra, *Responsa,* no. 1137; Moses Trani, *Responsa,* pt. 1, no. 123; Joseph Trani, *Responsa,* no. 60.

6. See D. G. Goffman, "The Maktu' System and the Jewish Community of Sixteenth Century Safed," *Journal of Ottoman Studies* 3 (1983): 81–90. On the problematics of taxation in Safed, see Hacker, "Payment of *Djizya,*" 90–98.

7. On the wine tax in the Mamluk period, see Strauss-Ashtor, *The Jews in Egypt and Syria,* 2:311–12.

8. See Cohen, *Jewish Life under Islam,* 33.

9. Strauss-Ashtor, *The Jews in Egypt and Syria,* 2:312.

10. This is the conclusion reached by Cohen, *Jewish Life under Islam,* 137.

11. The additions in parentheses are cited from the version found in the responsa collection *Zera Anashim,* ed. D. Fraenkel (Husiatyn, 1910), *Yoreh Deah,* no. 24.

12. See Strauss-Ashtor, *The Jews in Egypt and Syria,* 2:210–14, 216–17.

13. See David, "Letter of Israel Ashkenazi," 117–18. Where he wrote "green turban" he evidently meant a yellow one. See also Ish-Shalom, *Christian Travels,* 280, 310; Schur, "Christian Chronicles," 357, 361, 364, 370. Sharia court documents also provide information on the turban. See Cohen, *Ottoman Documents on Jerusalem,* English introduction, xvi, 47; idem, *Jewish Life under Islam,* 138; idem, *World Within,* 72, 78, 83, 97, 102, 105, 164, 176, 178; Cohen and Simon-Pikali, *Jews in the Moslem Religious Court,* 143–51.

14. See Cohen, *Ottoman Documents,* 47. David ibn Abi Zimra alluded to this matter in a responsum, no. 1315: "and if there is danger in these circumstances, as in Jerusalem, may it be speedily rebuilt and reestablished, where the Ishmaelites [Muslims] prevent them from covering their heads with woolen prayer shawls, one should wear a woolen *talit katan* [small fringed garment worn under the shirt—TRANS.] under his clothes and recite the blessing on donning it with the intention of fulfilling by this means the obligation of the blessing over the large linen prayer shawl that he dons in synagogue." This source seems to indicate that the problem with the woolen prayer shawl stemmed from its white color, whereas linen was not necessarily white.

15. See Cohen, *Ottoman Documents on Jerusalem,* English introduction, xvi; idem, *Jewish Life under Islam,* 73, 137–39; idem, *World Within,* 97, 105; Cohen and Simon-Pikali, *Jews in the Moslem Religious Court,* 147–48.

16. On this episode, see S. D. Goitein, "Ibn 'Ubbaya's Book Concerning the Destruction of the Synagogue of Jerusalem in 1474" (Hebrew), *Zion* 13–14 (1948/49): 18–32; Strauss-Ashtor, *The Jews in Egypt and Syria,* 2:401–16; idem, *Jerusalem in the Late Middle Ages,* 112–13.

17. See Cohen, *Ottoman Documents on Jerusalem,* English introduction, xiv–xv; idem, *Jewish Life under Islam,* 76–86; idem, *World Within,* index, s.v. "synagogue"; Cohen and Simon-Pikali, *Jews in the Moslem Religious Court,* 70–84.

18. See Cohen, *Ottoman Documents on Jerusalem,* 63–64; idem, *Jewish Life under Islam,* 82–84; idem, *World Within,* 46, 181, 184, 194–95, 196; Cohen and Simon-Pikali, *Jews in the Moslem Religious Court,* 82–87.

19. See Cohen, *Ottoman Documents on Jerusalem,* English introduction, xv; idem, *Jewish Life under Islam,* 83–86; idem, *World Within,* 201; Cohen and Simon-Pikali, *Jews in the Moslem Religious Court,* 88. However, a Christian source dating from 1599 appears to indicate the presence of a small synagogue in Jerusalem. See Schur, "Christian Chronicles," 370–71. Perhaps the reference was to one of the impromptu synagogues.

20. See A. Arce, "Restricciones impuestas a los judíos en Jerusalén (1534)," *Sefarad* 17 (1957): 49–72. [Appeared in Hebrew, "Restrictions upon the Freedom of Movements of Jews in Jerusalem (15th–16th Centuries)," in *Jerusalem in the Middle Ages,* ed. B. Z. Kedar, 206–20.]

21. Numerous firmans, dating from 1517 to the end of the sixteenth century, concerning the Jews of Jerusalem have been published in Hebrew and Turkish by Cohen, *Ottoman Documents on Jerusalem;* idem, *World Within,* index, s.v. "firman"; Cohen and Simon-Pikali, *Jews in the Moslem Religious Court,* passim. An additional warrant relating to Jerusalem's Jews (1589) as well as four warrants concerning Safed's Jews have been published in English translation by Heyd, *Ottoman Documents,* 163–71. See also his Hebrew article, "Turkish Documents Concerning Safed," 129–35.

22. For a summation of the central government's attitude, see Cohen, *Jewish Life under Islam,* 216–25; N. Schur, "The Privileged Position of the Jewish Yishuv in the 16th Century" (Hebrew), *Israel—People and Land* 2–3 (1985/86): 157–62. Sultanic firmans attest to the frequency with which local rulers, governors, kadis, or their representatives committed significant injury to Jews. Appalling testimony of persecution of Jews in Jerusalem in the 1540s (and perhaps later) is found in a *qinah* (elegy) composed by Moses Meali. Among the events and disasters he highlights the eviction of the Jews from the city at the kadi's command. See Y. Ratzhaby, "Troubles in Jerusalem in 1542" (Hebrew), *Shalem* 5 (1987): 265–72. No confirmatory evidence exists for this event, but it cannot be entirely dismissed inasmuch as the Ottomans often implemented a policy of eviction and resettlement. See Hacker, "The Ottoman System of Sürgün," 27–82. We know of the central government's intention to transfer 1,000 Jewish families from Safed to Cyprus in 1576, a plan that was never implemented. See chap. 9 below.

23. Cohen, *Jewish Life under Islam,* 36–45; idem, *World Within,* 83, 110, 116, 182, 194; Cohen and Simon-Pikali, *Jews in the Moslem Religious Court,* 7–8, 11–13. On the Jewish leadership in Jerusalem and Safed, see the chapters on communal organization that follow.

24. On the significance of Jewish legal autonomy and the dayyanim's administrative dependency on the local Muslim judicial system in the Ottoman empire in general, see J. R. Hacker, "Jewish Autonomy in the Ottoman Empire: Its Scope and Limits. Jewish Courts from the Sixteenth to the Eighteenth Centuries," in *The Jews of the Ottoman Empire,* ed. A. Levy (Princeton, 1994), 153–202. For Eretz-Israel in particular, see 168–74.

25. This attitude is reflected in the two known versions of the Jerusalem community's takkanot—on the tablet that hung in the synagogue, copied by Moses Basola, *Masot,* 83, and in the collection compiled by Freimann, "Taqqanot Yerushalayim," 206–7. See also n. 28 below.

26. Cohen, *Jewish Life under Islam,* 115–19, 126–27.

27. Ibid., 118–19. A sultanic firman relating to such a case in Safed has been published by Heyd, "Turkish Documents Concerning Safed," 128–29.

28. Basola, *Masot,* 83. The alternative version reads: "No Jew shall be turned over to the nations unless warned three times in the presence of seven communal notables" (Freimann, "Taqqanot Yerushalayim," 206–7). See also Moses Trani, *Responsa,* pt. 1, no. 22; pt. 3, nos. 207–8. The latter source deals with leasing by Jews. Only the Muslim judiciary had jurisdiction in these matters.

29. See Cohen, *Jewish Life under Islam,* 112–15; idem, *World Within,* 178, 182; Cohen and Simon-Pikali, *Jews in the Moslem Religious Court,* 157–58. Important evidence is given by Moses Trani, *Responsa,* pt. 1, no. 141, where he treats a case of litigation between a Jew and a Muslim over real estate

brought before the kadi, and the kadi ruled in the Jew's favor. Nonetheless, Moses Trani stressed that the kadi's judgment was influenced by a bribe.

30. Cohen, *Jewish Life under Islam,* 119–22.

CHAPTER 5. THE JEWISH QUARTER

1. See E. Reiner's brief excursus on the Jewish settlement in Jerusalem in Mamluk Eretz-Israel, "Ha-Temurot ba-Meah ha-15," in *The History of Eretz-Israel: Under the Mamluk and Ottoman Rule (1260–1804),* ed. A. Cohen (Hebrew; Jerusalem, 1981), 7:79–81; David, "New Sources on Jews During the Middle Ages," 289–91.

2. See Artom and David, "Obadiah mi-Bertinoro," 86 (Adler, *Jewish Travellers,* 236); David ibn Abi Zimra, *Responsa,* nos. 633, 731 for the use of Ẓion. For Ṣahyun, see ibid, no. 731. See also Moudjir-ed-dyn, *Histoire de Jérusalem et d'Hebron,* translated from the Arabic by H. Sauvaire (Paris, 1876), 175.

3. See n. 2 above.

4. Basola, *Masot,* 55.

5. Moudjir-ed-dyn, *Histoire de Jérusalem,* 174–75. Taḥrir register lists provide a breakdown according to neighborhood. Jews are mentioned as residing in three neighborhhoods. See Lewis, *Notes and Documents,* 7–8; Cohen and Lewis, *Population and Revenue,* 83–84, 88, 90, 94.

6. For a more detailed description of the Jewish quarter based on the above-mentioned sources, see Cohen, *Jewish Life under Islam,* xiii, 17–20; Cohen and Lewis, *Population and Revenue,* 80–104.

7. See Y. Elitzur, "Sources of the 'Nebi-Samuel' Tradition" (Hebrew), *Cathedra* 31 (1984): 75–90.

8. See Reiner, "Pilgrims and Pilgrimage," 306–20; A. David, "Qorot ha-Qehillah ha-Yehudit bi-Yerushalayim ba-Meah ha-15 lefi Teudah Ḥadashah min ha-Genizah," *Ariel* 119–20 (1997): 167–72. Many sources, spanning the medieval period to the mid-sixteenth century, attest to frequent gatherings here. See A. Yaari, "The Pilgrimage to Meron," 92–98; R. J. Z. Werblowsky, "Prayers at the Tomb of the Prophet Samuel" (Hebrew), *Sefunot* 8 (1964): 237–53; Reiner, "Jewish Community Leadership," 59–61.

9. See I. Ben-Zvi, "A Jewish Settlement near the Tomb of the Prophet Samuel" (Hebrew), *BJPES* 10 (1942–43): 15; Reiner, "Pilgrims and Pilgrimage," 311–15. These data are confirmed by a late-sixteenth-century Jerusalem letter, recently published by Rozen, *Jewish Community,* 411–13. See also Reiner, "Jewish Community Leadership," 61.

10. A Hebrew translation of a document dating from 1517 concerning this issue has been published by Cohen and Simon-Pikali, *Jews in the Moslem Religious Court,* 112. See also Cohen, *World Within,* 97, for an English precis.

11. Three sultanic firmans dating from November 1555 to April 1556 were sent to the governors and kadis of Jerusalem and Damascus, ordering them to prevent anti-Jewish disturbances at this site. See Cohen and Simon-Pikali, *Jews in the Moslem Religious Court,* 117–20; Cohen, *World Within,* 93, 102. On the other hand, another sultanic order, dated March 1556, prohibited visits by Jews to the prophet's tomb. See Cohen and Simon-Pikali, *Jews in the Moslem Religious Court,* 118–19; Cohen, *World Within,* 102.

12. D. Yellin, "Jewish Jerusalem Three Hundred Years Ago" (Hebrew), in *Yerushalayim: Journal of the Jewish Palestine Exploration Society, Dedicated to . . . A. M. Luncz,* ed. I. Press and E. L. Sukenik (Jerusalem, 1928), 94–96; Ben-Zvi, "The Tomb of the Prophet Samuel," 15.

13. David ibn Abi Zimra, *Responsa,* no. 608. On the time frame for its seizure from the Jews, see David, "Qorot ha-Qehillah," 167–72 (n. 8 above).

14. For a sultanic order from that year, see Cohen and Simon-Pikali, *Jews in the Moslem Religious Court,* 122–23; Cohen, *World Within,* 202. Christian traveler John Sanderson, who visited Jerusalem in 1601, mentioned that the Jews continued to hold ceremonies in Nabi Samuil, as in the past. See *The Travels of John Sanderson in the Levant, 1584–1602,* ed. W. Foster (London, 1931), 100.

15. As noted above (introduction, n. 5), B. Lewis has published these data in various contexts. For his latest treatment, which includes two additional censuses, see Cohen and Lewis, *Population and Revenue,* 81–94.

16. Basola, *Masot,* 61.

17. Yaari, *Letters,* 157.

18. See Cohen, "New Evidence on Demographic Change: The Jewish Community in 16th Century Jerusalem," in *Mémorial Ömer Lûtfi Barkan,* ed. O. Komlós, 62–64; idem, *Jewish Life under Islam,* 28–35; Hacker, "Payment of *Djizya,*" 90–98.

19. Cohen, *Jewish Life under Islam,* 32, believes that the figures should be at least 20 percent higher.

20. Cohen and Lewis, *Population and Revenue,* 94; Cohen, "New Evidence on Demographic Change," 59.

21. Ibid., 61–64; idem, *Jewish Life under Islam,* 20–27, 34–35.

22. This emerges from population censuses conducted by the Ottoman Turks. See Cohen and Lewis, *Population and Revenue,* 19–28, 84–91, 94; Cohen, *Jewish Life under Islam,* 14–17; Hacker, "Payment of *Djizya,*" 84.

23. See David, "Emissaries' Letters from Jerusalem," 325–31.

24. For the presumed date of his relocation, see Scheiber and Benayahu, "Communication to the Radbaz," 134; Cohen, *Jewish Life under Islam,* 44.

25. On conditions in Safed then and afterward, see M. Pachter, "'Ḥazut Kasha' of Rabbi Moshe Alsheikh" (Hebrew), *Shalem* 1 (1974): 157–93; and chap. 9, sec. B, below.

26. See Cohen and Lewis, *Population and Revenue,* 94; Cohen, "New Evidence on Demographic Change," 60; idem, *Jewish Life under Islam,* 17–20.

CHAPTER 6. THE COMMUNITIES

1. Basola, *Masot,* 61 (translation cited from David, "Spanish Exiles," 83). The latter three kehalim (who rarely cooperated with the Ashkenazi kahal) cooperated on legislative activity for the kehillah, a haskamah issued in 1534 "in the presence of R. Jacob Berab, may God preserve him, and in the presence of the leaders of the Sefardi kahal and the Maghrebi scholars and the Musta'rab notables." See Levi ibn Ḥabib, *Responsa,* no. 26.

2. See Braslawski (Braslvsky), *Studies in Our Country,* 137–53; I. Yuval, "Alms from Nuremberg to Jerusalem" (Hebrew), *Zion* 46 (1981): 182–97; Reiner, "Ashkenaz and Jerusalem," 27–62.

3. A. David, "The Ashkenazic Community in Jerusalem in the Sixteenth Century" (Hebrew), *Proceedings of the Sixth World Congress of Jewish Studies* (Jerusalem, 1976), 2:331–41.

4. See David, "Spanish Exiles," 82ff.; and below.

5. This state of affairs is attested to by a variety of sources. See David, "The Ashkenazic Community in Jerusalem," 334–38. Some data on the Ashkenazi community's institutional structure have survived in letters sent from Jerusalem found in the Geniza and published by David, "Ashkenazic Community in Jerusalem," *Vatiqin,* 27–32; Ch. Turniansky, "Correspondence in Yiddish," 158–59. The content of these letters will be discussed below.

6. Two sixteenth-century Ashkenazi emissaries are known by name: Uri Feyvush and David Tevlin. See David, "The Ashkenazic Community in Jerusalem," 336.

7. Because of its importance to Mediterranean trade, Venice served as the main Italian port for ships bound for the Orient. This also accounts for Venice's role as one of the major centers for collection and transfer of funds for Eretz-Israel. See David, "Emissaries' Letters from Jerusalem," 326, 331–32.

8. For a profound halakhic exposition of this issue, see Yom Tov Ṣahalon, *Responsa,* no. 160. See also David, "The Ashkenazic Community in Jerusalem," 335–37.

9. See Joseph Caro, *Shu"t Avqat Rokhel,* nos. 29, 115.

10. The query was dated 1610. On intercommunal marriages (between Ashkenazim and members of the other kehalim), see Turniansky, "Correspondence in Yiddish," 159. See also Jacob Berab, *Responsa,* no. 61, where he treats the case of "a North African man residing in Jerusalem who had an Ashkenazi sister-in-law [whom he was required to take in levirate marriage]."

11. Turniansky, "Correspondence in Yiddish," 204–5.

12. These Ashkenazi yeshivot will be discussed in sec. B below.

13. Regarding these figures, see David, "The Ashkenazic Community in Jerusalem," 339–41.

14. See David, "Ashkenazic Community in Jerusalem," *Vatiqin,* 25–32, and n. 15 below.

15. Three of the letters from this series have been published by S. Assaf, *Texts and Studies in Jewish History* (Hebrew; Jerusalem, 1946), 230–37. These letters were again published with an additional four letters from the same set of correspondence by Turniansky, "Correspondence in Yiddish," 149–209. The mother and son are mentioned in two additional Geniza documents, MS. Cambridge, University Library, T–S 13J 4, 19; MS. New York, Jewish Theological Seminary of America, ENA NS 43, 4, which were published in the Hebrew version of this book, 219–20.

16. These issues are discussed in depth by Turniansky, "Correspondence in Yiddish."

17. In the Hebrew sources, Germany is referred to as the land of Ashkenaz. Cf. Basola, *Masot,* 62. Evidence for the arrival of Jews from Ashkenaz—Germany and Bohemia—in the 1520s is found in Abraham ha-Levi's letter "On the Falashas and Martin Luther" (1525) cited above, chap. 1, sec. C. See also my comments above.

18. Several scholars of French origin whose families had settled in Italy several generations earlier resided in early-sixteenth-century Jerusalem, includ-

ing members of the Trèves family. See H. Chone, "Ḥakhamim mi-Mishpaḥat Trèves bi-Yerushalayim," *Sinai* 11 (1942–43): 183–213; David, "Ashkenazic Community in Jerusalem," *Vatiqin,* 32–33. Members of the Colon family were also present: Peretz ben Joseph Colon (the son of Joseph Colon, one of Italy's outstanding rabbis in the fifteenth century), and Peretz's son, Joseph Colon.

19. Regarding Bohemia, we know that one "Moses of Prague" lived in fifteenth-century Jerusalem. See Artom and David, "Obadiah mi-Bertinoro," 79 (Adler, *Jewish Travellers,* 232). At a later date, in the mid-sixteenth century, Rachel, wife of Eliezer Sussmann of the Ẓarit family of Prague, lived in Jerusalem. See Turniansky, "Correspondence in Yiddish," 189.

20. Evidence for the presence of Hungarian Jews in Jerusalem is found in two sources. See Turniansky, "Correspondence in Yiddish," 159, 206–7; and *Quntres Ḥiddushey Dinim mi-Rabbaney Ir Qodshenu Yerushalayim,* appended to *Ḥayyim va-Ḥesed* by Ḥayyim Musaphia (Leghorn, 1844), no. 63.

21. Data are extant on the arrival of several Ashkenazi scholars from Italy in Jerusalem in the late fifteenth century, including Joseph de Montagna and Jacob Colombano—both of Ashkenazi origin, who are mentioned by Meshullam of Volterra. See Yaari, *Massa Meshullam,* 76–77 (Adler, *Jewish Travellers,* 195, 196). The latter is also mentioned in Obadiah of Bertinoro's first letter. See Artom and David, "Obadiah mi-Bertinoro," 81 (Adler, *Jewish Travellers,* 234, where he is referred to as Jacob Calmann). For further information, see Kook, *Iyyunim,* 2:305–6. To this group we must also add Israel ben Yeḥiel Ashkenazi, who served as a rabbi and posek (decisor) in Perugia, Rome, and other Italian towns. See A. David, "On the Identity of R. Israel Ashkenazi of Jerusalem" (Hebrew), *Zion* 38 (1973): 172–73. For Samson Back, one of Isaac Luria's disciples, see Yaari, *Letters,* 188–89.

22. It appears that Polish scholars also lived and taught in Jerusalem; for example, Abraham Pollack headed one of the two Ashkenazi yeshivot in Jerusalem. See David, "Ashkenazic Community in Jerusalem," *Vatiqin,* 29, 31. It is possible that Ya'qub ibn Fallāq (=Jacob Pollack), who served as shaykh al-yahud in the 1530s and 1540s (see Cohen, *Jewish Life under Islam,* index, s.v. "Fallāq, Ya'qub ibn Ḥayim"), belonged to the same family and is to be identified with the Jacob Pollack who resided in Jerusalem in the first half of the sixteenth century. See T. Preschel, "Rabbi Yaakov Pollack's Aliyah to Jerusalem" (Hebrew), in *Jubilee Volume in Honor of R. Joseph B. Soloveitchik,* ed. S. Israeli, N. Lamm, and Y. Raphael (Jerusalem, 1984), 2:1124–29. Various suggestions have been tendered for this scholar's identity. Some claim he is to be identified with famed Polish scholar Jacob Pollack (*baal ha-ḥilluqim*—master of talmudic study based on fine distinctions—TRANS.). This seems unlikely. See ibid., 1126–29. It is possible, however, that his son resided in Jerusalem. See ibid., 1129. Bezalel Ashkenazi was also of Polish origin, as was Ephraim Fischel ben Moses Judah, the Maharshal's (Solomon ben Yeḥiel Luria) son-in-law. On a Jewish woman of Polish extraction in Jerusalem, see Turniansky, "Correspondence in Yiddish," 189.

23. The status of the Spanish exiles in these centers has been researched from various points of view. See H. Beinart, ed., *Moreshet Sepharad: The Sephardi Legacy* (Jerusalem, 1992), 2:11–133, 166–206, 217–39.

24. See Y. Baer, "Ha-Tenuah ha-Meshiḥit bi-Sefarad bi-Tequfat ha-Geyrush," *Zion* (*Me'asef*) 5 (1933): 76 n. 1.

25. This passage was published by E. Kupfer, "The Revelations of R. Asher b. R. Meir called Lemlein Roitlingen" (Hebrew), *Kobeẓ al Yad* 8 (1975): 387 n. 2.

26. He made this allusion in a previously unknown section of this letter recently published by David, "New Sources Describing Travel," 325.

27. See Yaari, *Letters,* 157. He also mentions "another Sefardi lad." Ibid., 156. In his second letter (1489), Obadiah of Bertinoro mentions "two Sephardic pupils [who] take uninterrupted part in my instruction." See Artom and David, "Obadiah mi-Bertinoro," 104 (Adler, *Jewish Travellers,* 248). Zechariah Sefardi was not the only preacher in Jerusalem at that time. Apparently, Obadiah of Bertinoro (Italy) was the foremost preacher of the day. He preached periodically in the synagogue, but only on specified occasions, mainly the festivals. See Artom and David, ibid. (Adler, ibid., 247), and the anonymous traveler's letter in Yaari, *Letters,* 157.

28. Their number included Jacob ben Isaac Mar-Ḥayyim the Sefardi, son of Spanish kabbalist Isaac Mar-Ḥayyim. The father reached Italy from Spain prior to the expulsion and made his way to Jerusalem via Salonika before 1503. Three additional Sefardi sages will be referred to below.

29. The takkanah and the ensuing haskamah were first published by Samuel d'Avila, *Keter Torah* (Amsterdam, 1725), introduction. On the takkanah and its social signficance, see Hacker, "Payment of *Djizya,*" 63–117.

30. See Benayahu, "Teudah," 109–25 where he pays specific attention to the history of those scholars, some of whom are known from other sources. See idem, "Yosef Garson," 98–103.

31. See Gottheil and Worrell, *Fragments from the Genizah,* 246–65. For the dating of this letter, see Benayahu, "Teudah," 112; idem, "Yosef Garson," 83–84. My investigations indicate that 1510 is the correct date. See my forthcoming study in *Te'udah* 15 (1999).

32. See Gottheil and Worrell, *Fragments from the* Genizah, 256–57.

33. See David, "The Identity of Israel Ashkenazi," 170–73; idem, "Letter of Israel Ashkenazi," 116.

34. Basola, *Masot,* 87.

35. These takkanot have been published by Freimann, "Taqqanot Yerushalayim," 206–14 (English citation from David, "Spanish Exiles," 84).

36. See David, "The Ashkenazic Community in Jerusalem," 333–34. A partial list of Ashkenazi scholars who lived in sixteenth-century Jerusalem can be found above.

37. See David, "The Ashkenazic Community in Jerusalem," 335; idem, "Spanish Exiles," 84–85.

38. Regarding the yeshivot, see David, "Jerusalem Academies," 143–44; Dimitrovsky, "Unknown Chapter," 119–21. These yeshivot will be discussed in greater detail in chap. 8, sec. A below.

39. He is not known from any other sources.

40. David, "Letter of Israel Ashkenazi," 113 (translation cited from David, "Spanish Exiles," 85).

41. The traditions of study in medieval Spain and Ashkenaz merit independent examination. Regarding the subject matter studied in these yeshivot, see David, "Jerusalem Academies," 149–52; Dimitrovsky, "Unknown Chapter," 110–12.

42. Recently published by Yaari, *Letters,* 160–66.

43. Published by David, "Sholal Family," 408–9.

44. See David, "A Letter from Jerusalem," 56 (English citation from David, "Spanish Exiles," 86).

45. See n. 8 above. See also David, "Spanish Exiles," 103–4.

46. Regarding his Ashkenazic extraction, see David, "The Ashkenazic Community in Jerusalem," 339 n. 55.

47. See Rozen, "Jewish Community," 102–8.

48. See D. Kaufmann, "Tofes Ketav she-nishlakh me-Ir ha-Qodesh le-Carpi," *Jerusalem Jahrbuch* 5 (1901), ed. A. M. Luncz, 82; Rozen, "Jewish Community," 105 (English citation from David, "Spanish Exiles," 104).

49. See Frumkin and Rivlin, *Ḥakhmey Yerushalayim,* pts. 1–2; Rozen, *Jewish Community.*

50. On the Musta'rabs in Eretz-Israel, see I. Ben-Zvi, *Studies and Documents* (Hebrew; Jerusalem, 1966), 15–20; Rozen, "The Musta'rabs," 73–101.

51. See David, "Spanish Exiles," 78–79.

52. See David, "The Ashkenazic Community in Jerusalem," 331–33; and my comments in sec. A above.

53. Basola, *Masot,* 63.

54. David, "Letter of Israel Ashkenazi," 110–11, 115.

55. See Yaari, *Letters,* 165–66. Samuel Masud is known to have headed a yeshivah in Jerusalem as early as 1512. See David, "Personalities in Jerusalem," 234–36.

56. Levi ibn Ḥabib, *Responsa,* no. 26. Nissim Ankari served as a rabbi and dayyan in Egypt for part of his life, but for unknown reasons he resigned from his position as dayyan in 1541. This emerges from a letter sent to David ibn Abi Zimra housed in the Geniza collection, MS. Cambridge, University Library, T-S NS 320, 114.

57. See David, "North African Jewry," 74–76; idem, "Sholal Family," 374–414; idem, "Personalities in Jerusalem," 233–35; idem, "New Genizah Documents," 30–31.

58. See also Frumkin and Rivlin, *Ḥakhmey Yerushalayim,* 1:77–78.

59. Bezalel Ashkenazi, *Responsa,* no. 14.

60. Levi ibn Ḥabib, *Responsa,* no. 93.

61. See Cohen, *Jewish Life under Islam,* 49–52, 197; idem, *World Within,* s.v. "maghāriba," "maghribī"; Cohen and Simon-Pikali, *Jews in the Moslem Religious Court,* s.v. "Mugrabim"; David, "Sholal Family," 382–83, 390–95, 408–14. On the pilgrims specifically, see Cohen, *Jewish Life under Islam,* 104–6.

62. This fragmentary letter, sent from Jerusalem to Egypt, is found in MS. Cambridge, University Library Geniza Collection, T-S Misc. 20, 166. It alludes to social tensions between Sefardim and Maghrebis in the Jerusalem community. The letter appeared in the Hebrew version of this book, 221.

63. Cf. Obadiah of Bertinoro's first letter, Artom and David, "Obadiah mi-Bertinoro," 91–92 (Adler, *Jewish Travellers,* 238–39); David ibn Abi Zimra, *Responsa,* no. 1290, pt. 7, nos. 5, 9.

64. There was a Christian Ethiopian community in Jerusalem at that time whose members may also have fled their homeland in the wake of the endemic warfare. See C. F. Beckingham, "Pantaleao de Aveiro and the Ethiopian Community in Jerusalem," *Journal of Semitic Studies* 7 (1962): 325–38.

65. David ha-Reuveni's origins remain an open question. M. D. U. Cassuto and others argue that he was of Ethiopian origin (See Cassuto, "David

ha-Reubeni," 339–58), whereas A. Shohat argues that he was from Yemen. See his "Notes on the David Reubeni Affair" (Hebrew), *Zion* 35 (1970): 96ff.

66. M. Beit-Arié and C. Sirat, *Manuscrits Médiévaux en Caractères Hébraïques* (Jerusalem and Paris, 1972), Part I, 73; M. Beit-Arié, "Hebrew Manuscripts Copied in Jerusalem before the Ottoman Conquest" (Hebrew), in *Jerusalem in the Middle Ages,* ed. B. Z. Kedar, 275–77; Cohen, *Jewish Life under Islam,* index, s.v. "Karaites"; idem, *World Within,* index, s.v. "Karaite"; Cohen and Simon-Pikali, *Jews in the Moslem Religious Court,* index, s.v. "Qaraim." On the Karaites in seventeenth-century Jerusalem, see M. L. Wilensky, "Rabbi Elijah Afeda Baghi and the Karaite Community of Jerusalem," *PAAJR* 40 (1972): 109–46. Cecil Roth has published a letter sent from Cairo to a Karaite family in Jerusalem. See his article, "A Letter from Cairo to a Karaite Family in Jerusalem" (Hebrew), *Yerushalayim* (*Review for Eretz-Israel Research*) 4 (1953): 138–40. Roth dates the document as no later than the sixteenth century; however, at present, it is not possible to determine whether the letter dates to the fifteenth or sixteenth century, or even earlier.

67. On this affair, see chap. 5, sec. A, above.

68. See Cohen, *Jewish Life under Islam,* 6–7, 28, 48–60, and passim.

CHAPTER 7. COMMUNAL ORGANIZATION

1. Meshullam of Volterra listed these officeholders in 1481. See Yaari, *Massa Meshullam,* 77 (Adler, *Jewish Travellers,* 196). On patterns of leadership and the role of the "elders" in the late-fifteenth-century Jerusalem kehillah, see David, "Historical Significance," 221–43; idem, "The Vice-Nagid of Jerusalem in the 15th and Early 16th Century" (Hebrew), *Zion* 45 (1980): 329–31; Reiner, "Jewish Community Leadership," 23–81.

2. See Artom and David, "Obadiah mi-Bertinoro," 82–87 (Adler, *Jewish Travellers,* 234–36).

3. Isaac Sholal's predecessor, his uncle and brother-in-law, Nathan Sholal, took some interest in Jerusalem's affairs. See David, "Sholal Family," 376, 388, 406–7. Nonetheless, his level of involvement in no way matched that of his successor. See Reiner, "Jewish Community Leadership," 34–35.

4. See David, "Sholal Family," 378–79. Aside from sages (ḥakhamim) and heads of yeshivot, we hear of no other public officeholders in Jerusalem during his tenure as nagid. It is quite likely that one Jerusalem public official was Moses Castro, who had direct dealings with Abraham ibn Sanji, a wealthy Egyptian Jew, concerning communal affairs. For correspondence between the two in 1513, including requests by Castro for individual and communal aid, as well as for funds for the rehabilitation of a synagogue in Jerusalem, see chap. 3, n. 73 above.

5. See chap. 3, n. 59 above.

6. See A. David, "A New Document Referring to the Yeshiva in Jerusalem in the Sixteenth Century" (Hebrew), *Cathedra* 68 (1993): 43–48, esp. 47.

7. See chap. 6, n. 29 above.

8. David ibn Abi Zimra, *Responsa,* no. 644. Regarding this takkanah, see David, "Historical Significance," 240–42.

9. See David, "The Office of *Nagid* in Egypt," 325–37.

10. See, for example, Elijah Mizraḥi, *Responsa,* no. 45; David ibn Abi Zimra, *Responsa,* nos. 628, 644, 1085; Moses Trani, *Responsa,* pt. 3, no. 1;

A. M. Luncz, "Issur laasot Peyrud be-ha-Qehillah mi-Shenat 1623," *Jerusalem Jahrbuch* 2 (1887): 147–48; E. Rivlin, "Taqqanot ha-Ezvonot bi-Yerushalayim u-ve-Ereẓ Yisrael," in *Azkkarah le-Nishmat Avraham Yiṣḥak ha-Kohen Kook* (Jerusalem, 1937), 5:559–69; Reiner, "Jewish Community Leadership," 41–52; M. Benayahu, "Ha-Taqqanah she-lo lehoṣi Sefarim mi-Yerushalayim ve-Hishtalshelutah," in *Minḥah le-Yehudah: Mugash le-ha-Rav Yehudah Leib Zlotnik,* ed. S. Assaf et al. (Jerusalem, 1950), 226–34.

11. Basola, *Masot,* 83–85.

12. See Freimann, "Taqqanot Yerushalayim," 206–14.

13. Documents from the Jerusalem sharia court contain references to individuals who held the position of shaykh al-yahud. See Cohen, *Jewish Life under Islam,* 36–42, and index; idem, *World Within,* index, s.v. "head of the Jewish community"; Cohen and Simon-Pikali, *Jews in the Moslem Religious Court,* 7–26, and index.

14. See Cohen and Simon-Pikali, *Jews in the Moslem Religious Court,* 13; Cohen, *World Within,* 194.

15. Cohen and Simon-Pikali, *Jews in the Moslem Religious Court,* 8; Cohen, *World Within,* 83.

16. See chap. 6, secs. A and B, above.

17. The title *shaykh* or *zaqen* (elder) is found in Hebrew sources. See Levi ibn Ḥabib, *Responsa,* no. 25; Moses Trani, *Responsa,* pt. 3, no. 188; and *Quntres Ḥiddushey Dinim,* no. 87.

18. On the "elders affair," see n. 1 above.

19. See Cohen, *Jewish Life under Islam,* index, s.v. "Shullāl, Salamun ibn Mūsā"; Cohen and Simon-Pikali, *Jews in the Moslem Religious Court,* index, s.v. "Salamun ben Mūsā Sholal."

20. On the dayyan's authority and status in the community, see Moses Trani, *Responsa,* pt. 3, nos. 188, 228, and *Quntres Ḥiddushey Dinim,* no. 87. See also Cohen, *Jewish Life under Islam,* 42–45, for this topic and his dependence on the kadi; idem, *World Within,* index, s.v. "dayyan"; Cohen and Simon-Pikali, *Jews in the Moslem Religious Court,* index, s.v. "diyan." The Hebrew sources relating to Ottoman policy have been treated by Hacker, "Jewish Autonomy in the Ottoman Empire," 153–202; on this matter specifically, see 168–74.

21. On the significance of punishment by excommunication in Jewish law, see G. Leibson, "Determining Factors in Herem and Nidui (Ban and Excommunication) During the Tannaitic and Amoraic Periods" (Hebrew), *Shenaton ha-Mishpat ha-Ivri* 2 (1975): 292–342; idem, "The Ban and Those Under It: Tannaitic and Amoraic Perspectives" (Hebrew), *Shenaton ha-Mishpat ha-Ivri* 5–6 (1979–80): 177–202; M. Gil, *A History of Palestine, 634–1099* (Cambridge, 1992), 522–25.

22. For the identification of this dayyan, see Rozen, *Jewish Community,* 125, 143–44; Hacker, "Jewish Autonomy in the Ottoman Empire," 171–74.

23. This episode is documented in sharia court documents. For a brief treatment, see Cohen, *Jewish Life under Islam,* 44. These documents show that at a later date, 1560, David ibn Abi Zimra's appointment as dayyan received the kadi's official approval. His term lasted until 1564 at least.

24. Cohen, *Jewish Life under Islam,* 44.

25. See David ibn Abi Zimra, *Responsa,* no. 1085.

26. Basola, *Masot,* 63.

27. David ibn Abi Zimra, *Responsa,* no. 644.

28. See David, "Letter of Israel Ashkenazi," 116, and my remarks below, chap. 8, sec. C.

29. On Ibn Ḥabib, see Cohen, *Jewish Life under Islam,* 42 n. 10, 44 n. 16, 130. For Ibn Abi Zimra, see ibid., 44, 81. At the inception of Ottoman rule, the following scholars served as dayyanim, Judah Albotini and Israel Ashkenazi. See David, "Letter of Israel Ashkenazi," 99, 116.

CHAPTER 8. INTELLECTUAL LIFE

1. See Gil, *History of Palestine,* 490–776.

2. The Jewish community in Jerusalem ceased to exist with the inception of Crusader rule in Eretz-Israel and was renewed with the city's capture by Saladin in 1187. Its subsequent development was gradual. See J. Prawer, *The History of the Jews in the Latin Kingdom of Jerusalem* (Oxford, 1988), index, s.v. "Jerusalem."

3. See Reiner, "Ashkenaz and Jerusalem," 27–62.

4. See David, "Jerusalem Academies," 141.

5. Zacuto's astronomical tables are located in MS. Sassoon 799 (IMHM, no. 9557). This citation has been published by S. D. Sassoon, *Ohel Dawid* (London, 1932), 1:510. This selection has also been cited and analyzed by A. Shochat, "Rabbi Abraham Zacuto in the Talmudical College of Rabbi Isaac Shulal in Jerusalem" (Hebrew), *Zion* 13–14 (1948–49): 43–46, and was mentioned by Strauss-Ashtor, *The Jews in Egypt and Syria,* 2:508. Shochat correctly dates Zacuto's comments to 1513. Abraham Zacuto died in Jerusalem a year later.

6. See David, introduction to "Letter of Israel Ashkenazi," 103 for a discussion of the addressee's identity.

7. I have revised the text in accord with MS. Oxford, Bodleian Library, Mich. 85 (1562) (IMHM, no. 16930), fol. 53r. Although this letter is usually referred to as the letter of "beney ha-yeshivah" (singular), it is more correctly the letter of "beney ha-yeshivot" (plural) as two yeshivot are mentioned in the letter, and its signatories noted that they were signing "in the name of each yeshivah."

8. A similar report is found in Basola, *Masot,* 62. See also David, "Jerusalem Academies," 148–49; idem, "Personalities in Jerusalem," 230–36; idem, "The Yeshivah in Jerusalem," 43–48; Dimitrovsky, "Unknown Chapter," 106–19.

9. For the text of this letter, see Benayahu, "Teudah," 122–25.

10. As attested to by the letter of beney ha-yeshivot mentioned above (n. 7). See David, "Jerusalem Academies," 143; Dimitrovsky, "Unknown Chapter," 108–10.

11. See the preceding discussion in chap. 7.

12. On the takkanah and its social significance, see I. Ta-Shma, "Al Petur Talmidey Ḥakhamim mi-Missim bi-Yemey ha-Beynayyim," in *Studies in Rabbinic Literature, Bible, and Jewish History Dedicated to E. Z. Melamed,* ed. Y. D. Gilat, Ch. Levine, and Z. M. Rabinowitz (Hebrew; Ramat Gan, 1982), 312–22; Hacker, "Payment of *Djizya,*" 63–117.

13. A letter sent by the nagid, Isaac Sholal, to "the scholars in the holy yeshivah in Jerusalem," at the end of the sixteenth century's first decade or the

beginning of the second, mentions Moses Alfaranji. There is, however, no evidence that he headed the yeshivah. See David, "The Yeshiva in Jerusalem," 45.

14. See chap. 6, sec. B, 67, for citations of Israel Ashkenazi's letter and of Moses Basola's account.

15. See chap. 6, sec. A.

16. On these individuals as successors to the previous heads of the Jerusalem yeshivot, see David, "Letter of Israel Ashkenazi," 113, 121. A system of dual leadership in the Jerusalem yeshivot emerges from another source, a letter sent from Jerusalem to Egypt by Joḥanan ben Solomon in the mid-sixteenth century. See David, "Ashkenazic Community in Jerusalem," *Vatiqin,* 27–32.

17. See my comments above, chap. 1, sec. A.

18. The chronology of Levi ibn Ḥabib's sojourns in Jersualem has recently been reexamined. See David, "Personalities in Jerusalem," 240–41.

19. Levi ibn Ḥabib, *Responsa,* no. 6. See also David Conforte, *Qore ha-Dorot* (Berlin, 1846), fol. 34r; and below.

20. In my article, "Ashkenazic Community in Jerusalem," *Vatiqin,* 29, I suggested that this Rabbi Yeḥiel can be identified as Yeḥiel ben Moses Castellazo Ashkenazi, a Jerusalem sage in the sixteenth century's third quarter, and perhaps earlier.

21. Rabbi Kalman has been tentatively identified as Kalonymos ben Jacob, an Ashkenazi scholar in the first half of the sixteenth century, and Rabbi David was none other than his contemporary, David ben Zechariah Frank.

22. See David, "Personalities in Jerusalem," 243–48.

23. Cited from an autobiographical MS by Solomon Adeni, MS. Warsaw 267 (IMHM, no. 11843), fol. 1r. An identical version is found in the printed text of the Mishnah (Romm, Vilna edition). The selection has been cited by Benayahu, "R. Ḥayyim Vital bi-Yerushalayim," *Sinai* 30 (1952): 66.

24. This letter has been published by A. Marx, "Zwei Briefe berühmter Gelehrter aus dem 16 Jahrhundert," in *Festschrift für Dr. J. Freimann* (Berlin, 1937), 169–70; and by L. (H. Z.) Dimitrovsky, "Notes to the History of the Jews in Italy" (Hebrew), *Zion* 20 (1955): 175–78.

25. Cf. M. Rozen, ed., *The Ruins of Jerusalem* (Hebrew; Tel Aviv, 1981), 108–9: "In the month of Ḥeshvan [5]386 [November 1625] the evil kadi thought of ways to increase his wealth, and thought to turn the synagogue [the so-called Naḥmanides synagogue] into a flour mill. Some forty years earlier, a mufti who hated the [Jewish] religion commanded that [the synagogue] be closed, since it was set aside to be a mosque . . . and to the present day, the Jews have not succeeded in restoring its glory."

26. The Hebrew word *hesger* was commonly used in Italy and the East to refer to bet midrash. In sixteenth-century Safed, for example, this term was used to refer to a yeshivah founded by Joseph Caro.

27. Samuel d'Avila, *Keter Torah,* introduction.

28. Yom Tov Ṣahalon, *Responsa,* no. 160. See also, David, "The Ashkenazic Community in Jerusalem," 340–41.

29. See David, "A Letter from Jerusalem," 59; idem, "Sholal Family," 378. See also chap. 3, sec. F, above.

30. For additional evidence of his philanthropic activities, see David, "Personalities in Jerusalem," 245–47; idem, "New Genizah Documents," 25 n. 34. See also the end of chap. 3 above.

31. The term *baaley Torah* appears in the takkanah exempting scholars

from taxes issued by the nagid's court in 1509. (On this takkanah, see chap. 7 above.) It is also found in the 1596 haskamah to this regulation by the Jerusalem scholars. In the 1509 haskamah of the Jerusalem scholars to this takkanah, they are also referred to as *beney ha-yeshivah. Ḥaverim maqshivim* was the term used in the opening of the letter sent by Safed scholars to their colleagues in Jerusalem in 1504 regarding the sabbatical year. See Benayahu, "Teudah," 122. The same term is used by Basola, *Masot,* 63, and in many other sources.

32. See H. Z. Dimitrovsky, "Rabbi Yaakov Berab's Academy" (Hebrew), *Sefunot* 7 (1963): 52–56, 78 n. 233; H. Bentov, "Methods of Study of Talmud in the Yeshivot of Salonica and Turkey after the Expulsion from Spain" (Hebrew), *Sefunot* 13 (1971–78): 40.

33. Cf. Dimitrovsky, "Yaakov Berab's Academy," 56. In the seventeenth century as well, the Jerusalem yeshivot served as a forum for scholars engaged in discussion of halakhic isssues. See Y. Y. Rivlin, "Rabbi Raphael Mordechay Malki's Proposal to Establish in Jerusalem a Yeshiva as a Centre for Judaism" (Hebrew), *Yerushalayim (Review)* 2/5 (1955): 187–94; S. Z. Havlin, "Jerusalem Yeshivot and Sages in the Late 17th Century" (Hebrew), *Shalem* 2 (1976): 115–17.

34. This letter has been published by Neubauer, "Qibuṣim," 45–50, and discussed by Prawer, "Jerusalem Letters," 145–48. J. R. Hacker has established that the signatories on the letter were not the parnassim as Prawer believed (ibid., 148), but rather the Jerusalem dayyanim. See Hacker, "The Connections of Spanish Jewry with Eretz-Israel between 1391 and 1492" (Hebrew), *Shalem* 1 (1974): 148 n. 85.

35. On Jacob Berab's yeshivah, see Dimitrovsky, "Yaakov Berab's Academy," 55, 78–80; and below, chap. 12, sec. C, 1. On the yeshivot in Turkey and Salonika, see ibid., 79–80; Bentov, "Yeshivot of Salonica and Turkey," 40.

36. See David, "Personalities in Jerusalem," 235–36. On the role of the melammed, see ibid., 231–32 n. 18.

37. Basola, *Masot,* 63. The latter figure is also mentioned as a teacher of young children by Israel Askenazi. See David, "Letter of Israel Ashkenazi," 114.

38. These letters were published as an appendix to Isaac ben Abraham ibn Latif's *Rav Pe'alim,* ed. S. Schönblum (Lemberg, 1885). The melammed noted his economic distress in his second letter. Moses ibn Latif's homilies were known to Azariah de Rossi, who wrote: "Also R. Moses Latif of Jerusalem delivered his homilies in public and then wrote them down himself as I have seen." See Azariah de Rossi, *Meor Einayim* (Jerusalem, 1970), 290. De Rossi cited Latif's comments in his treatise *Maṣref la-Kesef,* 9–10, which was printed together with *Meor Einayim.*

39. See David, "Jerusalem Academies," 149–51. In the Jerusalem yeshivah headed by Jacob Berab, the Spanish tradition of study as developed in the Castilian yeshivah of Isaac Canpanton was followed. See Dimitrovsky, "Unknown Chapter," 111–12. The same tradition was followed in his Safed yeshivah, as we shall see below, chap. 12, sec. C, 1.

40. David, "Letter of Israel Ashkenazi," 116.

41. Basola, *Masot,* 63.

42. On this issue, see David, "Historical Significance," 242, and chap. 7 above.

43. The text is cited according to MS. Oxford, Bodleian Library. Mich. 85 (1562) (IMHM no. 16930), fol. 53r–v.

44. Space does not permit further examination of this topic, which merits separate clarification. See chap. 12, sec. D, 6 below.

45. Yaari, *Letters,* 157.

46. See introduction to Artom and David, "Obadiah mi-Bertinoro," 37. See also E. Shochetman's pioneering study, "Is the Commentary of R. Obadiah of Bertinoro on the Mishna a Source for Halakhic Ruling?" (Hebrew), *Pe'amim* 37 (1988): 3–23.

47. David, "Letter of Israel Ashkenazi," 113. See also Dimitrovsky, "Unknown Chapter," 110–11. Dimitrovsky understands Israel Ashkenazi's comments as an attempt to stress the marked decline in the level of study following Jacob Berab's departure from Jerusalem in 1519.

48. In actuality, little is known about the curriculum of study in the Italian yeshivot during the Middle Ages. See R. Bonfil, *Rabbis and Jewish Communities in Renaissance Italy* (London and Washington, 1993), 14–26.

49. With the exception of an Ashkenazic kabbalist, Asher Lemlein Roitlingen, who prophesied in early-sixteenth-century Italy. His writings allude to a stay in Safed, and it appears likely that he visited Jerusalem as well. See Kupfer, "The Revelations of R. Asher Lemlein Roitlingen," 392; M. Idel, "On Mishmarot and Messianism in Jerusalem in the 16th–17th Centuries" (Hebrew), *Shalem* 5 (1987): 87.

50. Published by G. Polak, "Horaah al Sheelat ha-Malakhim," *Kerem Chemed* 9 (1856): 141–48. For the specific matter cited here, see ibid., 142.

51. On Joseph Ḥayyun, see A. Gross, *Rabbi Joseph ben Abraham Ḥayyun* (Hebrew; Jerusalem, 1993).

52. Some aspects of this issue have been addressed by M. Idel, "The Relationship of the Jerusalem Kabbalists and Israel Sarug of Safed" (Hebrew), *Shalem* 6 (1992): 165–73.

53. See G. Scholem's studies cited in chapter 13, s.v. "Abraham ben Eliezer ha-Levi." See also G. Scholem and M. Beit-Arié, introduction to *Maamar Meshare Qitrin le-Rabbi Avraham ben Eliezer ha-Levi* (Jerusalem, 1977).

54. For a summation of this treatise, see ibid., 31–36.

55. For summations of this topic, see Shulvass, *Roma vi-Yerushalayim,* 41–88; D. Tamar, *The Jewish People in Eretz Israel,* 11–38; H. H. Ben-Sasson, "The Reformation in Contemporary Jewish Eyes," *Proceedings of the Israel Academy of Sciences and Humanities* 4 (1970): 260–70; J. R. Hacker, "A New Letter on the Messianic Fervour in Eretz-Israel and the Diaspora in the Early 16th Century" (Hebrew), *Shalem* 2 (1976): 355–60; David, "A Letter from Jerusalem," 39–60; Idel, "Mishmarot and Messianism," 83–94; idem, introduction to Aescoly, *Jewish Messianic Movements,* 2d ed. (Hebrew; Jerusalem, 1988), 23–26.

56. Idel, introduction to Aescoly, *Jewish Messianic Movements,* 24–26.

57. See D. Tamar, "The Kabbalist Rabbi Avraham Halevy and His Contemporaries" (Hebrew), in *Chapters in the History of the Jewish Community in Jerusalem,* ed. Y. Ben Porat, B. Z. Yehoshua, and A. Kedar (Hebrew; Jerusalem, 1973), 1:313–14; idem, *Ha-Yehudim be-Ereẓ Yisrael u-ve-Arṣot ha-Mizraḥ,* 15–16; I. Robinson, "Messianic Prayer Vigils in Jerusalem in the Early Sixteenth Century," *JQR* 72 (1981): 32–42.

58. Regarding six of Abraham ha-Levi's letters, not all of which have been published, see Scholem and Beit-Arié, *Maamar Meshare Qitrin,* 38–42; David, "A Letter from Jerusalem," 39–60; Robinson, "Two Letters," 403–22. An additional letter, known as "The Secret Scroll sent to the *Ḥakham* R. Mordecai of Modena . . . and to R. Asher Segal . . . in the year 284 [1524]," is located in MS. Moscow, Russian State Library, Günzburg 62 (IMHM, no. 6880), fol. 76r–v. I intend to publish this letter in the near future.

59. See Scholem and Beit-Arié, *Maamar Meshare Qitrin,* 14, 26, 40; Tamar, *The Jewish People in Eretz Israel,* 12.

60. See M. Beit-Arié and M. Idel, "Treatise on Eschatology and Astrology by R. Abraham Zacut" (Hebrew), *Kiryat Sefer* 54 (1979): 174–94, 825–26.

61. See Idel, "Mishmarot and Messianism," 83–90. This premise has been fortified by the publication of a collection (*seder*) of prayers for the redemption, titled *Tefillah le-David,* which was in use in Jerusalem during the first third of the sixteenth century and which contains no hint of any ascription to Abraham ha-Levi. See I. Yudlov, "*Tefillah le-David:* A Collection of Prayers from Jerusalem, Constantinople 5295 or 5298" (Hebrew), *Kiryat Sefer* 61 (1986–87): 929–32.

62. See G. Scholem, "Chapters from the History of Cabbalistical Literature: New Researches on R. Abraham b. Eliezer Halevi" (Hebrew), *Kiryat Sefer* 7 (1930–31): 149; Scholem and Beit-Arié, *Maamar Meshare Qitrin,* 9.

63. Cf. A. Z. Aescoly, ed., *Sippur David ha-Reuveni* (Jerusalem, 1940), 25–27 (Adler, *Jewish Travellers,* 263–66). A considerable amount of attention has been devoted to reports of David ha-Reuveni's appearance in Jerusalem as reflected in other contemporary sources. See Cassuto, "David ha-Reubeni," 339ff.; Shohat, "David Reubeni Affair," 96–102.

64. Cf. *Midrasch Samuel,* ed. S. Buber (Cracow, 1893), *Parashah* 13, no. 4.

65. I have revised the text in accord with MS. Oxford, Bodleian Library,. Mich. 85 (1562) (IMHM, no. 16930), fol. 53v. The prayers recited at the vigils (*mishmarot*) instituted by Isaac Sholal in Jerusalem are extant in MS. Firenze, Biblioteca Mediceo Laurenziana, plut. 44.7 (IMHM, no. 17827), fols. 67v–73r. These prayers followed the composition of Abraham ha-Levi's treatises, *Peyrush le-Nevuot Naḥman* and *Iggeret Sod ha-Geulah.* See Robinson, "Messianic Prayer Vigils," 32–42, where he argues that Abraham ha-Levi was author of the above-mentioned prayers. M. Idel differs, arguing that Abraham ha-Levi was not necessarily the author of these prayers, given the prevailing messianic tension and atmosphere in Jerusalem as created by "precursors of the redemption." See Idel, "Mishmarot and Messianism," 83ff, and n. 61 above.

66. Legends regarding the Ten Tribes were rampant during the latter half of the fifteenth and the sixteenth centuries. A common feature of these legends was the attempt to locate the Sambatyon River, near which the Ten Tribes ostensibly resided. It was variously identified as being located in India, Cush, Yemen, the kingdom of Prester John (Ethiopia), or central Asia. Much has been written regarding the medieval conception of the Ten Tribes. See A. Gross, "The Ten Tribes and the Kingdom of Prester John—Rumors and Investigations Before and After the Expulsion from Spain" (Hebrew), *Pe'amim* 48 (1991): 5–41. Various anthologies regarding the Ten Tribes and the *Beney Moshe* (Sons of Moses) are included in the collected writings and copies made by Yoḥanan Alemano, MS. Oxford, Bodleian Library Reggio 23 (2234) (IMHM, no. 20517), fols. 39v–42r. A letter from this collection has been published by A. David, intro-

duction to Artom and David, "Obadiah mi-Bertinoro," 43. I intend to devote more space to these important collections in the future.

67. Aescoly, *Sippur David ha-Reuveni,* 54–56; Cassuto, "David ha-Reubeni," 339–58.

68. See Y. Baer's review of A. Z. Aescoly, *Sippur David ha-Reuveni,* in *Kiryat Sefer* 17 (1940): 304–6; Shohat, "David Reubeni Affair," 96–109.

CHAPTER 9. THE JEWISH QUARTER

1. Cohen and Lewis, *Population and Revenue,* 154, 156. For a map of the city's quarters, based on the *Survey of Palestine* (Jaffa, 1938), see ibid., 154. It is not clear to what extent this map reflects sixteenth-century reality.

2. David ibn Abi Zimra, *Responsa,* no. 25; Yom Tov Ṣahalon, *Responsa,* no. 251.

3. See Evliya Tshelebi's remarks cited below.

4. Information on this khan has been preserved in contemporary Jewish and non-Jewish sources. See I. Ben-Zvi, *Studies and Documents,* 26–29; Heyd, *Ottoman Documents,* 167–68.

5. This emerges from a sultanic order dating from 1578, published by Heyd, *Ottoman Documents,* 167–68.

6. Clearly, this Turkish tourist greatly exaggerated the number of the khan's residents. Not only did Safed's Jewish population never reach this size, as we shall see below, the construction of an edifice to house thousands of people was inconceivable in that era.

7. Yaari, *Letters,* 151.

8. This excerpt comes from a sermon delivered by Joseph Garson in Damascus (1517). See David, "The Pogrom of 1517," 190–94, and on this matter specifically, 193. Excerpts from this sermon have been published by Benayahu, "Yosef Garson," 188–90. David Tamar's claim that these events did not cause a decline in Safed's Jewish population is unfounded. See D. Tamar, "On the Jews of Safed in the Days of the Ottoman Conquest" (Hebrew), *Cathedra* 11 (1979): 181–82. See also Elijah Capsali's testimony, *Seder Eliyahu Zuta,* chap. 127, pp. 349–50.

9. Basola, *Masot,* 43. See also David, "The Pogrom of 1517," 193–94.

10. On the extant data and the difficulty of establishing the demographic reality, see Hütteroth and Abdulfattah, *Historical Geography,* 38–41, 52; Cohen and Lewis, *Population and Revenue,* 155–61; Hacker, "Payment of *Djizya,*" 90–98; David, "Demographic Changes in Safed," 83–93, and below.

11. As we saw in chap. 4 above.

12. Lewis, *Notes and Documents,* 28–34; Heyd, *Ottoman Documents,* 163–68. On the Ottoman regime's attempts to deport Safed Jews as a solution to social and economic problems as part of its policy of sürgün, see Hacker, "The Ottoman System of Sürgün," 65–66.

13. Hacker, "Payment of *Djizya,*" 98–104.

14. Pachter, "'Ḥazut Kasha,'" 168.

CHAPTER 10. THE COMMUNITIES

1. See Cohen and Lewis, *Population and Revenue,* 155–61.

2. Some information on the Musta'rab kahal can be extracted from a

fairly long letter found in the Cairo Geniza that was sent by Safed's Musta'rab sages to Nagid Isaac Sholal in Egypt in 1510. Published by Gottheil and Worrell, *Fragments from the Genizah,* 246–65.

3. Basola, *Masot,* 43.

4. Cohen and Lewis, *Population and Revenue,* 161. See also the section on Sefardim below, and David, "Demographic Changes in Safed," 85–86.

5. See Cohen and Lewis, *Population and Revenue,* 161.

6. See Gottheil and Worrell, *Fragments from the Genizah,* 256–57.

7. See ibid., 246–65, passim; Benayahu, "Teudah," 113–14.

8. See Benayahu, "Teudah," 115, 124.

9. Issachar ibn Susan, *Ibbur Shanim,* MS. Sassoon 689 (IMHM no. 9499), introduction, p. 96.

10. Evidence for this power struggle is found in Issachar ibn Susan, *Tiqqun Yissakhar* (Constantinople, 1564). See also Rozen, "Musta'rabs," 91–94; Hacker, "Pride and Depression," 572–79. For the early seventeenth century, see Yom Tov Ṣahalon, *Responsa,* no. 274; Rozen, "Musta'rabs," 94–96.

11. Regarding the Safed kehillah, Moses Basola mentions "a teacher of young children who came from Aden two years ago" [*Masot,* 89]. In the latter half of the sixteenth century Solomon Adeni resided in Safed, before moving to Hebron. On Jews from Kurdistan in Safed, see n. 62 below.

12. See Benayahu, "Teudah," 109–25, for a discussion of the history of these sages, some of whom are known from additional sources. See also idem, "Yosef Garson," 98–102.

13. See n. 6 above.

14. Gottheil and Worrell, *Fragments from the Genizah,* 256–57.

15. See David, "Spanish Exiles," 96–104.

16. See Cohen and Lewis, *Population and Revenue,* 161.

17. For a comprehensive discussion, see Kena'ani, "Ha-Ḥayyim ha-Kalkaliyyim," 195–201; Avitsur, "Safed," 41–69; Cohen and Lewis, *Population and Revenue,* 59–62; David, "Jews in Mediterranean Trade," 19–28. See also chap. 3, sec. B, above.

18. See David, "Conversos," 65–66; idem, "Shivat Anusim," 183–86; idem, "A Letter of Recommendation for a Converso Family Who Sought to Emigrate to Eretz Israel in 1521 [should read 1461—A. D.]" (Hebrew), *Pe'amim* 46–47 (1991): 190–95.

19. Don Isaac Abrabanel, commentary to Isa. 43:6. See chap. 6, sec. B for the citation.

20. See David, "Conversos," 66ff.; idem, "Shivat Anusim," 188ff. Very little is known concerning the settlement of conversos in sixteenth-century Jerusalem. See David, "Conversos," 66–67 n. 15a; idem, "Shivat Anusim," 187 n. 15a.

21. On the founding of the Portuguese Inquisition at that time, see A. Herculano, *History of the Origin and Establishment of the Inquisition in Portugal* (facsimile edition, New York, 1972), especially the prolegomenon by Y. H. Yerushalmi.

22. For the pertinent studies by Y. Baer, H. Beinart, and I. Tishby, see David, "Shivat Anusim," 194 n. 46.

23. The various midrashic traditions upon which Abraham ha-Levi's remarks were based have been surveyed by Tamar, *Ha-Yehudim be-Ereẓ Yisrael*

u-ve-Arṣot ha-Mizraḥ, 14–16. See also David, "Meqorot Ḥadashim le-Ḥiddush ha-Yishuv ha-Yehudi bi-Teveryah," 82–83.

24. Yom Tov Ṣahalon, *Shu"t Maharit ha-Ḥadashot,* no. 107, p. 22.

25. See David, "Conversos," 74–75; idem, "Shivat Anusim," 194–95.

26. For the text of the entire prayer, see R. J. Z. Werblowsky, "Solomon Alkabets," 148–53. See also the discussion, 139–42. On the attribution to Portuguese conversos, see ibid., 140–42; Tishby, *Messianism,* 41 n. 101. For further consideration of this prayer, see B. Sack, "Exile and Redemption in *Berit halevi* of R. Solomon Alkabeẓ" (Hebrew), *Eshel Beer-Sheva* 2 (1980): 265–69.

27. See Cohen and Lewis, *Population and Revenue,* 161.

28. See David, "Conversos," 72–73; idem, "Shivat Anusim," 196.

29. For the synagogue, see Jacob Berab, *Responsa,* no. 22. For the bet din, see Joseph Trani, *Responsa,* pt. 1, no. 39. See also David, "Conversos," 75; idem, "Shivat Anusim," 196.

30. See Gedaliah ibn Yaḥya, *Shalshelet ha-Qabbalah,* MS. Günzberg 652, fol. 130r: "Rabbi Moses Cordovero the Portuguese, a Safed kabbalist."

31. See I. Tishby, "Rabbi Moses Cordovero as He Appears in the Treatise of Rabbi Mordekhai Dato" (Hebrew), *Sefunot* 7 (1963): 124.

32. See David, "Conversos," 75–76; idem, "Shivat Anusim," 196–97.

33. See David, "Conversos," 76–79; idem, "Shivat Anusim," 197–200.

34. Basola, *Masot,* 43.

35. Jacob Berab's pesak is cited by Levi ibn Ḥabib, *Responsa,* no. 26. In another reference to the kehalim, made in a subsequent passage, they appear in a different order: "In the presence of the heads of the Sefardi congregations, and the Maghrebi wise men, and the Musta'rab notables, may God preserve and protect them."

36. See Gottheil and Worrell, *Fragments from the Genizah,* 252–53. See also Benayahu, "Teudah," 113.

37. See Cohen and Lewis, *Population and Revenue,* 159–61.

38. Beginning of his introduction to the first part of the translation, the Torah, MS. London, British Library, Or. 14020a (formerly Sassoon 159), (IMHM no. 9268). *Al-Sharḥ al-Susani* is an Arabic translation of the entire Bible. On the translation and its innovative character, see David Doron, "On the Arabic Translation of the Torah by Issachar ben-Susan Hamma'aravi" (Hebrew), *Sefunot* 18 (1985): 279–98.

39. In a later printed edition, this treatise was titled *Ibbur Shanim* (Venice, 1578).

40. On these two figures, see David, "North African Jewry," 81.

41. On the kabbalistic center in Dr'aa, see Elior, "Kabbalists of Dr'aa," 65. On the influence of these kabbalistic centers on the Jews of the Maghreb, see G. Scholem, *Sabbatai Ṣevi: The Mystical Messiah, 1626–1676* (Princeton, 1973), 570; M. Hallamish, "On the Categories of Kabbalistic Composition in Morocco" (Hebrew), *Pe'amim* 15 (1983): 29–46; idem, "The Kabbalists in Morocco" (Hebrew), *East and Maghreb* 2 (1980): 205–35; Elior, "Kabbalists of Dr'aa," 36–73. On links with Safed, see David, "North African Jewry," 81.

42. See Cohen and Lewis, *Population and Revenue,* 158, 160, 161. A document dating from 1576 published by Sonne, "Shadarim," 218, mentions an emissary sent by "two Italian congregations, may God protect and preserve them, in Safed." Sonne identified the two congregations as the Italian Ashkenazi con-

gregation and the congregation of *Beney Roma* (the Roman rite). However, I believe that the two congregations are those referred to in the taḥrir: the congregation of southerners (Apulia and Calabria), and the congregation from central and northern Italy, which differed significantly in nature. See Carpi, *Between Renaissance and Ghetto,* 236–37.

43. See Moses Trani, *Responsa,* pt. 1, no. 307; S. Assaf, "Iggerot mi-Ṣefat," *Kobeẓ al Yad* 3 (13) (1940): 131; Carpi, *Between Renaissance and Ghetto,* 231–81, and the literature cited therein; E. Kupfer, "The Jewish Community of Safed and the Activity of R. Menahem Azariah of Fano on Behalf of the Yishuv in Eretz-Israel" (Hebrew), *Shalem* 2 (1976): 361–64; David, "Emissaries' Letters from Jerusalem," 331–32; Rozen, "Musta'rabs," 96–97; and sec. I below.

44. Cohen and Lewis, *Population and Revenue,* 161.

45. A letter sent from Safed by Abraham Rafael Trabot has been published by Neubauer, "Qibuṣim," 32–34. The copyist notes that the writer resided in Jerusalem; however, the letter's contents clearly indicate that it was written in Safed. See J. Prawer, "On the Text of the 'Jerusalem Letters' in the 15th and 16th Centuries" (Hebrew), *Jerusalem (Quarterly)* 1 (1948): 143–44. Prawer dates the letter between Tevet (December) 1521 and Nisan (March) 1523. See ibid., 144. For further information on this letter, see Tamar, *The Jewish People in Eretz Israel,* 94.

46. See Cohen and Lewis, *Population and Revenue,* 156, 161, where they are called Ifranjiye. See also S. Schwarzfuchs, "Joseph Caro et la yeshiva provençale de Safed," *REJ* 150 (1991): 151–52.

47. On the Provençal kahal in the latter half of the sixteenth century and its ties with the Piedmont congregation, see David, "Community of Cuneo," 429–44. In the first half of the seventeenth century, we find the Provençal congregation mentioned along with three others in a letter sent in 1610 by "the rabbis and *geonim* of the Italian congregation" to the kabbalist Aaron Berachiah of Modena. See A. Elmaleh, "Mi-Ginzey he-Avar," *Mizraḥ ouMaarav* (Orient and Occident) 3 (1929): 320. This congregation, referred to as "the holy Franṣia [French] congregation," was still active in 1637 and maintained its Cuneo connection. See Schwarzfuchs, "Joseph Caro," 155–59.

48. See also ibid., 151–55.

49. See David, "The Ashkenazic Community in Jerusalem," 335–41; idem, "Spanish Exiles," 102–4.

50. See Cohen and Lewis, *Population and Revenue,* 161.

51. Moses Trani, *Responsa,* pt. 3, no. 96. These takkanot will be discussed in the chapter on communal organization immediately following. Regarding the special status of the Jerusalem Ashkenazi congregation, see chap. 6, sec. B.

52. Moses Trani, *Responsa,* pt. 3, no. 96, mentions scholars who studied in the synagogue. The letter was sent to Issachar Baer of Kremnitz in 1607. See Yaari, *Letters,* 203.

53. Naftali ben Joseph ha-Kohen, *Imrey Shefer* (Venice, 1601), fols. 16v–17r.

54. Contemporary rabbinic literature paid but scant attention to the Ashkenazim in Safed. Other than the above-mentioned sources, references to Ashkenazim are found in Joseph Caro, *Shu"t Beit Yosef, Even ha-Ezer,* "Laws of Levirate Marriage," no. 2; Yom Tov Ṣahalon, *Shu"t Maharit ha-Ḥadashot,* pt. 1, no. 24.

55. See David, "Ashkenazic Community in Jerusalem," *Vatiqin,* 30–31.

56. See M. Benayahu, "The Tax Concession Enjoyed by the Scholars of Safed" (Hebrew), *Sefunot* 7 (1963): 103–17; Hacker, "Payment of *Djizya*," 98–104.

57. See Cohen and Lewis, *Population and Revenue*, 161.

58. Yom Tov Ṣahalon, *Shu"t Maharit ha-Ḥadashot*, no. 227, p. 244. See also Hütteroth and Abdulfattah, *Historical Geography*, 39.

59. For random data on Hungarian sages who visited or settled in Safed during the seventeenth century, see M. A. Z. Kinstlicher, "The Yeshiva of 'The Benefactor of Ofen' in Safed and Jerusalem" (Hebrew), *Tzfunot* 1 (1989): 73–87.

60. See Issachar ibn Susan, *Ibbur Shanim*, MS. Sassoon 689 (IMHM no. 9499), introduction, p. 18; Hütteroth and Abdulfattah, *Historical Geography*, 39.

61. Members of the "holy Rumanian [Romaniot] congregation" signed a deed in 1605 related to a bequest made to this congregation. The deed was cited by Yom Tov Ṣahalon, *Responsa*, no. 259.

62. See Joseph Trani, *Responsa*, pt. 1, nos. 81–82, which date from the late sixteenth or early seventeenth century. See also M. Benayahu, "R. Samuel Barzani: Leader of Kurdistan Jewry" (Hebrew), *Sefunot* 9 (1964): 28–31.

63. Hütteroth and Abdulfattah, *Historical Geography*, 39.

64. Moses Trani, *Responsa*, pt. 1, no. 307.

65. See David, "Spanish Exiles," 102–3.

CHAPTER 11. COMMUNAL ORGANIZATION

1. For the term *memunim* and its significance, see below.

2. See also chap. 10, sec. G, above.

3. For fund-raising in the Diaspora by individual congregations, see Yaari, *Sheluḥey Ereẓ-Yisrael*, 233–55; Elmaleh, "Mi-Ginzey he-Avar," 320; Kupfer, "Jewish Community of Safed," 361–64; Carpi, *Between Renaissance and Ghetto*, 231–81; David, "Community of Cuneo," 429–44.

4. On communal taxation in Safed and related matters, see Benayahu, "Tax Concession," 103–17; Hacker, "Payment of *Djizya*," 63–117. On Safed in particular, see ibid., 90–98.

5. For the haskamot, see Benayahu, "Tax Concession," 114–15. Benayahu suggests that the takkanot issued in 1565 were done so at the initiative of Judah Aberlin, the leader of the Ashkenazi congregation at that time. Aberlin, then a recent arrival from Salonika, ruled the congregation with an iron hand. See ibid., 108–9, 113–17; Hacker, "Payment of *Djizya*," 101ff.

6. See the prior discussion, chap. 6, sec. B.

7. The relevant passage was cited above in the section on the Ashkenazi kahal. See chap. 10, sec. G.

8. See Heyd, *Ottoman Documents*, 169.

9. See Yaari, *Letters*, 197.

10. See Moses Trani, *Responsa*, pt. 3, no. 48. For the citation, see chap. 10, sec. B, above.

11. See Naftali ben Joseph ha-Kohen, *Imrey Shefer*, fols. 16v–17r for the Ashkenazi yeshivot. On Safed's yeshivot in general, see chap. 12, sec. A, below.

12. See, for example, Moses Trani, *Responsa*, pt. 1, no. 32; Joseph Caro, *Shu"t Beit Yosef*, "The Laws of a Gentile Speaking Innocently," no. 11.

13. See ibid., "Laws of Levirate Marriage," no. 2, where a court enactment

from 1565 signed by four Ashkenazi sages is cited. For a reference to the "bet din of the Portuguese (converso) congregation," see Joseph Trani, *Responsa,* pt. 1, no. 39, and above, chap. 10, sec. C.

14. In Safed, the term *memunim* was commonly used to refer to the members of the overall administration. See, for example, Jacob Berab, *Responsa,* no. 22; Moses Alshekh, *Responsa,* no. 139; Moses Trani, *Responsa,* pt. 1, no. 307; pt. 3, no. 96. See also a responsum written by Joseph ibn Ṣayyah, cited by Hacker, "Payment of *Djizya,*" 107ff. For further information on the memunim, see H. Z. Dimitrovsky, "A Dispute between Rabbi J. Caro and Rabbi M. Trani" (Hebrew), *Sefunot* 6 (1962): 108.

15. On the use of the term *kolel* in this sense, see Kupfer, "Jewish Community of Safed," 361–64.

16. Ibid. In the late 1560s we have evidence of attempts by the memunim in Safed to force scholars to pay the communal taxes, the opposition of the sages notwithstanding. See the responsum by Joseph ibn Ṣayyah, cited by Hacker, "Payment of *Djizya,*" 98ff.

17. The term *Bet ha-Vaad* is found in responsa written by Safed sages. See, for example, Moses Trani, *Responsa,* pt. 2, nos. 115, 131; Yom Tov Ṣahalon, *Responsa,* no. 33.

18. Scant information of a general nature is all that is available concerning the institution of the Bet ha-Vaad. See M. Benayahu, "The Revival of Ordination in Safed" (Hebrew), *Yitzhak F. Baer Jubilee Volume,* ed. S. W. Baron et al. (Jerusalem, 1960), 253–56; Dimitrovsky, "Yaakov Berab's Academy," 56–57 n. 95.

19. See Dimitrovsky, "Dispute," 90; Scheiber and Benayahu, "Communication to the Radbaz," 134; Cohen, *Jewish Life under Islam,* 44.

20. Regarding this halakhic decision, see Dimitrovsky, "Dispute," 91ff.

CHAPTER 12. CENTERS OF JEWISH LEARNING—STRUCTURE AND PROGRAM OF STUDY

1. For the dating of this responsum, see Benayahu, "Tax Concession," 113–14.

2. See the editor's introduction, 12, for the date of its composition.

3. See chap. 9, sec. B, above.

4. See Assaf, "Iggerot mi-Ṣefat," 136.

5. See Pachter, "'Ḥazut Kasha'," 163 n. 42, 174.

6. On philanthropic activity by Italian-Jewish communities on behalf of kehillot in Eretz-Israel, see chap. 3, n. 55. See also Kupfer, "Jewish Community of Safed," 361–64; David, "New Sources on Jews During the Middle Ages," 291–92. For additional bibliography, see ibid., 292 n. 2. Several responsa indicate that bequests were made to yeshivot in Eretz-Israel in wills, including yeshivot in Safed. See Kahane, *Sifrut ha-Teshuvot,* 206ff.; J. Geller, "The Economic Basis of the Yeshivot in the Ottoman Empire" (Hebrew), *Mi-Mizraḥ u-mi-Maarav (East and Maghreb)* 1 (1974): 202–11, passim. Various letters sent from Safed to raise funds for the yeshivot are extant. See Assaf, "Iggerot mi-Ṣefat," 140–41; David, "Community of Cuneo," 429–44.

7. Joseph Bagilar was already involved in commerce in the century's first half. See the letter sent to him by Joseph ha-Levi found among the Cairo

Geniza documents, MS. New York, Jewish Theological Seminary Library, ENA NS 52, 13.

8. Sambari, *Divrei Yosef,* 416.

9. See Sonne, "Shadarim," 214–17; Tamar, *The Jewish People in Eretz Israel,* 160–62; idem, *Ha-Yehudim be-Ereẓ Yisrael u-ve-Arṣot ha-Mizraḥ,* 194–96.

10. Abraham Monzon resided in Cairo. See E. Shochetman, introduction to the *Responsa of Rabbi Meir Gavizon* (Jerusalem, 1985), 1: 66–67.

11. This letter was published by Gottheil and Worrell, *Fragments from the Genizah,* 246–65. For the citation, see 256; for the English translation, 257.

12. Ibid. Translation mine—D. O.

13. Ibid., 260–61.

14. MS. Cambridge, University Library, T–S AS 218, 153. This letter has been published by David, "New Genizah Documents," 44–45.

15. Published by Benayahu, "Teudah," 122–25.

16. On Isaac Canpanton, an outstanding fifteenth-century Castilian scholar (d. 1463), who headed a yeshivah in Zamora, see A. David, "On R. Isaac Canpanton, One of the Great 15th Century Spanish Scholars" (Hebrew), *Kiryat Sefer* 51 (1976): 324–26; A. Gross, "A Sketch of the History of Yeshivot in Castile in the Fifteenth Century" (Hebrew), *Pe'amim* 31 (1987): 6–8.

17. For a list of and some data on Canpanton's disciples, see David, "Isaac Canpanton"; Gross, "Yeshivot in Castile," 6–8. On the Spanish method of speculation and study as practiced in Canpanton's yeshivah, see Dimitrovsky, "Yaakov Berab's Academy," 77–96; Bentov, "The Yeshivot of Salonica and Turkey," 5–102; Hacker, "Self-Perception of Spanish Jewry," 47–59; D. Boyarin, *Sephardi Speculation: A Study in Methods of Talmudic Interpretation* (Hebrew; Jerusalem, 1989).

18. See David, "Isaac Canpanton," 325; Gross, "Yeshivot in Castile," 11–12.

19. Dimitrovsky, "Yaakov Berab's Academy," 80–93.

20. See Dimitrovsky, "Yaakov Berab's Academy," 80–90; Katz, *Halakhah and Kabbalah* (Hebrew; Jerusalem, 1984), 87–89.

21. See sec. D below. For a similar phenomenon documented for Jerusalem in an earlier period, see Dimitrovsky, "Yaakov Berab's Academy," 50–51; and the discussion above, chap. 8, sec. C.

22. See Dimitrovsky, "Yaakov Berab's Academy," 48–50.

23. On the founding of Berab's yeshivah, see ibid., 50–52. On the students, see ibid., 56. For the citation, see p. 55.

24. Cited by Dimitrovsky, "Yaakov Berab's Academy," 55 n. 89.

25. For a general discussion of the methodology and framework for study in Berab's yeshivah, including the relationship between the ḥaverim and the head of the yeshivah, see ibid., 77–79.

26. Ibid., 52, 54–55, 57. See discussion in sec. E below about the plan to renew the ordination and to establish a Sanhedrin and the fierce opposition by Jerusalem's sages.

27. See Dimitrovsky, "Dispute," 112.

28. Conforte, *Qore ha-Dorot,* 36r. Cited by Dimitrovsky, "Yaakov Berab's Academy," 66.

29. Ibid., 94–96.

30. Joseph Caro, *Shu"t Avqat Rokhel,* no. 143. His bet midrash is mentioned in ibid., no. 126.

31. For a discussion of the Bet ha-Vaad, see chap. 11.

32. On Caro's bet din, see chap. 11.

33. Zacharia al-Dahri, *Sefer Hamussar,* 116–17.

34. See sec. C, 1 above.

35. Al-Dahri, *Sefer Hamussar,* 116–17.

36. For the full citation, see ibid., 117–23.

37. See ibid., editor's introduction, 31.

38. Caro's interest in kabbalah found expression in his treatise *Maggid Mesharim* as well as in the fact that his legal decisions were based in no small measure on the *Zohar* and other mystical works. This aspect of Caro's work has been studied in depth by various scholars. See R. J. Z. Werblowsky, *Joseph Caro: Lawyer and Mystic* (Philadelphia, 1980); J. Katz, *Halakhah and Kabbalah,* 34ff.; I. Ta-Shma, "Rabbi Joseph Caro and His *Beit Yosef:* Between Spain and Germany," in *The Sephardi Legacy,* ed. H. Beinart (Jerusalem, 1992), 2:192–206; M. Hallamish, "Joseph Karo—Kabbalah and Halakhic Decisions" (Hebrew), *Daat* 21 (1988): 85–102.

39. See sec. A above for the citation. See also David, "Community of Cuneo," 440.

40. Ibid.

41. On Moses Provençal (Provenẓali), see S. Simonsohn, *History of the Jews in the Duchy of Mantua* (Jerusalem, 1977), 729–30; E. Kupfer, "Haramat 'Keter Torah me-al Rosho' shel R. Moshe Provenẓali ve-Nusaḥ ha-Havdalah Shelo," *Sinai* 63 (1968): 137–60; R. Bonfil, "R. Moses Provenzalo's Commentary to Maimonides' 25 'Premises'" (Hebrew), *Kiryat Sefer* 50 (1974–75): 157–76; I. Yudlov, "Bibliographical Notes on the Tamari-Vintorozzo Affair" (Hebrew), *Alei Sefer* 2 (1976): 105–20; Y. Green, "Polemic Between Moshe ben Shoshan, Rabbi Moshe Provençal and the Printers of Sabionetta" (Hebrew), *Zion* 51 (1986): 223–40, and the extensive literature cited in these studies. The first part of Provenẓali's *Responsa* has been published by A. I. Yanni (Jerusalem, 1989).

42. David, "Community of Cuneo," 444. On the special relationship between Caro and Moses Provençal, see ibid., 438–39; Green, "Polemic," 223ff.

43. See David, "Bezalel Ashkenazi," 454–55.

44. See Joseph Caro, *Shu"t Avqat Rokhel,* no 124; Elijah Mizraḥi and Elijah ibn Ḥayyim, *Shu"t Mayim Amuqim,* no. 54; two letters sent from Safed to Avignon, cited in Isaac de Lattes, *Responsa,* pp. 16–18; a decision concerning the validity of the prohibition against bigamy for Ashkenazim found in a responsum of Isaac de Molina, published by S. Z. Havlin, "The Takkanot of Rabbenu Gershon Ma'or Hagola in Family Law in Spain and Provence (in the Light of Manuscripts of Responsa of RASHBA and R. Isaac de-Molina)" (Hebrew), *Shenaton ha-Mishpat ha-Ivri* 2 (1975): 245; a decision in the dispute between Moses ben Shoshan and Moses Provençal (1559) published by Green, "Polemic," 237–39; part of a decision in the Tamari-Ventorozzo affair (1568), which electrified Italian Jewry in the 1560s, was published by Z. Gartner, "Parashat ha-Get Tamari-Ventorozzo," *Moriah* 16, nos. 3–4 (1988): 9–15.

45. Abraham ibn Asher, Baruch [of Tivoli], Moses Alshekh, and Moses Saadiah are mentioned as being Caro's students by Mordecai ben Solomon Kalai, the proofreader of Caro's *Shu"t Beit Yosef,* "Laws of Marriage Contracts," no. 2, p. 103. See also Benayahu, *Yosef Beḥiri,* 233–55, 312–13, 316,

319. Moses Alshekh is mentioned elsewhere as a disciple of Caro; for example, in Caro's *Shu"t Avqat Rokhel,* no. 73. See sec. C, 4 below.

46. See Joseph Caro, *Shu"t Avqat Rokhel,* no. 85.

47. See ibid., nos. 85–89; Moses Trani, *Responsa,* pt. 2, nos. 133, 135. For additional information regarding Ibn Verga, see Dimitrovsky, "Dispute," 83 n. 37; Benayahu, *Yosef Beḥiri,* index, s.v. "Verga, Shemuel."

48. Some of Moses Baruch's responsa and decisions are found in Caro's *Shu"t Avqat Rokhel,* nos. 85, 113, 124. Moses Baruch served as a dayyan in Damascus for a time alongside Joseph ibn Ṣayyah. See Moses Trani, *Responsa,* pt. 2, no. 202. See also Benayahu, *Yosef Beḥiri,* 315. A fragmentary letter signed by Moses Baruch was found in the Cairo Geniza. See MS. New York, Jewish Theological Seminary Library, ENA 2739, 5.

49. See Tamar, *The Jewish People in Eretz Israel,* 152.

50. See, for example, the decision issued in the disagreement between Moses ben Shoshan and Moses Provençal (1559), published by Green, "Polemic," 237–39; the decision in the Tamari-Ventorozzo affair, published by Gartner, "Parashat ha-Get Tamari-Ventorozzo," 9–18; two letters sent by Joseph Caro to Italian and German kehillot (1567) concerning laxity of observance of the prohibition against drinking Christian wine, included in Ḥayyim Sitehon, *Sefer Ereṣ Ḥayyim* (Jerusalem, 1908), *Yoreh Deah,* no. 123. In 1575, when Caro was on his deathbed, two of his disciples, Elisha Gallico and Moses Alshekh, issued a decision in Caro's name. This decision concerned the banning of the unique historiographical work *Meor Einayim* written by Azariah de Rossi, published in Mantua in the previous year. This decision was first published by A. Kahana, *Sifrut ha-Historiya ha-Yisraelit* (Warsaw, 1923), 2:255, according to a copy made by Abraham Joseph Solomon Graziano. See also R. Bonfil, *"Azaria De" Rossi: Selected Chapters from Sefer Me'or 'Einayim and Matsref la-Kessef* (Hebrew; Jerusalem, 1991), introduction, 115–17.

51. See, for example, Joseph Caro, *Shu"t Avqat Rokhel,* no. 67, concerning wine imported from Crete, among many others. For some of these responsa, see Scheiber and Benayahu, "Communication to the Radbaz," 125–34; Benayahu, *Yosef Beḥiri,* 67–75. See also the compact of perpetual friendship between members of Samuel ibn Sid's synagogue in Cairo, achieved through the intervention of Safed's sages in 1564. Published by J. Mann, *Texts and Studies* (Cincinnati, 1931), 1:472–74.

52. See, for example, Joseph Caro, *Shu"t Avqat Rokhel,* nos. 204, 205, regarding tax payments in the cities of Tokat and Amasya; ibid., no. 206, concerning a teacher of Torah in the city of Manissa (Magnesia).

53. See, for example, Joseph Caro, *Shu"t Avqat Rokhel,* no. 147, for a query sent from Salonika regarding a claim for one hundred lead ingots.

54. See, for example, a query forwarded by Elijah Capsali to Joseph Caro concerning the issue of permitting stone reliefs of animals to placed in the synagogue, *Shu"t Avqat Rokhel,* nos. 63–66; or, concerning "a hedge against licentiousness and against calling his friend an apostate." See E. S. Artom and M. D. Cassuto, *Taqqanot Candia ve-Zikhronoteha* (Jerusalem, 1943), 147–48.

55. Safed's rabbis were queried by the leaders of Avignon's Jewish community concerning permission for a man who released his sister-in-law from a levirate marriage to marry this woman's daughter (1558). Their two decisions were cited by Isaac de Lattes, *Responsa,* pp. 16–18. Joseph Caro sent a letter to

the leaders and parnassim of Venisse in Provence concerning tax payments by those who had left the city. Published by D. Kaufmann, "Une lettre de Josef Caro adressée aux juifs de Carpentras," *REJ* 18 (1889): 133–36; Schwarzfuchs, "Josef Caro," 151–59.

56. See the discussion of communal organization, near the end of chap. 11 above.

57. The conflict between these two figures has been treated at length by Dimitrovsky, "Dispute," 71–123; Benayahu, *Yosef Beḥiri,* 7–98, 108–14.

58. See chap. 10, sec. B, for the citation. See also Benayahu, *Introduction to the Facsimile Edition of R. Moses Trani's Responsa* (Hebrew; Venice, 1629–30; Jerusalem, 1990), 11, 19–20.

59. Moses Trani, *Responsa,* pt. 2, no. 138.

60. See Dimitrovsky, "Yaakov Berab's Academy," 78 n. 233; Benayahu, introduction to Moses Trani, *Responsa,* 17–19.

61. For Isaac Mishan, see Moses Trani, *Responsa,* pt. 2, no. 127; on Moses ha-Levi, see ibid., pt. 3, no. 89. See also Benayahu, introduction to Moses Trani, *Responsa,* 18, for both men.

62. Ibid., 18–19. This matter requires further investigation.

63. Moses Trani, *Responsa,* pt. 1, no. 180.

64. Moses Alshekh, introduction to *Rav Peninim* (Venice, 1592).

65. Elisha Gallico, title page of his *Commentary on Qohelet* (Hebrew; Venice, 1578).

66. Joseph Caro, *Shu"t Avqat Rokhel,* no. 85.

67. Yom Tov Ṣahalon, *Responsa,* no. 54.

68. Ḥiyya Rofe, introduction to *Ḿaaseh Hiyya* (Venice, 1652), fols. 15v, 47r, 104r. See also M. Benayahu, "Rabbi Chiya Rophe and His Book 'Mase Chija'" (Hebrew), *Aresheth* 2 (1960): 120.

69. Samuel de Uceda, introduction to *Iggeret Shmuel* (Kuru-Chesme, 1597).

70. Moses Galante, *Responsa,* no. 52. See also Benayahu, "Revival of Ordination," 262.

71. Ḥiyya Rofe, *Maaseh Ḥiyya,* fol. 83r. See also Benayahu, "Chiya Rophe," 109, 121.

72. See David, "Bezalel Ashkenazi," 454–55, where this testimony is dated to c. 1575.

73. See Benayahu, "Chiya Rophe," 109; David, "Bezalel Ashkenazi," 454–55.

74. See David, "Community of Cuneo," 432, 440, and the discussion above, sec. C, 2.

75. See chap. 10, sec. C for the citation.

76. Menaḥem Azariah Fano, *Asis Rimmonim* (Jerusalem, 1962), introduction. See also M. Benayahu, *The Toledoth Ha-Ari and Luria's 'Manner of Life' (Hanhagot)* (Hebrew; Jerusalem, 1967), 178–79.

77. See Benayahu, *Toledoth ha-Ari,* 163, 319–21. See also Katz, *Halakhah and Kabbalah,* 93; David, "Halakhah and Commerce in the Biography of Isaac Luria" (Hebrew), *Jerusalem Studies in Jewish Thought* 10 (1992): 291–92.

78. Sambari, *Divrei Yosef,* 416.

79. See Yaari, *Letters,* 202, 207. Both Masud the Blind and Solomon Maaravi were born in Fez, Morocco. Evidently, both men were ordained by Jacob Berab II in the late 1590s. See Benayahu, "Revival of Ordination," 258, 268–69. See also David, "North African Jewry," 81.

80. See Meroz, "Moshe ben Makhir," 40–51.

81. See chap. 8, sec. C.

82. For the Mamluk period, see David, "Jerusalem Academies," 149–52, and the discussion above, chap. 8, sec. C. See also Meroz, "Moshe ben Makhir," 48.

83. As we saw above, in the opening of sec. C.

84. The term *halakhah* was also used for the study of Talmud by Elijah of Massa Lombarda. See Hacker, "Elija of Massa Lombarda," 259. See also Dimitrovsky, "Yaakov Berab's Academy," 50–51.

85. Abraham Azulay, introduction to *Or ha-Ḥamah* (Jerusalem, 1876). See also Meroz, "Moshe ben Makhir," 47. Meroz did not relate to Solomon Shlomil Meinstral of Dreznitz's letter cited herein.

86. See Hacker, "Self-Perception of Spanish Jewry," 52–56.

87. See Katz, *Halakhah and Kabbalah,* 89–96; Meroz, "Moshe ben Makhir," 47.

88. See S. D. Goitein, *Jewish Education in Muslim Countries* (Hebrew; Jerusalem, 1962), 148–53; idem, *A Mediterranean Society* (Berkeley, Los Angeles, London, 1971), 2:205–7.

89. See Katz, *Halakhah and Kabbalah,* 70ff.; A. F. Kleinberger, *The Educational Theory of the Maharal of Prague* (Hebrew; Jerusalem, 1962), 24–25 and passim.; E. Kanarfogel, *Jewish Education and Society in the High Middle Ages* (Detroit, 1992), 78–85, 88–90; Bonfil, *Rabbis and Jewish Communities in Renaissance Italy,* 16–31; idem, "Tiyutat Haṣaah li-Yisud Yeshivah bi-Derom Italyah be-Shalhey ha-Meah ha-15," *Studies in Memory of the Rishon le-Zion R. Yitzhak Nissim,* ed. M. Benayahu (Jerusalem, 1985), 4:185–204.

90. See, for example, Joseph Trani's autobiographical notes in Bentov, "Josef Trani," 215.

91. The first part of Ibn Susan's work on the Bible, which contains the introduction, is found in MS. London, British Library, Or. 14020a (formerly, Sassoon 159), (IMHM, no. 9268). The introduction was published in the catalog of the Sassoon collection. See *Ohel Dawid—Descriptive Catalogue of the Hebrew and Samaritan Manuscripts in the Sassoon Library,* pt. 1 (Oxford and London, 1932), 62–68.

92. See Moshe ben Makhir, *Seder ha-Yom* (Venice, 1599), fol. 65v. See also Meroz, "Moshe ben Makhir," 45–46.

93. See David, "Jerusalem Academies," 151.

94. On Mishnaic study in Jerusalem's yeshivot in the early 1520s, see David, "Jerusalem Academies," 151–52; and the discussion above, chap. 8, sec. C. Kabbalistic sources indicate that study of Mishnah was undertaken in Safed. These sources were collected by Werblowsky, *Joseph Caro.* See index. Joseph Trani devoted much of his time to Mishnaic study. See Bentov, "Josef Trani," 213.

95. See Werblowsky, *Joseph Caro,* 206–33; Meroz, "Moshe ben Makhir," 45–47.

96. See Werblowsky, *Joseph Caro.*

97. For Joseph Ashkenazi's role in proofreading the text of the Mishnah, see Y. N. Epstein, *Mavo le-Nusaḥ ha-Mishnah* (Tel Aviv, 1964), 2:1284–85; G. Scholem, "New Contributions to the Biography of Rabbi Joseph Ashkenazi" (Hebrew), *Tarbiẓ* 28 (1958–59): 60–61.

98. For a brief survey of the efforts of these proofreaders, see Epstein, *Mavo,* 2:1286–90.

99. Benayahu, "Teudah," 109–25.

100. Ibid., 121.

101. Tamar, *The Jewish People in Eretz Israel,* 72–74.

102. Benayahu, "Teudah," 123.

103. The main source of information on the ordination controversy is *Quntres ha-Semikhah* (Ordination pamphlet), which contains some of the pesakim and exchanges between the two main players in this controversy. The pamphlet itself was appended to Levi ibn Ḥabib's *Responsa.* This episode has been the subject of extensive study. See Katz, *Halakhah and Kabbalah,* 213–36. Additional halakhic material related to a polemic between Jacob Berab and his student Moses Castro, which sheds new light on the affair as a whole, has been published by H. Z. Dimitrovsky, "New Documents Regarding the *Semicha* Controversy in Safed" (Hebrew), *Sefunot* 10 (1966): 113–92.

104. On the conversos in Safed, see chap. 10, sec. C above.

105. See Katz, *Halakhah and Kabbalah,* 230–32.

106. On the role of the messianic aspect in the rationale for the renewal of ordination, see Katz, *Halakhah and Kabbalah,* 226–29.

107. See also Maimonides' commentary on the Mishnah, *Sanhedrin* 1:3: "Both the person being ordained and those who are ordaining him must be together in Eretz-Israel. When a person has been ordained in Eretz-Israel he has the right to adjudicate cases involving fines in the Diaspora as well, according to the principle that the Sanhedrin has authority in Eretz-Israel and the Diaspora as shall be explained below. But whether all three [who sit as judges] must be ordained and it will then be possible for them to ordain another, this is doubtful. It appears that according to the Talmud the chief [judge] among them must be ordained, and he can then have two join him in appointing whomever they wish. I am of the opinion that if all the students and ḥakhamim agree to appoint one person from the yeshivah, that is, to make him the head, on condition that this occurs in Eretz-Israel as I said earlier . . . then this person will be ordained and empowered to ordain others as he wishes." (Translated according to the Y. Kafah edition of Maimonides' commentary to the Mishnah [Jerusalem, 1964].)

108. The dispute between Berab and Ibn Ḥabib concerning the interpretation of Maimonides has recently been reexamined by E. Shochetman, "Renewal of the Semicha According to Maimonides" (Hebrew), *Shenaton ha-Mishpat ha-Ivri* 14–15 (1988–89): 217–43.

109. See Katz, *Halakhah and Kabbalah,* 225–27.

110. See Benayahu, "Revival of Ordination," 248–69.

CHAPTER 13. BRIEF BIOGRAPHIES OF RABBINIC PERSONALITIES IN ERETZ-ISRAEL

Abraham Abzardiel

1. For the chronology of his life, see Benayahu, "Yosef Garson," 96, 98, 198.

2. See Samuel d'Avila, *Keter Torah,* introduction. See also Benayahu, "Yosef Garson," 97.

3. For a list of his decisions, see ibid., 97–98. Abzardiel is mentioned by David ibn Abi Zimra, *Responsa,* no. 1108.

Abraham ben Eliezer ha-Levi

4. For the chronology of his life, see Scholem and Beit-Arié, *Maamar Meshare Qitrin,* 16–17; David, "Sholal Family," 376; idem, "Personalities in Jerusalem," 238–39, 242; and the studies in n. 5 below.

5. See Scholem "Kabbalistical Miscellaneous Notes: Bi-Devar Ḥokhmata Rabbatah de-Shelomoh ve-Rabbi Avraham ha-Levi ha-Zaqen" (Hebrew), *Kiryat Sefer* 1 (1924): 163–64; idem, "The Cabbalist Rabbi Abraham Halevi" (Hebrew), *Kiryat Sefer* 2 (1925): 101–41, 269–73; idem, "Chapters from Cabbalistical Literature," 149–65, 440–56. For a summation of Scholem's studies of this kabbalist, see Scholem and Beit-Arié, *Maamar Meshare Qitrin,* and the references cited there. See also David, "A Letter from Jerusalem," 39–60; I. Robinson, "Abraham ben Eliezer Halevi: Kabbalist and Messianic Visionary of the Early Sixteenth Century" (Ph.D. diss., Cambridge, Mass., 1980). See also n. 9 below.

6. David, "Personalities in Jerusalem," 242.

7. See Yaari, *Letters,* 162–66. G. Scholem has already shown that the letter was actually written by Abraham ha-Levi. See Scholem, "The Cabbalist Abraham Halevi," 106; Scholem and Beit-Arié, *Maamar Meshare Qitrin,* 14, 38; David, "A Letter from Jerusalem," 46–47.

8. See Basola, *Masot,* 62.

9. See Robinson, "Abraham ben Eliezer Halevi"; idem, "Messianic Prayer Vigils," 32–42; Idel, "Mishmarot and Messianism," 83–94.

10. On *Nevuot ha-Yeled,* see Scholem and Beit-Arié, *Maamar Meshare Qitrin,* 14, 31–36. Most of his letters have been published in critical editions and have been reexamined by Scholem and Beit-Arié, *Maamar Meshare Qitrin,* 36–42. See also David, "A Letter from Jerusalem," 39–60; Robinson, "Two Letters," 403–22.

Abraham ben Gedaliah ibn Asher

11. Joseph Caro, *Shu"t Avqat Rokhel,* no. 72; idem, *Shu"t Beit Yosef,* "Laws of Marriage Contracts," no. 2. See also Benayahu, *Yosef Beḥiri,* 312–13.

Abraham ben Mordecai Galante

12. In Galante's commentary on Lamentations (Venice, 1589), the blessing for the dead is appended to his name.

13. In 1559 Galante copied Menaḥem ha-Meiri's *Bet ha-Beḥirah* in Safed. MS. Moscow, Russian State Library, Günzburg 952 (IMHM, no. 28006).

14. See B. Zak (Sack), "Notes Regarding the Relationship of R. Abraham Galante's Commentaries to the Works of His Teachers" (Hebrew), in *Misgav Yerushalayim Studies in Jewish Literature* (Jerusalem, 1987), 61–86; idem, *The Kabbalah of Rabbi Moshe Cordevero* [*sic*] (Hebrew; Jerusalem, 1995), 291–98.

15. This emerges from a letter sent by the community of Cuneo to the heads of the Provençal yeshivah in Safed. See David, "Community of Cuneo," 434.

16. A single copy of this work on the *Zohar* is extant, MS. Jerusalem, Jewish National and University Library, Heb. 8° 493. Only part of the commentary has survived, until the weekly portion *Terumah* (Exod. 25). See Scholem, *Kitvey Yad be-Qabbalah,* no. 41, pp. 102–4. An abridged version of this commentary was written by Abraham Azulay, *Sefer Zoharey Ḥammah* (Przemysl, 1882). On his kabbalistic commentaries, see the brief discussion in Zak (Sack),

"Abraham Galante's Commentaries," 61–86; idem, *Kabbalah of Rabbi Moshe Cordevero,* 291–98. The anthology is found in MS. Jerusalem, National and University Library, Heb. 8° 539. See Scholem, *Kitvey Yad be-Qabbalah,* no. 42, pp. 104–6.

17. These *hanhagot* have been published along with others attributed to his teacher Moses Cordovero and others. See S. Schechter, "Safed in the Sixteenth Century—A City of Legists and Mystics," in *Studies in Judaism,* 2d series (Philadelphia, 1938), 294–97; M. Hallamish, "On the Text of Behavioral Mannerisms of the Sages of Safed" (Hebrew), *Alei Sefer* 14 (1987): 89–97.

Abraham ben Samuel Zacuto

18. For the chronology of his life, see Shochat, "Abraham Zacuto," 43–44; Beit-Arié and Idel, "Treatise by Abraham Zacut," 177 n. 13; Benayahu, "Yosef Garson," 89–92, 174–79; Hacker, "Self-Perception of Spanish Jewry," 90–92.

19. *Al Talikat* is mentioned in a letter written by Jacob Gavison (MS. Oxford, Bodleian Library, Pocock 74 [2000]; [IMHM, no. 19285]). For a summation of Zacuto's accomplishments in the field of astronomy, see Luis de Albuquerque's introduction to the facsmile edition of *Almanach Perpetuum* (Lisbon, 1986), 7–59. See also B. R. Goldstein, "The Hebrew Astronomical Tradition: New Sources," *Isis* 72 (1981): 237–51.

20. The latter has been published by Beit-Arié and Idel, "Treatise by Abraham Zacut," 174–94, 825–26. For a substantive discussion of Zacuto's astrological conceptions, see ibid., 174–82.

21. Zacuto and his *Sefer Yuḥasin* have been the subject of research; the definitive study of his historiographical corpus, however, has yet to be written. See A. H. Freimann, introduction to *Sefer Yuḥasin ha-Shalem,* 2d ed., edited by A. H. Freimann (Jerusalem, 1963), ix–xxiv; A. A. Neuman, "Abraham Zacuto—Historiographer," in *Harry Austryn Wolfson Jubilee Volume,* ed. S. Lieberman et al. (Jerusalem, 1965), 2:597–629; idem, "The Paradoxes and Fate of a Jewish Medievalist," in *The Seventy-fifth Anniversary Volume of the Jewish Quarterly Review* (Philadelphia, 1967), 398–408; J. L. Lacave, "Las fuentes cristianas del Sefer Yuḥasin," *Proceedings of the Fifth World Congress of Jewish Studies* 2 (1972): 92–98.

22. Gedaliah ibn Yaḥya, *Shalshelet ha-Qabbalah* (printed edition), fol. 63v, stresses that Zacuto taught in Saragossa. It is possible that he taught there at a later date. This matter requires further investigation.

23. See Albuquerque, introduction to *Almanach Perpetuum,* 35ff.

24. See Tishby, *Messianism,* 37–39.

25. See Zacuto, *Sefer Yuḥasin ha-Shalem* (Freimann ed.), 22, col. a.

26. See Shochat, "Abraham Zacuto," 43–46; David, "Jerusalem Academies," 142.

27. On his relationship to Abraham ha-Levi, see Scholem and Beit-Arié, *Maamar Meshare Qitrin,* 10; Tamar, *Ha-Yehudim be-Ereẓ Yisrael u-ve-Arṣot ha-Mizraḥ,* 167; David, "Personalities in Jerusalem," 239, 242. On his nephew, Moses Castro, see David, "Personalities in Jerusalem, 238–39, 242.

28. Ibid., 239, 242. See biography no. 2 for the citation (n. 6).

29. MS. Jerusalem, National and University Library, Heb. 8° 6424. This treatise has been described by A. Kohut, introduction to *Sefer he-Arukh ha-Shalem* (Vienna, 1878), pt. 1, xli–xlii.

Abraham Besodo

30. On Besodo's family, and his reported demise in Ein Zitun, see Benayahu, "Yosef Garson," 99–101, 167.

31. See Benayahu, "Teudah," 122–25.

Abraham Castro

32. For studies of the man and his role in sixteenth-century Egypt and Jerusalem, see A. N. Pollack, "The Jews and the Egyptian Treasury in the Times of the Mamelukes and the Beginning of the Turkish Regime" (Hebrew), *Zion* 1 (1935): 24–36; David, "The Office of *Nagid* in Egypt," 325–37; idem, "Abraham Qastro," 147–62; H. Gerber, "An Unknown Turkish Document on Abraham di Castro" (Hebrew), *Zion* 45 (1980): 158–63; Cohen, "Abraham Castro," 407–18; E. Shochetman, "Additional Information on the Life of R. Abraham Castro" (Hebrew), *Zion* 48 (1983): 387–405.

33. See chap. 3, n. 69, above.

34. Sambari, *Divrei Yosef,* 285. See introduction, n. 12, above.

35. See Shochetman, "Additional Information on Abraham Castro," 387–90.

36. Venetian documents clearly indicate that it was a different Abraham Castro who converted to Islam in Jerusalem. See B. Arbel, "Abraham Castro Multiplied: Venetian Traders and Jewish Customs Farmers in the Levant, c. 1530–c. 1540," in *Trading Nations: Jews and Venetians in the Early Modern Eastern Mediterranean* (Leiden, 1995), 28–54.

37. See David, "Abraham Qastro," 154, 161–62. On Jacob Castro specifically, see J. S. Spiegel, "Rabbi Jacob Castro (*Maharikas*) and His Works" (Hebrew), *Alei Sefer* 16 (1989/90): 5–36, 58.

Abraham Gabriel

38. On this individual, see Benayahu, "Revival of Ordination," 262–63; Bentov, "Josef Trani," 223.

Abraham ha-Levi Berukhim

39. On him, see Tamar, *The Jewish People in Eretz Israel,* 175; Scholem and Beit-Arié, *Maamar Meshare Qitrin,* 17; Hallamish, "The Kabbalists in Morocco," 210–11; R. Elior, "Response to D. Tamar" (Hebrew), *Jerusalem Studies in Jewish Thought* 3 (1983/84): 494–97.

40. This ascription, made one generation after Berukhim by Joseph Solomon Delmedigo of Candia (Crete), has been refuted by G. Scholem. See Scholem and Beit-Arié, *Maamar Meshare Qitrin,* 19–20. D. Tamar reiterated this mistaken view in his review of "A Critical Edition of Galya Raza: Galya Raza, ed. R. Elior, Jerusalem, 1982" (Hebrew), *Jerusalem Studies in Jewish Thought* 2 (1982/83): 646–47. See Elior's reply, "Response to D. Tamar," 493–506.

41. These regimen vitae were first published by S. Schechter along with others ascribed to his teacher, Moses Cordovero. See Schechter, "Safed in the Sixteenth Century," 297–99. See also Hallamish, "Behavioral Mannerisms," 89–97.

42. See Benayahu, *Toledoth ha-Ari,* index, s.v. "Berukhim, Avraham ha-Levi." See also A. Wineman, "The Metamorphosis of Narrative Traditions: Two

Stories from Sixteenth-Century Safed," *AJS Review* 10 (1985): 171–80 for a legendary tradition associated with Berukhim.

Abraham Shalom

43. See Dimitrovsky, "Yaakov Berab's Academy," 49 n. 45, 66; Benayahu, "Revival of Ordination," 249. Shalom probably spent time in Egypt. See E. Gutwirt, "A Judeo-Spanish Letter from the Genizah," in *Judeo-Romance Languages,* ed. I. Benabu and J. Sermoneta (Jerusalem, 1985), 127–38.

44. See Yaari, *Sheluḥey Ereẓ-Yisrael,* 243–44.

Bezalel ben Abraham Ashkenazi

45. On the date of his death, see David, "The Ashkenazic Community in Jerusalem," 336 n. 38. From an allusion in a poem by Ashkenazi's contemporay Israel Najara, E. Rivlin concludes that Ashkenazi was born in Eretz-Israel, presumably in Safed. See Frumkin and Rivlin, *Ḥakhmey Yerushalayim,* 1:116. In my opinion, however, the evidence is inconclusive and requires further investigation.

46. See Bezalel Ashkenazi, *Responsa,* no. 1; Conforte, *Qore ha-Dorot,* fol. 41r.

47. On his studies, yeshivah, and students in Egypt, see the previous note; Sambari, *Divrei Yosef,* 412; Shochetman, introduction to *Responsa of Rabbi Meir Gavizon,* 1:66, 73.

48. On this obscure episode, see David, "The Office of *Nagid* in Egypt," 327–29.

49. See Frumkin and Rivlin, *Ḥakhmey Yerushalayim,* 1:115–18; David, "The Office of *Nagid* in Egypt," 328 n. 22; idem, "Jerusalem Academies," 159 n. 71.

50. Shochetman, introduction to *Responsa of Meir Gavizon,* 1:71–72, argues that Ashkenazi was the rabbi of the Sefardi kahal in Jerusalem. Nonetheless, the evidence cited by Shochetman can also be interpreted as indicating that Ashkenazi headed the entire kehillah.

51. As evidenced by his disciple, Solomon Adeni. See chap. 8, sec. A for the citation. See also David, "Jerusalem Academies," 144–45.

52. See A. Marx, "Die *Kelaley ha-Talmud* des R. Bezalel Aschkenasi," in *Festschrift zum Siebzigsten Geburtstage David Hoffmann's,* ed. S. Eppenstein et al. (Berlin, 1914); Hebrew section, 201. At that date Ashkenazi was apparently a recent arrival in Safed, for in the previous paragraph, he had written: "And I finished it on Monday, the twelfth of Tishri in the year 5335 to the creation [28 Sept. 1574], here in Egypt."

53. See David, "Bezalel Ashkenazi," 455.

54. A bibliographical list of the *Shitah Mequbbeṣet* on the various tractates, both published and in manuscript, has been compiled by H. Michael, *Or ha-Ḥayyim: The Sages of Israel and Their Literary Works* (Hebrew; Jerusalem, 1965), 286–88; A. Freimann, "List of the Early Commentaries on the Talmud" (Hebrew), in *Louis Ginzberg Jubilee Volume,* ed. S. Lieberman et al. (New York, 1946), Hebrew section, 323–54; M. M. Kasher and J. B. Mandelbaum, *Sarei ha-Elef,* 2d ed. (Jerusalem, 1978), index, s.v. "Shitah Mequbbeṣet." A comprehensive study of this corpus has yet to be undertaken; moreover, an accurate bibliographical listing is also a desideratum. See also E. Shochetman,

"'Binyan-Shlomo Lehokhmat-Bezalel' by R. Shlomo Adani" (Hebrew), *Alei Sefer* 3 (1976): 63–93.

55. See Epstein, *Mavo,* 2:1289–90; Y. L. Ha-Kohen Maimon, "Rabbi Beṣalel Ashqenazi u-Sefarav," *Sinai: Sefer Yovel* (Jerusalem, 1958), 89–125; idem, *Rabbi Moshe ben Maimon* (Hebrew; Jerusalem, 1960), 251–92; Benayahu, "Hagahoteyhem she-le-Rabbi Beṣalel Ashqenazi ve-Rabbi Yehosef Ashqenazi ve-tofes ha-Av Shelahem," *Asufot* 1 (1987) 47–104; idem, "Hagahot Mishneh Torah min ha-tofes she-la-Rambam ve-Hagahot hameyuḥasot le-Rabbi Beṣalel Ashqenazi ve-ha-Ari," *Sinai* 100 (Jubilee Volume, 1987): 135–42; Shochetman, "'Binyan-Shlomo Lehokhmat-Bezalel'," 63–93.

56. *Kelaley ha-Talmud* has appeared in two editions. See A. Marx, "Die *Kelaley ha-Talmud* des Bezalel Aschkenasi," Hebrew section, 179–217; German section, 369–82; and E. Shochetman, "Kelalei Hatalmud of R. Bezalel Ashkenazi" (Hebrew), *Shenaton ha-Mishpat ha-Ivri* 8 (1981): 247–308.

57. His collected sermons are found in MS. Oxford, Bodleian Library, Opp. Add. 4° 33 (1015), (IMHM, no. 22501). See Shochetman, "'Binyan-Shlomo Lehokhmat-Bezalel'," 63 n. 1. These sermons have recently been published by Y. Bochbot, *Derashot u-Maamarim shel ha-Rav . . . Beṣalel Ashqenazi* (Jerusalem, 1996).

David ben Solomon ibn Abi Zimra (RaDBaZ)

58. See H. J. Zimmels, *Rabbi David Ibn Abi Simra* (Breslau, 1932); I. M. Goldman, *The Life and Times of Rabbi David Ibn Abi Zimra* (New York, 1970), 1–28; Strauss-Ashtor, *The Jews in Egypt and Syria,* 2:458–70.

59. No information is available regarding this yeshivah in Abi Zimra's writings or in the writings of his contemporaries. Recently, I discovered an explicit reference to Abi Zimra's yeshivah in Egypt in Issachar ibn Susan's *Tiqqun Yissakhar,* fol. 23r–v (a photocopy of which is in my possession): "When I was in Egypt I heard that our teacher, the great rabbi and perfect scholar R. David ben Zamiru, may God preserve him, used to do thus in his home where he always prayed with the students who attended his yeshivah." On his commercial activities, see Assaf, *Texts and Studies,* 199–203; A. David, "More on the Commercial Activities of R. David Ibn Zimra—According to an Unknown Document from the Cairo Geniza" (Hebrew), *Pe'amim* 32 (1987): 131–34.

60. See David ibn Abi Zimra, *Responsa,* no. 644.

61. Isaac ben Abraham Akrish, introduction to three commentaries to the Song of Songs, which he published in Istanbul, 1575(?).

62. This chronology has been contested by other scholars, who argue for a later date for Abi Zimra's arrival in Jerusalem, either 1558, or 1561–62. Their arguments are definitely refuted by Akrish's statement. See A. David, "The Economic Status of Egyptian Jewry in the 16th Century According to the Responsa of Radbaz," *Miqqedem umiyyam* 1 (1981): 86 n. 2.

63. See Hacker, "Jewish Autonomy in the Ottoman Empire," 170–74. See above, chap. 7, "the dayyan"; Cohen, *Jewish Life under Islam,* 44.

64. See David ibn Abi Zimra, *Responsa,* no. 1085. See also Hacker, "Payment of *Djizya,*" 84–85. On the scholars' refusal to remit the levy, see David ibn Abi Zimra, *Responsa,* no. 752.

65. Ibn Ṣayyaḥ's responsum was cited by Hacker, "Payment of *Djizya,*" 105–17. For the specific citation, see ibid., 116. Excerpts from this responsum

were published earlier by S. Assaf, "On Various Manuscripts" (Hebrew), *Kiryat Sefer* 11 (1935), 493–95.

66. See Dimitrovsky, "Dispute," 90 n. 71; Scheiber and Benayahu, "Communication to the Radbaz," 134; Cohen, *Jewish Life under Islam,* 44.

67. Isaac Akrish; see n. 61 above.

68. See Bentov, "Josef Trani," 215.

69. He cosigned a decision concerning the agreement of the butchers in Damascus with "Joseph Caro" and "R. Moses . . . Trani." See Joseph Caro, *Shu"t Avqat Rokhel,* no. 187. His name also appears with the forementioned sages on a pesak from 1568 concerning "a hedge against licentiousness and against calling his friend an apostate," signed also by "Israel . . . Curiel." See Artom and Cassuto, *Taqqanot Candia ve-Zikhronoteha,* 147–48.

70. Abi Zimra's responsa have been published in several volumes. A complete edition of Abi Zimra's published responsa appeared in Sudylkow, 1836 and Warsaw, 1882. An additional volume of responsa, mainly those not included in the printed editions, appeared in Bnei Brak, 1975. Individual responsa published over the years have been surveyed by Goldman, *David Ibn Abi Zimra,* 17–18. For an additional responsum, see A. Scheiber, "An Unknown Responsum of David Ibn Abi Zimra," in *Essays on the Occasion of the Seventieth Anniversary of the Dropsie University,* ed. A. I. Katsh and L. Nemoy (Philadelphia, 1979), 397–403.

71. Abi Zimra's *Yeqar Tiferet* has appeared with Maimonides' Code from the publication of the Romm (Vilna) edition, 1900. He completed his commentary to *Zeraim* (Book of Agriculture) in Jerusalem in 1561. See M. Assis, "Mashehu al 'Kesef Mishneh' le-Sefer Zeraim ve-al Nusaḥ Sefer Zeraim shel Mefarshey ha-Rambam bi-Zemano shel Maran," *Asufot* 3 (1989): 316–22. His *Kelaley ha-Gemara* was first published in Abraham Aqra, *Me-Harerey Nemerim* (Venice, 1599). Abi Zimra mentions his commentary on the Pentateuch in the introduction to his *Magen David* (Amsterdam, 1713).

72. For a look at his kabbalistic ideas, see M. Helner, "Transmigration of Souls in the Kabbalistic Writings of R. David ibn Zimra" (Hebrew), *Pe'amim* 43 (1990): 16–50.

73. For a brief survey of Abi Zimra's piyyutim, see Goldman, *David Ibn Abi Zimra,* 20–21.

David ben Zechariah Frank

74. On David Frank, see David, "Ashkenazic Community in Jerusalem," *Vatiqin,* 30–32; Dimitrovsky, "Dispute," 87.

75. Samuel d'Avila, *Keter Torah,* introduction.

76. Joseph Caro, *Shu"t Avqat Rokhel,* no. 115; idem, *Shu"t Beit Yosef,* "Laws of Levirate Marriage," no. 2.

David ibn Shoshan

77. Samuel d'Avila, *Keter Torah,* introduction.

78. See Basola, *Masot,* 62; David, "Letter of Israel Ashkenazi," 113. See also David, "Jerusalem Academies," 143–44.

79. Levi ibn Ḥabib, *Responsa,* no. 25. See also David, "Historical Significance," 232.

80. See David, "The Identity of Israel Ashkenazi," 171 n. 10; idem, "Sholal Family," 382.

81. Ibn Shoshan's sermons are located in MS. Moscow, Russian State Library, Günzburg 313 (IMHM, no. 27962), fols. 18r–54r.

Eleazar ben Moses Azikri (Azkari)

82. For the chronology of his life, see S. Lieberman, "The Old Commentators of the Yerushalmi," *Alexander Marx Jubilee Volume,* ed. S. Lieberman (New York, 1950), Hebrew section, 306; J. Franzos, ed., *Talmud Yerushalmi, Beṣah,* with commentary by Eleazar Azikri (Hebrew; New York, 1967), introduction, 50; M. Pachter, "The Life and Personality of R. Elazar Azikri According to His Mystical Diary" (Hebrew), *Shalem* 3 (1981): 131–32. For a detailed examination of his biography and literary works, see idem, *Milei De-Shemaya by Rabbi Elazar Azikri* (Hebrew; Tel Aviv, 1991), 11–69. On Azikri's birthplace, see Pachter, *Milei De-Shemaya,* 24. For his death, see Lieberman, "Old Commentators," 305.

83. In *Sefer Ḥaredim* (Venice, 1601), fol. 65r, Azikri explicitly mentions his rabbi. See also Pachter, *Milei De-Shemaya,* 25.

84. For the former society, see Azikri, *Sefer Ḥaredim,* fol. 2r–v; Benayahu, "Revival of Ordination," 262; Pachter, "Elazar Azikri," 133ff., 143ff.; idem, *Milei De-Shemaya,* 44. For the latter, see ibid.; idem, "Elazar Azikri," 142ff.

85. See Benayahu, "Revival of Ordination," 257, 266.

86. See Pachter, "Elazar Azikri," 142; idem, "Homiletic and Ethical Literature," 379–97.

87. For a comprehensive treatment of his commentaries on the Jerusalem Talmud and their citations by Solomon Adeni, see Lieberman, "Old Commentators," 304–13; Franzos, introduction to *Talmud Yerushalmi, Beṣah,* 52–61.

88. Azikri's extant commentaries to the Babylonian Talmud, his sermons, and his *Milei De-Shemaya* are bound together in an autograph copy, MS. New York, Jewish Theological Seminary, Mic. 3541, (ENA 74) (IMHM, no. 29346). A brief description of these works can be found in Pachter, "Elazar Azikri," 128–30. *Milei De-Shemaya* has recently been published by M. Pachter.

89. See Pachter, "Elazar Azikri," 128–47.

Eleazar ben Solomon ben Yoḥai

90. See Schepansky, *Eretz Israel in the Responsa Literature,* 2:417 n. 2.

91. On Samuel ben Benveniste, see Benayahu, "Teudah," 116.

92. Contemporary sources place Eleazar ben Yoḥai in Tiberias. See Zechariah al-Ḍāhiri, *Sefer Hamussar,* 287, as well as various responsa exchanged in the framework of halakhic correspondence between Ben Yoḥai and Joseph Caro, Joseph ibn Ṣayyaḥ, Moses Trani, and Levi ibn Ḥabib. See Joseph Caro, *Shu"t Avqat Rokhel,* nos. 52–55, on the question of the purity of the ritual bath in Hamat, Tiberias, evidently raised in 1558, and on another matter, ibid., no. 105; Moses Trani, *Responsa,* pt. 1, nos. 34–35, 92; pt. 2, no. 64; pt. 3, no. 29; Levi ibn Ḥabib, *Responsa,* no 101. In Joseph Caro's *Shu"t Avqat Rokhel,* no. 85, we find mention of "the yeshivah of the perfect sage R. Eleazar ibn Yoḥai." From the context, it is clear that this yeshivah was located in Tiberias.

Elijah ben Moses de Vidas

93. See Azulay, *Shem ha-Gedolim,* s.v. "Elijah de Vidas."

94. See M. Pachter, "The Book 'Reshit Ḥokhmah' by R. Eliyahu De-Vidas and Its Epitomes" (Hebrew), *Kiryat Sefer* 47 (1971/72): 686–710; idem, "Con-

cerning the Quotations from 'Orḥot Tsadikim' in the Ethical Writings of the Safed Scholars" (Hebrew), ibid., 489–92. For a more comprehensive discussion of this treatise, see idem, "Homiletic and Ethical Literature," 369–78.

Elisha ben Gabriel Gallico

95. For general treatments of Gallico and his thought, see Pachter, "Homiletic and Ethical Literature," 194–212; Benayahu, *Yosef Beḥiri,* 259–90. On his arrival in Safed, see M. Benayahu, "He-Hagut she-be-Peyrushey ha-Megillot le-Rabbi Elisha Gallico," *Asufot* 4 (1990): 73.

96. In 1575, when Caro was on his deathbed, Elisha Gallico and Moses Alshekh issued a halakhic ruling in his name banning the historiosophic work *Meor Einayim* by Azariah de Rossi (Mantua, 1574). For the publication of the ruling, see chap. 12, n. 50. On his ordination, see Benayahu, "Revival of Ordination," 256.

97. On the title page of his commentary on Lamentations (Venice, 1578), Gallico is referred to as the "head of a yeshivah in Safed." On Benveniste, see Tamar, *The Jewish People in Eretz Israel,* 144–45.

98. On his commentaries, see Benayahu, "Elisha Gallico," 74, 98. The recently discovered fragments have been published by S. Regev, "Sarid mi-Peyrush Megillat Rut le-Rabbi Elisha Gallico," *Asufot* 4 (1990): 99–126. On his halakhic works, see Benayahu, "Elisha Gallico," 73; Pachter, "Homiletic and Ethical Literature," 195 n. 5. A responsum of Gallico is cited by Moses Trani, *Responsa,* pt. 3, no. 205. See also David, "Shivat Anusim," 198 n. 62.

Ephraim Fish ben Moses Judah

99. On Ephraim Fish, see Solomon Adeni, *Melekhet Shelomo,* introduction. See also Frumkin and Rivlin, *Ḥakhmey Yerushalayim,* 1:107–8, on him and his teachers; S. Assaf, "A Contribution to the Biography of R. Solomon Luria" (Hebrew), in *Louis Ginzberg Jubilee Volume,* Hebrew section, 61.

100. Yom Tov Ṣahalon, *Responsa,* no. 160. Perhaps Ṣahalon was referring to the total number of Ephraim Fish's students, including those who studied under him in Lithuania. See also Joseph Trani, *Responsa,* pt. 2, no. 52.

101. Samuel d'Avila, *Keter Torah,* introduction.

102. Excerpts from his commentary on tractate *Avot* are embedded in Samuel de Uceda's *Midrash Shemuel* (Venice, 1579), whereas some of his glosses and comments on the Mishnah are found in Solomon Adeni's *Melekhet Shelomo.* See Assaf, "Biography of Solomon Luria," 61, for the citations.

Gedaliah ben Moses Cordovero

103. For details on his life, see Gedaliah ben Moses Cordovero, introduction to Moses Cordovero, *Peyrush Avodat Yom ha-Kippurim* (Venice, 1587); M. Benayahu, "Le-toledot R. Gedalyah Cordovero," *Sinai* 16 (1945): 82–90; Tishby, "Moses Cordovero," 126 n. 21; Rozen, *Jewish Community,* 140, and index.

104. Thus he states explicitly in the introduction to his father's work *Or ha-Neerav* (Venice, 1587): "like the opinion of the pious sage, my mother's brother, Rashba [R. Solomon Alkabetz] ha-Levi of blessed memory."

105. On this episode, see Benayahu, "Gedalyah Cordovero," 86–88; Sonne, "Shadarim," 197–203.

106. Sonne, "Shadarim," 199–203, published a document relating to this

trip but mistakenly read the date as 1608. Yaari, *Sheluḥey Ereẓ-Yisrael,* 841–42, based his dating of the letter on Sonne. Careful examination of the document reveals the correct date to be 1617. See Carpi, *Between Renaissance and Ghetto,* 145; and in light of his determination, Rozen, *Jewish Community,* 140.

107. See Rozen, *The Ruins of Jerusalem,* 94–95.

Ḥayyim ben Joseph Vital

108. For autobiographical information, see his *Sefer ha-Ḥezyonot,* ed. A. Z. Aescoly (Jerusalem, 1954). See also Azulay, *Shem ha-Gedolim,* s.v. "Ḥayyim Vital"; M. Oron, "Dream, Vision and Reality in Haim Vital's *Sefer ha-Ḥezyonot*" (Hebrew), *Jerusalem Studies in Jewish Thought* 10 (1992): 299–309. On Vital's life in Jerusalem, see G. Scholem, "A Document by the Disciples of Isaac Luria" (Hebrew), *Zion* 5 (1940): 138–39; Benayahu, "Ḥayyim Vital," 65–75, esp. 65.

109. This was the eponym used by Solomon Shlomil Meinstral of Dreznitz. See Assaf, "Iggerot mi-Ṣefat," 129.

110. See the opening section of *Sefer ha-Ḥezyonot.*

111. Adeni's testimony is found in the introduction to his *Melekhet Shelomo,* cited above, chap. 8, sec. A. See also Benayahu, "Ḥayyim Vital," 66–67.

112. See Azulay, *Shem ha-Gedolim,* s.v. "Moses Alshekh." See also Benayahu, "Revival of Ordination," 256, 266.

113. Samuel d'Avila, *Keter Torah,* introduction. See also Benayahu, "Ḥayyim Vital," 67.

114. This suggestion, which has been put forth by Benayahu, "Ḥayyim Vital," 67, requires further investigation.

115. Ibid.; Vital, *Sefer ha-Ḥezyonot,* 92, 116.

116. *Ḥayyim Shenayim* was preserved in a copy by his son Samuel Vital. MS. Moscow, Russian State Library, Günzburg 67 (IMHM, no. 6747). It is also mentioned by I. Nissim, "Teshuvot Rabbi Ḥayyim Vital," in *Sefer Yovel le-Rabbi Ḥanokh Albeck* (Jerusalem, 1963), 332. Ḥayyim Vital's responsa are found in the collected responsa of his son, Samuel Vital, *Beer Mayim Ḥayyim,* MS. Oxford, Bodleian Library, Mich. 463 (832), (IMHM, no. 21593), nos. 82–86. These responsa have been published by Nissim, "Teshuvot Ḥayyim Vital," 332–51, and appear in the printed edition of the entire collection of Samuel Vital's responsa (New York, 1966).

117. For a detailed treatment of Vital's exegetical works, see Pachter, "Homiletic and Ethical Literature," 294–303.

118. See W. Rabinowitsch, "Manuscripts from an Archive in Stolin" (Hebrew), *Zion* 5 (1940): 125–26. On this agreement and its implications, see Scholem, "Disciples of Isaac Luria," 133–60.

119. On the dissemination of Vital's writings in the Orient, see S. Z. Havlin, "Intellectual Creativity" (Hebrew), in *The Jews in Ottoman Egypt (1517–1914),* ed. J. M. Landau (Hebrew; Jerusalem, 1988), 302–6. On Italy, see J. Avivi, "The Writing [*sic*] of R. Isaac Luria in Italy before 1620" (Hebrew), *Alei Sefer* 11 (1984): 91–134.

120. The bibliographical issues related to the collection, reworking, and interpretation of Lurianic texts by Vital and others have been discussed by J. Avivi, *Binyan Ariel: Introduction to the Homilies of R. Isaac Luria* (Hebrew; Jerusalem, 1987).

Ḥiyya Rofe

121. On the man and his works, see Benayahu, "Chiya Rophe," 109–29.

122. On Solomon Sagis, see ibid., 109. For Ḥayyim Vital, see ibid., 111.

123. Benayahu, "Revival of Ordination," 263, 266; idem, "Chiya Rofe," 109.

Isaac ben Mordecai Gershon

124. Confusion has arisen concerning Isaac Gershon and Isaac Treves, contemporaries who were both employed as proofreaders in the Italian-Jewish press. This has given rise to the mistaken conclusion that they were actually one and the same person. See Yudlov, "Isaac Gershon and Isaac Treves," 247–51; E. Horowitz, "Isaac ben Gershon Treves in Venice," 252–57.

125. See Yaari, *Sheluḥey Ereẓ-Yisrael,* 251; Yudlov, "Isaac Gershon and Isaac Treves," 247–51.

Isaac ben Solomon Ashkenazi (Isaac Luria; Ha-Ari)

126. The only information available on Luria's biography is in the form of pseudo-epigraphic material based on legendary traditions that were preserved in the popular treatise *Toledot ha-Ari* and its offshoots, in addition to oral traditions that combine fact and fancy. These genres have been compiled by Benayahu, *Toledoth ha-Ari.* See also Tamar's critique, *The Jewish People in Eretz Israel,* 166–93. On Luria's stay in Egypt and his involvement in commerce there, see David, "Halakhah and Commerce," 287–97.

127. Ḥayyim Vital, *Shaar ha-Pesuqim,* weekly portion of *Be-Haalotekha,* no. 12. Cited by Frumkin and Rivlin, *Ḥakhmey Yerushalayim,* 1:98. Luria's other scholarly biographers, like Benayahu and Tamar, did not single out this important detail. See also David, "Halakhah and Commerce," 288–89.

128. A deed of sale issued in Egypt in 1554 mentions "the honored rabbi, Isaac Luria Ashkenazi." MS. Cambridge, University Library Geniza Collection, T–S Glass 12,589. Published by E. J. Worman, "Un document concernant Isaac Louria," *REJ* 57 (1909): 281–82. On David ibn Abi Zimra as his teacher, see Conforte, *Qore ha-Dorot,* fol. 40v; Tamar, *Ha-Yehudim be-Ereẓ Yisrael u-ve-Arṣot ha-Mizraḥ,* 71–72, 74–76. On his teacher-colleague, Bezalel Ashkenazi, see Sambari, *Divrei Yosef,* 412; Conforte, *Qore ha-Dorot,* fol. 40v.

129. Ibid. See also David, "Halakhah and Commerce," 289.

130. See Judah Aryeh Modena, *Ari Nohem,* ed. N. S. Libowitz (Jerusalem, 1929), 80; Worman, "Isaac Louria," 281 n. 1; Assaf, *Texts and Studies,* 204–5; E. Shochetman, "New Sources from the Genizah on the Economic Activity of R. Isaac Luria in Egypt" (Hebrew), *Pe'amim* 16 (1983): 56–64; M. Benayahu, "Teudot min ha-Genizah al Iskey Misḥar she-la-Ari ve-al Beney Mishpaḥto be-Miṣrayim," *Studies in Memory of the Rishon Le-Zion R. Yitzhak Nissim,* 4:225–53 (Benayahu included previously published as well as newly discovered documents along with some whose attribution to Luria is doubtful); A. David, "More on the History of the Ari in Egypt in Light of Geniza Documents" (Hebrew), *Alei Sefer* 14 (1987): 135–37; idem, "Halakhah and Commerce," 292–97.

131. See David, "Halakhah and Commerce," 295–96.

132. See Benayahu, *Toledoth ha-Ari,* 283, 286; Tamar, *Ha-Yehudim be-Ereẓ Yisrael u-ve-Arṣot ha-Mizraḥ,* 71.

133. See Sambari, *Divrei Yosef,* 416. Luria's student Ḥayyim Vital testifies to this emphasis on kabbalah. See Benayahu, *Toledoth ha-Ari,* 163, 320–21. See

also Katz, *Halakhah and Kabbalah,* 92–94; David, "Halakhah and Commerce," 291–92.

134. Azulay, *Shem ha-Gedolim,* s.v. "Rabbenu ha-Ari (R. Isaac Luria)," notes that Luria's novellae to tractate *Zevaḥim* were destroyed by fire in Izmir along with Bezalel Ashkenazi's. It seems likely that Luria wrote novellae to additional tractates as well. See David, "Halakhah and Commerce," 290–91.

135. See M. Idel, "R. Yehudah Ḥallewa and his 'Zafenat Pa'aneaḥ'" (Hebrew), *Shalem* 4 (1984): 120; Helner, "Transmigration of Souls," 20. At present, no in-depth study clarifying the relationship between David ibn Abi Zimra's mystical doctrine and that of Isaac Luria has been undertaken. This remains an area for new research. See also biography no. 12 above.

136. See G. Scholem, "R. Isaac Luria's Authentic Works" (Hebrew), *Kiryat Sefer* 19 (1942/43): 188; Avivi, *Binyan Ariel,* 19.

137. On the editions of Luria's doctrines, see Avivi's comprehensive bibliographic study *Binyan Ariel.*

Isaac ibn Ḥayyim

138. See Benayahu, "Teudah," 123. Benayahu mistakenly identifies this sage with Isaac Mar-Ḥayyim (ibid., 117), as D. Tamar has already noted. See Tamar, *The Jewish People in Eretz Israel,* 110–11.

139. Samuel d'Avila, *Keter Torah,* introduction.

140. Levi ibn Ḥabib, *Responsa,* no. 93. See also Tamar, *The Jewish People in Eretz Israel,* 111.

Isaac Mar-Ḥayyim

141. See J. R. Hacker, "Some Letters on the Expulsion of the Jews from Spain and Sicily" (Hebrew), in *Studies in the History of Jewish Society Presented to Prof. Jacob Katz,* ed. E. Etkes and Y. Salmon (Hebrew; Jerusalem, 1980), 77–78. On Mar-Ḥayyim's kabbalistic doctrines, see G. Scholem, "The Kabbalistic Responsa of R. Yosef Alcastiel to R. Yehuda Hayyat" (Hebrew), *Tarbiẓ* 24 (1955): 168–69; Y. Nadav, "An Epistle of the Qabbalist R. Isaac Mar Ḥayyim Concerning the Doctrine of 'Supernal Lights'" (Hebrew), *Tarbiẓ* 26 (1957): 440–58; E. Gottlieb, *Studies in the Kabbala Literature,* ed. J. Hacker (Hebrew; Tel Aviv, 1976), 397ff.; M. Idel, "Iggarto shel R. Yiṣḥak mi-Pisa (?) bi-Shelosh Nusḥaoteha," *Kobeẓ al Yad,* n.s., 10 (1982): 163–214.

142. Hacker, "Letters on the Expulsion," 77 n. 78; David, "Jerusalem Academies," 161 n. 99. In his introduction to his commentary on Psalms (Venice, 1549), Solomon Atiyah mentions several sages who "went from Salonika to Eretz-Israel," including Isaac Mar-Ḥayyim.

143. See n. 138 above.

144. Samuel d'Avila, *Keter Torah,* introduction. The presence of Isaac ibn Ḥayyim's name on the list contributed to the earlier-mentioned confusion between the two.

Isaac Sholal

145. For a comprehensive study of Sholal, see David, "Sholal Family," 377ff.; Dimitrovsky, "Unknown Chapter," 106ff.

146. See Assaf, *Texts and Studies,* 191–92, 195–96.

147. David, "Sholal Family," 378–79. See also Idel, "Mishmarot and Messianism," 84–85. On his support for yeshivot in Eretz-Israel and the change in

his personal circumstances after the Ottoman conquest, see chap. 3, sec. F. On his role in administering the Jerusalem kehillah, see chap. 7. On his interest in hastening redemption and in its harbingers, see chap. 8, sec. E.

Israel ben Meir di Curiel

148. For biographical details, see M. Benayahu, Historical Introduction to *Rabbi Israel Di-Koriel: Sermons and Homilies,* ed. S. Regev (Hebrew; Jerusalem, 1992), 9–21; Bentov, "Josef Trani," 201–2, 216.

149. See Benayahu, "Revival of Ordination," 249.

150. Some of his signed decisions are cited in his contemporaries' responsa. See the end of chap. 11.

151. Conforte, *Qore ha-Dorot,* fol. 41r.

152. On di Curiel's literary corpus, see M. Pachter, "Identification of the Author of the Sermons in Sefer *Or Ẓaddikim,* Attributed to R. Joseph Caro, and the Homiletic Writings of R. Israel di Curiel" (Hebrew), *Kiryat Sefer* 55 (1980): 802–10. Selected sermons have been published by S. Regev, *Rabbi Israel di-Koriel: Sermons and Homilies* (Hebrew; Jerusalem, 1992). See also Benayahu's historical introduction, ibid., 9–21.

153. M. Benayahu, "Rabbi Yisrael Najara," *Asufot* 4 (1990): 204–5.

Israel ben Moses Najara

154. For his biography, see Benayahu, "Yisrael Najara," 205–17.

155. On the inclusion of Najara's poetry in the Karaite ritual, see ibid., 283. On the Shabbatean use of his poetry, see G. Scholem, "Shir shel Yisrael Najara be-fi ha-Shabbtaim," *Ignace Goldziher Memorial Volume,* ed. S. Löwinger and J. Somogyi (Budapest, 1948), pt. 1, Hebrew section, 41–44; idem, *Sabbatai Ṣevi,* 355–56; Benayahu, "Yisrael Najara," 281–82.

156. Najara's poetry, a large portion of which still remains in manuscript, awaits comprehensive study. Nonetheless, his poetry has captured the interest of contemporary scholars, who have tried to characterize its unique stylistic and musical features and have published dozens of his poems. On the publication of Najara's poems, see J. Yahalom, "Hebrew Mystical Poetry and Its Turkish Background" (Hebrew), *Tarbiẓ* 60 (1991): 625–48; Benayahu, "Yisrael Najara," 217–84; E. Seroussi, "Rabbi Yisrael Najara Meaṣev Zimrat ha-Qodesh Aḥarey Geyrush Sefarad," *Asufot* 4 (1990): 285–310; T. Beeri, "'Olat Ḥodesh' le-Rabbi Yisrael Najara—Nosim u-Tekhanim," ibid., 311–24; idem, "The Spanish Elements in the Poetry of R. Israel Najara" (Hebrew), *Pe'amim* 49 (1991): 54–67.

157. See Benayahu, "Yisrael Najara," 243–48. The extant portions of the commentary from both the printed edition and the manuscript have been published by S. Regev, "'Piṣey Ohev' le-R. Yisrael Najara," *Asufot* 4 (1990): 225–56.

158. This treatise is extant in two mss., one of which is complete, located in MS. Budapest, Rabbinical Seminary Library, 30 (IMHM, no. 47022). Four sermons were published by Abraham Bick (Pressburg, 1890). See Benayahu, "Yisrael Najara," 248–49.

159. David Conforte mentions having seen this treatise at the home of the author's son in Gaza in 1645. See Conforte, *Qore ha-Dorot,* fol. 49v. See also Benayahu, "Yisrael Najara," 249.

160. First published with Moses Ventura's *Yemin Moshe* (Amsterdam, 1718).

161. See J. Yahalom, "R. Israel Najarah and the Revival of Hebrew Poetry in the East after the Expulsion from Spain" (Hebrew), *Pe'amim* 13 (1982): 124; Beeri, "'Olat Ḥodesh,'" 319.

162. Later printed editions of *Zemirot Yisrael* saw the addition of many poems. See Benayahu, "Yisrael Najara," 251–56.

163. Benayahu described twenty mss. of this treatise. See ibid., 256–71.

164. Two of his responsa were included in Yom Tov Ṣahalon's *Shu"t Maharit ha-Ḥadashot,* vol. 1, pp. 1–2, 85–87. See Benayahu, "Yisrael Najara," 250–51.

Israel ben Yeḥiel Ashkenazi

165. On Israel Ashkenazi's career in Italy, see David, "The Identity of Israel Ashkenazi," 170–73; idem, "Letter of Israel Ashkenazi," introduction, 98. On Ashkenazi's career in Jerusalem, see ibid., 97–101.

166. On his role as dayyan in Jerusalem, see David, "Letter of Israel Askenazi," 116; idem, "Sholal Family," 389, 408. At that time, the office of dayyan was the most important administrative post in the Jerusalem kehillah. See the earlier discussion in chap. 7, "the dayyan."

167. See David, "Letter of Israel Ashkenazi," introduction, 101.

168. For the responsa, see David, "The Identity of Israel Ashkenazi," 172–73. Ashkenazi's letter has been published in several editions, most recently in 1990. See David, "Letter of Israel Ashkenazi."

Issachar ben Mordecai ibn Susan

169. For his biography, see Doron, "Issachar ben Susan," 280–82; for additional details, see David, "North African Jewry," 77, 79.

170. According to the autograph copy of *Tiqqun Yissakhar* (a photocopy of which is in my possession): "From me, the youth, son of his servant, who has written and revised this book which he advised me to begin, helping me to finish it this day, Tuesday, the 9th of Marḥeshvan, 5300 to the Creation [21 Oct. 1539] in Damascus . . . copied here in Safed . . . in the Upper Galilee . . . this day, Friday, the 4th of Nisan 5334 to the Creation [26 Mar. 1574], I the youth Issachar son of my master and father the eminent sage Mordecai, may God preserve him, known as Ben Susan."

171. An autograph copy of *Al-Sharḥ al-Susani* on the entire Bible is extant. On the Pentateuch: MS. London, British Library, Or. 14020a (formerly Sasson 159), (IMHM, no. 9268); on the Prophets: MS. London, British Library, Or. 5434 (1115), (IMHM, no. 6488); on the Writings: MS. London, British Library, Or.14020g (formerly Sasson 160), (IMHM, no. 9269). In his concluding remarks in the different sections, the author notes various dates between 1571 and 1574. For a brief discussion of the treatise and its nature, see Doron, "Issachar ben Susan," 283–98.

Jacob Abulafia

172. See Tamar, *Ha-Yehudim be-Ereẓ Yisrael u-ve-Arṣot ha-Mizraḥ,* 162 n. 13.

173. See Conforte, *Qore ha-Dorot,* fol. 42r.

174. See Sambari, *Divrei Yosef,* 361.

175. Yom Tov Ṣahalon, *Responsa,* no. 203; Benayahu, "Revival of Ordination," 263.

176. Benayahu, "Revival of Ordination," 263. On the ordination of his disciples, see ibid., 260, 266–67.

177. See Benayahu, *Toledoth ha-Ari,* index; Tamar, *The Jewish People in Eretz Israel,* 188–89.

178. Jacob Berab I's estate derived from Moses ibn Saida's charitable trust. The dispute between the brothers-in-law was discussed by Dimitrovsky, "Yaakov Berab's Academy," 54 n. 84. Judah Abulafia's cloth-beating establishment is mentioned in the context of the dispute. See Moses Trani, *Responsa,* pt. 1, no. 94.

Jacob Berab

179. Some biographical details are provided by Berab himself in one of the halakhic decisions related to the ordination controversy, "From the time of the expulsion and forced conversion in Spain I have been a rabbi in Israel, rabbi to five thousand Jewish households in the city of Fez. . . . I was then eighteen years old." See *Quntres ha-Semikhah,* appended to Levi ibn Ḥabib's responsa. Maqueda is located near Toledo. Berab's surname and birthplace are mentioned in his *Responsa,* no. 1. See also David, "The Year of Rabbi J. BeiRav's Death," 132.

180. See Dimitrovsky, "Yaakov Berab's Academy," 84. Isaac Aboab headed yeshivot in two Spanish cities. In the 1460s he was head of a yeshivah in Buitrago. See David, "Isaac Canpanton," 325 n. 15. At a later date he headed a yeshivah in Guadalajara, where Jacob Berab was a student. See Gross, "Yeshivot in Castile," 11–12.

181. See *Quntres ha-Semikhah,* n. 179 above, for his residence in Fez. For his move to Algeria, see Abraham Gavison, *Omer ha-Shikheḥah* (Leghorn, 1748), fol. 68v. On his relocation in Egypt, see Strauss-Ashtor, *The Jews in Egypt and Syria,* 2:470ff.; Dimitrovsky, "Yaakov Berab's Academy," 49 n. 49.

182. On the dispute, see Dimitrovsky, "Unknown Chapter," 83–105. In any event, in 1513 we find Berab serving as dayyan. He was one of two signatories on a regulation issued by the nagid's court, published by Assaf, *Texts and Studies,* 198–99.

183. Benayahu's contention that Berab was in Jerusalem as early as 1507/08 is unsubstantiated. See Benayahu, "Yosef Garson," 82–84.

184. Important data on Berab's yeshivah in Jerusalem are found in a fragmentary deed from the Cairo Geniza, MS. Cambridge, University Library Geniza Collection, T–S 8J 35, 2. Published by Assaf, *Texts and Studies,* 196. On Berab's yeshivah in Jerusalem, see Dimitrovsky, "Unknown Chapter," 109–21. On his temporary move to Egypt, see David, "Letter of Israel Ashkenazi," 113–14 (see chap. 8, sec. A for the citation); idem, "A Letter from Jerusalem," 50–51; Dimitrovsky, "Unknown Chapter," 114–17.

185. See David, "Sholal Family," 389, 408; idem, "Halakhah and Commerce," 296–97.

186. See Dimitrovsky, "Yaakov Berab's Academy," 45–48. For an extensive examination of Berab's yeshivah in Safed, see ibid., 41–102. See also chap. 12, sec. C, 1.

187. See Katz, *Halakhah and Kabbalah,* 213–36; Dimitrovsky, "New Documents Regarding the *Semicha* Controversy," 113–92. For a summation of this issue, see chap. 12, sec. E. On the practice of ordination, see Benayahu, "Revival of Ordination," 248–69.

188. A more complete version of his commentary on *Kiddushin* is found in MS. Moscow, Russian State Library, Günzburg 17 (IMHM, no. 6698). Published by G. Hassida, *Hidushei Rabenu Yaacob BeRav on the Tractate of Kidushin* (Hebrew; Jerusalem, 1981).

189. Berab's commentary is extant in manuscript: on *Sefer ha-Mada* (The Book of Knowledge)—MS. Cambridge, University Library, Add. 1179 (IMHM, no. 17045), fols. 1r–168r. Published by Y. L. Maimon, "Aqdamot Milin," *Sinai* 36 (1955): 275–357; on "The Laws of Oaths"—MS. Moscow, Russian State Library, Günzburg 322 (IMHM, no. 27966), fols. 35r–39v.

190. Some sermons have been compiled in MS. Moscow, Russian State Library, Günzburg 1055 (IMHM, no. 28070).

191. MS. London, British Library, Or. 10771 (IMHM, no. 8086).

Jacob ben Abraham Berab II

192. See Bentov, "Josef Trani," 222 n. 71. It is not clear why Bentov writes that Berab died in 1600.

193. See Joseph Caro, *Shu"t Avqat Rokhel,* no. 146. See also Benayahu, *Yosef Beḥiri,* 293–97; idem, "Revival of Ordination," 255.

194. On Jacob Berab II's ordination of his students, see ibid., 255–62, 264–66.

195. See Meir Gavison, *Responsa,* vol. 2, letter 14.

Jacob of Triel

196. On Triel, see Benayahu, "Teudah," 117–18; for the letter (mentioned below) sent by the Safed sages in 1504, see ibid., 122–25. Benayahu's contention (117) that Triel was of Spanish origin is unsubstantiated.

197. See *Quntres Ḥiddushey Dinim,* no. 80.

198. See Samuel d'Avila, *Keter Torah,* introduction.

199. For the citations of his halakhic decisions, see Benayahu, "Teudah," 117–18.

Jeremiah ben Levi Maurogonato (Mavrogonato)

200. For biographical details, see Conforte, *Qore ha-Dorot,* fol. 48v; David, "Bezalel Ashkenazi," 455; Benayahu, *Yosef Beḥiri,* 318.

201. Other family members are known to have been living in Crete in the late Middle Ages. See Artom and Cassuto, *Taqqanot Candia ve-Zikhronoteha,* 42, 156.

202. See Yeḥiel Bassan, *Responsa* (Istanbul, 1737), nos. 118, 122.

Joseph Ashkenazi

203. See Samson Back's letter from 1582, published by D. Kaufmann, "Iggerot R. Shimson Back mi-Shenot 1582, 1584," *Jerusalem Jahrbuch* 1 (1887): 145, where "R. Joseph of Verona," to be identified with Joseph Ashkenazi, is mentioned as no longer being among the living.

204. This designation was applied to Ashkenazi by Samson Back in 1582. See ibid.

205. On Ashkenazi's virulent anti-Maimonidean stance, see D. Kaufmann, "R. Josef Aschkenas, der Mischnakritiker von Safet," *MGWJ* 42 (1898): 38–46; P. Bloch, "Der Streit um den Moreh des Maimonides in der Gemeinde Posen um die Mitte des 16. Jahrhunderts," ibid. 47 (1903): 153–69, 263–79, 346–56; J. Elbaum, *Openness and Insularity: Late Sixteenth Century Jewish Literature*

in Poland and Ashkenaz (Hebrew; Jerusalem, 1990), 161–65, 295–98. Ashkenazi wrote a sixty-chapter-long treatise in answer to his opponents, whose chief protagonist was Abraham Horowitz (father of Isaiah Horowitz, "the Holy Shelah"). Excerpts from this treatise, still in manuscript, have been published by G. Scholem, who also identified its author. See Scholem, "Joseph Ashkenazi," 59–89, 201–35. A written rejoinder to Ashkenazi's virulent anti-philosophical stance has been discovered and published by E. Kupfer, "Hasagot min Ḥakham Eḥad al Divrey he-Ḥakham R. Yosef ben ha-Qadosh R. Yosef ha-Loazi she-katav ve-qara be-Qol Gadol neged ha-Rambam," *Kobeẓ al Yad,* n.s., 11 (21) (1985): 213–88. Kupfer, 221, suggests that Baruch Uziel Ḥezqito of Ferrara wrote the rejoinder. On his challenge to Maimonides' code, see I. Twersky, "R. Joseph Ashkenazi and the Mishne Tora by Maimonides" (Hebrew), *Salo Wittmayer Baron Jubilee Volume,* ed. S. Lieberman (Jerusalem, 1974), 3:183–94.

206. See Scholem, "Joseph Ashkenazi," 68.

207. For his period in Egypt, and his arrival in Safed, see Benayahu, *Toledoth ha-Ari,* 107; idem, "Bezalel Ashkenazi," 94.

208. See Z. Horowitz, "Toledot Rabbi Yosef Ashqenazi ha-'Tanna' mi-Ṣefat," *Sinai* 7 (1941): 325–28; Benayahu, "Bezalel Ashkenazi," 98–99.

209. Many of Ashkenazi's glosses and readings are cited by Solomon Adeni, *Melekhet Shelomo.* See Epstein, *Mavo,* 2:1284–85; Benayahu, "Bezalel Ashkenazi," 84, 88. On his proofreading of talmudic and midrashic texts, see ibid., 66–67, 89–91.

Joseph ben Abraham ibn Ṣayyaḥ (Ṣiyyaḥ)

210. MS. Jerusalem, Jewish National and University Library, Yah. Heb. 94 contains a prayerbook with kabbalistic commentaries copied in Jerusalem in 1518 for Ibn Ṣayyaḥ by the scribe Aaron ben Azuz. There is substantial confusion concerning Ibn Ṣayyaḥ's biography. See C. Hirschensohn, "Yediot Sefarim Kitvey Yad," 192–201, 255–59; Frumkin and Rivlin, *Ḥakhmey Yerushalayim,* 1:67–69, esp. Rivlin's notes there, 67–68.

211. MS. Jerusalem, Jewish National and University Library, Heb. 8° 416. This text has been described by Scholem, *Kitvey Yad be-Qabbalah,* 89–91, no. 33. An additional copy of this treatise is found in the manuscript collection of the Bar-Ilan University Library, MS. 598 (IMHM, no. 36544).

212. See Scholem, *Kitvey Yad be-Qabbalah,* 90–91; David, "The Office of *Nagid* in Egypt," 335–36; Shochetman, "Additional Information on Abraham Castro," 387–89.

213. MS. London, Jews College, Montefiore 318 (IMHM, no. 5262).

214. This work is otherwise unknown. See Scholem, *Kitvey Yad be-Qabbalah,* 90.

215. Autograph copy, MS. Warsaw, Jewish Historical Institute, 229 (IMHM, no. 12006; photostat 2795).

216. See Hirschensohn, "Yediot Sefarim Kitvey Yad," 193ff. for citations of his responsa in the works of his contemporaries. For his collected responsa, see MS. Jerusalem, Jewish National and University Library, Heb. 4° 1446, which has been described by Assaf, "On Various Manuscripts," 492–96. Excerpts from the responsa also appear there. A responsum relating to the dispute on whether scholars should be exempted from taxes in Jerusalem and Safed has been published by Hacker, "Payment of *Djizya,* 105–17.

Joseph ben Abraham Saragossi

217. See Benayahu, "Teudah, 114." Saragossi was eulogized by Joseph Garson. See Benayahu, "Yosef Garson," 162–64.

218. See Yaari, *Letters,* 149.

219. As per the anonymous traveler's testimony, ibid.

220. See Benayahu, "Teudah," 114; idem, "Yosef Garson," 98–99.

Joseph ben Ephraim Caro

221. For biographical details, see Werblowsky, *Joseph Caro;* A. David, "New Data on the Biography of R. Joseph Caro" (Hebrew), *Proceedings of the Tenth World Congress of Jewish Studies* (Jerusalem, 1990), Division C, 1:201–7. Caro died in Safed in 1575 at the age of eighty-seven; he was therefore born in 1488. See Conforte, *Qore ha-Dorot,* fol. 35v; Bentov, "Josef Trani," 215–16. Caro's birthplace cannot be determined with certainty. Although Toledo was formerly thought to be his birthplace, there is no tradition or evidence for his birth anywhere in Spain. Caro's putative Spanish origins have been questioned by R. J. Z. Werblowsky, *Joseph Caro,* 86, where he posits that Caro was born in Portugal. See also my article, cited above.

222. David, "Biography of Joseph Caro," 203–4.

223. MS. Cambridge, University Library, T–S Misc. 10, 80. "The pearl from Shutira [?] which we purchased through Judah was sent with R. Joseph Caro." See David, "Biography of Joseph Caro," 203–4.

224. See chap. 12, sec. C, 2 for the citations. An additional oblique reference to Caro's public activity, probably intercession with the authorities, is found in a fragmentary Geniza document, MS. Manchester, John Rylands University Library, Gaster A 852. This document appeared in the Hebrew version of this book, 216.

225. See earlier discussion on both these institutions, chap. 11 above.

226. On queries addressed to Caro, and his replies, see chap. 12, sec. C, 2.

227. See David, "Community of Cuneo," 432ff.; idem, "Biography of Joseph Caro," 206.

228. The *Beit Yosef* has yet to merit a definitive study. At present, see Benayahu, *Yosef Beḥiri,* 335–64. Caro proofread this treatise personally. Following his death, Caro's son published his father's corrections under the title *Bedek ha-Bayit* (Salonika, 1605). See Benayahu, *Yosef Beḥiri,* 351–54.

229. This important work awaits intense scholarly study. See Assis' pioneering study, "Mashehu al 'Kesef Mishneh' le-Sefer Zeraim," 275–322.

230. For a summation of Caro's extraordinary influence in the halahkhic realm, see M. Elon, *Jewish Law: History, Sources, Principle,* trans. B. Auerbach and M. J. Sykes (Philadelphia, 1994), 3:1309–1452; I. Twersky, "Ha-Rav R. Yosef Qaro Baal ha-Shulḥan Arukh," *Asufot* 3 (1989): 245–62; I. Ta-Shma, "Rabbi Joseph Caro and His *Beit Yosef,*" 192–206. One of Caro's sharpest critics was Moses Trani. See Dimitrovsky, "Dispute," 71–123; Benayahu, *Yosef Beḥiri,* 9–98.

231. This treatise has been the subject of scholarly interest. Scholars differ however as to the nature of this work. Werblowsky, *Joseph Caro,* views it as essentially kabbalistic, whereas Pachter argues for a strong ethical component. See M. Pachter, "Joseph Karo's *Maggid Mesharim* as a Book of Ethics" (Hebrew), *Daat* 21 (1988): 57–83.

232. Caro's work was intended as a companion to Yeshua ben Joseph ha-Levi's *Halikhot Olam* and was published together with this treatise (Salonika, 1598).

Joseph ben Moses Trani

233. For biographical details, see his son Moses' introduction to Joseph Trani, *Responsa* (Istanbul, 1641), pt. 1; and Trani's autobiographical notes, published by Bentov, "Joseph Trani," 195–228.

234. See David, "New Genizah Documents," 47–48, 50.

235. Bentov, "Joseph Trani," 208–10.

236. Although Joseph's son places this mission in 1600, Yaari points out that he must have meant 1599. See Yaari, *Sheluḥey Ereẓ-Yisrael,* 243–44, and n. 51. Yaari also submits that with the completion of his mission in 1604, Trani decided to settle in Aleppo. However, Trani's autobiographical notes indicate that his mission began in 1597 and that he returned to Safed in 1599, when he left for Syria and returned in that same year. See Bentov, "Josef Trani," 222, 227–28.

237. See his son's introduction to his responsa, cited earlier.

238. Tz. Leitner, ed., *Responsa and Decisions of R. Joseph Trani (Maharit)* (Hebrew; Jerusalem, 1978). In addition to responsa, Leitner published Trani's *Ṣurat ha-Bayit,* ibid., 249–89; and *Shemot Gittin,* ibid., 203–48.

239. In his autobiographical notes, Trani comments that he began to write novellae and decisions in 1586, when he was "about seventeen years old." See Bentov, "Josef Trani," 219.

240. Ibid., 221.

241. *Sefer ha-Miṣvot* is mentioned in Trani's novellae to Alfasi on *Kiddushin.* See Bentov, "Josef Trani," 212, 220. On *Nimmuqey Masekhet Negaim,* see ibid., 221. For *Ḥiddushey Sheviit,* see ibid., 222–23. On *Ḥiddushey Yebamot,* see ibid., 223.

Joseph ben Peretz Colon

242. See David, "Personalities in Jerusalem," 230–36.

243. See Yaari, *Letters,* 162–66. See also chap. 6, sec. B, n. 42.

244. See David, "Sholal Family," 389, 408.

245. See Levi ibn Ḥabib, *Responsa,* no. 25.

246. On Joseph Colon ben Moses Latif, see David, "Historical Significance," 232–33 n. 49. On the Latif family, see Kook, *Iyyunim,* 2:142–46.

Joseph Corcos

247. For biographical details, see David, "Personalities in Jerusalem," 243–48. On the date of his death, see Assis, "Mashehu al 'Kesef Mishneh' le-Sefer Zeraim," 307 n. 59.

248. *Leshonot ha-Rambam* was published by H. D. Azulay, *Quntres Ḥayyim Shaal la-Ḥida* (Leghorn, 1792). For additional information on his treatises, see David, "Personalities in Jerusalem," 244 n. 123; Assis, "Mashehu al 'Kesef Mishneh' le-Sefer Zeraim," 307–16.

Joseph ibn Tabul

249. See Scholem, "Disciples of Isaac Luria," 149 n. 35; Elior, "Kabbalists of Dr'aa," 52.

250. Concerning Ibn Tabul and his treatises, see Scholem, "Disciples of

Isaac Luria," 149–60; I. Weinstock, "Peyrush ha-Idra Rabbah le-R. Yosef ibn Tabul," *Temirin* 2 (1981): 123–67; Elior, "Kabbalists of Dr'aa," 65; Y. Avivi, "Derushey ha-Kavvanot le-Rabbi Yosef Tabul," *Studies in Memory of the Rishon Le-Zion R. Yitzhak Nissim* (Hebrew; Jerusalem, 1985), 4:75–108; idem, "The Writing of Isaac Luria," 101–5; Z. Rubin, "The Zoharic Commentaries of Joseph Ibn Tabul" (Hebrew), *Jerusalem Studies in Jewish Thought* 10 (1992): 363–87.

Joseph Iscandari

251. Jacob Berab, *Responsa,* no. 55.

252. David ibn Abi Zimra, *Responsa,* no. 596. Abi Zimra's birthdate is unknown, so we are unable to ascertain the date of his visit to Safed.

253. See Benayahu, "Teudah," 122–25.

254. See Gottheil and Worrell, *Fragments from the Genizah,* 246–59.

255. See Benayahu, "Teudah," 113 n. 26.

Joseph Sagis

256. This is attested by his student Eleazar Azikri. MS. New York, Jewish Theological Seminary Library, Mic. 3541 (ENA 74), (IMHM, no. 29346), fol. 216r. For the date of his death, see S. A. Horodezky, "R. Eliezer Azikri," in *Ṣiyyunim: Qoveṣ le-Zikhrono shel J. N. Simhoni* (Berlin, 1929), 149 n. 5.

257. See Benayahu, "Revival of Ordination," 249 n. 9; Tamar, *The Jewish People in Eretz Israel,* 80.

258. On his disciples and his colleagues, see Benayahu, "Revival of Ordination," 262.

Judah Albotini

259. In his letter, Israel Ashkenazi appends the blessing for the dead to Albotini's name. See David, "Letter of Israel Ashkenazi," 116.

260. On Joseph Ḥayyun, see Gross, *Rabbi Joseph ben Abraham Ḥayyun.*

261. Samuel d'Avila, *Keter Torah,* introduction.

262. See David, "Letter of Israel Ashkenazi," 116. See also the editor's introduction, ibid., 99, for a discussion of this passage.

263. Two parts of this work are extant in autograph. The first part (MS Moscow, Günzburg 980 [IMHM, no. 48895]) contains "Laws of the Sabbath" and was completed in Jerusalem in 1519. The second part, completed there in the same year, which contains the "Book of Women" until the middle of the fourth chapter on divorce, is found in MS. New York, Jewish Theological Seminary, Rab. 474 (IMHM, no. 37501). Excerpts from this commentary have been published by M. Benayahu, "Rabbi Yehudah ben Rabbi Moshe Albotini ve-Sifro *Yesod Mishneh Torah,*" *Sinai* 36 (1955): 240–74. The introduction was published by Maimon, *Moshe ben Maimon,* 93–97.

264. The text has been published by J. E. E. Parush, *Sefer Sullam ha-Aliyyah* (Jerusalem, 1989). See also Scholem and Beit-Arié, *Maamar Meshare Qitrin,* 15–16 n. 35.

Judah Ḥallewa

265. On his life and works in Safed, see Idel, "Yehudah Ḥallewa," 119–48. On his life in Jerusalem, see David, "Personalities in Jerusalem," 246–47; idem, "New Genizah Documents," 35–36.

266. See Joseph Caro, *Shu"t Beit Yosef,* "Laws of Divorce," no. 4.

Judah Mishan

267. See Conforte, *Qore ha-Dorot,* fol. 40v.

268. On Mishan and the kabbalistic traditions preserved in his writings and those of Ḥayyim Vital, see Scholem, "Disciples of Isaac Luria," 146–48. MS. New York, Jewish Theological Seminary, EMC. 683 (IMHM, no. 10867) contains an autograph copy of his writings where he compiled the kabbalistic traditions of Isaac Luria, Solomon Alkabetz, and Moses Cordovero. Also found in this text are three of Mishan's treatises: a kabbalistic commentary on the Passover Haggadah, a commentary on *Midrash ha-Neelam,* and one on *Raaya Meheimna* as well. See Scholem, ibid., 140, 147–48.

Kalonymus

269. Joseph Caro, *Shu"t Beit Yosef,* "Laws of Marriage Contracts," no. 14. See also David, "Ashkenazic Community in Jerusalem," *Vatiqin,* 29–30.

270. Samuel d'Avila, *Keter Torah,* introduction.

271. See David, "Ashkenazic Community in Jerusalem," *Vatiqin,* 29–30. See the citation, chap. 8, sec. A.

272. See biography no. 24, "Isaac Luria" above; David, "Halakhah and Commerce," 288.

273. Tales of his marvelous deeds, including miraculous acts, have been related throughout the generations. See Rivlin, *Ḥakhmey Yerushalayim,* 1:98–100 n. 3; T. Alexander, "The Judeo-Spanish Legend about Rabbi Kalonimus in Jerusalem—A Study of Processes of Folk-Tale Adaptation" (Hebrew), *Jerusalem Studies in Jewish Folklore* 5–6 (1984): 85–122.

274. Rivlin, *Ḥakhmey Yerushalayim,* 1:98–100 n. 3. See also Assaf, "Biography of Solomon Luria," 45–46.

Levi ben Jacob ibn Ḥabib (Ralbaḥ)

275. Ibn Ḥabib's biography has not been properly explored. The existing biographical data do not pass muster. See Frumkin and Rivlin, *Ḥakhmey Yerushalayim,* 1:38–51; Y. R. Molcho, "R. Levi Ben Ḥabib Ish Yerushalayim mi-Shomrey ha-Ḥomot," in *Ḥemdat Yisrael: Qoveṣ le-Zikhro shel Maran Ḥayyim Ḥizqiyahu Medini,* ed. A. Elmaleh (Jerusalem, 1946), 33–42. Various suggestions for Ibn Ḥabib's date of death have been tendered, but none is convincing. In any event, he was definitely no longer alive in 1549. See David, "Spanish Exiles," 88 n. 73. Concerning his conversion to Christianity, see Tishby, *Messianism,* 44–46; Hacker, "Self-Perception of Spanish Jewry," 35. For a summary of the chronology of his moves, mentioned below, see David, "Personalities in Jerusalem," 240–41; idem, "Spanish Exiles," 87–88.

276. See J. Hacker, "Rabbi Jacob b. Solomon Ibn Ḥabib—An Analysis of Leadership in the Jewish Community of Salonika in the XVIth Century" (Hebrew), *Proceedings of the Sixth World Congress of Jewish Studies* (1975), 2:117–26.

277. See Hacker, "Self-Perception of Spanish Jewry," 42–43.

278. See chap. 12, sec. E, above.

279. On this honorific, see David ibn Abi Zimra, *Responsa,* no. 1085. Sharia court documents indicate that Levi ibn Ḥabib held this office from 1533 to 1536. See Cohen, *Jewish Life under Islam,* 234 n. 16.

280. See Ibn Susan's *Ibbur Shanim,* fol. 27.

281. Levi ibn Ḥabib, *Responsa,* no. 144. A slightly different version titled *Derekh ha-Qodesh* is found in MS. Cambridge, University Library, Add. 1179 (IMHM, no. 17045), fols. 187r–196v.

282. Ibn Ḥabib's sermons are extant in two manuscripts: (1) MS. Oxford, Bodleian Library, Hunt. 412 (969) (IMHM, no. 21929), fols. 135r–141r; (2) MS. London, Montefiore Collection 14 (IMHM, no. 4537), fols. 147r–151v. Two sermons from MS. Oxford have been published by A. David, "The Sermons of R. Levi Ibn Haviv" (Hebrew), *Kiryat Sefer* 61 (1986–87): 933–35.

Malkiel Ashkenazi

283. Azulay, *Shem ha-Gedolim,* s.v. "Malkiel Ashkenazi"; David, "New Genizah Documents," 39–40.

284. See Yaari, *Massa Meshullam,* 69 (Adler, *Jewish Travellers,* 186); Artom and David, "Obadiah mi-Bertinoro," 81 (Adler, *Jewish Travellers,* 233); Basola, *Masot,* 58.

285. See chap. 2, "Hebron," above.

286. See Avivi, *Binyan Ariel,* 24.

287. In his entry for Malkiel Ashkenazi in *Shem ha-Gedolim,* Azulay notes that Isaiah Horowitz, author of *Sheney Luḥot ha-Berit,* cited Ashkenazi's treatise. This collection is located in MS. Oxford, Bodleian Library, Opp. 445 (2301) (IMHM, no. 20993), fols. 76v–81v.

288. For his textual notations on the Talmud, see Benayahu, "Bezalel Ashkenazi," 59–60. On his halakhic decisions, see Conforte, *Qore ha-Dorot,* fol. 43v. A laconic reference to Ashkenazi is found in Solomon Shlomil Meinstral of Dreznitz's letter from Safed (1607). See Yaari, *Letters,* 201.

Meir ben Samuel Back Ashkenazi

289. On this dispute, which was documented by Yom Tov Ṣahalon, *Responsa,* no. 160, see David, "The Ashkenazic Community in Jerusalem," 335–37, and the discussion above, chap. 6, sec. B.

290. Samuel d'Avila, *Keter Torah,* introduction.

291. This letter was published by A. Danon, "Shivah Mikhtavim mi-Rabbaney Yerushalayim mi-Shenat 1591–1801," *Jerusalem Jahrbuch* 7 (1906): 347–51.

Menaḥem ben Moses ha-Bavli

292. On his origins, see E. Roth, "Menaḥem Babli or Romi?" (Hebrew), *Kiryat Sefer* 31 (1955–56): 399. On his time in Greece, see A. Ben-Yaakov, "Le-Toledot Beney Bavel be-Ḥevron," in *Ḥemdat Yisrael: Qoveṣ le-Zikhro shel Maran Ḥayyim Ḥizqiyahu Medini,* ed. A. Elmaleh, 89–90; M. Benayahu, "Whence Came R. Menahem Bavli to Hebron?" (Hebrew), *Kiryat Sefer* 29 (1953–54): 173–74; idem, "Answer to E. Roth's Note: Menaḥem Babli or Romi?" (Hebrew), *Kiryat Sefer* 31 (1955–56): 399–400.

293. See Moses Trani, *Responsa,* pt. 1, no. 43.

294. This responsa was published in Joseph Caro's *Shu"t Beit Yosef,* "Laws of Divorce," no. 14.

Menaḥem de Lonzano

295. For the date of his death, see Kook, *Iyyunim,* 1:242. On his period in Jerusalem, see Frumkin and Rivlin, *Ḥakhmey Yerushalayim,* 1:134–45;

Rozen, *Jewish Community,* 176, 209–10. On the dispute with Gedaliah Cordovero and its background, see Sonne, "Shadarim," 197–204, and biography no. 20 above, "Gedaliah Cordovero." On de Lonzano's reinstatement, see Sonne, "Shadarim," 199.

296. For a bibliography of de Lonzano's published works and those still in manuscript, see Frumkin and Rivlin, *Ḥakhmey Yerushalayim,* 1:143–45. Concerning one collection of midrashim published by de Lonzano, see Kook, *Iyyunim,* 1:241–45.

297. See J. Hacker, "Agitation Against Philosophy in Istanbul in the 16th Century—Studies in Menachem de Lonsano's *Derech Ḥayyim*" (Hebrew), in *Studies in Jewish Mysticism, Philosophy, and Ethical Literature: Presented to Isaiah Tishby on His Seventy-Fifth Birthday,* ed. Y. Dan and J. R. Hacker (Hebrew; Jerusalem, 1986), 507–36.

Moses ben Abraham Berab

298. See Benayahu, "Revival of Ordination," 257, 262, 266.

299. On Berab's involvement in wool, see Moses Galante, *Responsa,* no. 43. See also M. Benayahu, "Oniyot Teunot Ṣemer ve-Khesef sheshalḥah Qehillat Qushta le-Ezratah shel Ṣefat," *Oṣar Yehudey Sefarad* 5 (1962): 102–3. On Moses Berab's involvement in leasing in Egypt, see Moses Trani, *Responsa,* pt. 3, nos. 207–9. See also Shtober, "'Customs Collectors in Egypt,'" 76–80. Berab's signature is found on a fragmentary deed in a Geniza document, MS. Manchester, John Rylands University Library, Gaster A 1390. It seems likely that the deed was issued in Egypt.

300. Cambridge, University Library, T–S Glass 16, 348.

Moses ben Ḥayyim Alshekh

301. For his biography, see S. Shalem, *Rabbi Moshe Alsheikh* (Hebrew; Jerusalem, 1966), 21; Benayahu, *Yosef Beḥiri,* 233. On Vital as his student, see Vital, *Sefer ha-Ḥezyonot* (Aescoly ed.), 2, par. c; Benayahu, "Ḥayyim Vital," 68. For the date of his death, see Bentov, "Josef Trani," 220.

302. On Alshekh as Caro's student, see Joseph Caro, *Shu"t Avqat Rokhel,* no. 73. See also Benayahu, *Yosef Beḥiri,* 233ff. For a halakhic ruling issued in Caro's name by Moses Alshekh and Elisha Gallico, see chap. 12, n. 50. For his ordination by Caro, see Benayahu, "Revival of Ordination," 255–56. We find Alshekh as a signatory to decisions handed down by Caro's court. See Ḥayyim Sitehon, *Ereṣ Ḥayyim, Yoreh Deah,* no. 123; Isaac de Lattes, *Responsa* (Vienna, 1860), pp. 16–18 (from 1562). He also gave his approval to one of Moses Trani's rulings. See Moses Trani, *Responsa,* pt. 2, no. 100.

303. Alshekh imparts this information in a responsum (see Moses Alshekh, *Responsa,* no. 84) and in the introduction to his *Rav Peninim* (Venice, 1592). See also Benayahu, *Yosef Beḥiri,* 235–36.

304. See Benayahu, "Revival of Ordination," 256, 266.

305. The date of the mission is not clear from the sources. Pachter believes that Alshekh left in 1591. See Pachter, "'Ḥazut Kasha,'" 159. Benayahu, *Yosef Beḥiri,* 241–42, makes the unfounded assertion that Alshekh left at an earlier date. This letter has been discussed above. See chap. 9. For the text of the letter, see Pachter, "'Ḥazut Kasha,'" 174–93. It is almost certain that this letter was never published. See ibid., 158 n. 6. However, we cannot entirely rule

out the possibility that this letter was published and that no copies have survived.

306. See Pachter, "'Ḥazut Kasha,'" 160.

307. For a comprehensive discussion of Alshekh's spiritual nature and his exegetical and homiletical methods, see Shalem, *Rabbi Moshe Alsheikh;* Pachter, "Homiletic and Ethical Literature," 262–93; Benayahu, *Yosef Beḥiri,* 244–55. On Alshekh as a kabbalist, see Shalem, *Rabbi Moshe Alsheikh,* 22–23; Benayahu, *Yosef Beḥiri,* 239–40.

308. For a list of Alshekh's published works, see N. Ben-Menahem's appendix to Shalem, *Rabbi Moshe Alsheikh,* 235–72. For a list of Alshekh's works, including those extant in manuscript, see Benayahu, *Yosef Beḥiri,* 244–54.

309. See Shalem, *Rabbi Moshe Alsheikh,* 24–25; Benayahu, *Yosef Beḥiri,* 253–54.

Moses ben Isaac Alashkar

310. Cf. Ṣemah and Simeon ben Solomon Duran, *Responsa, Shu"t Yakhin u-Boaz* (Leghorn, 1782), pt. 2, no. 23.

311. On his life, see Dimitrovsky, "Dispute," 117–18, 120–23; Frumkin and Rivlin, *Ḥakhmey Yerushalayim,* 1:57–59.

312. The letter and Alashkar's reply are found in MS. Vienna, Österreichische Nationalbibliothek, 111/72 (IMHM, no. 1349), fols. 200v–201v.

313. An autograph copy is located in MS. Moscow, Russian State Library, Günzburg 989 (IMHM, no. 28010). Regarding this commentary, see J. S. Spiegel, "Rabbi Moshe Alshaker's 'Geon Jacob' on Tur Orach Chaim" (Hebrew), *Tzfunot* 4 (1989): 24–30. Included in this article is Alashkar's commentary on the laws of the ninth of Av.

314. See Davidson, *Thesaurus of Mediaeval Hebrew Poetry* (Hebrew; New York, 1933), 4:443 (index).

315. This critique was included in Alashkar's *Responsa,* no. 117. See also M. Benayahu, "A New Source Concerning the Spanish Refugees in Portugal and Their Move to Saloniki" (Hebrew), *Sefunot* 11 (1971–77): 239–43.

Moses ben Jacob Cordovero (RaMaK)

316. On his birthdate, see J. Ben-Shlomo, *The Mystical Theology of Moses Cordovero,* 2d ed. (Hebrew; Jerusalem, 1986), 8; Benayahu, *Yosef Beḥiri,* 190. For the date of his death, see his son Gedaliah's concluding remarks in *Sefer Peyrush Avodat Yom ha-Kippurim* (Venice, 1587). On his family origins, see Gedaliah ibn Yaḥya, *Shalshelet ha-Qabbalah,* MS. Moscow, Russian State Library, Günzburg 652, fol. 130r. See also David, "Shivat Anusim," 197.

317. On his teacher, Solomon Alkabetz, see Cordovero's introduction to *Sefer Pardes Rimmonim* (Venice, 1586). On Joseph Caro as Cordovero's teacher, see Menaḥem Azariah Fano, introduction to *Asis Rimmonim* (Jerusalem, 1962): "His particular teacher was R. Joseph Caro of blessed memory." Cordovero himself stressed this relationship in his writings. See also Benayahu, *Yosef Beḥiri,* 190–91.

318. On his role as dayyan, see A. David, "A Legal Decision from the Court of R. Moses Cordovero in Safed" (Hebrew), *Zion* 56 (1991): 441–46. For his disciple Mordecai Dato's reference to the Portuguese yeshivah, see chap. 10, sec. C, and n. 31. See also Tishby, "Moses Cordovero," 124. On Menaḥem

Azariah Fano's allusion to Cordovero's yeshivah, see chap. 12, sec. C, 4 and n. 76. See also Benayahu, *Toledoth ha-Ari,* 178–79.

319. See Joseph Caro, *Shu"t Beit Yosef,* "Laws of Marriage Contracts," no. 2; idem, *Shu"t Avqat Rokhel,* no. 91.

320. On Dato, see Tishby, "Moses Cordovero," 119–66. For Abraham Galante, see ibid., 122 n. 13. On Moses Galante, see Tamar, *The Jewish People in Eretz Israel,* 150–51; Benayahu, *Yosef Beḥiri,* 194–95. For Luria, see Benayahu, *Toledoth ha-Ari,* 283, 286; Tamar, *Ha-Yehudim be-Ereẓ Yisrael u-ve-Arṣot ha-Mizraḥ,* 71. For Gallico, see Conforte, *Qore ha-Dorot,* fol. 42v. On De Vidas' citations of his mentor's teachings in his *Reshit Ḥokhmah,* see Tishby, "Moses Cordovero," 122 n. 13; Pachter, "Homiletic and Ethical Literature," 363, 372; idem, "'Reshit Ḥokhmah,'" 687.

321. A clearer picture of Cordovero's kabbalistic doctrine has emerged from recent studies. A representative sample can be found in Ben-Shlomo, *Mystical Theology of Moses Cordovero;* Benayahu, *Yosef Beḥiri,* 189–229; Sack, *Kabbalah of Rabbi Moshe Cordevero.*

322. See Pachter, "Homiletic and Ethical Literature," 356–62.

323. These regimen vitae were first published along with other hanhagot by Schechter, "Safed in the Sixteenth Century," 292–94. On the hanhagot of Safed's sages in general, see Hallamish, "Behavioral Mannerisms," 89–97.

Moses ben Joseph Trani (Ha-Mabbit)

324. See Moses Trani, *Responsa,* pt. 1, no. 180.

325. For biographical details, see Dimitrovsky, "Dispute," 115–17; Benayahu, introduction to Moses Trani, *Responsa,* 7–8, 10–12, 21–25 (hereafter, Benayahu, Introduction; this bibliographical unit appeared as a separate chapter in Benayahu's *Yosef Beḥiri,* 101–51; all future references will be to the first publication); the introduction to Joseph ben Moses Trani's *Ṣafenat Paaneaḥ* written by Mabbit's grandson, Moses ben Joseph Trani (Venice, 1648); Bentov, "Josef Trani," 210, 217.

326. See Benayahu, "Revival of Ordination," 249; idem, Introduction, 12.

327. On his role as a teacher in the Bet Yaakov congregation, see Moses Trani, *Responsa,* pt. 3, no 48. For the citation, see chap. 10, sec. B. See also Benayahu, Introduction, 11, 19–20. For his yeshivah, see Moses Trani, *Responsa,* pt. 2, no. 138; pt. 3, no 15. For an excerpt, see chap. 12, sec. C, 3. See also Dimitrovsky, "Yaakov Berab's Academy," 78 n. 233; Benayahu, Introduction, 17–19.

328. For Mishan, see Moses Trani, *Responsa,* pt. 2, no. 39. Mishan sent an additional query to his teacher; in this instance, however, he did not address Trani as his teacher. See Moses Trani, *Responsa,* pt. 2, no. 127. On Isaac Mishan, see Benayahu, Introduction, 18. For ha-Levi, see Moses Trani, *Responsa,* pt. 3, no. 89. Joḥanan Kaṣin was a late-sixteenth/early-seventeenth-century sage in Egypt, of whom it was said that Moses Trani "raised and taught him like a merciful father." See David, "New Genizah Documents," 47–48, 50.

329. See Moses Trani, *Responsa,* pt. 2, nos. 115 (see chap. 11 for an excerpt), 131.

330. At present, scant information is available concerning the Bet ha-Vaad. See the previous discussion in chap. 11.

331. See Dimitrovsky, "Dispute," 116–17; Bentov, "Josef Trani," 210; Benayahu, Introduction, 23–25; David, "New Genizah Documents," 47, 50.

332. For a brief treatment of this important treatise, see Benayahu, Introduction, 27–29.

333. This printed edition is very rare. See Benayahu, Introduction, 29–30. Concerning this ethical treatise, see Pachter, "Homiletical and Ethical Literature," 325–29.

334. For a discussion of this treatise, see Pachter, "Homiletical and Ethical Literature," 330–43; idem, "The Land of Israel in the Homiletic Literature of Sixteenth Century Safed" (Hebrew), in *The Land of Israel in Medieval Jewish Thought*, ed. M. Hallamish and A. Ravitzky (Hebrew; Jerusalem, 1991), 290–96.

335. On this commentary, see M. Beit-Arié, "Perek Shira: Introductions and Critical Edition" (Hebrew) (Ph.D. diss., Jerusalem, 1966), 22–24.

336. Moses Trani, *Bet Elohim*, chap. 51, fol. 102v.

337. See Pachter, "Homiletic and Ethical Literature," 341–42; C. Horowitz, "Notes on the Attitude of Moshe De Trani Toward Pietist Circles in Safed" (Hebrew), *Shalem* 5 (1987): 283–84. Even Trani's comments on the intrinsically kabbalistic book *Sefer ha-Peliah*—extant in MS. Jerusalem, Jewish National and University Library, Heb. 8° 5637, fols. 197r–v, 198r, 205r—do not conclusively indicate that he was a kabbalist. In this I differ with Benayahu, Introduction, 30–31, where, from information in Trani's notes to *Sefer ha-Peliah*, he claims "equal prowess for Trani as a kabbalist and as a halakhist."

338. Dozens of such practices were recorded by Safed kabbalists in the last quarter of the sixteenth century. These notes have been published by Shechter, "Safed in the Sixteenth Century," 292–301. Additional tikkunim and regimen vitae dating from 1577 have been published by J. M. Toledano, *Oṣar Genazim* (Jerusalem, 1960), 48–51. These takkanot and hanhagot have been reexamined by Hallamish, "Behavioral Mannerisms," 89–97. For Trani's objections, see Horowitz, "Attitude of Moshe De Trani Toward Pietist Circles," 273–84.

Moses ben Levi Najara

339. See Benayahu, *Yosef Beḥiri*, 44–45.

340. See Benayahu, "Yisrael Najara," 204.

Moses ben Mordecai Basola

341. For his biography, see R. Lamdan, "Rabbi Moshe Basola—His Life and Work" (Hebrew), (master's thesis, Tel Aviv, 1983), 74–77; idem, "'Boycott of Ancona,'" 135–54.

342. Basola's diary was edited and published by I. Ben-Zvi, *Masot Ereẓ-Yisrael le-Rabbi Moshe Basola* (Jerusalem, 1938).

343. Basola's halakhic rulings and sermons are surveyed in Lamdan, "Rabbi Moshe Basola," 78–146; idem, "Two Writings by R. Moshe Basula" (Hebrew), *Michael* 9 (1985): 171–93.

Moses ben Mordecai Galante

344. For his life, see Tamar, *Ha-Yehudim be-Ereẓ Yisrael u-ve-Arṣot ha-Mizraḥ*, 99; Benayahu, "Revival of Ordination," 255–57, 262, 266; idem, *Yosef Beḥiri*, 298–302.

345. For Caro as his mentor, see Moses Galante, *Responsa*, no. 124. See also David, "Community of Cuneo," 440; Benayahu, *Yosef Beḥiri*, 298–99. See

Caro's letter to the "the appointed officials, parnassim, and leaders of the Provençal congregation in the Piedmont," published by David, "Community of Cuneo," 432–33, 439–40. For excerpts, see chap. 10, sec. F; chap. 12, sec. C, 2.

346. This emerges from a letter sent by members of the Cuneo congregation to the heads of the Provençal yeshivah in Safed. See N. Allony and E. Kupfer, "Additional Hebrew MSS. in the 'Ambrosiana'" (Hebrew), *Aresheth* 4 (1966): 267–68; David, "Community of Cuneo," 434.

347. See Tamar, *The Jewish People in Eretz Israel,* 150–54; idem, *Ha-Yehudim be-Ereẓ Yisrael u-ve-Arṣot ha-Mizraḥ,* 31–37.

348. See Tamar, *The Jewish People in Eretz Israel,* 154–55. For additional references to Galante's interest in the kabbalistic realm, see Benayahu, *Yosef Beḥiri,* 302–4.

349. Another sermon is extant in MS. Hamburg, Staats- und Universitätsbibliothek, Levy Collection 67 (IMHM, no. 1530), fols. 2r–v.

Moses ben Shem Tov Alfaranji

350. For his life, see Benayahu, "Yosef Garson," 86–87, 169–70. (Benayahu's assertion that Alfaranji was born c. 1435 is unsubstantiated.)

351. See *Sefer ha-Qabbalah le-Rabbi Avraham ben Shelomo mi-Torrutiel,* in *Two Chronicles from the Generation of the Spanish Exile,* ed. A. David (Hebrew; Jerusalem, 1979), 30.

352. According to the testimony of Ḥayyim Gagin. See Benayahu, "Teudah," 110; idem, "Yosef Garson," 86.

353. See Benayahu, "Teudah," 122–25.

354. See David, "The Yeshiva in Jerusalem," 45, 48.

355. On Shem Tov Alfaranji, see ibid., 45, 48; Benayahu, "Teudah," 124–25; idem, "Yosef Garson," 87–88.

Moses ben Ẓaddik Castro

356. For his biography, see Dimitrovsky, "New Documents Regarding the *Semicha* Controversy," 119–20, 146; David, "Personalities in Jerusalem," 236–43; idem, "Moses Castro," 342–51.

357. See David, "Personalities in Jerusalem," 241–43.

358. See Yaari, *Letters,* 162–66.

359. In Levi ibn Ḥabib's *Quntres ha-Semikhah,* which was appended to his collected responsa, we find the reaction of both Ibn Ḥabib and Jacob Berab to Castro's responsum. The responsum itself has been published by Dimitrovsky, "New Documents Regarding the *Semicha* Controversy," 113–92. For a reexamination of this responsum, see Katz, *Halakhah and Kabbalah,* 215ff. On the *semikha* controversy, see chap. 12, sec. E above.

Moses Deleiria

360. I made this suggestion in my article, "Shivat Anusim," 197.

361. These hanhagot are included among the ones published by Schechter, "Safed in the Sixteenth Century," 299–301. Concerning these hanhagot, see Hallamish, "Behavioral Mannerisms," 89–97.

362. See David, "Jews in Mediterranean Trade," 23–28.

363. On Yehosef Deleiria, see J. S. Spiegel, ed., *Teshuvot Rabbi Yehosef mi-Leiria ve-Ḥakhmey ha-Dor bi-Ṣefat* (Jerusalem, 1988), introduction.

Moses ibn Makhir

364. See Boksenboim, *Letters of Rabbi Leon Modena,* 29–30, 208. On the yeshivah, see chap. 2 above, "Ein Zeitim."

365. See Sonne, "Shadarim," 214–17; Tamar, *Ha-Yehudim be-Ereẓ Yisrael u-ve-Arṣot ha-Mizraḥ,* 194–96; Boksenboim, *Letters of Rabbi Leon Modena,* 29–30, 208.

366. On the curriculum and method of study pursued in Makhir's yeshivah, see Meroz, "Moshe ben Makhir," 40–61. For a discussion of a parable found in Makhir's *Seder ha-Yom,* see Wineman, "Metamorphosis of Narrative Traditions," 165–71.

Peretz ben Joseph Colon

367. Yaari, *Letters,* 151–52.

368. For biographical details, see David, "Personalities in Jerusalem," 230–32.

Samson Bacchi (Back)

369. Members of the Bacchi family were active in Italy. Bacchi's origins may have been from Ashkenaz. A contemporary Jerusalem sage was named "Samson Ashkenazi," and I believe the reference is to Bacchi. See n. 374 below.

370. Two letters sent by Bacchi from Safed in 1582 are extant. See Kaufmann, "Iggerot Shimshon Back," 144–47. Scholem, "Disciples of Isaac Luria," 150, makes the unsubstantiated assertion that Bacchi's arrival in Safed can definitely be dated to 1579. In these letters, Bacchi stresses that Ibn Tabul was his teacher, calling him "R. Joseph Maghrebi."

371. This is explicitly stated in a letter sent by Bacchi from Jerusalem, first published by Kaufmann, "Iggerot Shimshon Back," 143–44, and by Yaari, *Letters,* 188–89 (see chap. 5, sec. B for an excerpt), where the date 1584 appears. In MS. Leghorn, Talmud Tora 74 (IMHM, no. 12467), 1583 appears as the date of the letter. At present, no firm determination can be made either way.

372. See Scholem, "Disciples of Isaac Luria," 155.

373. Many copies of this treatise are extant. See Scholem, "Disciples of Isaac Luria," 155–58; I. Tishby, "The Confrontation between Lurianic Kabbalah and Cordoverian Kabbalah in the Writings and Life of Rabbi Aaron Berechiah of Modena" (Hebrew), *Zion* 39 (1974): 78–79 n. 282; Avivi, "The Writing of Isaac Luria," 104.

374. MS. Oxford, Bodleian Library, Opp. 551 (1742) (IMHM, no. 17773), fol. 149r. Additional information regarding Bacchi's period of residence in Jerusalem until 1591 has been compiled by E. Rivlin. See Frumkin and Rivlin, *Ḥakhmey Yerushalayim,* 1:111. A personal letter, located in a collection of letters concerning Eretz-Israel in the seventeenth century (and perhaps earlier), addressed to "the sage R. Samson Ashkenazi, may his light shine, in Jerusalem, regarding his monetary affairs," may have been intended for Samson Bacchi. MS. Jerusalem, Jewish National and University Library, Heb. 8° 61, pp. 318–20.

Samuel ben Isaac de Uceda

375. See Scholem, "Disciples of Isaac Luria," 145; M. Pachter, "Rabbi Isaac Luria (Ha-Ari) as Portrayed in Rabbi Samuel Ucedah's Eulogy" (Hebrew), *Zion* 37 (1972): 22–40; idem, "Homiletic and Ethical Literature," 224; Tamar,

Ha-Yehudim be-Ereẓ Yisrael u-ve-Arṣot ha-Mizraḥ, 114–15. Tamar, ibid., 112–13, argues that de Uceda was not one of Luria's close disciples.

376. See Tamar, *The Jewish People in Eretz Israel,* 144–47.

377. See Pachter, "Homiletic and Ethical Literature," 225; Tamar, *Ha-Yehudim be-Ereẓ Yisrael u-ve-Arṣot ha-Mizraḥ,* 171–73.

378. MS. New York, Jewish Theological Seminary Library, L 1065 (Ad. 1613) (IMHM, no. 24267). See also Pachter, "Homiletic and Ethical Literature," 227.

379. MS. Moscow, Russian State Library, Günzburg 1054 (IMHM, no. 28014). See Pachter, "Samuel Ucedah's Eulogy," 32–33. On de Uceda as an exegete and homilist, see Pachter, "Homiletic and Ethical Literature," 227–59.

380. See E. Shochetman, "Taqqanat Ṣefat u-Teshuvot Ḥakhmey Ṣefat be-Inyan Shinui Erekh ha-Matbea," *Sinai* 82 (1978): 119–22.

Samuel Masud

381. For the chronology of his life, see Benayahu, "Teudah," 118; David, "Personalities in Jerusalem," 234, 236; Dimitrovsky, "Unknown Chapter," 106, 114, 117–20.

382. Samuel d'Avila, *Keter Torah,* introduction.

383. See David, "Personalities in Jerusalem," 234, 236; Yaari, *Letters,* 165.

384. See Frumkin and Rivlin, *Ḥakhmey Yerushalayim,* 1:60.

Simeon ben Isaac Eshenberg ha-Levi

385. This letter was published by Danon, "Shivah Mikhtavim mi-Rabbaney Yerushalayim," 347–51.

386. Yom Tov Ṣahalon, *Responsa,* no. 160. On Eshenberg, see Frumkin and Rivlin, *Ḥakhmey Yerushalayim,* 1:109; Elbaum, *Openness and Insularity,* 61–62 n. 118.

Solomon Absaban

387. Benayahu, "Revival of Ordination," 255, mentions Absaban as one of Caro's ordinees. His responsa are scattered in the works of his contemporaries. See, for example, Joseph Caro, *Shu"t Avqat Rokhel,* no. 141; Gartner, "Parashat ha-Get Tamari-Ventorozzo," 12. One of his responsa is extant in MS. London, Jews College, Montefiore Collection 116 (IMHM, no. 4629), fol. 176ff. It may have been sent by the Safed kehillah to Venice in 1591. See Pachter, "'Ḥazut Kasha,'" 161 n. 31. See also Benayahu, *Yosef Beḥiri,* 306–8. Absaban was Abulafia's teacher. See Sambari, *Divrei Yosef,* 361.

Solomon ben Jeshua Adeni (Adani)

388. Biographical details are found in Adeni's introduction to his commentary on the Mishnah, first published in the printed edition of the Mishnah (Romm, Vilna ed., 1887) See also Frumkin and Rivlin, *Ḥakhmey Yerushalayim,* 1:132–33.

389. This commentary has yet to be the subject of a comprehensive scholarly study. At present, see Epstein, *Mavo,* 2:1290; E. Z. Melamed, "Melekhet Shelomo le-R. Shelomo Adeni," *Sinai* 44 (1959): 346–63; I. Z. Feintuch, *Versions and Traditions in the Talmud* (Hebrew; Ramat Gan, 1985), 179–86; Benayahu, "Bezalel Ashkenazi," 60; Y. Ratzaby, "R. Shelomo Adeni ve-Ḥibburo Melekhet Shelomo," *Sinai* 106 (1990): 243–54.

390. The authorship of this treatise, which was characterized as a *shitah mequbbeṣet* on *Seder Kodashim*, was mistakenly attributed to Bezalel Ashkenazi in the printed editions. Solomon Adeni's authorship of this work has been correctly established by Shochetman, "'Binyan-Shlomo Lehokhmat-Bezalel,'" 63–93.

Solomon ben Joseph Sirillo

391. See Frumkin and Rivlin, *Ḥakhmey Yerushalayim*, 1:64–67; A. Samuel, "The First Commentator on the Jerusalem Talmud—On the Personality and Work of Rabbi Shelomo Serilio, an Exile from Spain" (Hebrew), *Pe'amim* 49 (1991): 35–36.

392. Samuel, "Shelomo Serilio," 32–34.

393. For the list of citations, see Frumkin and Rivlin, *Ḥakhmey Yerushalayim*, 1:64–67.

394. This letter has been published by Assaf, *Texts and Studies*, 257. See also Samuel, "Shelomo Serilio," 36.

395. Several copies of this treatise are extant, one of which apparently dates to the period when Sirillo resided in Safed. MS. Paris, Bibliothèque nationale, Heb. 1389 (IMHM, no. 26884). This commentary was published between 1934 and 1967. The commentary on tractate *Berakhot* was first published by M. Lehmann (Mainz, 1875). See Samuel, "Shelomo Serilio," 36–52.

396. See Lieberman, "Old Commentators," 301–2; M. Assis, "Le-Nusaḥ ha-Yerushalmi shel Rabbi Shelomo Sirillo be-Masekhet Sheqalim," in *Studies in Memory of the Rishon Le-Zion R. Yitzhak Nissim*, ed. M. Benayahu (Jerusalem, 1985), 2:119–59; Samuel, "Shelomo Serilio," 36–52.

397. The unpublished manuscript of this commentary is located in MS. Moscow, Russian State Library, Günzburg 1133 (IMHM, no. 28022).

Solomon ben Moses ha-Levi Alkabetz

398. For his biography, see M. Pachter, "R. Shelomo Alkabetz's Departure Sermon from Salonika to Eretz Israel" (Hebrew), *Shalem* 5 (1987): 251–55; Tamar, *Ha-Yehudim be-Ereẓ Yisrael u-ve-Arṣot ha-Mizraḥ*, 94–95; B. Sack, "The Mystical Theology of Solomon Alkabeẓ" (Hebrew; Ph.D. diss., Brandeis University, 1977), 5, 195 n. 26.

399. Alkabetz's departing sermon, delivered in Salonika, can be seen as part of this propaganda campaign for aliyah. The sermon has been published by Pachter, "Shelomo Alkabetz's Departure Sermon," 255–63.

400. Alkabetz composed various prayers, including one for redemption that he wrote following his arrival in Safed, which expresses Alkabetz's intense longing for redemption. It also singled out the massive numbers of Portuguese conversos who were then making their way to Eretz-Israel, a phenomenon Alkabetz perceived as an important stage in the process of redemption. See Werblowsky, "Solomon Alkabets," 139–42, 148–53. (Excerpts were cited in chap. 1, sec. A; chap. 10, sec. C.) On his idea of redemption as reflected in his writings, in his *Berit ha-Levi* in particular, see Sack, "*Berit halevi* of Solomon Alkabeẓ," 265–86.

401. On Alkabetz's achievements as a kabbalist and homilist, see Ben-Shlomo, *Mystical Theology of Moses Cordovero*, 264–70 and index; Sack, "Mystical Theology of Solomon Alkabeẓ"; idem, "*Berit halevi* of Solomon Alkabeẓ"; idem, "R. Solomon Alkabetz' Attitude Towards Philosophic Studies" (Hebrew),

Eshel Beer-Sheva 1 (1976): 288–306; Pachter, "Homiletic and Ethical Literature," 138–93. For a survey of his written works, see Sack, "Mystical Theology of Solomon Alkabeẓ," 6–14, 195–97, 266–67.

402. See I. J. Cohen, "The Order of the Friday Evening Service and the 'Lecho Dodi'—A Comparative Liturgreat [*sic*] Study" (Hebrew), in *The Adam Noah Braun Memorial Volume* (Jerusalem, 1969), 321–57; Sack, "Mystical Theology of Solomon Alkabeẓ," 184–91, 264–65.

403. In 1562, along with Joseph Caro's court and other disciples, Alkabetz signed one of two copies of a halakhic decision sent from Safed to Avignon. For the decision, see Isaac de Lattes, *Responsa,* pp. 17–18. Alkabetz signed the copy: "Solomon ha-Levi."

Solomon Sagis

404. See Bentov, "Josef Trani," 219.

405. See Benayahu, *Toledoth ha-Ari,* 366. There is a strong likelihood that Solomon's son Moses was the dayyan Moses Sagis who sat on Moses Cordovero's court. See David, "Legal Decision from the Court of Moses Cordovero," 442, 444–46.

406. See Benayahu, "Chiya Rophe," 109; David, "Bezalel Ashkenazi," 455.

407. See Avivi, "The Writing of Isaac Luria," 119 n. 66.

Yeḥiel Ashkenazi Castellazzo

408. For his biography, see A. David, "Mishpaḥat Castellazzo," *Sinai* 64 (1969): 283–85; idem, "Ashkenazic Community in Jerusalem," *Vatiqin,* 29.

409. See David, "Ashkenazic Community in Jerusalem," *Vatiqin,* 28–29, 31–32. (See chap. 8, sec. A for an excerpt.)

410. See David, "Mishpaḥat Castellazzo," 283–84; idem, "R. Isaac di Molina (with one of his responsa, from a MS)" (Hebrew), *Kiryat Sefer* 44 (1968–69): 555–56; Havlin, "Takkanot of Rabbenu Gershom," 226–29, 244–50.

Yom Tov ben Moses Ṣahalon

411. For a summary of Ṣahalon's biography, see Tamar, *Ha-Yehudim be-Ereẓ Yisrael u-ve-Arṣot ha-Mizraḥ,* 26ff.; J. S. Spiegel, introduction to *Sheelot u-Teshuvot Maharit Ṣahalon ha-Ḥadashot* (Jerusalem, 1980), 1:13–31 (hereafter: Spiegel, introduction).

412. See Benayahu, "Revival of Ordination," 257, 266.

413. This work is still in manuscript and is located in MS. Oxford, Bodleian Library, Heb. C. 24 (2635) (IMHM, no. 22679). On this treatise, which Ṣahalon wrote when he was seventeen, see Spiegel, introduction, 1:17–18.

414. Ṣahalon wrote this treatise when he was eighteen. See Tamar, *Ha-Yehudim be-Ereẓ Yisrael u-ve-Arṣot ha-Mizraḥ,* 26–31; Spiegel, introduction, 1:18–19.

415. For a detailed description of the collection, see Spiegel, introduction, 1:21–31.

416. Ibid., 1:23–24.

Glossary

aliyah (pl. **aliyot**) — immigration or a series of waves of immigration to Eretz-Israel.

Ashkenaz — Germany.

Ashkenazim — Jews originating from Germany and the nearby lands.

asper — a Turkish coin.

av bet din — head of the rabbinic court.

bet din — a rabbinic court of law.

Bet ha-Vaad — umbrella organization that administered the Safed kehillah.

bet midrash — school for higher rabbinic learning, often attached to a synagogue.

conversos — Spanish and Portuguese Jews who adopted Christianity in public but continued to practice Judaism in secret.

dayyan — a rabbi qualified to serve as a judge on a rabbinic court.

defterdar — provincial director of finances in the Ottoman Empire.

dhimmi/ahl-al-dhimma — the unenslaved population that does not embrace Islam in a country under Muslim conquest, subject to special taxes and restrictions (essentially, Jews and Christians).

firman — a decree, mandate, order, license, or grant issued by the ruler of an Oriental country.

gabbai — synagogal official.

gaon (pl. **geonim**) — outstanding talmudical scholar.

Geniza — the Cairo Geniza, a storeroom for old and defective books and documents in the synagogue in Fustat.

ḥakham sage; rabbi.

halakhah the legal side of Judaism that embraces personal, social, national, and international relationships, as well as the practices and observances of Judaism.

hanhagot regimen vitae, conduct literature.

haskamah (pl. **haskamot**) agreement to accept or renew a regulation (see **takkanah**).

ḥaver(im) title given to the mature sages who studied in the rabbinical academy.

ḥavurah/ḥavurot societies founded for a specific purpose.

hekdesh/hekdeshot dedication of property for a charitable purpose.

ḥerem excommunication.

jizya (**djizya**) poll tax levied by the Ottoman authorities on the dhimmi.

kabbalah Jewish mysticism.

kadi Muslim judge who interprets and administers the religious law of Islam.

kahal/kehalim congregation; or group bound by a common land or area of origin; for example, a community of Sefardim, Ashkenazim, Moriscos, as well as smaller subdivisions based on town of origin.

ḳānūn Islamic civil law.

kehillah (pl. **kehillot**) the organized Jewish community of a city, overseeing the administration of communal affairs.

ketubbah marriage contract.

khafar (**ghafar**) toll or protection tax levied on dhimmi at various checkpoints.

kohen (pl. **kohanim**) individual of priestly descent.

kolel the overall administration of the Safed kehillah.

liwā see **sanjak.**

Maghrebis Jews of North African origin.

melammed (pl. **melamdim**) teacher of young children.

memunim	the appointed congregational officials in Safed.
Musta'rabim	Moriscos; local Jews of Oriental origin.
nagid	title applied in Muslim countries in the Middle Ages to a leader recognized by the state as head of the Jewish community.
parnassim	congregational functionaries, elected lay leaders.
pasha	provincial governor.
piyyut	liturgical poem.
pesak(im)	a halakhic decision handed down by a rabbi.
posek(im)	decisor; codifier or rabbinic scholar who pronounces decisions in disputes and on questions of Jewish law.
rishonim	older rabbinic authorities; the early commentators on the Talmud.
sanjak	a district; Ottoman administrative unit.
Sefardim	Jews originating from the Iberian peninsula.
sefirah (pl. **sefirot**)	mystical term denoting the ten spheres or emanations through which the Divine manifests itself.
shadar(im)	rabbinic emissary sent to collect funds for Eretz-Israeli communities.
sharia	the body of formally established sacred law in Islam, governing not only religious but also political, economic, civil, criminal, ethical, social, and domestic affairs.
Shavuot	Pentecost; Feast of Weeks. Second of the three annual pilgrim festivals, it commemorates the receiving of the Torah at Mt. Sinai.
shaykh al-yahud	elder of Jews; official representative of the Jerusalem Jewish community to the Ottoman authorities.
shekhinah	presence of God in the world, often apprehended by a personal mystical experience.
Shu"t- Sheelot u-Teshuvot	responsa. Written opinions given to questions on aspects of Jewish law by qualified

	authorities; collections of such queries and opinions in book form.
sijill	records of a kadi's court sentences.
Sukkot	Feast of Booths (or Tabernacles). Last of the three pilgrim festivals.
sürgün	Ottoman policy of transfer of population groups.
taḥrir registers	the Ottoman records of the data collected by commissions sent to survey the tax-paying population, lands, crops, and revenues in the towns and villages for fiscal purposes.
takkanah (pl. **takkanot**)	regulation supplementing the Law of the Torah; regulations governing the internal life of communities and congregations.
Talmud Torah	Jewish school for youths.
tanna	rabbinic teacher of the Mishnaic period; epithet occasionally applied to later authorities as an honorific.
tikkun(im)	("restitution," "reintegration"). Order of service for certain occasions, recited mostly at night; mystical term denoting the restoration of the right order and true unity after the spiritual "catastrophe" that occurred in the cosmos.
Tikkun Leil Shavuot	custom of staying awake on the night of Shavuot in order to study Torah, introduced in sixteenth-century Safed.
waqf	an Islamic endowment of property to be held in trust and used for a charitable or religious purpose.
yeshivah (pl. **yeshivot**)	Traditional Jewish academy primarily devoted to the study of the Talmud and rabbinic literature.
yishuv	the Jewish settlement in Eretz-Israel.

Bibliography

This bibliography contains three sections: primary sources, secondary sources, and manuscript collections. Boldface has been used to indicate the short titles used for works that appear repeatedly in the notes. These short titles appear after the appropriate entries. Whereas English title pages were used in the notes and for the short titles, all references to Hebrew works in the bibliography have been provided in transliteration alone.

PRIMARY SOURCES

Abraham Azulay. *Or ha-Ḥamah.* Jerusalem, 1876.

Abraham Gavison. *Omer ha-Shikheḥa.* Leghorn, 1748.

Abraham Zacuto. *Sefer Yuḥasin ha-Shalem.* 2d edition. Edited by A. H. Freimann. Jerusalem, 1963.

Artom, M. E., and A. David. "R. Ovadyah mi-Bertinoro ve-Igrotav me-Ereẓ Yisrael." In *Jews in Italy: Studies Dedicated to the Memory of U. Cassuto,* edited by H. Beinart, 24–108. Jerusalem, 1988. (Reprint: *Me-Italyah li-Yerushalayim: Iggerotav shel R. Ovadyah me-Bertinoro me-Ereẓ Yisrael.* Ramat Gan, 1997).

Artom and David, "Obadiah mi-Bertinoro"

Azariah de Rossi. *Meor Einayim.* 2d edition. Jerusalem, 1970.

Azulay, Ḥayyim Joseph David. *Shem ha-Gedolim.* Jerusalem, 1960.

Azulay, *Shem ha-Gedolim*

Basola, Moshe. *Masot Ereẓ-Yisrael le-Rabbi Moshe Basola.* Edited by I. Ben-Zvi. Jerusalem, 1938.

Basola, *Masot*

Benjamin ben Abraham Motal. Introduction to *Tummat Yesharim* by Tam ibn Yaḥya. Venice, 1622.

Biddulph, W. *Travel into Africa, Asia, and to the Blacke Sea.* London, 1619. Reprint, Da Capo Press: Amsterdam, New York, 1968.

Boksenboim, Y., ed. *Iggerot Melamdim: Italyah 1555–1591.* Tel Aviv, 1985.

Boksenboim, *Letters of Jewish Teachers*

———. *Iggerot Rabbi Yehudah Aryeh mi-Modena.* Tel Aviv, 1984.

Boksenboim, *Letters of Rabbi Leon Modena*

Bonifacio Stefani Ragusino. *Liber de Perenni Cultu Terrae Sanctae.* Venice, 1875.

David, A., ed. "Iggeret R. Yisrael Ashqenazi mi-Yerushalayim le-Rabbi Avraham mi-Perusha." *Alei Sefer* 16 (1990): 95–122.

David, "Letter of Israel Ashkenazi"

David Conforte. *Qore ha-Dorot.* Berlin, 1846.

Duff, E. G., ed. *Information for Pilgrims unto the Holy Land.* London, 1893.

Eleazar ben Moses Azikri. *Sefer Ḥaredim.* Venice, 1601.

Elijah Capsali. *Seder Eliyahu Zuta.* 2 vols. Edited by A. Shmuelevitz, S. Simonsohn, and M. Benayahu. Jerusalem, 1976–77.

Elisha Gallico. *Peyrush le-Qohelet.* Venice, 1578.

Gedaliah ben Moses Cordovero. Introduction to *Peyrush Avodat Yom ha-Kippurim* by Moses Cordovero. Venice, 1587.

Gedaliah ibn Yaḥya. *Shalshelet ha-Qabbalah.* MS. Russian State Library, Günzburg 652. Printed edition, Venice, 1587.

Gottheil, R., and W. H. Worrell. *Fragments from the Cairo Genizah in the Freer Collection.* New York, 1927.

Gottheil and Worrell, *Fragments from the Genizah*

Ḥayyim Sitehon. *Sefer Ereṣ Ḥayyim.* Jerusalem, 1908.

Ḥiyya Rofe. *Maaseh Ḥiyya.* Venice, 1652.

Isaac ben Abraham Akrish, compiler. Introduction to *Sheloshah Peyrushim le-Shir ha-Shirim.* Constantinople, 1575(?).

Isaac ben Abraham ibn Latif. *Rav Pealim.* Edited by S. Schönblum. Lemberg, 1885.

Israel Isserlein. *Pesaqim u-Khetavim.* Venice, 1519.

Issachar ibn Susan. *Ibbur Shanim.* Venice, 1579.

———. Introduction to *Al-Sharḥ al-Susani.* MS. London, British Library, Or. 14020a.

———. *Tiqqun Yissakhar.* Istanbul, 1564.

Joseph ha-Kohen. *Divrey ha-Yamim le-Malkhey Ṣorfat u-Malkhey beyt Ottoman ha-Tugar.* Vols. 1–2. Sabbioneta, 1554.

Joseph ha-Kohen, *Divrey ha-Yamim*

———. *Emeq ha-Bakha.* Edited by K. Almbladh. Uppsala, 1981.

———. *Vale of Tears.* Translated by H. S. May. The Hague, 1971.

Judah Albotini. *Sullam ha-Aliyyah.* Edited by J. E. E. Parush. Jerusalem, 1989.

Judah Aryeh Modena. *Ari Nohem.* Edited by N. S. Libowitz. Jerusalem, 1929.

Menaḥem Azariah Fano. Introduction to *Asis Rimmonim.* Jerusalem, 1962.

Moses Alshekh. *Rav Peninim.* Venice, 1592.

Moses ibn Makhir. *Seder ha-Yom.* Venice, 1599.

Moudjir-ed-dyn. *Histoire de Jérusalem et d'Hebron.* Translated by H. Sauvaire. Paris, 1876.

Naftali ben Joseph ha-Kohen. *Imrey Shefer.* Venice, 1601.

Quntres Ḥiddushey Dinim mi-Rabbaney Ir Qodshenu Yerushalayim. Appended to *Ḥayyim va-Ḥesed,* by Ḥayyim Musaphia. Pt. 1. Leghorn, 1844.

Quntres *Ḥiddushey Dinim*

Rabbi Yisrael di-Quriel: Derashot u-Maamarim. Edited by S. Regev. Jerusalem, 1992.

Rozen, M., ed. *Ḥorvot Yerushalayim.* Tel Aviv, 1981.

Rozen, *The Ruins of Jerusalem*

Sambari, Joseph. *Sefer Divrei Yosef le-R. Yosef ben Yitzḥak Sambari.* Edited by S. Shtober. Jerusalem, 1994.

Sambari, *Divrei Yosef*

Samuel d'Avila. *Keter Torah.* Amsterdam, 1725.

Samuel de Uceda. *Iggeret Shemuel.* Kuru-Chesme, 1597.

——. *Leḥem Dimah.* Venice, 1605.

Sanderson, John. *The Travels of John Sanderson in the Levant, 1584–1602.* Edited by W. Foster. London, 1931.

Schepansky, I. *Ereẓ-Yisrael be-Sifrut ha-Teshuvot.* 2 vols. Jerusalem, 1966–68.

Schepansky, *Eretz Israel in the Responsa Literature*

Solomon Adeni. *Melekhet Shelomo.* (Mishnah, Romm edition, Vilna, 1887).

Solomon Atiyah. Introduction to *Peyrush le-Tehillim.* Venice, 1549.

Tshelebi, Evliya. *Evliya Tshelebi's Travels in Palestine (1648–1650).* Translated by St. H. Stephan. Jerusalem, 1980.

Vital, Ḥayyim. *Sefer ha-Ḥezyonot.* Edited by A. Z. Aescoly. Jerusalem, 1954.

Vital, *Sefer ha-Ḥezyonot*

Yaari, A., ed. *Iggerot Ereẓ-Yisrael.* 2d edition. Ramat Gan, 1971.

Yaari, *Letters*

——. *Masot Ereẓ Yisrael shel Olim Yehudim.* 2d edition. Ramat Gan, 1976.

Yaari, *Masot*

——. *Massa Meshullam mi-Volterra be-Ereẓ Yisrael.* Jerusalem, 1949.

Yaari, *Massa Meshullam*

Yellinek, A. *Quntres Gezeyrot Tatnu.* Leipzig, 1854.

Zacharia al-Dahri (Zechariah al-Ḍāhiri). *Sefer Hammusar.* Edited by Y. Ratzaby. Jerusalem, 1965.

RESPONSA LITERATURE

(Unless the collection has a specific title, responsa are cited in the notes under the author's name, *Responsa,* and the number. The abbreviation *Shu"t* stands for *Sheelot u-Teshuvot.*)

Bezalel Ashkenazi. *Sheelot u-Teshuvot.* Jerusalem, 1968.

David ibn Abi Zimra. *Sheelot u-Teshuvot.* Warsaw, 1882.

——. *Shu"t ha-Radbaz.* Part 8. Bnei-Brak, 1975.
Elijah ibn Ḥayyim. *Sheelot u-Teshuvot.* Istanbul, n.d.
Elijah Mizraḥi. *Sheelot u-Teshuvot.* Jerusalem, 1984.
Elijah Mizraḥi, and Elijah ibn Ḥayyim. *Mayyim Amuqim.* Berlin, 1778.
Isaac de Lattes. *Sheelot u-Teshuvot.* Vienna, 1860.
Jacob Berab. *Sheelot u-Teshuvot.* Jerusalem, 1958.
Jacob Castro. *Shu"t Ohaley Yaaqov.* Leghorn, 1783.
Joseph Caro. *Shu"t Avqat Rokhel.* Jerusalem, 1960.
——. *Shu"t Beit Yosef.* Jerusalem, 1987.
Joseph Trani. *Sheelot u-Teshuvot.* Istanbul, 1641.
——. *Teshuvot u-Pisqey Maharit ha-Ḥadashim.* Edited by Tz. Leitner. Jerusalem, 1978.
Joshua Ṣunṣin. *Naḥalah li-Yehoshua.* Istanbul, 1731.
Levi ibn Ḥabib. *Sheelot u-Teshuvot.* Venice, 1565.
Meir Gavison. *Sheelot u-Teshuvot.* Edited by E. Shochetman. 2 vols. Jerusalem, 1985.
Moses Alashkar. *Sheelot u-Teshuvot.* Jerusalem, 1988.
Moses Alshekh. *Sheelot u-Teshuvot.* Venice, 1605.
Moses Galante. *Sheelot u-Teshuvot.* Jerusalem, 1988.
Moses Trani. *Sheelot u-Teshuvot.* Lvov, 1861.
Samuel de Medina. *Sheelot u-Teshuvot.* Lvov, 1862.
Ṣemah Duran and Simeon ben Solomon Duran. *Shu"t Yakhin u-Boaz.* Leghorn, 1782.
Sheelot u-Teshuvot Zera Anashim. Edited by D. Frankel. Husiatyn, 1910.
Yom Tov Ṣahalon. *Sheelot u-Teshuvot.* Venice, 1694.
——. *Sheelot u-Teshuvot Maharit ha-Ḥadashot.* 2 vols. Edited by J. Buksbaum, M. Ben-Shimon, M. Rubinstein. Jerusalem, 1980–81.

SECONDARY SOURCES

(Entries with asterisks are collections of articles.)

Adler, E. N. *Jewish Travellers.* 2d edition. New York, 1966.
Aescoly, A. Z., ed. *Sefer ha-Ḥezyonot,* by Ḥayyim Vital. Jerusalem, 1954.
——. *Sippur David ha-Reuveni.* Jerusalem, 1940.
Albuquerque, L., ed. *Almanach Perpetuum De Abraão Zacuto.* Lisbon, 1986.
Alexander, T. "Ha-Aggadah ha-Sefaradit ha-Yehudit al Rabbenu Kalonymus bi-Yerushalayim—Le-Ḥeqer Darkhey Histaglut shel ha-Sippur ha-Amami." *Meḥqarey Yerushalayim be-Folqlor Yehudi* 5–6 (1984): 85–122.
Allony, N., and E. Kupfer. "Kitvey Yad Ivriyyim Nosafim be-'Ambrosiana' be-Milano shelo nikhlelu bi-Reshimat Bernheimer." *Aresheth* 4 (1966): 234–70.
Ammar, Z. "Hearot al ha-Ṣomeah ve-ha-Ḥaklaut shel Ereẓ Yisrael ba-Tequfah

ha-Mamlukit." In *Ereẓ Yisrael ba-Tequfah ha-Mamlukit,* edited by J. Drory, 220–36. Jerusalem, 1992.

Ankori, Z., ed. *Mi-Lisbon le-Saloniqi ve-Qushta.* Tel Aviv, 1988.

Arbel, B. "Abraham Castro Multiplied: Venetian Traders and Jewish Customs Farmers in the Levant." In *Trading Nations: Jews and Venetians in Early Modern Mediterranean,* by B. Arbel, 28–54. Leiden, 1995.

Arce, A. "Restricciones impuestas a los judíos en Jerusalén (1534)." *Sefarad* 17 (1957): 49–72. Published in Hebrew, "Hagbalot al Ḥofesh Tenuatam shel Yehudey Yerushalayim be-Shalhey Yemey ha-Mamlukim u-ve-Reshit ha-Tequfah ha-Ottmanit," in B. Z. Kedar, *Peraqim be-Toledot Yerushalayim bi-Yemey ha-Beynayyim* (Jerusalem, 1979), 206–20.

Artom, E. S., and M. D. Cassuto. *Taqqanot Candia ve-Zikhronoteha.* Jerusalem, 1943.

Artom, M. E. "Reshimat Masa Italqit me-ha-Meah ha-15." *Italy,* ed. M. A. Szulwas. Vol. 1 (1945): 21–23.

Ashtor, E. "Europäischer Handel im Spätmittelalterlichen Palästina." In *Das Heilige Land im Mittelalter,* ed. W. Fischer and J. Schneider, 107–26. Neustadt a. d. Aisch, 1982.

——. "Yerushalayim bi-Yemey ha-Beynayyim ha-Meuḥarim." *Yerushalayim (Meḥqarey Ereẓ Yisrael)* 2/5 (1955): 71–116.
Ashtor, "Jerusalem in the Late Middle Ages"

——. "The Venetian Supremacy in Levantine Trade: Monopoly or Pre-Colonialism?" *Journal of European Economic History* 3 (1974): 5–53.

——. "Venezia e il pellegrinaggio in Terrasanta nell basso Medioevo." *Archivio Storico Italiano* 143 (1985): 197–223.
Ashtor, "Venezia"

——. "Die Verbreitung des englischen Wolltuches in den Mittelmeerländern im Spätmittelalter." *Vierteljahrschrift für Sozial und Wirtschaftgeschichte* 71 (1984): 1–29.

Assaf, S., *Be-Ohaley Yaaqov.* Jerusalem, 1943.

——. "Mashehu le-Toledot Maharshal." In *Louis Ginzberg Jubilee Volume,* ed. S. Lieberman et al., Hebrew section, 45–63. New York, 1946.
Assaf, "Biography of Solomon Luria"

——. "Iggerot mi-Ṣefat." *Kobeẓ al Yad,* n.s., 3 (13) (1939): 113–42.
Assaf, "Iggerot mi-Ṣefat"

——. "Le-Toledot Beyt ha-Keneset al Qivro shel Shmuel ha-Navi." *BJPES* 6 (1939): 141–42.

——. "Al Kitvey Yad Shonim." *Kiryat Sefer* 11 (1935): 492–98.
Assaf, "On Various Manuscripts"

*——. *Meqorot u-Meḥqarim be-Toledot Yisrael.* Jerusalem, 1946.
Assaf, *Texts and Studies*

Assis, M. "Le-Nusaḥ ha-Yerushalmi shel Rabbi Shelomo Sirillo be-Masekhet Sheqalim." In *Sefer Zikkaron le-ha-Rav Yiṣḥak Nissim,* ed. M. Benayahu, 2:119–59. Jerusalem, 1985.

——. "Mashehu al 'Kesef Mishneh' le-Sefer Zeraim ve-al Nusaḥ Sefer Zeraim shel Mefarshey ha-Rambam bi-Zemano shel Maran." *Asufot* 3 (1989): 275–322.

Assis, "Mashehu al 'Kesef Mishneh' le-Sefer Zeraim"

Avitsur, S. "Ṣefat Merkaz le-Taasiyat Arigey Ṣemer ba-Meah ha-15 [should read ha-16]." *Sefunot* 6 (1962): 41–69.

Avitsur, "Safed"

Avivi, J. *Binyan Ariel: Mavo Derushey ha-Elohi Rabbi Yiṣḥak Luria.* Jerusalem, 1987.

Avivi, *Binyan Ariel*

——. "Derushey ha-Kavvanot le-Rabbi Yosef ibn Tabul." In *Sefer Zikkaron le-ha-Rav Yiṣḥak Nissim,* ed. M. Benayahu, 4:75–108. Jerusalem, 1985.

——. "Kitvey ha-Ari be-Italyah ad Shnat 1620." *Alei Sefer* 11 (1984): 91–134.

Avivi, "The Writing [sic] of Isaac Luria"

Ayalon, D. "Ha-Ṣava ha-Mamluki be-Reshit ha-Kibbush ha-Ottmani." *Tarbiẓ* 23 (1952): 221–26.

Baer, Y. "Al *Sippur David ha-Reuveni* le-A. Z. Aescoly" (review article). *Kiryat Sefer* 17 (1940): 302–12.

——. "Ha-Tenuah ha-Meshiḥit bi-Sefarad bi-Tequfat ha-Geyrush." *Zion (Me'asef)* 5 (1933): 61–77.

Balog, P. *The Coinage of the Mamluk Sultans of Egypt and Syria.* New York, 1964.

Barkan, O. L. "The Price Revolution of the Sixteenth Century: A Turning Point in the Economic History of the Near East." *IJMES* 6 (1975): 3–28.

Baron, S. W. "Solomon Ibn Yaish and Sultan Suleiman the Magnificent." In *Joshua Finkel Festschrift,* ed. S. B. Hoenig and L. D. Stitskin, 29–36. New York, 1974.

Bashan, E. "Ha-Aliyot mi-Saloniqi le-Ereẓ Yisrael ba-Meot ha-16–ha-18." In *Yehudey Yavan le-Dorotham,* ed. Z. Ankori, 73–83. Tel Aviv, 1984.

——. *Shivyah u-Fedut ba-Ḥevrah ha-Yehudit be-Arṣot ha-Yam ha-Tikhon (1391–1830).* Jerusalem, 1980.

Bashan, *Captivity and Ransom*

——. "Ḥayyey ha-Kalkalah ba-Meot ha-16–ha-18." In *Toledot Yehudey Miṣrayim ba-Tequfah ha-Ottmanit,* ed. J. M. Landau, 63–112. Jerusalem, 1988.

Bashan, "Economic Life from the 16th to 18th Century"

——. "Ha-Mashber ha-Medini ve-ha-Kalkali ba-Imperiyah ha-Ottmanit haḥel ba-Shlish ha-Aḥaron shel ha-Meah ha-16 le-or Sifrut ha-Shu"t." *Proceedings of the Sixth World Congress of Jewish Studies,* 2:107–15. Jerusalem, 1975.

——. "Shemot Arey Ereẓ Yisrael ke-Kinuyyim le-Arim be-Ḥu"l be-Sifrut ha-Shu"t shel ha-Tequfah ha-Ottmanit." *Bar-Ilan* 12 (1974): 137–65.

——. "Teudah mi-Shenat [5]384 al ha-Vikuaḥ bi-Devar Halvaah la-Noṣrim bi-Yerushalayim." In *Peraqim be-Toledot ha-Yishuv ha-Yehudi bi-Yerushalayim,* ed. M. Friedman, B. Z. Yehoshua, and Y. Tobi, 2:77–96. Jerusalem, 1976.

Bat Yeor. *The Dhimmi: Jews and Christians under Islam.* Rutherford, New Jersey, c. 1985.

Beckingham, C. F. "Pantaleao de Aveiro and the Ethiopian Community in Jerusalem." *Journal of Semitic Studies* 7 (1962): 325–38.

Beeri, T. "'Olat Ḥodesh' le-Rabbi Yisrael Najara—Nosim u-Tekhanim." *Asufot* 4 (1990): 311–24.

Beeri, "'Olat Ḥodesh'"

——. "Ha-Yesodot ha-Sefaradiyyim be-Shirat R. Yisrael Najara." *Pe'amim* 49 (1991): 54–67.

Beinart, H. "Fez—Merkaz le-Giyur u-le-Shivat Anusim la-Yahadut ba-Meah ha-16." *Sefunot* 8 (1964): 319–34.

——. "Iggron Ivri mi-Sefarad min ha-Meah ha-15." *Sefunot* 5 (1961): 75–134.

Beit-Arié, M. "Kitvey Yad Ivriyyim shehuatqu bi-Yerushalayim o al yedey Yoṣey Yerushalayim ad ha-Kibbush ha-Ottmani." In *Peraqim be-Toledot Yerushalayim bi-Yemey ha-Beynayyim,* ed. B. Z. Kedar, 244–78. Jerusalem, 1979.

——. "*Pereq Shirah:* Mevoot u-Mahadurah Biqortit." Ph.D. diss., Jerusalem, 1966.

Beit-Arié, M., and M. Idel. "Maamar al ha-Qeṣ ve-ha-Iṣtagninut me-et R. Avraham Zakut." *Kiryat Sefer* 54 (1979): 174–94, 825–26.

Beit-Arié and Idel, "Treatise by Abraham Zacut"

Beit-Arié, M., and C. Sirat. *Manuscrits Médiévaux en Caractères Hébraïques.* Part One. Jerusalem and Paris, 1972.

Ben-Menaḥem, N. "Iggeret R. Yiṣḥak b. R. Meir Latif mi-Yerushalayim." *Sinai* 53 (1963): 258–62.

Ben-Sasson, H. H. "Galut u-Geulah be-Eynav shel Dor Goley Sefarad." In *Sefer Yovel le-Yiṣḥak Baer,* ed. S. W. Baron et al., 216–27. Jerusalem, 1960.

——. "The Reformation in Contemporary Eyes." *Proceedings of the Israel Academy of Sciences and Humanities* 4 (1970): 260–70.

Ben-Shlomo, J. *Torat ha-Elohut shel R. Moshe Cordovero.* 2d edition. Jerusalem, 1986.

Ben-Shlomo, *Mystical Theology of Moses Cordovero*

Ben-Yaakov, A. "Le-Toledot Beney Bavel be-Ḥevron." In *Ḥemdat Yisrael: Qoveṣ le-Zikhro shel Maran Ḥayyim Ḥizqiyahu Medini,* ed. A. Elmaleh, 89–90. Jerusalem, 1946.

Ben-Zvi, I. *Ereẓ Yisrael ve-Yishuvah taḥat ha-Shilton ha-Ottmani.* 2d edition. Jerusalem, 1967.

Ben-Zvi, *Eretz-Israel under Ottoman Rule*

——. "Meṣudat ha-Yehudim ba-Meah ha-16 ve-ha-Qesariya she-bi-Ṣefat." *BJPES* 10 (1942–43): 113–16.
Ben-Zvi, "The Jewish Fortress in Safed"
——. *Shear Yashuv.* Jerusalem, 1967.
Ben-Zvi, *Remnants of Ancient Jewish Communities*
*——. *Meḥqarim u-Meqorot.* Jerusalem, 1967.
Ben-Zvi, *Studies and Documents*
——. "Yishuv Yehudi le-Yad Qever Shmuel ha-Navi." *BJPES* 10 (1942–43): 12–18.
Ben-Zvi, "Tomb of the Prophet Samuel"
——, ed. *Masot Ereẓ-Yisrael le-Rabbi Moshe Basola.* Jerusalem, 1938.
Benayahu, M. "Hagahoteyhem she-le-Rabbi Beṣalel Ashqenazi ve-Rabbi Yehosef Ashqenazi ve-Tofes ha-Av Shelahem." *Asufot* 1 (1987): 47–104.
Benayahu, "Bezalel Ashkenazi"
——. "Rabbi Ḥiyya Rofe ve-Sifro 'Maaseh Ḥiyya.'" *Aresheth* 2 (1960): 109–29.
Benayahu, "Chiya Rophe"
——. "He-Hagut she-be-Peyrushey ha-Megillot le-Rabbi Elisha Gallico." *Asufot* 4 (1990): 73–98.
Benayahu, "Elisha Gallico"
——. "Le-Toledot R. Gedalyah Cordovero." *Sinai* 16 (1945): 82–90.
Benayahu, "Gedalyah Cordovero"
——. "Hagahot Mishneh Torah min ha-Tofes she-la-Rambam ve-Hagahot hameyuḥasot le-Rabbi Beṣalel Ashqenazi ve-ha-Ari." *Sinai* 100 (1987): 135–42.
——. "Halvaat Kesafim be-Ribit le-Minzarim bi-Yerushalayim." *Yerushalayim: Rivon le-Ḥeqer Ereẓ-Yisrael* 1 (1948): 86–88, 221.
——. "R. Ḥayyim Vital bi-Yerushalayim." *Sinai* 30 (1952): 65–75.
Benayahu, "Ḥayyim Vital"
——. Historical Introduction to *Rabbi Yisrael di Quriel: Derashot u-Maamarim.* Edited by S. Regev. Jerusalem, 1992.
——. Introduction to the facsimile edition of *Rabbi Moshe Trani, Sheelot u-Teshuvot.* Venice, 1629–30. Jerusalem, 1990.
Benayahu, Introduction to Moses Trani, *Responsa*
——. "Hanhagot Mequbbaley Ṣefat be-Meyron." *Sefunot* 6 (1962): 9–40.
Benayahu, "Kabbalists of Safed in Meron"
——. "Maqor al Megorashey Sefarad be-Portugal ve-Ṣetam aḥarey Gezeyrot 1506 le-Saloniqi." *Sefunot* 11 (1971–77): 231–65.
——. "Me-Heykhan Ba Rabbi Menaḥem ha-Bavli le-Ḥevron?" *Kiryat Sefer* 29 (1953–54): 173–74. Ibid., 31 (1955–56): 399–400.
——. "Oniyot Teunot Ṣemer ve-Khesef sheshalḥah Qehillat Qushta le-Ezratah shel Ṣefat." *Oṣar Yehudey Sefarad* 5 (1962): 101–8.
——. "R. Shmuel Barzani Rosh Golat Kurdistan." *Sefunot* 9 (1964): 21–125.
——. "Rabbi Yehudah ben Rabbi Moshe Albotini ve-Sifro *Yesod Mishneh Torah.*" *Sinai* 36 (1955): 240–74.

——. "Ḥidushah shel ha-Semikha bi-Ṣefat." In *Sefer Yovel le-Yiṣḥak Baer,* ed. S. W. Baron et al., 248–69. Jerusalem, 1960.
Benayahu, "Revival of Ordination"
——. "Ha-Taqqanah she-lo lehoṣi Sefarim mi-Yerushalayim ve-Hishtalshelutah." In *Minhah le-Yehudah: Mugash le-ha-Rav Yehudah Leib Zlotnik,* ed. S. Assaf et al., 226–34. Jerusalem, 1950.
——. "Haskamat Ṣefat le-Pitur Talmidey Ḥakhamim mi-Misim ve-Nisyono shel R. Yehudah Aberlin levatlah." *Sefunot* 7 (1963): 103–17.
Benayahu, "Tax Concession"
——. "Teudah min ha-Dor ha-Rishon shel Megorashey Sefarad bi-Ṣefat. In *Sefer Assaf,* ed. M. D. Cassuto, J. Klausner, and J. Gutman, 109–25. Jerusalem, 1953.
Benayahu, "Teudah"
——. "Teudot min ha-Genizah al Iskey Misḥar she-la-Ari ve-al Beney Mishpaḥto be-Miṣrayim." In *Sefer Zikkaron le-ha-Rav Yiṣḥak Nissim,* ed. M. Benayahu, 4:225–53. Jerusalem, 1985.
——. *Sefer Toledot ha-Ari.* Jerusalem, 1967.
Benayahu, *Toledoth ha-Ari*
——. "R. Yisrael Najara." *Asufot* 4 (1990): 203–84.
Benayahu, "Yisrael Najara"
*——. *Yosef Beḥiri: Maran Rabbi Yosef Qaro.* Jerusalem, 1991.
Benayahu, *Yosef Beḥiri*
——. "Derushav she-le-Rabbi Yosef ben Meir Garson." *Michael* 7 (1981): 42–205.
Benayahu, "Yosef Garson"
——, ed. *Seder Eliyahu Zuta,* by Elijah Capsali. 2 vols. Jerusalem, 1976–77.
Bentov, H. "Reshimot Autobiografiyot ve-Historiyot shel Rabbi Yosef mi-Trani." *Shalem* 1 (1974): 195–228.
Bentov, "Josef Trani"
——. "Shitat Limud ha-Talmud bi-Yeshivot Saloniqi ve-Turkiyah." *Sefunot* 13 (1971–78): 5–102.
Bentov, "Yeshivot of Salonica and Turkey"
Bloch, P. "Der Streit um den Moreh des Maimonides in Der Gemeinde Posen um die Mitte des 16. Jahrhunderts." *MGWJ* 47 (1903): 153–69, 263–79, 346–56.
Boksenboim, Y., ed. *Iggerot Melamdim: Italyah 1555–1591.* Tel Aviv, 1985.
——. *Iggerot Rabbi Yehudah Aryeh mi-Modena.* Tel-Aviv, 1984.
Boksenboim, *Letters of Rabbi Leon Modena*
Bonfil, R. *Kitvey Azaryah min ha-Adummim.* Jerusalem, 1991.
——. "Peyrush R. Moshe Provenẓalo le-25 Haqdamot ha-Rambam." *Kiryat Sefer* 50 (1974–75): 157–76.
——. *Rabbis and Jewish Communities in Renaissance Italy.* Trans. Jonathan Chipman. London and Washington, 1993.
——. Tiyutat Haṣaah le-Yisud Yeshivah bi-Derom Italyah be-Shalhey ha-

Meah ha-15." In *Sefer Zikkaron le-ha-Rav Yiṣḥak Nissim,* ed. M. Benayahu, 4:185–204. Jerusalem, 1985.

Boyarin, D. *Ha-Iyyun ha-Sefaradi.* Jerusalem, 1989.

Braslawski (Braslvsky), J. "Ereẓ Yisrael be-Tirgum Ivri shel 'Histoire de Juifs' le-Basnage." *Eretz-Israel* 6 (1960): 168–73.

*——. *Le-Ḥeqer Arṣenu, Avar u-Seridim.* Tel Aviv, 1954.
Braslvsky, *Studies in Our Country*

Braude, B. "International Competition and Domestic Cloth in the Ottoman Empire, 1500–1650: A Study in Undevelopment." *Review* 2 (1979): 437–51.

Braudel, F. *The Mediterranean and the Mediterranean World in the Age of Philip II.* Vol. 2. London, 1981.

*Carpi, D. *Be-Tarbut ha-Renaissance u-veyn Ḥomot ha-Geto.* Tel Aviv, 1989.
Carpi, *Between Renaissance and Ghetto*

——. "Geyrush ha-Yehudim mi-Medinat ha-Keneysiyyah bi-Yemey ha-Afifyor Pius ha-Ḥamishi u-Mishpatey ha-Ḥaqirah neged Yehudey Bologna (1566–1569)." In *Scritti in Memoria di Enzo Sereni,* ed. D. Carpi, A. Milano, and U. Nahon, 145–65. Jerusalem, 1970.

Cassuto, M. D. U. "Mi Hayah David ha-Reuveni?" *Tarbiẓ* 32 (1963): 339–58.
Cassuto, "David ha-Reubeni"

Charriere, E. *Negociations de la France, Dans le Levant.* Vol. 3. Paris, n.d.

Chone, H. "Ḥakhamim mi-Mishpaḥat Trèves bi-Yerushalayim." *Sinai* 11 (1942–43): 183–213.
Chone, "Mishpaḥat Trèves"

Cohen, A. "Ha-Omnam Nivnu Ḥomot Yerushalayim al yedey Avraham Castro?" *Zion* 47 (1982): 407–18.
Cohen, "Abraham Castro"

——. "Arkhiyonim Turkiyyim ve-Arviyyim ke-Maqor le-Toledot Yehudey Ereẓ-Yisrael ba-Tequfah ha-Ottmanit." In *Miqqedem umiyyam* 1 (1981): 39–48.

——. "Dameseq vi-Yerushalayim." *Sefunot* 17 (1983): 97–104.
Cohen, "Damascus and Jerusalem"

——. "Temurot Demografiyot ba-Qehillah ha-Yehudit bi-Yerushalayim ba-Meah ha-16, al pi Meqorot Turkiyyim ve-Arviyyim." In *Peraqim be-Toledot Yerushalayim be-Reshit ha-Tequfah ha-Ottmanit,* ed. A. Cohen, 93–111. Jerusalem, 1979.
Cohen, "Demographic Changes"

——. "Mifaley Pituaḥ bi-Yerushalayim be-Reshit ha-Shilton ha-Ottmani." *Cathedra* 8 (1978): 179–87.
Cohen, "Development Projects"

——. *Economic Life in Ottoman Jerusalem.* Cambridge, 1989.
Cohen, *Economic Life*

——. "Biṣurah shel Yerushalayim ha-Ottmanit: Ha-Meymad ha-Eyropi." *Cathedra* 63 (1992): 52–64.

Cohen, "Fortifications of Suleiman in Jerusalem"

——. *Jewish Life under Islam.* Cambridge, Mass., 1984.

Cohen, *Jewish Life under Islam*

——. "Local Trade, International Trade and Government Involvement in Jerusalem during the Early Ottoman Period." *AAS* 12 (1978): 5–12.

Cohen, "Local Trade, International Trade and Government Involvement"

——. "Ha-Misḥar shel Ereẓ-Yisrael ba-Tequfah ha-Ottmanit." In *Peraqim be-Toledot ha-Misḥar shel Ereẓ-Yisrael,* ed. B. Z. Kedar, T. Dothan, and S. Safrai, 300–308. Jerusalem, 1990.

Cohen, "Ha-Misḥar shel Erez-Yisrael"

——. "New Evidence on Demographic Change: The Jewish Community in 16th Century Jerusalem." *Mémorial Ömer Lûtfi Barkan,* ed. O. Komlós, 57–64. Paris, 1980.

Cohen, "New Evidence on Demographic Change"

——. *Yehudey Yerushalayim ba-Meah ha-16: Lefi Teudot Turkiyot shel Beyt ha-Din ha-Shari.* Jerusalem, 1976.

Cohen, *Ottoman Documents on Jerusalem*

——. "Ottoman Sources for the History of Ottoman Jews: How Important?" In *The Jews of the Ottoman Empire,* ed. A. Levy, 687–704. Princeton, 1994.

——. "Beyt Melakhah le-Yiṣur Sabon bi-Yerushalayim ha-Ottmanit." *Cathedra* 52 (1989): 120–24.

Cohen, "Soap Factory"

——. "The Walls of Jerusalem." In *The Islamic World from Classical to Modern Times: Essays in Honor of Bernard Lewis,* ed. C. E. Bosworth, 467–77. Princeton, 1989.

——. *A World Within: Jewish Life as Reflected in Muslim Court Documents from the Sijill of Jerusalem (XVIth Century).* 2 vols. Jewish Quarterly Review Supplement, 1994. Philadelphia, 1994.

Cohen, *World Within*

Cohen, A., and B. Lewis. *Population and Revenue in the Towns of Palestine in the Sixteenth Century.* Princeton, 1978.

Cohen and Lewis, *Population and Revenue*

Cohen, A., and E. Simon-Pikali, *Yehudim be-Veyt ha-Mishpat ha-Muslemi.* Jerusalem, 1993.

Cohen and Simon-Pikali, *Jews in the Moslem Religious Court*

Cohen, I. J. "Seder Qabbalat Shabbat u-Fizmon 'Lekha Dodi' be-Minhagey Yisrael." In *Sefer Adam Noah Braun,* ed. H. Lifshitz, S. Y. Cohen, and Z. Kaplan, 321–57. Jerusalem, 1969.

Cohen, M. R. *Under Crescent and Cross.* Princeton, 1994.

Cook, M. A. *A History of the Ottoman Empire to 1730.* Cambridge, 1976.

Corcos, D. "Yehudey Maroqo mi-Geyrush Sefarad ve-ad Emṣaah shel ha-Meah ha-16." *Sefunot* 10 (1966): 53–111.

Danon, A. "Shivah Mikhtavim mi-Rabbaney Yerushalayim mi-Shenat 1591–1801." *Jerusalem Jahrbuch* 7 (1906): 345–60.

David, A. "Le-Toldotav shel Avraham Qastro le-or Mismakhim min ha-Geniza." *Michael* 9 (1985): 147–62.

David, "Abraham Qastro"

———. "Od le-Toledot ha-Ari be-Miṣrayim le-or Mismekhey ha-Genizah." *Alei Sefer* 14 (1987): 135–37.

David, "The Ari in Egypt"

———. "Qavim li-Demutah shel ha-Qehillah ha-Ashqenazit bi-Yerushalayim ba-Meah ha-16." *Proceedings of the Sixth World Congress of Jewish Studies,* 2:331–41. Jerusalem, 1976.

David, "The Ashkenazic Community in Jerusalem"

———. "Le-Toledot ha-Qehillah ha-Ashqenazit bi-Yerushalayim ba-Meah ha-16." In *Vatiqin: Meḥqarim be-Toledot ha-Yishuv,* ed. H. Z. Hirschberg with Y. Kaniel, 25–33. Ramat Gan, 1975.

David, "Ashkenazic Community in Jerusalem," *Vatiqin*

———. "Aza—Merkaz le-Saḥar beyn Miṣrayim le-Ereẓ Yisrael ba-Meah ha-16." *Maḥanayim,* n.s., 2 (1992): 184–91.

David, "Aza"

———. "Yeshivato shel R. Beṣalel Ashqenazi bi-Ṣefat." *Tarbiẓ* 55 (1986): 454–55.

David, "Bezalel Ashkenazi"

———. "Yediot Ḥadashot le-Toldotav shel R. Yosef Qaro." *Proceedings of the Tenth World Congress of Jewish Studies. Division C.* Vol. 1, 201–7. Jerusalem, 1990.

David, "Biography of Joseph Caro"

———. "Ezratah shel Qehillat Qoni li-Yeshivat K"K Provenṣalish bi-Ṣefat ba-Meah ha-16." *Shalem* 4 (1984): 429–44.

David, "Community of Cuneo"

———. "Safed, foyer de retour au judaïsme de *conversos* au xvie siècle." *REJ* 146 (1987): 63–83.

David, "Conversos"

———. "Demographic Changes in the Safed Jewish Community of the Sixteenth Century." In *Occident and Orient: A Tribute to the Memory of A. Scheiber,* ed. R. Dan, 83–93. Budapest, 1988.

David, "Demographic Changes in Safed"

———. "Derushav shel R. Levi ibn Ḥabib." *Kiryat Sefer* 61 (1986–87): 933–35.

———. "Shtey Iggerot Ereẓ-Yisraeliyot min ha-Meah ha-16." *Shalem* 3 (1981): 325–32.

David, "Emissaries' Letters from Jerusalem"

———. "Fifteenth and Sixteenth Century Pilgrim and Immigrant Journey Routes to the Land of Israel." In *Jewish Studies in a New Europe: Proceedings of the Fifth Congress of Jewish Studies in Copenhagen 1994,* 163–74. Copenhagen, 1998.

——. "Halakhah u-Fraqmatiyah be-Toledot ha-Ari." *Meḥqarey Yerushalayim be-Maḥshevet Yisrael* 10 (1992): 287–97.

David, "Halakhah and Commerce"

——. "Ha-Mashmaut ha-Historit shel 'ha-Zeqenim' be-Divrey R. Ovadyah mi-Bertinoro." In *Peraqim be-Toledot Yerushalayim bi-Yemey ha-Beynayyim,* ed. B. Z. Kedar, 221–43. Jerusalem, 1979.

David, "Historical Significance"

——. "Le-Veyrur Zehuto shel R. Yisrael Ashqenazi." *Zion* 38 (1973): 170–73.

David, "The Identity of Israel Ashkenazi"

——. "Iggeret mi-shel ha-Meshorer R. Shelomo Da Piera be-Inyan ha-Aliyah le-Ereẓ Yisrael mi-Sefarad." *Tarbiẓ* 52 (1983): 655–59.

——. "Le-Qorotav shel R. Yiṣḥak Canpanton, mi-Gedoley Ḥakhmey Sefarad ba-Meah ha-15." *Kiryat Sefer* 51 (1976): 324–26.

David, "Isaac Canpanton"

——. "Qavvim li-Demut ha-Yeshivot u-Vatey ha-Midrash bi-Yerushalayim ba-Meot ha-15 ve-ha-16." *Iyyunim be-Ḥinukh* 34 (1982): 139–64.

David, "Jerusalem Academies"

——. "Hishtalvut Yehudey Ereẓ-Yisrael ba-Saḥar ha-Yam Tikhony be-Reshit ha-Tequfah ha-Ottmanit." In *The Mediterranean and the Jews: Banking, Finance, and International Trade (16th–18th Centuries),* ed. A. Toaff and S. Schwarzfuchs, Hebrew section, 15–28. Ramat Gan, 1989.

David, "Jews in Mediterranean Trade"

——. "Meoravut Yehudey Ereẓ-Yisrael be-Ḥayyey ha-Kalkalah ba-Meot ha-15 ve-ha-16." In *Meḥqarey Yehudah ve-Shromron: Divrey ha-Kenes ha-Shevii, 1997,* ed. Y. Eshel, 265–78. Kedumin-Ariel, 1998.

——. "Ketav Hamlaṣah mi-Shenat 1461 be-Inyanah shel Mishpaḥat Anusim mi-Sefarad hamevaqeshet Laalot le-Ereẓ-Yisrael." *Pe'amim* 46–47 (1991): 190–95.

——. "Maaseh Beyt-Din mi-Beyt Dino shel R. Moshe Cordovero bi-Ṣefat." *Zion* 56 (1991): 441–46.

David, "Legal Decision from the Court of Moses Cordovero"

——. "Le-Qorot Yehudey Italyah be-Ṣilah shel ha-Reyaqṣiyah ha- Qatolit ba-Meah ha-16 le-or Teudot Ḥadashot." *Tarbiẓ* 49 (1979–80): 376–83.

——. "Iggeret Yerushalmit mi-Reshit ha-Shilton ha-Ottmani be-Ereẓ Yisrael." In *Peraqim be-Toledot Yerushalayim be-Reshit ha-Tequfah ha-Ottmanit,* ed. A. Cohen, 39–60. Jerusalem, 1979.

David, "A Letter from Jerusalem"

——. "Le-Veyrur Shenat Petirato shel R. Yaaqov Berav." *Alei Sefer* 12 (1986): 132.

——. "Meqorot ha-Genizah le-Ḥeqer Yehudey Miṣrayim ve-Ereẓ Yisrael be-Sof Yemey ha-Beynayyim." *Zemanim* 38 (1991): 62–69.

——. "Meqorot Ḥadashim le-Ḥiddush ha-Yishuv ha-Yehudi bi-Teveryah ba-Meah ha-16." *Ariel* 105–6 (1994): 81–86.

———. "Mishpaḥat Castellazzo." *Sinai* 64 (1969): 282–87.

———. "Od le-toldotav shel R. Moshe Qastro—Mi-Ḥakhmey Yerushalayim ba-Meah ha-16 le-or Mismakh min ha-Genizah." *Te'udah* 7 (1991): 347–51.

David, "Moses Castro"

———. "Teudot Ḥadashot min ha-Genizah le-Toledot ha-Qesharim beyn Yehudey Ereẓ-Yisrael vi-Yehudey Miṣrayim ba-Meot ha-16–17." *Cathedra* 59 (1991): 19–55.

David, "New Genizah Documents"

———. "Meqorot Ḥadashim al Haflagat ha-Yehudim mi-Veneṣiyah la-Mizraḥ u-le-Ereẓ Yisrael ba-Meot ha-15 ve-ha-17." *Shalem* 6 (1992): 319–33.

David, "New Sources Describing Travel"

———. "New Sources on the History of the Jews of Egypt and Their Ties with the Land of Israel in the Sixteenth Century." *Bulletin of the Israeli Academic Center in Cairo* 13 (1990): 10–15.

———. "Meqorot Ḥadashim le-Toledot ha-Yishuv ha-Yehudi be-Ereẓ Yisrael bi-Yemey ha-Beynayyim." In *Sefer Zev Vilnay*, ed. E. Schiller, 1:289–92. Jerusalem, 1984.

David, "New Sources on Jews During the Middle Ages"

———. "Ha-Qesharim beyn Yehudey Ṣefon Afriqah le-Ereẓ Yisrael ba-Meot ha-15 ve-ha-16." *Pe'amim* 24 (1985): 74–86.

David, "North African Jewry"

———. "Od le-Iskey ha-Misḥar shel ha-Radbaz al pi Teudah Bilti-yeduah min ha-Genizah." *Pe'amim* 32 (1987): 131–34.

———. "Le-Siyumah shel ha-Negidut be-Miṣrayim u-le-Toldotav shel Avraham di Castro." *Tarbiẓ* 41 (1972): 325–37.

David, "The Office of *Nagid* in Egypt"

———. "Le-Toledot Ḥakhamim bi-Yerushalayim ba-Meah ha-16." *Shalem* 5 (1987): 229–49.

David, "Personalities in Jerusalem"

———. "Yediot Nosafot al Peraot bi-Yehudey Ṣefat bi-Shenat 1517." *Cathedra* 8 (1978): 190–94.

David, "The Pogrom of 1517"

———. "Qorot ha-Qehillah ha-Yehudit bi-Yerushalayim ba-Meah ha-15 lefi Teudah Ḥadashah min ha-Genizah." *Ariel* 119–20 (1997): 167–72.

———. "Rabbi Yiṣḥak di Molina." *Kiryat Sefer* 44 (1968–69): 553–59.

———. "Maamadam ha-Kalkali shel Yehudey Miṣrayim ba-Meah ha-16 le-or Teshuvot ha-Radbaz." *Miqqedem umiyyam* 1 (1981): 85–99.

David, "Responsa of Radbaz"

———. "Seridim mi-Sefer Masotav shel Nosea Yehudi be-Ereẓ Yisrael be-Mifneh ha-Meot ha-15 ve-ha-16." *Yisrael—Am va-Areẓ* 7–8 (1990–93): 223–30.

———. "Ṣefat ke-Merkaz le-Shivat Anusim ba-Meah ha-16." In *Society*

and Community, Proceedings of the Second International Congress for Research of the Sephardi and Oriental Jewish Heritage, 1984, ed. A. Haim, Hebrew section, 183–204. Jerusalem, 1991.
David, "Shivat Anusim"

——. "Le-Toledot Beney Mishpaḥat Sholal be-Miṣrayim ve-Ereẓ Yisrael be-Sof ha-Tequfah ha-Mamlukit ve-Reshit ha-Tequfah ha-Ottmanit, Le-or Mismakhim Ḥadashim min ha-Genizah." In *Galut aḥar Golah: Meḥqarim be-Toledot Am Yisrael mugashim le-Professor H. Beinart,* ed. A. Mirsky, A. Grossman, and Y. Kaplan, 374–414. Jerusalem, 1988.
David, "Sholal Family"

——. "The Spanish Exiles in the Holy Land." In *The Sephardi Legacy,* ed. H. Beinart, 2:77–108. Jerusalem, 1992.
David, "Spanish Exiles"

——. "Teudot Ḥadashot al Megorashey Medinat ha-Keneysiyyah bi-Shenat 1569 ve-ha-Gezeyrot shekadmu la-Geyrush." *Italia* 10 (1993): 17–36.

——. "Meoravutam shel Yehudey Miṣrayim ba-Misḥar im Veneṣiyah ba-Meah ha-16 al pi Mismekhey ha-Genizah ha-Qahirit u-Meqorot Aḥerim." *PAAJR* 60 (1994): 1–29.
David, "Trade with Venice"

——. "Viṣo Nagid [The Vice-Nagid] ba-Hanhagah ha-Yehudit bi-Yerushalayim ba-Meah ha-15 u-ve-Reshit ha-Meah ha-16." *Zion* 45 (1980): 327–31.
David, "The Vice-Nagid of Jerusalem"

——. "Teudah Ḥadashah le-Qorot ha-Yeshivah ha-Yerushalmit mi-Reshit ha-Meah ha-16." *Cathedra* 68 (1993): 43–48.
David, "The Yeshivah in Jerusalem"

——, ed. "Iggeret R. Yisrael Ashqenazi mi-Yerushalayim le-Rabbi Avraham mi-Perusha." *Alei Sefer* 16 (1990): 95–122.
David, "Letter of Israel Ashkenazi"

——, ed. *Shetey Kroniqot Ivriyot mi-Dor Geyrush Sefarad.* Jerusalem, 1979.

Davidson, I. *Oṣar ha-Shirah ve-ha-Piyyut.* New York, 1933.

Dimitrovsky, H. Z. "Vikuaḥ she-avar beyn Maran Rabbi Yosef Qaro ve-ha-Mabbit." *Sefunot* 6 (1962): 71–123.
Dimitrovsky, "Dispute"

——. "Shtey Teudot Ḥadashot al Vikuaḥ ha-Semikhah bi-Ṣefat." *Sefunot* 10 (1966): 113–92.
Dimitrovsky, "New Documents Regarding the *Semicha* Controversy"

——. "Le-Toledot ha-Yehudim be-Italyah ba-Meah ha-16." *Zion* 20 (1955): 175–81.
Dimitrovsky, "Notes to the History of the Jews in Italy"

——. "Parashah Alumah be-Yaḥasey ha-Nagid R. Yiṣḥak Sholal ve-R.

Yaaqov Berab ve-Toledot Yeshivot Yerushalayim be-Reshit ha-Meah ha-16." *Shalem* 6 (1992): 83–163.
Dimitrovsky, "Unknown Chapter"

——. "Beyt Midrasho shel R. Yaaqov Berab bi-Ṣefat." *Sefunot* 7 (1963): 41–102.
Dimitrovsky, "Yaakov Berab's Academy"

Doron, D. "Al Targum ha-Torah le-Aravit shel R. Yissakhar ben Susan ha-Maaravi." *Sefunot* 18 (1985): 279–98.
Doron, "Issachar ben Susan"

Drory, J. "Yerushalayim ba-Tequfah ha-Mamlukit." In *Peraqim be-Toledot Yerushalayim bi-Yemey ha-Beynayyim,* ed. B. Z. Kedar, 148–77. Jerusalem, 1979.
Drory, "Jerusalem in the Mamluk Period"

Elad, A. *Medieval Jerusalem and Islamic Worship.* Leiden, 1995.

Elbaum, J. *Petiḥut ve-Histagrut.* Jerusalem, 1990.
Elbaum, *Openness and Insularity*

Elior, R. "Mequbbaley Dr'aa." *Pe'amim* 24 (1985): 36–73.
Elior, "Kabbalists of Dr'aa"

——. "Teshuvah le-Biqoret: D. Tamar, 'Mahadurah Biqortit shel Galya Raza.' Meḥqarey Yerushalayim be-Maḥshevet Yisrael 2 (1983)." *Meḥqarey Yerushalayim be-Maḥshevet Yisrael* 3 (1983/84): 493–506.
Elior, "Response to D. Tamar"

Elitzur, Y. "Meqor ha-Masoret al 'Nebi Samuil.'" *Cathedra* 31 (1984): 75–90.

Elmaleh, A. "Mi-Ginzey he-Avar." *Mizraḥ ouMaarav* 3 (1929): 311–24.

Elon, M. *Jewish Law: History, Sources, Principles.* Trans. B. Auerbach and M. J. Sykes. 4 vols. Philadelphia, 1994.

Epstein, Y. N. ha-Levi. *Mavo le-Nusaḥ ha-Mishnah.* Vol. 2. Tel Aviv, 1964.
Epstein, *Mavo*

Feintuch, I. Z. *Masorot ve-Nusḥaot ba-Talmud.* Ramat Gan, 1985.

Ferorelli, N. *Gli ebrei nell Italia meridionale.* Torino, 1915.

Fischer, G. *Barbary Legend: War, Trade, and Piracy in North Africa (1415–1830).* Oxford, 1957.

Franzos, J., ed. Introduction to *Talmud Yerushalmi, Beṣah,* with commentary by Eleazar Azikri. New York, 1967.
Franzos, Introduction to *Talmud Yerushalmi, Beṣah*

Freimann, A. H. "Quntres ha-Mefaresh ha-Shalem." In *Louis Ginzberg Jubilee Volume,* ed. S. Lieberman et al. Hebrew section, 323–54. New York, 1946.

——. "Taqqanot Yerushalayim." In *Sefer Dinaburg,* ed. Y. Baer, J. Gutman, and M. Schwabe, 206–14. Jerusalem, 1949.
Freimann, "Taqqanot Yerushalayim"

——, ed. Introduction to *Sefer Yuḥasin ha-Shalem.* 2d ed. Jerusalem, 1963.

Fried, N. "Le-Toledot ha-Yishuv ha-Yehudi be-Ḥevron." *Sinai* 53 (1963): 108–11.

Friedman, Y. "Ereẓ-Yisrael vi-Yerushalayim Erev ha-Kibbush ha-Ottmani." In *Peraqim be-Toledot Yerushalayim be-Reshit ha-Tequfah ha-Ottmanit,* ed. A. Cohen, 7–38. Jerusalem, 1979.

Frumkin, A. L., and E. Rivlin. *Toledot Ḥakhmey Yerushalayim.* 2 vols. Jerusalem, 1928–30.

Frumkin and Rivlin, *Ḥakhmey Yerushalayim*

Galanté, A. *Don Salomon Aben Yaèch: Duc de Mételin.* Istanbul, 1936.

Gartner, Z. "Parashat ha-Get Tamari-Ventorozzo." *Moriah* 16, nos. 3–4 (1988): 9–18.

Geller, J. "Qiyumam ha-Kalkali shel ha-Yeshivot ve-Talmudey ha-Torah be-Qeysarut ha-Ottmanit ba-Meah ha-16 u-va-Maḥaṣit ha-Rishonah ba-Meah ha-17." *Mi-Mizraḥ u-mi-Maarav* 1 (1974): 167–221.

Gerber, H. "Mismakh Turki al Avraham di Castro—Manhig Yehudey Miṣrayim ba-Meah ha-16." *Zion* 45 (1980): 158–63.

——. *Yehudey ha-Imperiyah ha-Ottmanit ba-Meot ha-16–17: Kalkalah ve-Ḥevrah.* Jerusalem, 1982.

——. "Yozmah u-Misḥar Biynleumi be-Peilut ha-Kalkalit shel Yehudey ha-Imperiyah ha-Ottmanit ba-Meot 16–17." *Zion* 43 (1978): 38–67.

Gil, M. *A History of Palestine, 634–1099.* Cambridge, 1992.

Goffman, D. G. "The Maktu' System and the Jewish Community of Sixteenth-Century Safed." *Journal of Ottoman Studies* 3 (1983): 81–90.

Goitein, S. D. *A Mediterranean Society.* Vol. 2, *The Community.* Berkeley, Los Angeles, London, 1971.

——. *Sidrey Ḥinukh bi-Yemey ha-Geonim u-Veyt ha-Rambam.* Jerusalem, 1962.

——. "Sifro shel Ibn 'Ubbaya al Harisat Beyt ha-Keneset ha-Yehudi bi-Yerushalayim bi-Shenat 1474." *Zion* 13–14 (1948/49): 18–32.

Goldman, I. M. *The Life and Times of Rabbi David Ibn Abi Zimra.* New York, 1970.

Goldman, *David Ibn Abi Zimra*

Goldstein, B. R. "The Hebrew Astronomical Tradition: New Sources." *Isis* 72 (1981): 237–51.

*Gottlieb, E. *Meḥqarim be-Sifrut ha-Qabbalah.* Edited by J. Hacker. Tel Aviv, 1976.

Grabois, A. "Mi-Nosim ba-Sefinah le-Sefinat ha-Nosim; Temurot be-Hashatat Ṣalyyanim le-Ereẓ Yisrael bi-Yemey ha-Beynayyim." *Yisrael—Am va-Areẓ* 5–6 (1987–89): 155–64.

Grabois, "Passengers"

Graetz, H. *History of the Jews.* Vol. 4. Philadelphia, 1956.

Green, Y. "Pulmus R. Moshe ben Shoshan, R. Moshe Provenṣali u-Madpisey Sabbioneta." *Zion* 51 (1986): 223–40.

Green, "Polemic"

Gross, A. "Aseret ha-Shevatim u-Malkhut Prester John—Shemuot ve-Ḥippusim lifney Geyrush Sefarad ve-Aḥarav." *Pe'amim* 48 (1991): 5–41.

———. *Rabbi Yosef ben Avraham Ḥayyun.* Jerusalem, 1993.

———. "Qavvim le-Toledot ha-Yeshivot be-Qastiliyah ba-Meah ha-15." *Pe'amim* 31 (1987): 3–21.

Gross, "Yeshivot in Castile"

Grossman, A. "Iggeret Ḥazon ve-Tokheḥah me-Ashqenaz ba-Meah ha-14." *Cathedra* 4 (1977): 190–98.

Gutwirt, E. "A Judeo-Spanish Letter from the Genizah." In *Judeo-Romance Languages,* ed. I. Benabu and J. Sermoneta, 127–38. Jerusalem, 1985.

Hacker, J. R. "Aliyat Yehudey Sefarad le-Ereẓ Yisrael ve-Ziqatam eleha beyn 1391 le-1492." *Shalem* 1 (1974): 105–56.

Hacker, "Connections"

———. "R. Eliyahu mi-La Massa bi-Yerushalayim." *Zion* 50 (1985): 241–63.

Hacker, "Elija of Massa Lombarda"

———. "Ha-Ḥevrah ha-Yehudit be-Saloniqi ve-Agafeha ba-Meot ha-15 ve-ha-16." Ph.D. diss., Jerusalem, 1978.

———. "Jewish Autonomy in the Ottoman Empire: Its Scope and Limits. Jewish Courts from the Sixteenth to the Eighteenth Centuries." In *The Jews of the Ottoman Empire,* ed. A Levy, 153–202. Princeton, 1994.

Hacker, "Jewish Autonomy in the Ottoman Empire"

———. "Qevuṣat Iggerot al Geyrush ha-Yehudim mi-Sefarad u-mi-Siṣilyah ve-al Goral ha-Megorashim." In *Peraqim be-Toledot ha-Ḥevrah ha-Yehudit: Muqdashim le-Professor Yaaqov Katz,* ed. E. Etkes and Y. Salmon, 64–97. Jerusalem, 1980.

Hacker, "Letters on the Expulsion"

———. "Links between Spanish Jewry and Palestine, 1391–1492." In *Vision and Conflict in the Holy Land,* ed. R. I. Cohen, 111–39. Jerusalem, 1985.

Hacker, "Links"

———. "Mikhtav Ḥadash al Tesisah Meshiḥit be-Ereẓ Yisrael u-va-Golah be-Reshit ha-Meah ha-16." *Shalem* 2 (1976): 355–60.

———. "Ha-Negidut bi-Ṣefon Afriqah be-Sof ha-Meah ha-15." *Zion* 45 (1980): 118–32.

———. "Shitat ha-Sürgün ve-Haspaatah al ha-Ḥevrah ha-Yehudit ba-Imperiyah ha-Ottmanit ba-Meot ha-15–17." *Zion* 55 (1990): 27–82.

Hacker, "The Ottoman System of Sürgün"

———. "Ein Puranut Baah la-Olam ela bishvil Amei ha-Areṣ." *Shalem* 4 (1984): 63–117.

Hacker, "Payment of *Djizya*"

———. "Gaon ve-Dikaon—Qotavim be-Havayatam ha-Ruḥanit ve-ha-Ḥevratit shel Yoṣey Sefarad u-Portugal ba-Imperiyah ha-Ottmanit." In *Tarbut ve-Ḥevrah be-Toledot Yisrael bi-Yemey ha-Beynayyim: Qoveṣ*

Maamarim le-Zikhro shel Ḥayyim Hillel Ben-Sasson, ed. M. Ben-Sasson, R. Bonfil, and J. R. Hacker, 541–86. Jerusalem, 1989.

Hacker, "Pride and Depression"

——. "Pulmus ke-Neged ha-Filosofiyah be-Istanbul ba-Meah ha-16." In *Meḥqarim be-Qabbalah, be-Filosofia Yehudit u-be-Sifrut ha-Musar ve-he-Hagut: Mugashim le-Yeshayahu Tishby bimlot lo Shivim ve-Ḥamesh Shanim,* ed. Y. Dan and J. R. Hacker, 507–36. Jerusalem, 1986.

——. "Rabbi Yaaqov ibn Ḥabib—Li-Demutah shel ha-Hanhagah ha-Yehudit be-Saloniqi be-Reshit ha-Meah ha-16." *Proceedings of the Sixth World Congress of Jewish Studies,* 2:117–26. Jerusalem, 1975.

——. "Li-Demutam ha-Ruḥanit shel Yehudey Sefarad be-Sof ha-Meah ha-15." *Sefunot* 17 (n.s., 2) (1983): 21–95.

Hacker, "Self-Perception of Spanish Jewry"

——. "Spiritual and Material Links between Egyptian and Palestinian Jewry in the Sixteenth Century." In *Egypt and Palestine,* ed. A. Cohen and G. Baer, 241–51. Jerusalem, 1984.

Hallamish, M. "Le-Nusaḥ Hanhagot Ḥakhmey Ṣefat." *Alei Sefer* 14 (1987): 89–97.

Hallamish, "Behavioral Mannerisms"

——. "Ha-Yeṣirah ha-Qabbalit be-Maroqo." *Pe'amim* 15 (1983): 29–46.

Hallamish, "Kabbalistic Composition in Morocco"

——. "Ha-Mequbbalim be-Maroqo." *Mi-Mizraḥ u-mi-Maarav* 2 (1980): 205–35.

Hallamish, "The Kabbalists in Morocco"

——. "Qabbalah ba-Pesiqah shel R. Yosef Qaro." *Daat* 21 (1988): 85–102.

Ḥason, I. "Shivḥey Yerushalayim ba-Islam." In *Sugyot be-Toledot Ereẓ-Yisrael taḥat Shilton ha-Islam,* ed. M. Sharon, 33–75. Jerusalem, 1976.

Havlin, S. Z. "Le-Toledot Yeshivot Yerushalayim ve-Ḥakhameha be-Shalhey ha-Meah ha-16 ve-Reshit ha-Meah ha-18." *Shalem* 2 (1976): 113–92.

Havlin, "Jerusalem Yeshivot"

——. "Taqqanot Rabbenu Gershom Meor ha-Golah be-Inyaney Ishut bi-Teḥumey Sefarad u-Provence." *Shenaton ha-Mishpat ha-Ivri* 2 (1975): 200–57.

Havlin, "Takkanot of Rabbenu Gershom"

——. "Ha-Yeṣirah ha-Ruḥanit." In *Toledot Yehudey Miṣrayim ba-Tequfah ha-Ottmanit (1517–1914),* ed. J. M. Landau, 245–310. Jerusalem, 1988.

Helner, M. "Torat ha-Gilgul be-Sifrey ha-Qabbalah shel R. David ibn Zimra." *Pe'amim* 43 (1990): 16–50.

Helner, "Transmigration of Souls"

Herculano, A. *History of the Origin and Establishment of the Inquisition in Portugal.* New York, 1972.

Heyd, U. *Ottoman Documents on Palestine, 1522–1615.* Oxford, 1960.
Heyd, *Ottoman Documents*

———. "Teudot Turkiyot al Yehudey Ṣefat ba-Meah ha-16 al pi Teudot me-ha-Arkhiyon ha-Ottmani." *Yerushalayim: Meḥqarey Ereẓ-Yisrael* 2/5 (1955): 128–35.
Heyd, "Turkish Documents Concerning Safed"

———. "Teudot Turkiyot al Binyanah shel Teveryah ba-Meah ha-16." *Sefunot* 10 (1966): 193–210.
Heyd, "Turkish Documents on Tiberias"

———. "Yerushalayim bi-Yemey ha-Mamlukim ve-ha-Turkim." In *Yerushalayim le-Doroteha,* ed. Y. Aviram, 194–96. Jerusalem, 1968.

Hirschberg, H. Z. (J. W.) *A History of the Jews in North Africa.* Vol. 1. Leiden, 1974.

———. "Ottoman Rule in the Light of Firmans and Sharia Documents, Preliminary Note." *IEJ* 2 (1952): 237–48.

Hirschensohn, C. "Yediot Sefarim Kitvey Yad." *Hamisderonah* 1 (1885): 192–201, 255–59.

Holt, P. M. *Egypt and the Fertile Crescent.* London, 1966.

Horodezky, S. A. "R. Eliezer Azikri." In *Ṣiyyunim: Qoveṣ le-Zikhrono shel J. N. Simhoni,* 149–58. Berlin, 1929.

Horowitz, C. "Hearot le-Yaḥas ha-Mabbit el Ḥasidey Ṣefat." *Shalem* 5 (1987): 273–84.
Horowitz, "Attitude of Moshe de Trani Toward Pietist Circles"

Horowitz, E. "Al R. Yiṣḥak ben Gershon Treves be-Veneṣiyah." *Kiryat Sefer* 59 (1984): 252–57.

Horowitz, Z. "Toledot Rabbi Yosef Ashqenazi ha-'Tanna' mi-Ṣefat." *Sinai* 7 (1941): 311–30.

Hütteroth, W. D., and K. Abdulfattah. *Historical Geography of Palestine, Transjordan, and Southern Syria in the Late Sixteenth Century.* Erlangen, 1977.
Hütteroth and Abdulfattah, *Historical Geography*

Idel, M. "Beyn Qabbalat Yerushalayim le-Qabbalat R. Yisrael Saruq." *Shalem* 6 (1992): 165–73.

———. "Iggarto shel R. Yiṣḥak mi-Pisa(?) bi-Shelosh Nusḥaoteha." *Kobeẓ al Yad,* n.s., 10 (1982): 163–214.

———. Introduction to A. Z. Aescoly, *Ha-Tenuot ha-Meshiḥiyot be-Yisrael.* 2d edition. Jerusalem, 1988.
Idel, Introduction to Aescoly, *Jewish Messianic Movements*

———. "Al Mishmarot u-Meshiḥiyut bi-Yerushalayim ba-Meot ha-16–ha-17." *Shalem* 5 (1987): 83–94.
Idel, "Mishmarot and Messianism"

———. "R. Yehudah Ḥallewa ve-Ḥibburo Sefer Ṣafenat Paaneaḥ." *Shalem* 4 (1984): 119–48.
Idel, "Yehudah Ḥallewa"

Ish-Shalom, M. *Masey Noṣrim le-Ereẓ Yisrael.* Tel Aviv, 1965.
Ish-Shalom, *Christian Travels*

Jacoby, D. "Ha-Yehudim u-Vaayat Har Ṣiyyon ba-Meah ha-15; Iyyun Meḥudash." *Cathedra* 39 (1986): 51–70.

Kahana, A. *Sifrut ha-Historiya ha-Yisraelit.* Book 2. Warsaw, 1923.

*Kahane, Y. Z. *Meḥqarim be-Sifrut ha-Teshuvot.* Jerusalem, 1973.

Kanarfogel, E. *Jewish Education and Society in the High Middle Ages.* Detroit, 1992.

Kasher, M. M., and J. B. Mandelbaum. *Sarei ha-Elef.* 2d edition. 2 vols. Jerusalem, 1978.

*Katz, J. *Halakhah ve-Qabbalah.* Jerusalem, 1984.
Katz, *Halakhah and Kabbalah*

Kaufmann, D. "Contributions à l'histoire des Juifs en Italie." *REJ* 20 (1890): 35–72.

——. "Don Joseph Nassi, Founder of Colonies in the Holy Land, and the Community of Cori in the Campagna." *JQR* 2 (1890): 291–310.
Kaufmann, "Don Joseph Nassi"

——. "Iggerot R. Shimshon Back mi-Shenot 1582, 1584." *Jerusalem Jahrbuch* 1 (1887): 141–47.
Kaufmann, "Iggerot Shimshon Back"

——. "A Letter from the Community of Pesaro to Don Joseph Nassi." *JQR* 4 (1891–92): 509–12.
Kaufmann, "A Letter from Pesaro"

——. "R. Josef Aschkenas, der Mischnakritiker von Safet." *MGWJ* 42 (1898): 38–46.

——. "Tofes Ketav she-nishlakh me-Ir ha-Qodesh le-Carpi." *Jerusalem Jahrbuch* 5 (1901): 70–88.

——. "Une lettre de Josef Caro adressée aux juifs de Carpentras." *REJ* 18 (1889): 133–36.

Kedar, B. Z. "Yehudey Yerushalayim 1187–1267 ve-Ḥelqo shel ha-Ramban be-Shiqum Qehillatam." In *Peraqim be-Toledot Yerushalayim bi-Yemey ha-Beynayyim,* ed. B. Z. Kedar, 122–36. Jerusalem, 1979.

Kena'ani, Y. "Ha-Ḥayyim ha-Kalkaliyyim bi-Ṣefat u-ve-sevivoteha ba-Meah ha-16 ve-haṣi ha-Meah ha-17." *Zion (Me'asef)* 6 (1934): 172–217.
Kena'ani, "Ha-Ḥayyim ha-Kalkaliyyim

——. "Ha-Yishuv ha-Yehudi be-Akko." *BJPES* 2 (1935): 29–31.
Kena'ani, "Jewish Population in Acre"

——. "Le-Toledot ha-Yishuv be-Aza." *BJPES* 5 (1937–38): 33–41.
Kena'ani, "Jewish Population of Gaza"

Kinstlicher, M. A. Z. "Beyn Ofen le-Ereẓ ha-Qodesh." *Tzfunot* 1 (1989): 73–87.

Kleinberger, A. F. *Ha-Maḥshavah ha-Pedagogit shel ha-Maharal mi-Prag.* Jerusalem, 1962.

Kobler, F. *A Treasury of Jewish Letters.* 2 vols. Philadelphia, 1953.

Kohut, A. Introduction to *Sefer he-Arukh ha-Shalem.* Part 1. Vienna, 1878.

*Kook, S. H. *Iyyunim u-Meḥqarim.* 2 vols. Jerusalem, 1959–63.

Kook, *Iyyunim*

Kupfer, E. "Haramat 'Keter Torah me-al Rosho' shel R. Moshe Provenẓali ve-Nusaḥ ha-Havdalah Shelo." *Sinai* 63 (1968): 137–60.

——. "Hasagot min Ḥakham Eḥad al Divrey he-Ḥakham R. Yosef ben ha-Qadosh R. Yosef ha-Loazi she-katav ve-qara be-Qol Gadol neged ha-Rambam." *Kobeẓ al Yad,* n.s., 11 (21) (1985): 213–88.

——. "Qehillat Ṣefat u-Feulat R. Menaḥem Azaryah mi-Fano lemaan ha-Yishuv be-Ereẓ Yisrael." *Shalem* 2 (1976): 361–64.

Kupfer, "Jewish Community of Safed"

——. "Ḥezyonotav shel R. Asher b. R. Meir ha-mekhuneh Lemlein Roitlingen." *Kobeẓ al Yad* 8 (1975): 385–423.

Kupfer, "The Revelations of Asher Lemlein Roitlingen"

Lacave, J. L. "Las fuentes cristianas del Sefer Yuḥasin." *Proceedings of the Fifth World Congress of Jewish Studies* 2 (1972): 92–98.

Lamdan, R. "Parshat Ḥerem Anqona—Ha-Ṣad ha-Sheni shel ha-Matbea." In *Mi-Lisbon le-Saloniqi ve-Qushta,* ed. Z. Ankori, 135–54. Tel Aviv, 1988.

Lamdan, "Boycott of Ancona"

——. "R. Moshe Basola—Ḥayyav vi-Yeṣirato." Master's thesis, Tel Aviv, 1983.

Lamdan, "Rabbi Moshe Basola"

——. "Sheney Ketavim mi-shel R. Moshe Basola." *Michael* 9 (1985): Hebrew section, 171–93.

Lamdan, "Two Writings by Moshe Basola"

Lane, F. C. *Venice: A Maritime Republic.* Baltimore, 1977.

Leibson, G. "Al Mah Menadim." *Shenaton ha-Mishpat ha-Ivri* 2 (1975): 292–342.

——. "Niduy u-Menudeh be-Eyney ha-Tannaim ve-ha-Amoraim." *Shenaton ha-Mishpat ha-Ivri* 5–6 (1979/80): 177–202.

Lewis, B. "Acre in the Sixteenth Century According to the Ottoman *Tapu* Registers." In *Mémorial Ömer Lûtfi Barkan,* ed. O. Komlós, 135–39. Paris, 1980.

——. *The Emergence of Modern Turkey.* 2d ed. London, 1968.

——. "Jaffa in the Sixteenth Century According to Ottoman Tahrir Registers." In *Studies in Classical and Ottoman Islam,* ed. B. Lewis, article 18: 435–36. London: Variorum Reprints, 1976.

——. "Nazareth in the Sixteenth Century According to the Ottoman *Tapu* Registers." In *Studies in Classical and Ottoman Islam,* ed. B. Lewis, article 17: 416–25. London: Variorum Reprints, 1976.

——. *Notes and Documents from the Turkish Archives.* Jerusalem, 1952.

Lewis, *Notes and Documents*

——. "The Ottoman Archives as a Source for the History of Palestine." *JRAS* (Oct. 1951): 139–55.

——. "The Ottoman Archives as a Source for Jewish History." In *Studies in Classical and Ottoman Islam,* ed. B. Lewis, article 20: 1–52. London: Variorum Reprints, 1976.

——. "Palestine: On the History and Geography of a Name." *International History Review* 2, no. 1 (Jan. 1980): 1–12.

——. "Some Statistical Surveys of 16th Century Palestine." In *A Felicitation Volume for Professor J. D. Pearson,* ed. B.C. Bloomfield, 115–22. London, 1980.

——. "Studies in the Ottoman Archives—1." *BSOAS* 16 (1954): 469–501.
Lewis, "Studies in the Ottoman Archives"

——. "Ha-Ukhlusiyah ve-Hakhnasot ha-Missim be-Ereẓ Yisrael al pi Teudot Turkiyot." *Yerushalayim: Rivon le-Ḥeqer Ereẓ-Yisrael* 4 (1953): 133–37.

Lieberman, S. "Mashehu al Mefarshim Qadmonim la-Yerushalmi." In *Alexander Marx Jubilee Volume,* ed. S. Lieberman, Hebrew section, 287–319. New York, 1950.
Lieberman, "Old Commentators"

Littman, M. "Ha-Aliyot Le-Ereẓ Yisrael mi-Miṣrayim be-Shalhey ha-Tequfah ha-Mamlukit ve-Reshit ha-Shilton ha-Ottmani." *Cathedra* 23 (1982): 47–56.
Littman, "Aliyot from Egypt"

Luncz, A. M. "Issur laasot Peyrud be-ha-Qehillah mi-Shenat 1623." *Jerusalem Jahrbuch* 2 (1887): 147–48.
Luncz, "Issur laasot Peyrud"

Maimon, Y. L. "Aqdamot Milin." *Sinai* 36 (1955): 275–357.

——. "Rabbi Beṣalel Ashqenazi u-Sefarav." *Sinai: Sefer Yovel,* 89–125. Jerusalem, 1958.

——. *Rabbi Moshe ben Maimon.* Jerusalem, 1960.

Mann, J. *Texts and Studies.* Vol. 1. Cincinnati, 1931.

Marx, A. "Die *Kelaley ha-Talmud* des R. Bezalel Aschkenasi." In *Festschrift zum Siebzigsten Geburtstage David Hoffman's,* ed. S. Eppenstein et al., German section, 369–82; Hebrew section, 179–217. Berlin, 1914.

——. "Zwei Briefe berühmter Gelehrter aus dem 16 Jahrhundert." In *Festschrift für Dr. Jakob Freimann,* 167–71. Berlin, 1937.
Marx, "Zwei Briefe"

Melamed, E. Z. "Melekhet Shelomo le-R. Shelomo Adeni." *Sinai* 44 (1959): 346–63.

Merchavia, Ch. *Qolot Qorim le-Ṣiyyon.* Jerusalem, 1980.

Meroz, R. "Ḥavurat R. Moshe ben Makhir ve-Taqqanoteha." *Pe'amim* 31 (1987): 40–61.
Meroz, "Moshe ben Makhir"

Merriman, R. B. *Suleiman the Magnificent.* Cambridge, Mass., 1944.

Michael, H. *Or ha-Ḥayyim.* 2d edition. Jerusalem, 1965.

Molcho, Y. R. "R. Levi Ben Ḥabib Ish Yerushalayim mi-Shomrey ha-Ḥomot." In *Ḥemdat Yisrael: Qoveṣ le-Zikhro shel Maran Ḥayyim Ḥizqiyahu Medini,* ed. A. Elmaleh, 33–42. Jerusalem, 1946.

Nadav, Y. "Iggeret ha-Mequbbal R. Yiṣḥak Mar Ḥayyim al Torat ha-Ṣaḥṣaḥot." *Tarbiẓ* 26 (1957): 440–58.

Neubauer, A. "Reiseroute." *Hebräische Bibliographie* 21 (1881–82): 136.

——. "Qibuṣim al Inyaney Aseret ha-Shevatim u-Veney Moshe." *Kobeẓ al Yad* 4 (1888): 9–74.
Neubauer, "Qibuṣim"

Neuman, A. A. "Abraham Zacuto—Historiographer." In *Harry Austryn Wolfson Jubilee Volume,* ed. S. Lieberman et al., 2:597–629. Jerusalem, 1965.

——. "The Paradoxes and Fate of a Jewish Medievalist." In *The Seventy-fifth Anniversary Volume of the Jewish Quarterly Review,* 398–408. Philadelphia, 1967.

Newett, M. M., ed. Introduction to *Canon Pietro Casola's Pilgrimage to Jerusalem in the Year 1494.* Manchester, 1907.

Nissim, I. "Teshuvot Rabbi Yom Tov Ṣahalon be-Inyaney Avodat Adamah be-Ḥaṣbeyah u-va-Galil." *Sefunot* 9 (*Sefer Ben-Zvi* 2, 1965): 7–20.

——. "Teshuvot Rabbi Ḥayyim Vital." In *Sefer Yovel le-Rabbi Ḥanokh Albeck,* 331–51. Jerusalem, 1963.

Ovadya, A. "R. Eliyahu Mizraḥi." *Sinai* 6 (1940): 510–16.

Oron, M. "Ḥalom, Ḥazon u-Meṣiut be-Sefer ha-Ḥezyonot le-Ḥayyim Vital." *Meḥqarey Yerushalayim be-Maḥshevet Yisrael* 10 (1992): 299–309.

Pachter, M. "Ḥayyav ve-Ishiyuto shel R. Elazar Azikri bi-Rei Yomano ha-Misti ve-Sefer 'Ḥaredim.'" *Shalem* 3 (1981): 127–47.
Pachter, "Elazar Azikri"

——. "Ereẓ-Yisrael be-Sifrut ha-Derush ve-ha-Musar shel Ḥakhmey Ṣefat ba-Meah ha-16." In *Ereẓ-Yisrael ba-Hagut ha-Yehudit bi-Yemey ha-Beynayyim,* ed. M. Hallamish and A. Ravitsky, 290–319. Jerusalem, 1991.

——. "'Ḥazut Kasha' le-Rabbi Moshe Alsheikh." *Shalem* 1 (1974): 157–93.
Pachter, "'Ḥazut Kasha'"

——. "Sifrut ha-Derush ve-ha-Musar shel Ḥakhmey Ṣefat ba-Meah ha-16 u-Maarekhet Rayonoteha ha-Merkaziyyim." Ph.D. diss., Jerusalem, 1976.
Pachter, "Homiletic and Ethical Literature"

——. "Yeṣirato ha-Darshanit shel R. Yisrael di Quriel ve-zihui Meḥabro ha-Amiti shel Qoveṣ ha-Derushim she-ba-Sefer 'Or Ṣaddiqim' hame-yuḥas le-Rabbi Yosef Qaro." *Kiryat Sefer* 55 (1980): 802–10.
Pachter, "Israel di Curiel"

——. "Sefer 'Maggid Mesharim' le-R. Yosef Qaro ke-Sefer Musar." *Daat* 21 (1988): 57–83.

Pachter, "Karo's *Maggid Mesharim*"

——. "Le-Inyan ha-Muvaot mi-'Orḥot Ṣaddiqim' be-Sifrey ha-Musar shel Ḥakhmey Ṣefat." *Kiryat Sefer* 47 (1971/72): 487–92.

——. "Demuto shel ha-Ari ba-Hesped she-hispido R. Shmuel Ucedah." *Zion* 37 (1972): 22–40.

Pachter, "Samuel Ucedah's Eulogy"

——. "Aliyato shel R. Shelomo Alqabeṣ le-Ereẓ Yisrael u-Derashat ha-Preydah shelo be-Saloniqi." *Shalem* 5 (1987): 251–63.

Pachter, "Shelomo Alkabetz's Departure Sermon"

——. "Sefer 'Reshit Ḥokhmah' le-R. Eliyahu de Vidas ve-Qiṣurav." *Kiryat Sefer* 47 (1971–72): 686–710.

Pachter, "'Reshit Ḥokhmah'"

——, ed. *Milei De-Shemaya le-Rabbi Elazar Azikri.* Tel Aviv, 1991.

Pachter, *Milei De-Shemaya*

Parkes, J. *A History of Palestine from 135 to Modern Times.* New York, 1949.

Peles, H. Y. "Birya ha-Atiqah mitokh ha-Meqorot." *Morasha* 2 (1972): 36–47.

Polak, G. "Horaah al Sheelat ha-Malakhim." *Kerem Chemed* 9 (1856): 141–48.

Pollack, A. N. "Ha-Yehudim u-Veyt ha-Matbeot be-Miṣrayim bi-Yemey ha-Mamlukim u-ve-Reshit Shilton ha-Turkim." *Zion* 1 (1935): 24–36.

Prawer, J. J. *The History of the Jews in the Latin Kingdom of Jerusalem.* Oxford, 1988.

——. "Le-Biqoret Iggerot Yerushalmiyot min ha-Meah ha-15 ve-ha-16." *Yerushalayim: Rivon le-Ḥeqer Yerushalayim ve-Toldoteha* 1 (1948): 139–59.

Prawer, "Jerusalem Letters"

——. "Minzar ha-Franṣisqanim be-'Har Ṣiyyon' vi-Yehudey Yerushalayim ba-Meah ha-15." *BJPES* 14 (1947): 15–24.

Preschel, Tuvia. "Aliyato shel R. Yaaqov Pollack li-Yerushalayim." In *Sefer Yovel le-ha-Gaon Rabbi Yosef Dov Soloveitchik,* ed. S. Israeli, N. Lamm, and Y. Raphael, 2:1124–29. Jerusalem, 1984.

Purgstall, J. von Hammer. *Histoire de l'Empire Ottoman.* Trans. J. J. Hellert. Vol. 4. Paris, 1836.

Rabinowitsch, W. "Min ha-Genizah ha-Stolinait." *Zion* 5 (1940): 125–32.

Rabinowitsch, "Manuscripts from an Archive in Stolin"

Ratzaby (Ratzhaby), Y. "Meoraot Yerushalayim bi-Shenat 1542." *Shalem* 5 (1987): 265–72.

——. "R. Shelomo Adeni ve-Ḥibburo Melekhet Shelomo." *Sinai* 106 (1990): 243–54.

——, ed. *Sefer Hammusar* by Zacharia al-Dahri. Jerusalem, 1965.

Regev, S. "'Piṣey Ohev' le-R. Yisrael Najara." *Asufot* 4 (1990): 225–56.

——. "Sarid mi-Peyrush Megillat Rut le-Rabbi Elisha Gallico." *Asufot* 4 (1990): 99–126.

——, ed. *Rabbi Yisrael di-Quriel: Derashot u-Maamarim.* Jerusalem, 1992.

Reiner, E. "Beyn Ashqenaz li-Yerushalayim." *Shalem* 4 (1984): 27–62.

Reiner, "Ashkenaz and Jerusalem"

——. "Hanhagat ha-Qehillah bi-Yerushalayim be-Shalhey ha-Tequfah ha-Mamlukit: Teudot u-Veyrurim be-Shuley 'Parashat ha-Zeqenim.'" *Shalem* 6 (1992): 23–81.

Reiner, "Jewish Community Leadership"

——. "Aliyah va-Aliyah le-Regel le-Ereẓ Yisrael, 1099–1517." Ph.D. diss., Jerusalem, 1988.

Reiner, "Pilgrims and Pilgrimage"

——. "Ha-Temurot ba-Meah ha-15." In *Ha-Historiyah shel Ereẓ-Yisrael.* Vol. 7, *Shilton ha-Mamlukim ve-ha-Ottmanim (1260–1804),* ed. A. Cohen, 59–90. Jerusalem, 1981.

Rhode, H. "The Geography of the Sixteenth Century Sancak of Safed." *Archivum Ottomanicum* 10 (1985–87): 179–218.

Rivlin, E. "Taqqanot ha-Ezvonot bi-Yerushalayim u-ve-Ereẓ Yisrael." In *Azkkarah le-Nishmat Avraham Yiṣḥak ha-Kohen Kook,* ed. Y. L. Fishman, 5:559–69. Jerusalem, 1937.

Rivlin, Y. Y. "Haṣaat R. Refael Mordekhai Malki le-Yisud Yeshivah bi-Yerushalayim ke-Merkaz le-Yahadut." *Yerushalayim: Meḥqarey Ereẓ-Yisrael* 2/5 (1955): 187–94.

Robinson, I. "Abraham ben Eliezer Halevi: Kabbalist and Messianic Visionary of the Early Sixteenth Century." Ph.D. diss., Cambridge, Mass., 1980.

Robinson, "Abraham ben Eliezer ha-Levi"

——. "Messianic Prayer Vigils in Jerusalem in the Early Sixteenth Century." *JQR* 72 (1981): 32–42.

Robinson, "Messianic Prayer Vigils"

——. "Two Letters of Abraham ben Eliezer Halevi." In *Studies in Medieval Jewish History and Literature,* ed. I. Twersky, 2:403–22. Cambridge, Mass., 1984.

Robinson, "Two Letters"

Röhricht, R., and H. Meisner. *Deutsche Pilgerreisen nach dem heiligen Lande.* Berlin, 1880.

Roth, C. *The House of Nasi: The Duke of Naxos.* Philadelphia, 1948.

——. "Mikhtav mi-Qahir le-Mishpaḥat ha-Qaraim bi-Yerushalayim." *Yerushalayim: Meḥqarey Ereẓ-Yisrael* 4 (1953): 138–40.

Roth, E. "Menaḥem ha-Bavli o Romi?" *Kiryat Sefer* 31 (1955–56): 399.

Rozen (Rosen), M. "Ha-Fattoria—Pereq be-Toledot ha-Misḥar ha-Yam Tikhony ba-Meot ha-16–17." *Miqqedem umiyyam* 1 (1981): 101–31.

——. *Ha-Qehillah ha-Yehudit bi-Yerushalayim ba-Meah ha-17.* Tel Aviv, 1984.

Rozen, *Jewish Community*

——. "Maamad ha-Musta'rabim ve-ha-Yeḥasim beyn ha-Edot be-Ereẓ Yisrael mi-Shalhey ha-Meah ha-15 ve-ad Shalhey ha-Meah ha-17." *Cathedra* 17 (1980): 73–101.

Rozen, "Musta'rabs"

——. "The Relations between Egyptian Jewry and the Jewish Community of Jerusalem in the Seventeenth Century." In *Egypt and Palestine,* ed. A. Cohen and G. Baer, 251–65. Jerusalem, 1984.

——. "Yehudim be-Sheyrut Faḥr ed-Din ha-Sheni Shalit ha-Levanon (1586–1635)." *Pe'amim* 14 (1982): 32–44.

——, ed. *Ḥorvot Yerushalayim.* Tel Aviv, 1981.

Rubin, Z. "Darko shel R. Yosef ibn Tabul ke-Farshan ha-Zohar." *Meḥqarey Yerushalayim be-Maḥshevet Yisrael* 10 (1992): 363–87.

Sack (Zak), B. "Al Peyrushav shel R. Avraham Galante—Kamah Hearot al Ziqatam le-Kitvey Rabotav." In *Meḥqarey Yerushalayim be-Sifruyot Am Yisrael,* ed. E. Ḥazan, 61–86. Jerusalem, 1987.

Sack, "Abraham Galante's Commentaries"

——. "Galut u-Geulah bi-'Verit ha-Levi' le-R. Shelomo ha-Levi Alqabeṣ." *Eshel Beer-Sheva* 2 (1980): 265–86.

Sack, "*Berit halevi* of Solomon Alkabez"

*——. *Be-Shaarey ha-Qabbalah shel R. Moshe Cordevero [sic].* Jerusalem, 1995.

Sack, *Kabbalah of Rabbi Moshe Cordevero*

——. "The Mystical Theology of Solomon Alkabeẓ" (Hebrew). Ph.D. diss., Brandeis University, 1977.

Sack, "Mystical Theology of Solomon Alkabeẓ"

——. "Yaḥaso shel R. Shelomo Alqabeṣ la-Ḥaqirah ha-Filosofit." *Eshel Beer-Sheva* 1 (1976): 288–306.

Salmon, W. H. *An Account of the Ottoman Conquest of Egypt in the Year A. H. 922 (1516).* London, 1921.

Samuel, A. "Rishon Parshaney ha-Yerushalmi, Qavvim li-Demuto u-le-Foalo shel R. Shelomo Sirillo, mi-Megorashey Sefarad." *Pe'amim* 49 (1991): 32–53.

Samuel, "Shelomo Serilio"

Sassoon, S. D. *Ohel Dawid: Descriptive Catalogue of the Hebrew and Samaritan Manuscripts in the Sassoon Library.* Vol. 1. London, 1932.

Schechter, S. "Safed in the Sixteenth Century—A City of Legists and Mystics." In *Studies in Judaism.* 2d series. Ed. S. Schechter, 202–306. Philadelphia, 1938.

Schechter, "Safed in the Sixteenth Century"

Scheiber, A. "An Unknown Responsum of David Ibn Abi Zimra." In *Es-*

says on the Occasion of the Seventieth Anniversary of the Dropsie University, ed. A. I. Katsh and L. Nemoy, 397–403. Philadelphia, 1979.

Scheiber, A., and M. Benayahu. "Peniyyat Ḥakhmey Miṣrayim el ha-Radbaz ve-Ḥakhmey Ṣefat lehashqit Maḥloqet she-parṣah be-Qehillatam." *Sefunot* 6 (1962): 125–34.
Scheiber and Benayahu, "Communication to the Radbaz"

Scholem, G. "Ha-Mequbbal Rabbi Avraham ben Eliezer ha-Levi." *Kiryat Sefer* 2 (1925): 101–41, 269–73.
Scholem, "The Cabbalist Abraham Halevi"

——. "Peraqim mi-Toledot Sifrut ha-Qabbalah: Ḥaqirot Ḥadashot al R. Avraham b. Eliezer ha-Levi." *Kiryat Sefer* 7 (1930–31): 149–65, 440–65.
Scholem, "Chapters from Cabbalistical Literature"

——. "Shetar ha-Hitqashrut shel Talmidey ha-Ari." *Zion* 5 (1940): 133–60.
Scholem, "Disciples of Isaac Luria"

——. "Yediot Ḥadashot al R. Yosef Ashqenazi ha-'Tanna' mi-Ṣefat." *Tarbiẓ* 28 (1958–59): 58–89, 201–35.
Scholem, "Joseph Ashkenazi"

——. "Hearot Shonot le-Sifrut ha-Qabbalah: Bi-Devar Ḥokhmata Rabbatah de-Shelomo ve-Rabbi Avraham ha-Levi ha-Zaqen." *Kiryat Sefer* 1 (1924): 163–64.
Scholem, "Kabbalistical Miscellaneous Notes"

——. "Ketavav ha-Amitiyyim shel ha-Ari." *Kiryat Sefer* 19 (1942–43): 184–99.

——. *Kitvey Yad be-Qabbalah ha-Nimṣaim be-Veyt ha-Sefarim ha-Leumi ve-ha-Universitai bi-Yerushalayim.* Jerusalem, 1930.
Scholem, *Kitvey Yad be-Qabbalah*

——. "Li-Yediat ha-Qabbalah bi-Sefarad Erev ha-Geyrush." *Tarbiẓ* 24 (1955): 167–206.

——. *Sabbatai Ṣevi: The Mystical Messiah, 1626–1676.* Princeton, 1973.

——. "Shir shel Yisrael Najara be-fi ha-Shabbtaim." In *Ignace Goldziher Memorial Volume,* ed. S. Löwinger and J. Somogyi, pt. 1, Hebrew section, 41–44. Budapest, 1948.

Scholem, G., and M. Beit-Arié. Introduction to *Maamar Meshare Qitrin le-Rabbi Avraham ben Eliezer ha-Levi.* Jerusalem, 1977.
Scholem and Beit-Arié, *Maamar Meshare Qitrin*

Schur, N. "Ha-Yishuv ha-Yehudi bi-Yerushalayim ba-Meot ha-16–18 al pi Khroniqot Franṣisqaniyot ve-Khitvey Nosim Qatoliyyim u-Protestantiyyim." In *Peraqim be-Toledot Yerushalayim be-Reshit ha-Tequfah ha-Ottmanit,* ed. A. Cohen, 343–434. Jerusalem, 1979.
Schur, "Christian Chronicles"

——. *Jerusalem in Pilgrims and Travellers' Accounts: A Thematic Bibliography of Western Christian Itineraries, 1300–1917.* Jerusalem, 1980.

——. "Ha-Nisayon le-Haqamat 'Medinah Yehudit' bi-Teveryah al-yedey

Dona Gracia Mendes ve-Don Yosef Nasi ve-Hakhshalato bi-yedey ha-Franṣisqanim." *Ariel* 53–54 (1988): 44–50.

——. "Toledot Yehudey Aza ba-Tequfot ha-Mamlukit ve-ha-Ottmanit." *Yisrael—Am Va-Areẓ* 5–6 (1987–89): 199–218.

——. "Yaḥas Meyuḥad mi-Ṣad ha-Shilton ha-Turki la-Yishuv ha-Yehudi ba-Meah ha-16." *Yisrael—Am Va-Areẓ* 2–3 (1985–86): 157–62.

——. "Madrikh Bibliografi: Aṣey ha-Pri ve-Giduley ha-Sadeh she-be-Ereẓ Yisrael ba-Tequfah ha-Mamlukit ve-ha-Ottmanit lefi Kitveyhem shel Nosim Noṣriyyim min ha-Maarav." *Nofim* 11–12 (1979): 138–60.

——. "Toledot Yehudey Shekhem bi-Yemey ha-Beynayyim u-va-Et ha-Ḥadashah." In *Meḥqarey Shomron,* ed. S. Dar and Z. Safrai, 229–301. Tel Aviv, 1986.

——. "Yehudey ha-Levanon ba-Tequfah ha-Ottmanit bi-Rei Sifrut ha-Nosim." *Pe'amim* 24 (1985): 117–44.

Schwarzfuchs, S. "Joseph Caro et la yeshiva provençale de Safed." *REJ* 150 (1991): 151–59.

Schwarzfuchs, "Joseph Caro"

——. "La décadence de la Galilée Juive du XVIe siècle et la crise du textile au Proche-Orient." *REJ* 121 (1962): 169–79.

Seroussi, E. "Rabbi Yisrael Najara Meaṣev Zimrat ha-Qodesh Aḥarey Geyrush Sefarad." *Asufot* 4 (1990): 285–310.

Shalem, S. *Rabbi Moshe Alsheikh.* Jerusalem, 1966.

Sharon, M. "Tahalikhey Ḥurban ve-Nomadizaṣiyah be-Ereẓ Yisrael taḥat Shilton ha-Islam." In *Sugyot be-Toledot Ereẓ-Yisrael taḥat Shilton ha-Islam,* ed. M. Sharon, 9–32. Jerusalem, 1976.

Sharon, "Processes of Destruction"

Shatzmiller, J. "Travelling in the Mediterranean in 1563: The Testimony of Eliahu of Pesaro." In *The Mediterranean and the Jews . . . 16th–18th Centuries,* ed. A. Toaff and S. Schwarzfuchs, 237–48. Ramat Gan, 1989.

Shochat (Shohat), A. "R. Avraham Zakut bi-Yeshivat R. Yiṣḥak Sholal bi-Yerushalayim." *Zion* 13–14 (1948–49): 43–46.

Shochat, "Abraham Zacuto"

——. "Le-Farashat David ha-Reuveni." *Zion* 35 (1970): 96–116.

Shochat, "David Reubeni Affair"

Shochetman, E. "Od li-Demuto u-le-Qorotav shel R. Avraham Qastro." *Zion* 48 (1983): 387–405.

Shochetman, "Additional Information on Abraham Castro"

——. "'Binyan Shelomo le-Ḥokhmat Beṣalel le-Rabbi Shelomo Adeni ve-Hagahot R. Beṣalel Ashqenazi le-Seder Kodashim." *Alei Sefer* 3 (1976): 63–93.

Shochetman, "'Binyan-Shlomo Lehokhmat-Bezalel'"

——. "Kelaley ha-Talmud le-Rabbi Beṣalel Ashqenazi." *Shenaton ha-Mishpat ha-Ivri* 8 (1981): 247–308.

——. "Meqorot Ḥadashim min ha-Genizah li-Feiluto ha-Misḥarit shel ha-Ari be-Miṣrayim." *Pe'amim* 16 (1983): 56–64.

——. "R. Ovadyah mi-Bertinoro—Parshan o gam Poseq?" *Pe'amim* 37 (1988): 3–23.

——. "Taqqanat Ṣefat u-Teshuvot Ḥakhmey Ṣefat be-Inyan Shinui Erekh ha-Matbea." *Sinai* 82 (1978): 109–22.

——. "'Ve-ha-Davar Ṣarikh Hekhra'—Le-Veyrur Daat ha-Rambam bi-Shealat Ḥiddush ha-Semikhah." *Shenaton ha-Mishpat ha-Ivri* 14–15 (1988/89): 217–43.

——, ed. *Responsa of Rabbi Meir Gavizon.* 2 vols. Jerusalem, 1985.

Shtober, S. "'Al Devar ha-Mokhsin asher be-Miṣrayim.'" *Pe'amim* 38 (1989): 68–94.

Shtober, "'Customs Collectors in Egypt'"

——, ed. *Sefer Divrei Yosef,* by Yosef ben Yitzhak Sambari. Jerusalem, 1994.

Shulvass (Szulwas), M. A. *Roma vi-Yerushalayim.* Jerusalem, 1944.

——. "Al Reshimat ha-Massa ha-Italqit." *Kiryat Sefer* 23 (1946–47): 73–74.

Simonsohn, S. "Divieto di trasportare ebrei in Palestina." *Italia Judaica* 2 (1986): 39–53.

——. *History of the Jews in the Duchy of Mantua.* Jerusalem, 1977.

Singer, A. *Palestinian Peasants and Ottoman Officials.* Cambridge, 1994.

Sonne, I. *Mi-Paulus ha-Revii ad Pius ha-Ḥamishi.* Jerusalem, 1954.

Sonne, *Mi-Paulus ad Pius*

——. "Teudot al Shadarim Aḥadim be-Italyah." *Kobeẓ al Yad* 5 (1951): 197–218.

Sonne, "Shadarim"

Spiegel, J. S. "'Geon Yaaqov' le-Rabbi Moshe Alashqar al Tur Oraḥ Ḥayyim." *Tzfunot* 4 (1989): 24–30.

——. "Ha-Rav R. Yaaqov Qastro (Maharikas) ve-Ḥibburav." *Alei Sefer* 16 (1989/90): 5–36, 58.

——. Introduction to *Sheelot u-Teshuvot Maharit Ṣahalon ha-Ḥadashot.* Jerusalem, 1980.

——, ed. Introduction to *Teshuvot Rabbi Yehosef mi-Leiria ve-Ḥakhmey ha-Dor bi-Ṣefat.* Jerusalem, 1988.

Stern, M. *Urkundliche beiträge über die Stellung der Päpste zu den Juden.* Kiel, 1893.

Stillman, N. *The Jews of Arab Lands.* Philadelphia, 1979.

Strauss-Ashtor, E. *Toledot ha-Yehudim be-Miṣrayim ve-Suriyah taḥat Shilton ha-Mamlukim.* 3 vols. Jerusalem, 1944–70.

Strauss-Ashtor, *The Jews in Egypt and Syria*

——. "The Social Isolation of Ahl-Adh-Dhimma." In *Etudes Orientales à la Mémoire de Paul Hirschler,* ed. O. Komlós, 73–94. Budapest, 1950.

Ta-Shma, I. "Al Petur Talmidey Ḥakhamim mi-Missim bi-Yemey ha-Beynayyim." In *Iyyunim be-Sifrut Ḥaza"l, ba-Miqra u-ve-Toledot Yisrael: Muqdash le-E. Z. Melamed,* ed. Y. D. Gilat, Ch. Levine, Z. M. Rabinowitz, 312–22. Ramat Gan, 1982.

——. "Rabbi Joseph Caro and His *Beit Yosef:* Between Spain and Germany." In *The Sephardi Legacy,* ed. H. Beinart, 2:192–206. Jerusalem, 1992.

Tamar, D. "Al Yehudey Ṣefat bi-Yemey ha-Kibbush ha-Ottmani." *Cathedra* 11 (1979): 181–82.

*——. *Meḥqarim be-Toledot ha-Yehudim be-Ereẓ Yisrael u-ve-Italyah.* Jerusalem, 1970.

Tamar, *The Jewish People in Eretz Israel*

——. "Mahadurah Biqortit shel *Galya Raza*—Raḥel Elior, *Galya Raza . . .* Yerushalayim, 1982." *Meḥqarey Yerushalayim be-Maḥshevet Yisrael* 2 (1982/83): 645–55.

——. "Ha-Mequbbal R. Avraham ha-Levi u-Zemano. In *Peraqim be-Toledot ha-Yishuv ha-Yehudi bi-Yerushalayim,* ed. Y. Ben Porat, B. Z. Yehoshua, and A. Kedar, 1:310–21. Jerusalem, 1973.

*——. *Meḥqarim be-Toledot ha-Yehudim be-Ereẓ Yisrael u-ve-Arṣot ha-Mizraḥ.* Jerusalem, 1981.

Tamar, *Ha-Yehudim be-Ereẓ Yisrael u-ve-Arṣot ha-Mizraḥ*

Tishby, I. "Ha-Iymut beyn Qabbalat ha-Ari le-Qabbalat ha-Remaq bi-Khetavav u-be-Ḥayyav shel R. Aharon Berekhiyah mi-Modena." *Zion* 39 (1974): 8–85.

Tishby, "Confrontation between Lurianic and Cordoverian Kabbalah"

——. *Meshiḥiyut be-Dor Geyrushey Sefarad u-Portugal.* Jerusalem, 1985.

Tishby, *Messianism*

——. "Demuto shel Rabbi Moshe Qordovero ba-Ḥibbur shel R. Mordekhai Dato." *Sefunot* 7 (1963): 119–66.

Tishby, "Moses Cordovero"

Toledano, E. "The Sanjaq of Jerusalem in the Sixteenth Century: Aspects of Topography and Population." *Archivum Ottomanicum* 9 (1977): 279–319.

*Toledano, J. M. *Oṣar Genazim.* Jerusalem, 1960.

——. "Teudot mi-Khitvey Yad." *HUCA* 4 (1927): 449–66.

Turniansky, Ch. "Ṣeror Iggerot be-Yiddish mi-Yerushalayim mi-Shenot ha-Shishim shel ha-Meah ha-16." *Shalem* 4 (1984): 149–209.

Turniansky, "Correspondence in Yiddish"

Twersky, I. "Ha-Rav R. Yosef Qaro Baal ha-Shulḥan Arukh." *Asufot* 3 (1989): 245–62.

——. "R. Yosef Ashqenazi ve-Sefer Mishneh Torah la-Rambam." In *Salo Wittmayer Baron Jubilee Volume,* ed. S. Lieberman, Hebrew section, 183–94. Jerusalem, 1974.

Twersky, "Joseph Ashkenazi and the Mishne Tora"

Vilnay, Z. *Derom Levanon.* Tel Aviv, 1982.

——. *Yerushalayim: Ha-Ir ha-Atiqah.* Jerusalem, 1971.

Weinstock, I. "Peyrush ha-Idra Rabbah le-Rabbi Yosef ibn Tabul." *Temirin* 2 (1981): 123–67.

Werblowsky, R. J. Z. *Joseph Caro: Lawyer and Mystic.* Philadelphia, 1980.
Werblowsky, *Joseph Caro*

——. "Tiqquney Tefillah le-Rabbi Shelomo ha-Levi Alqabeṣ." *Sefunot* 6 (1962): 135–72.
Werblowsky, "Solomon Alkabets"

——. "Tefilot al Qever Shmuel ha-Navi." *Sefunot* 8 (1964): 237–53.

Wilensky, M. L. "Rabbi Elijah Afeda Baghi and the Karaite Community of Jerusalem." *PAAJR* 40 (1972): 109–46.

Wineman, A. "The Metamorphosis of Narrative Traditions: Two Stories from Sixteenth-Century Safed." *AJS Review* 10 (1985): 165–80.

Worman, E. J. "Un document concernant Isaac Louria." *REJ* 57 (1909): 281–82.

Yaari, A. *Sheluḥey Ereẓ-Yisrael.* Jerusalem, 1951.
Yaari, *Sheluḥey Ereẓ-Yisrael*

——. "Teveryah ve-Ṣippori ki-Reuven ve-Shimon." *Tarbiẓ* 18 (1947): 64.

——. "Toledot ha-Hilula be-Meron." *Tarbiẓ* 31 (1961): 72–101.

——. "Toledot ha-Yishuv ha-Yehudi be-Ḥevron." *Maḥanayim* 72 (1962): 84–96.

——. "Toledot ha-Yishuv ha-Yehudi bi-Shekhem." *Sinai* 36 (1955): 166–87.

——, ed. *Iggerot Ereẓ-Yisrael.* 2d edition. Ramat Gan, 1971.
Yaari, *Letters*

——. *Masot Ereẓ Yisrael shel Olim Yehudim.* 2d edition. Ramat Gan, 1976.
Yaari, *Masot*

——. *Massa Meshullam mi-Volterra be-Ereẓ Yisrael.* Jerusalem, 1949.
Yaari, *Massa Meshullam*

Yahalom, J. "Rabbi Yisrael Najara ve-Hitḥadshut ha-Shirah ha-Ivrit ba-Mizraḥ le-Aḥar Geyrush Sefarad." *Pe'amim* 13 (1982): 96–124.

——. "Shirah Ivrit Mistit ve-ha-Reqa ha-Turki Shelah." *Tarbiẓ* 60 (1991): 625–48.

Yellin, D. "Yerushalayim ha-Yehudit lifney Shelosh Meot Shanah." *Yerushalayim: Qoveṣ le-Zikhro shel A. M. Luncz,* ed. I. Press and E. L. Sukenik, 78–105. Jerusalem, 1928.

Yudlov, I. "Hearot Bibliografiyot le-Parashat ha-Get Tamari-Ventorozzo." *Alei Sefer* 2 (1976): 105–20.

——. "R. Yiṣḥak Gershon ve-Rabbi Yiṣḥak Treves—Shenayim she-hem Shenayim." *Kiryat Sefer* 59 (1984): 247–51.
Yudlov, "Isaac Gershon and Isaac Treves

——. "'Tefillah le-David'—Qoveṣ Tefilot mi-Yerushalayim, Qushta 5295 o 5298." *Kiryat Sefer* 61 (1986–87): 929–32.

Yuval, I. "Terumot mi-Nuremberg li-Yerushalayim." *Zion* 46 (1981): 182–97.

Zimmels, H. J. *Rabbi David Ibn Abi Simra.* Breslau, 1932.

MANUSCRIPT COLLECTIONS

Budapest, Rabbinical Seminary
30
Cambridge, University Library
Ad. 10. 46
Add. 1179
T-S 6J 10, 6
T-S 13J 4, 19
T-S 13J 24, 25
T-S AS 145, 313
T-S AS 218, 153
T-S Glass 8J 35, 2
T-S Glass 12, 589
T-S Glass 16, 348
T-S Misc. 10, 80
T-S Misc. 20, 166
T-S Misc. 28, 168
T-S NS 320, 114
Firenze, Biblioteca Mediceo Laurenziana
Plut. 44.7
Hamburg, Staats- und Universitätsbibliothek, Levy Collection
67
Jerusalem, Jewish National and University Library
Heb. 4° 1446
Heb. 8° 61
Heb. 8° 416
Heb. 8° 493
Heb. 8° 539
Heb. 8° 1783
Heb. 8° 5637
Heb. 8° 6424
Yah. Heb. 94
Leghorn, Talmud Tora
74
London, British Library
Add. 26966 (1071)
Or. 5434
Or. 14020a
Or. 104020g
Or. 10771
London, Jews College, Montefiore Collection
14
116
318
488
Manchester, John Rylands University Library
Gaster A 852
Gaster A 1390
Moscow, Russian State Library, Günzburg Collection
17
62
67
313
322
652
952
980
989
1054
1055
1133
New York, Jewish Theological Seminary
EMC 683
ENA 2050
ENA 2739, 5
ENA NS 43, 14
ENA NS 52, 13
L 1065 (Ad. 1613)
Mic. 2324 (Acc. 3637)
Mic. 3541 (ENA 74)
Rab. 474
Oxford, Bodleian Library
Heb. C. 24 (2635)
Hunt. 412 (969)
Mich. 85 (1562)
Mich. 463 (832)
Mich. Add. 67 (2317)
Opp. 445 (2301)
Opp. 551 (1742)

Opp. Add. 4° 33 (1015)
Opp. Add. 8° 26 (2417)
Pocock 74 (2000)
Reggio 23

Paris, Bibliothèque nationale
Heb. 1389

Parma, Biblioteca Palatina
2095 (1377)

Ramat Gan, Bar-Ilan University Library
598

Sassoon Collection
689
799

Vienna, Österreiche Nationalbibliothek
111/72

Warsaw, Jewish Historical Institute
229
267

Index of Persons and Places

Index of Subjects